D1405124

JOHN BROWN

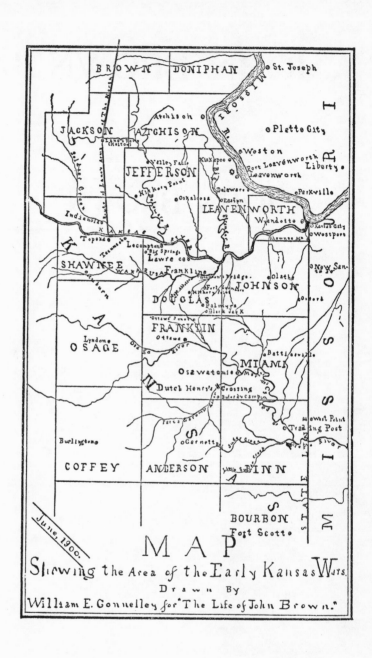

MAP
Showing the Area of the Early Kansas Wars.
Drawn By
William E. Connelley for "The Life of John Brown."

JOHN BROWN

BY

WILLIAM ELSEY CONNELLEY

Sic itur ad astra

" From boulevards
O'erlooking both Nyanzas,
The statured bronze shall glitter in the sun,
With rugged lettering:

' John Brown of Kansas:
he dared begin;
he lost,
But, losing, won.' "

—*Eugene F. Ware.*

The Black Heritage Library Collection

BOOKS FOR LIBRARIES PRESS
FREEPORT, NEW YORK
1971

First Published 1900
Reprinted 1971

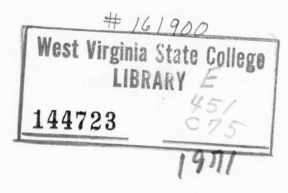
Reprinted from a copy in the
Fisk University Library Negro Collection

INTERNATIONAL STANDARD BOOK NUMBER:
0-8369-8842-6

LIBRARY OF CONGRESS CATALOG CARD NUMBER:
71-164383

PRINTED IN THE UNITED STATES OF AMERICA

PREFACE.

"Await the issue. In all battles, if you await the issue, each fighter has prospered according to his right. His right and his might, at the close of the account, were one and the same. He has fought with all his might, and in exact proportion to all his right he has prevailed. His very death is no victory over him. He dies indeed; but his work lives, very truly lives. A heroic Wallace, quartered on the scaffold, cannot hinder that Scotland become, one day, a part of England: but he does hinder that it become, on unfair terms, a part of it; commands still, as with a god's voice, from his old Valhalla and Temple of the Brave, that there be a just real union as of brother and brother, not a false and merely semblant one as of slave and master."

—*Carlyle.*

EMERSON says that all history resolves itself into the biographies of a few strong characters. This makes it imperative that those who would have a right understanding of the history of their country should study carefully the life of John Brown. For it is rare that any country produces a man who deliberately, even joyously, lays down his life for a principle—for an idea. When such a character appears among men he is first maligned and misunderstood, afterwards driven and persecuted, and often "gibbeted as a felon." After his death the people come gradually to see and understand the great truths he willingly went to the scaffold for. It becomes apparent that, after all, though in conflict with accredited forms and established and recognized conventionalities which regu-

(5)

late and prescribe the relations between men in their social state, he was right. This realization presses upon the people; the cause in their interest which cost human blood becomes vital to their existence, as the martyr insisted. It becomes known by all that he was the first to discern in its true magnitude and proportion the evil which threatened the progress of the race. It is perceived that he alone proposed an adequate remedy, and so deep were laid the foundations of his faith that he willingly sealed with his blood the cause which the people could but reject until the broad sunlight which he saw from his mountain-top flooded the valleys in which dwelt those of his generation. Men gather about the standard he reared and carry it to a triumphant issue and victory for the cause for which he suffered martyrdom at their hands. Thus, wonderfully and fearfully is man made, and strangely is society constituted.

John Brown perished on a scaffold of ignominy, in conformity to the exactions of recognized and accredited systems and at the instance of reactionary institutions poisoning and drying up the fountains of our national life, and in so doing died a martyr for human liberty. Such men remain potent forces in individual and national life. They touch and quicken in man and nation truth, justice, patriotism. When the wiles of greed and avarice would tempt us to cast loose from the safe havens of liberty and justice in pursuit of pomp and grandeur on the glittering and deceptive seas of questionable or unjust enterprises, the lives of such men blaze and burn a beacon on the eternal shores of truth to entreat us to return to accord with laws human and divine.

John Brown comes with a message to one and all to-day.
If we can get some correct comprehension of the motives
by which his life was ordered and the principles which
led him to sacrifice himself for high and noble purposes,—
if we can apprehend why he sought the relief of the poor,
the weak, the despised, rather than the plaudits of the rich,
the mighty, the unjust, and that in so doing he but sought
to bring us back to the truth and simplicity of the fathers
of our country,—then we may profit by the important
lessons his life holds for us. He was a man, and not, as
some are inclined to say, a saint whose every act was just,
who was incapable of doing wrong, who alone and un-
aided saved Kansas to freedom and America to liberty.
And we insist that those who seek to sink him to the
level of the criminal and the malefactor, who distort their
country's history with malice and venom to gratify private
animosity or exalt at his expense an inferior contemporary,
are equally in error. The efforts of both are futile. Posterity invariably comes to a right verdict on the actions
of men. Every fact that will in any way affect this verdict becomes fully known. In such an instance it is as impossible to conceal a wrong or suppress a virtue as to blot
out the sun. John Brown was human, and as such was
burdened with human weaknesses. That he often erred,
must be admitted. That his faults were grievous, none
so well knew as he himself; and his letters are full of
confessions. He made no claim to perfection; who would
place him in a position so false would do him immeasura-
ble injustice. He eschewed evil, and strove daily with his
own shortcomings. He never for a moment sought to
evade the full responsibility of any act committed by him-

self or at his instance. Long before he left Kansas for Harper's Ferry he said without evasion or reservation that if the killing on the Pottawatomie was murder, he was not guiltless. He said this without any injunction to secrecy, and with the full consciousness of the rectitude of his own purpose and the unfaltering faith that a right understanding of the facts would vindicate his course in the eyes of right-thinking men, and that history would not fail to justify him.

The strength of John Brown's life and the grandeur of his character lie not in his having been always right. No man has ever been so. But they lie in his having done his duty as he saw it. Perhaps he failed in judgment, but never in intention, nor by evasion. In Kansas, patriotic men differed from him in the policy to be pursued. They would have been satisfied with a temporary peace, and any compromise which would have made Kansas alone a free State. And indeed this would have been a great, and when accomplished was, a wonderful achievement over seemingly insurmountable obstacles. John Brown believed it his duty and the duty of every man to demand freedom for the whole people. He was aware that we might patch a compromise and cry "peace! peace!" as we had done before, but he knew there would be no peace and no possibility of permanent peace in Kansas or any other State or Territory so long as our government was an absurdity—so long as we proclaimed freedom and practiced slavery. When he came to Kansas he was an old man, and his experience taught him that we had been trying compromise and proclaiming peace for half a century, during which slavery had made conquest after conquest,—marched from triumph to triumph,—until those forces of our country resting upon justice, humanity, the Declaration, the Constitution, and the Christian religion, said that it was useless to continue longer the deception. Without claiming more than that he was acting in obedience and conformity to God's will, John Brown represented these forces, which were our only hope for preservation. He believed that God commanded him to make war upon the wickedness of slavery. Not only that; he believed this command was universal, that it was to all men. I find no evidence that John Brown assumed to be the *only* man with a divine commission to fight slavery. But John Brown *heeded* this call, and acted upon it; therein lies his glory.

John Brown was right. He was an intense revolutionist and an incisive reformer. He went back to the first principles of simple justice; and having done so, self-deception and the temporizing of others became impossible for him. He saw the inconsistency and injustice of a government founded upon liberty enslaving millions of its people. He very properly concluded that it was better that such a government cease to exist altogether if it could not be brought to conform to its expressed and underlying principles. Some will ask wherein he differed from the secessionist, who sought the destruction of the Union. John Brown would have destroyed it because of its injustice, and have built of its ruins the temple of truth, justice, liberty, and honor. The secessionist would have destroyed it because of its justice, in the hope that he would be enabled to build from the fragments the dishonorable structure of injustice and the brutality of human slavery—a

monstrous empire of iniquity. John Brown believed that
God called him and every other man to work as in him lay,
to the end that our country might rise to the divine heights
of enduring truth and become in fact what the fathers
designed it—the beacon to lead the world to higher conceptions of liberty. In this world obedience to the call
of duty, and the defense of the inalienable rights of humanity, are due from every man. How few of us respond
to even the conceptions we attain! And our universal
indifference adds the greater glory to the individual who
says in his weakness: Here am I; send me; I will do
what I can. John Brown said that. In sickness and in
health, through evil and good report; maligned, misrep-
resented, persecuted and ridiculed; beset and weighted
down by poverty; surrounded by obstacles none other
could have overcome; without any hope, desire or expectation of reward in this life; not for himself nor his family nor for the rich, the powerful, and the great, but for
the poor, the driven, the bondman and the slave who toiled
in a sore and bitter thralldom, he did struggle onward and
upward in the steep and rugged path appointed to him.
There is little doubt that he often saw the scaffold, or a
file of soldiers in front of himself with a coffin at his
feet, at the end of the way. But he turned not aside.
So devoted to his Master's work was he that he could
exclaim, with Saint Paul: "For I am persuaded, that
neither death, nor life, nor angels, nor principalities, nor
powers, nor things present, nor things to come, nor height,
nor depth, nor any other creature, shall be able to separate
us." And therein lies the nobility, the majesty, and the
sublimity of the character of John Brown. God had given

him the cup, and until He let it pass it must be drained
to the last drop. When it was manifest that this cup contained the bitterness of death, it was given him to see
that he was right, that his work had not been in vain,
and the power to exclaim in triumph and in great faith
with another servant of God who perished at the hands
of a wicked and unjust state: " I have fought the good
fight, I have finished my course, I have kept the faith:
Henceforth there is laid up for me a crown of righteousness, which the Lord, the righteous judge, shall give me at
that day: and not to me only, but unto all them that love
his appearing."

So much in advance of his age was John Brown, that
it took the Civil War to show us that he was right, and to
reveal to the world the divine height of justice, humanity
and liberty upon which he stood and looked down with
horror upon the sodden iniquity of our land. He was
strangled on the border-land between liberty and slavery.
His blood maddened the South. It fell to them according
to the true proverb, " Whom the gods would destroy they
first make mad." A year later the Southern people cried:
Kill! burn! slay! Away with the Union! We will have
none of it! What is it to us or our children? We will
build us a country the foundation-stone of which shall be
human slavery! Truly, it was upon the second day of
December, 1859, as though the noonday sun had broken
there over a field of moles! But for the North, solemn
and serious was the day! Good men everywhere clothed
themselves with sackcloth and sat in ashes in repentance
for the sins of the land. They stood upon the walls of
the cities to warn the people to flee from the manifest

wrath of Heaven. They girded on the sword of the Lord
and of Gideon. When the voice of incendiarism was
raised in the temple by the South, the spirit of John Brown
stalked abroad and became the inspiration of the armies
marching to bring back the nation to its starting-point.
Hill and dale resounded with patriotic songs,—" Tramp,
tramp, tramp, the boys are marching," and " We are coming, father Abraham, three hundred thousand more."
But when the grim and grisly columns grew faint and
road-worn; when armies met in battle-shock which shook
the solid earth and the day was doubtful; when the long
lines of blood-stained Blue would staunch the wound and

> "Lend the eye a terrible aspect;
> Let it pry through the portage of the head
> Like the brass cannon; let the brow o'erwhelm it
> As fearfully as doth a galled rock
> O'erhang and jutty his confounded base,
> Swill'd with the wild and wasteful ocean,"

and nerve the terrible arm of war to do or die,—then
arose the war-cry of the North,—that weird, soul-thrilling
strain, bearing over the weary way, on the field of blood
and carnage, the solemn chant,

> "John Brown's body lies mouldering in the grave,
> But his soul goes marching on."

As the volume of this grim Marseillaise of America
rose and rolled, filling the valleys and overflowing the re-
straining hills with a fearful menace like the eagle's
scream, courage filled every heart, daring shone in every
eye, and the armies of the Republic became invincible.

The Kansas Historical Society has one of the finest

libraries in America. Its vaults are rich in documents relating to John Brown, his men and his times. The obliging and efficient Secretary, Hon. George W. Martin, placed all these at my service. He that would know John Brown as he really was must pore over these papers; and this John Brown Collection is the most complete in the country.

I rest, also, under deep obligations to F. B. Sanborn, Esq., of Concord, Massachusetts, author of *Life and Letters of John Brown.* His work is the most extensive and exhaustive biography of John Brown ever written. It is particularly rich in letters and other original documents. Mr. Sanborn had unusual opportunities to gather this invaluable material, and all students of American history have cause to thank him for the fidelity with which he has performed the work. His burning pages have ever been an incentive to me to dig and delve in this interesting historical field. During his recent visit to our city we discussed the work of John Brown; since his return home he has sent me books and papers.

And I am no less bound to Colonel Richard J. Hinton, of Brooklyn, N. Y. While he was in attendance upon the sessions of the annual meeting of the State Historical Society we had many conferences upon this subject. Since his return home, Colonel Hinton has continued to assist me. He is one of John Brown's men, and but one other man now living has so great a personal knowledge of the martyr. Colonel Hinton is the author of *John Brown and His Men,* the best book ever published for information of those who followed the old hero to Harper's Ferry. Kansas owes much to Colonel Hinton. He fought for her through the dark days of the Territorial period, with pen and sword. He fought in the ranks of her armies through the Civil War; and he has fought her battles with the pen every day since the close of the Rebellion. Kansas never had a truer friend than Colonel Hinton.

Very few States or countries have been favored with so complete a record of the events constituting their history as can be found in *Wilder's Annals of Kansas,* gathered, compiled, and written by the Honorable D. W. Wilder, of Hiawatha. It is by far the greatest work ever prepared upon the history of Kansas; all others sink into insignificance when compared with it. It is an imperishable monument to the genius and industry of its author. Mr. Wilder brought greater talents and learning to his task, and longer experience in the field he covered so thoroughly, than can be boasted of any other Kansas work. The genius of an author is as much displayed in what he omits as in what he writes; Mr. Wilder seizes the vital thread of Kansas history and holds it to the end. Nothing superfluous is tolerated. Every vital fact is stated. In this great work we see accomplished the most delicate and difficult feat known to literature—a work at once indispensable to the busy man at his desk, seeking the barest statement, and to the student poring at his table by the midnight oil. No Kansas writer has ever equaled Mr. Wilder in the use of short, sharp, clear-cut, meaty sentences. His words take their places like polished blocks in a granite wall. The pages of Kansas history are filled with illustrious names; and that of D. W. Wilder will outlive and outshine all others. Aside from his work, the book of Kansas books, I have had the benefit of Mr.

Wilder's personal interest in this Life of John Brown; his vast knowledge of the subject has been at all times at my disposal.

I am under obligations to Mrs. Sara T. D. Robinson, of Lawrence, for aid in preparing this work. She kindly sent me books and pamphlets which it would have been difficult for me to find elsewhere than in her vast collection relating to Kansas history. One of the earliest and best books written on Kansas is her *Kansas: Its Interior and Exterior Life*. It was not the least of the causes which made Kansas free. And in addition to her literary work for " bleeding Kansas," she rendered services which were a credit to her head and heart, and of vast benefit to us who enjoy the fruits of them.

The list of brilliant Kansas writers to whom I am under obligations for aid in preparing this work contains no more illustrious name than that of Eugene F. Ware. Mr. Ware insists that he is only a business man who turns occasionally to the delights of literature as he is moved by his muse. It may be so; but he is perfectly familiar with every phase of Kansas life and development, and has investigated and written well on many of our important historical subjects. His writings are not all in verse, although he is our earliest eminent Kansas poet. The keepers of the true traditions were the first poets, and the founders of all literature. In ancient times, as in the days of Homer, the songs they chanted had imbedded in them the history of their country, and they were national characters. Our mother country still adheres to this ancient usage, and recognizes a national bard. It is the boast of Kansas that she has everything good possessed by any

other land. Our Poet Laureate is Mr. Ware, than whom
Kansas has no more talented nor loyal son. His poem,
John Brown, is second in popularity only to the great
song which inspired the legions on the battlefield, where
Mr. Ware doubtless often sang it. Every student of Kan-
sas history must read well the writings of Eugene F. Ware.

The Rev. Thomas C. Richards, pastor of the Congre-
gational Church in West Torrington, Connecticut, to
which John Brown's father and mother belonged, sent me
valuable papers. The Historical Department of Iowa,
Des Moines, sent me books and papers which I found indispensable in writing this work. Mrs. Elvira Gaston Platt,
formerly of Nebraska and Iowa, residing now in Oberlin,
Ohio, was long engaged in benevolent and charitable work
in the West. In the days when John Brown was laboring for Kansas she lived on the road through Iowa taken
by Free-State people in passing to and from the Territory.
She knew the old hero, and her roof gave him shelter.
She is now in the evening of a noble and beautiful Christian life; and forgetting the weight of her many years,
has taken her pen in hand to give me the benefit of her
knowledge. Major J. B. Remington, of Osawatomie, married the daughter of the Rev. S. L. Adair, who was the
brother-in-law of John Brown. There remain some of the
letters of the martyr in the family. These, together with
papers and pictures, Mr. Remington sent me, for which I
acknowledge here my obligations. I have talked with a
great number of persons who knew John Brown in Kansas
and elsewhere, and from them I obtained much of value.
Some of these are the oldest and most respected citizens
of the State. Among the many so consulted I desire to

mention the following: Edward P. Harris, John Armstrong, G. W. W. Yates, Harvey D. Rice, Edwin R. Partridge, Jacob Willets, and Samuel J. Reader. I am indebted to Captain Joseph G. Waters for many useful suggestions.

This work was originally prepared for the Twentieth Century Classics, a monthly educational publication issued by Crane & Company, Topeka. The Classics are issued under the editorial supervision of William M. Davidson, Superintendent of the Topeka public schools, and are rapidly finding favor with the general readers of the country, as well as with the thorough investigators and students. Mr. Davidson is well equipped by nature and training for his responsible position. I have had the benefit of his perfect knowledge of the subject in the writing of this work, and am under deep debt to him for assistance.

I am in duty bound to acknowledge the deep interest taken in this work by the house of Crane & Company, for whom it was prepared. They have given me every facility at the command of their great establishment, for the collection of material for this volume. They assisted me to secure all that the latest and most thorough research could offer. They have ever been the true friends of Kansas writers, and have published more Kansas books than all other Kansas houses combined. Their publications have covered every field, and they deserve well of the State. They left nothing undone to help me make this work all it should be.

WILLIAM ELSEY CONNELLEY.

TOPEKA, KANSAS, September 3, 1900.

—2

TABLE OF CONTENTS.

CHAPTER I.

SLAVERY IN AMERICA.

The abhorred Form
Whose scarlet robe was stiff with earthly pomp,
Who drank iniquity in cups of gold,
Whose names were many and all blasphemous.
—*Coleridge.*

The origin of moral law must be sought in the dawn
of intelligence and at that point in human progress where
man is first conscious of human dignity. In the condition anterior to this, man was a savage with a remote
social instinct. He was a hunter, and prowled from the
same necessity that impels the wolf. As war is a relation
between state and state and not a relation between man
and man,[1] his conflicts in this early stage of his development are to be regarded as single combats, duels, and
encounters;[2] and in these he could capture prisoners but
could not make them slaves. Having no occupation nor
industry in which one held by force could be profitably
employed, he slew his captives on the field of battle or
reserved them for torture or sacrifice. If any escaped
these ends, they were adopted, and became competent
members of the victorious band or family. But death
might not await females, for in this period of social progress (or the want of it) whatever of labor is necessary to
life is performed by the women. And in the animal king-

dom the first and chief contention between the males arises
for possession of the females; in even the crudest forms
of society females may be held by force, but their deten-
tion is not slavery as we understand the term, and their
lot is not more wretched than that of the women born in
the family or band holding them.

In the path of human progress the barbarian follows
the savage; the advance is chiefly due to the tending of
such animals as may have been domesticated. Men are
congregated into rude governments, the distinguishing
features of which are patriarchal; men are associated
along the lines of consanguinity. Man is here nomadic,
but usually the wanderings of a band or community do
not extend beyond the bounds of a circumscribed and well-
defined district; and such rovings are often to find pas-
turage for herds and flocks. The outlines of a state are
discernible and a rude and savage warfare is possible.
Captives are reserved for barter to adjoining tribes, and
a few are retained to assist in whatever of agriculture
may be practiced; some may be even intrusted with the
care of animals.

In the third period of human progress society becomes
sedentary and man fixes himself to the soil of a particular
locality, and in the main he keeps to this. This is the
result of several causes; as the nomadic families and
clans of the barbarous increase, more dependence is had
upon the soil for existence. The warlike characteristics
are retained, and as slaves cannot be expected to battle
valiantly for their masters, they are forced to cultivate
the land, and are also given care of the herds and flocks
which the masters have deserted for war and conquest.

The divine decree, " In the sweat of thy face shalt thou eat bread," was considered by the ancients a punishment of sufficient magnitude for disobedience to God's specific command. This judgment is founded in the nature of man, for in him there is no inherent love of work. Regular and sustained labor is a characteristic which it has taken man ages to acquire. "Antipathy to regular and sustained labor is deeply rooted in human nature, especially in the earlier stages of the social movement, when insouciance is so common a trait, and irresponsibility is hailed as a welcome relief." [3]

Productive industry has always been the result of slavery, and has become a fixed characteristic in a people only after ages of labor performed by the helpless under the strong hand of force and oppression. Nowhere has a system of economics arisen by voluntary effort. When the decadence of force enabled the lower strata of society to rise and throw off their bonds, the whole community was compelled to work,—to unite in labor to supply the necessaries and wants resulting from the labor of a portion, now become indispensable to the existence of all. Slavery is reëstablished by further conquest, or, perhaps, has not been allowed to become altogether obsolete. But as slavery presupposes the existence of a condition or state of war, it becomes now deleterious to the society founded upon the industries its presence developed. For, in the development of these industries human dignity appears and moral law is perceived; this the moral reaction of slavery tends to subvert, and if involuntary servitude is persisted in as an institution, society is thrown back on itself and industrial and moral development becomes impossible.

And the mental powers being different in different individuals, or becoming so by occupations in different industries or by certain conventionalities instituted and im-
posed by the masters, society divides along the .line of
mental strength or upon the basis of conventionalities,
and this results in the enslavement of a portion of society
by caste or custom.   The accumulations of ages fall into
the hands and under the control of a few.   If the inferior
classes escape the slavery of caste, slaves are imported,
and the free citizens are sent to war.   The property of
the state, including the land, falls into the hands of the
class who rule politically, and who are supported by the
labor of the weak and the helpless.   They become a class of
idlers and cruel oppressors who lead lives of ease, indulgence, and often of excess and wickedness.   War is entered upon for conquest and weaker nations are enslaved
or destroyed.   In this period of human progress slavery
becomes a curse to all classes, and must cease, or end in
disorder or, even, the destruction of society.

Though the evil effects of slavery always manifest
themselves so clearly in this period of progress and are
cried out against by the just and the humane, the interests
of property are usually paramount to the rights of man,
and only the most enlightened nations have abolished
slavery.[4]

Only the political effects of slavery and its aid in the
development of productive industry have been noticed
here.   The moral effects of the institution have been
scarcely considered in the foregoing.   While it must be
admitted that politically slavery was indispensable in
the early periods of social progress, in that productive

industry is wholly the result of it, it is true that its moral effects have always been debasing and disastrous, and equally so to the master and the slave. It always afforded unusual opportunities for the indulgence of the basest propensities of human nature.[5] Another evil of slavery, more manifest to society than the preceding one, was the development of tyranny. Absolute rule—the exercise of absolute power—is ruinous to man's nature, and the arrogance and intolerance it develops in a class are always subversive of patriotism. It engenders and develops all the brutal tendencies of unrestrained human nature. Flattery is sought and vanity becomes characteristic. True conditions of moral life become obscured, society becomes distorted, and tendencies to decay and demoralization are hailed as signs of social and political progress. The rights of others are wholly disregarded, and this characteristic is carried into all intercourse with institutions and states. Constraint in even its mildest forms is irksome,—not to be endured or even thought of,—and the policy of the slave-owner comes to be expressed in two words—*rule* or *ruin.*[6] Reason is dethroned and tyranny set on the throne in the temple of human liberty. The voice of protest is stifled and the right of free speech denied. In ancient times the sages commented on "the little humanity commonly observed in persons accustomed from their infancy to exercise so great authority over their fellow-creatures and to trample upon human nature. Nor can a more probable reason be assigned for the severe, I might say, barbarous manners of ancient times than the practice of domestic slavery, by which every man of rank was rendered a petty tyrant, and educated amidst the flattery, submission, and low debasement of his slaves." [7]

Slavery was introduced into the New World by the Spaniards. They enslaved the natives, and in many places exterminated them by this barbarous system. Before the discovery of America (in 1492), the Portuguese had begun to enslave the Africans. One Antam Gonsalves captured some Moors while exploring the Atlantic coast of Africa, and carried them to his own country. Prince Henry the Navigator ordered them returned to their own land; and as a reward for this act of justice the Moors of that country gave Gonsalves ten negroes and some gold dust. Here was discovered by accident an opportunity for enterprise in a new field of commerce, and many Portuguese embraced it. Forts were built and manned along the Atlantic coast of Africa, to serve as bases for the slave trade. From these points many negroes were sent into Portugal and Spain, and their descendants were carried slaves to the Spanish and Portuguese colonies in America. Early in the sixteenth century the King of Spain granted a patent to a favorite courtier, giving him the exclusive right to carry negro slaves to the West Indies. This patent allowed the importation of four thousand slaves per annum; it was sold to Genoese navigators, who procured their negroes from the Portuguese. The practice became from this time systematic, and was eagerly entered by many of the nations of Europe. The first Englishman to engage in this odious traffic was Captain John Hawkins, who amassed a great estate, and was knighted by Queen Elizabeth. England had no colonies in America at that time, and Sir John's business was with the Spanish settlements. His manner of barter is said to have been somewhat arbitrary. It is recorded of him that he would land with his human chattels at some unfortified town, train the cannon of his ships upon the principal buildings, and then demand that he be instantly paid so much for his human cargo. His conditions were complied with from necessity, and the bluff old Captain sailed away with great satisfaction.

Those portions of our country acquired from Spain, or some of them, contained slaves before the English planted colonies in America. But in 1620 a Dutch ship landed at Jamestown, in the colony of Virginia, with slaves obtained on the coast of Guinea. A part of this cargo was sold to the tobacco-planters of Virginia. The trade here commenced was carried into all the colonies of Great Britain in America; and in 1790 Virginia contained two hundred thousand negro slaves.

The greatest men of England condemned the slave trade in the last half of the seventeenth century, and in 1772 Lord Mansfield defined the legal status of an English slave in his famous decision rendered for the whole bench. He declared that "as soon as a slave set his foot on the soil of the British Islands he was free."

The first action taken in England by an organization or body against the slave trade was had by the Quakers, who declared in their meeting of 1727 that it was a practice "not to be commended or allowed." In 1761 they prohibited their members from engaging in it. They formed an association of their members in 1783 having for its object "the relief and liberation of the negro slaves in the West Indies, and for the discouragement of the slave-trade on the coast of Africa." The practice was not, however, abolished and prohibited by England until 1811. Denmark was the first country to abolish the loathsome traffic; May 16, 1792, it was decreed that it cease in the Danish possessions at the end of 1802.

The Quakers in Pennsylvania advocated the abolition of the slave-trade before those in England considered the question. Their first opposition to it was formulated in 1696; and they continued to take advanced ground upon the subject until 1776, when they excluded slaveholders from membership in their society. The United States finally prohibited the importation of slaves; the law was passed March 2d, 1807, to become effective January 1st, 1808.

Washington, Jefferson, Franklin, Madison, Hamilton, and many others of the founders of the Republic opposed slavery and saw in it the source of evil and trouble to our country. Jefferson was the most active of its eminent adversaries. In 1784 he proposed to the Continental Congress a plan of government for the territory included now in the States of Alabama, Mississippi, and Tennessee, in which it was provided that "after the year 1800 there shall be neither slavery nor involuntary servitude in any of said States, otherwise than in punishment for crime." This humane and patriotic measure was lost. The convention which met in Philadelphia in 1787 and formed our Constitution was opposed to slavery. The fathers of the Republic there assembled would have provided for its extinction but for the States of South Carolina and Georgia. Both of these States, the latter probably at the instance

of the former, insisted upon its retention as a condition
to their becoming members of the new Union. In the
same year slavery had been excluded from the territory
northwest of the Ohio river by the last Continental Congress. Slavery was gradually extinguished in the North.[8]

Slavery having survived the establishment of the Republic, it soon became aggressive. Its tenacious depravity
was aided by many favorable circumstances. The influences which augmented the increasing power of the
slave-owners and slave States are marked in our national
growth by (1) The acquisition of Louisiana, although the
purchase was not made in the interest of slavery; (2) The
Missouri Compromise of 1820; (3) The annexation of
Texas, in 1845; (4) The Fugitive Slave Law, slavery
legalized in New Mexico, and the other measures of the
Compromise of 1850; (5) The Kansas-Nebraska bill,
1854; (6) The Ostend Manifesto, 1854; (7) The attempt to reopen the slave-trade, 1859–60.[9] While the
measures of 1854 were in the interest of slavery,
they precipitated the conflict which ended in its extinction. There were many subordinate causes for the
growth of slavery, not the least of which was the
invention of the cotton-gin by Whitney, the profits
of which were almost all filched from him by the
slave States. The South apostatized from the faith
of Jefferson, and chiefly through the efforts of Calhoun.
The tariff was made the cause in 1828, when Calhoun declared that the resolutions of '98 inculcated the doctrine
of secession as a remedy against obnoxious or unsatis-
factory Federal laws. His construction was soon made
applicable to slavery by Southern statesmen, who were

determined to make this institution the underlying principle of a league or cabal for the control of the Government.

It is wonderful to realize the completeness of the infatuation of the South with the institution of negro slavery. It is strange and seems almost incredible that the truth of history allows us to say that in this free land, up to 1860, freedom of speech was absolutely prohibited in more than one-half of it. Yet such is the fact. No minister dared to lift up his voice there against slavery or any of its evil consequences. Sermons were always prepared to meet the approval of the slave-owners.[10] Mob law and such punishments as burning at the stake were advocated by the aristocratic press of the South as suitable for those who opposed their institution on its own ground.[11] The non-slaveholding whites were terrorized and brutally hung without trial.[12] Many persons of Northern birth were put to death in the South upon mere suspicion and without even mob trial. The Government mails were rifled and anti-slavery literature seized and publicly burned by the clergy and prominent men in public assembly. The Rev. Elijah P. Lovejoy was slain in Alton, Illinois, and anti-abolition riots occurred in many Northern cities, including Boston. Never in our history have the arrogance and intolerance of the slave-power been equaled. It was boasted that the masters would again call the rolls of their slaves in the shadow of the Bunker Hill monument. Public moneys were embezzled and purloined to buy newspapers to speak for slavery.[13] It was asserted that could Washington have returned to life he would have been mobbed in Virginia.[14] A lawyer sent from

Massachusetts to South Carolina to perform a mission
for the State was forced to depart from Charleston after
a mob had been for days warning him to quit the city; he
and his daughter were forcibly placed in a carriage, driven
to the wharf, placed on a boat and sent away.[15] Slavery
was carried into our foreign relations, and we stood in
the eyes of the world what we in fact were—a *slave*
Nation.[16] At the close of the Missouri struggle in 1820
a Governmental policy was formulated which prevented
the North from reaping any advantage accruing from that
Compromise. The arable portion of the country north of
the Compromise line in the Louisiana Purchase was assigned to emigrant tribes of Indians, to be by them held
"as long as grass grows or water runs." As opposed to
this policy for the North, Texas was annexed to afford
slavery a field for expansion. Cuba was coveted, and the
slave-power committed the Government to its acquisition.
The Mexican war brought vast territory to slavery; and as
a last resort the Compromise was repealed. The supreme
tribunal of the land was made the ally of slavery, and
announced that the institution could not be excluded by
law from any territory in the United States. Slavery
dominated the Government; up to 1860 the South had
held the Presidency forty-eight years—more than two-
thirds of the time to 1860—eleven of sixteen terms. The
South had seventeen of the twenty-eight Justices of the
Supreme Court, fourteen of the nineteen Attorneys-
General, sixty-one of the seventy-seven Presidents of the
Senate, twenty-one of the thirty-three Speakers of the
House, and eighty of the one hundred and thirty-four
Foreign Ministers.

Nature never made a fairer country nor a more fertile one than that portion of the United States south of Mason and Dixon's line. No material natural resource is wanting. Gold, silver, lead, zinc, copper, iron, coal, oil, building-stone, timber, natural gas, water-power, fertile soil, beautiful and grand scenery, a healthful and pleasant climate, navigable rivers in great abundance, and an ocean line of remarkable extent,—all these invited for the South an industrial development second to no other equal area on the globe. At the time of the adoption of the Federal Constitution the South was the most populous portion of the Union, and, too, the most prosperous and wealthy. In 1790 Virginia contained 748,308 inhabitants and New York but 340,120. The census for 1850 showed 3,097,394 for New York and 1,421,661 for Virginia. Commerce made a similar transfer of preponderance. In 1791 the exports of Virginia amounted to $3,130,865, while those of New York were only $2,505,465. The figures in 1852 were, for New York $87,484,456, and for Virginia, $2,-724,657, a decrease of $406,208 from the amount for the year 1791.[17] The comparisons between Massachusetts and North Carolina, Pennsylvania and South Carolina, show even greater paralysis and stagnation in those Southern States and the same vigor and progress in the corresponding Northern States. No manufactures were established in the South;[18] in fact, they were discouraged; by public sentiment, prohibited.[19]

Not alone did slavery blight agriculture and commerce in the South. Where the foot of the slave pressed it the soil was accursed. In 1850 the value of land in New Jersey was $28.76 per acre; in South Carolina, considered the queen of the slave States, the value of land in the same year was *one dollar and thirty-two cents per acre,* and almost the same proportion prevailed between the other Northern and Southern States.[20]

The slaveholders were always a great minority of the white population of the South; but they succeeded in overriding and debasing the non-slaveholding whites to that degree that they were eliminated from any participation in public affairs. No schools were provided, and so ignorant and sodden became the "poor whites" that they were held in contempt by even the slaves. This condition existed in all portions of the South, except what may be termed Appalachian America. Here there was a hardy people imbued with the principles of liberty, and who bitterly hated slavery. When the opportunity came they fought for its destruction, and they have never been in sympathy with the slave portion of the South. The Southern planters sold their own children by slave mothers into slavery, and the knowledge of this fact brought no disgrace. Indeed, it secured honor; for Richard M. Johnson, of Kentucky, was elected Vice-President of the United States after it was publicly known that many of his children were slaves.[21] Wendell Phillips said: "Virginia is only another Algiers. The barbarous horde who gag each other, imprison women for teaching children to read, prohibit the Bible, sell men on the auction-block, abolish marriage, condemn half their women to prostitution, and devote themselves to the breeding of human beings for sale, is only a larger and blacker Algiers."

It will be asked why slavery was permitted and so fiercely fought for as to lead men to look to a dissolution

—3

of the Union in order to perpetuate it, if it was so great an evil. Slavery benefitted the individual slave-owners. Through it they seized all political power where the institution existed; they were the landholders, ministers, merchants, and planters. By their insolent intolerance they moulded the sentiment of the South, and there it was made to favor the institution with a unanimity remarkable, and never before surpassed in any part of any country on any subject. They cared nothing for the general decay of their country so long as they flourished individually.[22] Their white non-slaveholding neighbors increased enormously, but there was nothing for them to follow in the way of honorable calling, and there existed no schools for their children; but this was brutally disregarded, for to their own children would fall slaves to cultivate the soil, and an education in Northern colleges. They utterly ignored and disregarded that axiom of republican governments, that the injury to one is the injury of the whole. In the South violence was done to the rights of a vast majority of the people, and this violence benefitted a class upon which it finally reacted morally, and the reaction destroyed the institution by which the wrong existed.

Every law is the result of some social instinct in the nature of man. What conflicts with his nature and social instinct cannot long remain a law. As man is the only animal endowed with any considerable degree of reason, he is the only animal in which different environment and degrees of progress beget variety and modification in instinct to an appreciable degree. Progress in man modifies his social instinct, and this modification makes social advancement possible—necessary—imperative. Man will

battle in one age to throw off and rise above what cost blood
and treasure in a preceding age.   There is no stationary
ground for man socially, morally, or mentally; he must
advance, to avoid retrocession.   Institutions suited to one
condition of society become the bane and destruction of a
higher condition.   Governments that do not learn and
heed this law perish from the earth.   We may see this
exemplified in the tendencies of our own country under
slavery.   We founded a free government—a republican
democracy—with slavery as an institution, an institution
so alien to our Declaration of Independence and all our
avowed principles and recognized tenets, that only the
patriotism developed in our people by the War of the Revolution enabled us to survive for even a short time.   In the
generation succeeding the Revolutionary fathers, the poison
manifested itself in symptoms of some violence.   Before
1850 the decadence of the Republic was plainly visible;
and between 1850 and 1860 the Government was a slave
oligarchy.   From the time of the beginning of the Administration of Jackson the nationality of the country and the
sentiment of the people for the Union fell into a rapid
and almost fatal decline.   This may be said to have begun
with the adoption of the Missouri Compromise.   It took
civil war to save us; that cleared away falsehoods and
gave us a true conception of what our Union means.   It
righted us about, and from the devious paths through the
quagmires of nullification, State-rights, human bondage,
and secession, brought us to the solid highway of liberty
and nationality.   Von Holst finds slavery in a democratic
republic to be such a political inconsistency as could only
end in violent revolution.

The opposition to slavery in the early days of the Republic was of the type which tolerated it while recognizing its evils and its dangers to free institutions. The fathers of our country were opposed to it,[23] but they feared to take action looking to its extinction: that step might have prevented the formation of a more perfect Union. They contented themselves with leaving to posterity their recorded convictions, and the hope that time would set right what they could not then with safety undertake. Their action was the choice of the least of two evils.

No direct anti-slavery movement, or even advocate, was anywhere found in our country until about the year 1815. A New Jersey Quaker named Benjamin Lurdy organized the "Union Humane Society" in Wheeling, Virginia, in that year. So much engrossed with his work in this field did he become that he spent his life in it. He founded papers for the exposition of his views. He organized anti-slavery societies in the South in 1824, principally among the Quakers there, and visited Hayti in 1825 in the interest of his work. He was followed by William Lloyd Garrison, who was the most radical and impracticable of all the opponents of slavery; many opponents of the institution could not agree with him in either method or sentiment.[24] A "Liberty party" arose, composed of men who believed the Federal Constitution was in spirit anti-slavery. They supported only such men as were in favor of "liberty for all," and were the most practical and effective in their work against slavery, of the Northern " parties." There were many organizations formed in the North having for their purpose agitation against the further extension of slavery, not so radical as the "Garrisonians" nor so liberal

as the "Liberal party." They were never independently
nor collectively of sufficient strength to materially influence
public sentiment, and served more to indicate the growing
discontent with the institution than as a means to its abolition. The agitation commenced in the North by Lundy,
and carried forward by those "societies" and "parties,"
bore fruit in later years. There began to be a conservative
and independent element there that grew steadily and took
a practical view of the situation; they did not separate
themselves from existing parties, but sought the election
of such men as they believed would turn every favorable
incident to advantage and work consistently against the
further extension of slavery. Of this great body such men
as Lincoln, Greeley, and Giddings were leaders; their
adherents constantly increased in numbers and influence,
and finally in the development of events, and, fired by the
martyrdom of John Brown, they arose in their might and
accomplished the redemption and purification of our country.[25]

By slaveholders everywhere in the South these people,
"societies" and "parties" were called "abolitionists" indiscriminately. No distinctions were made; and the people
there were taught that these Northern opponents of slavery
were in hostility to the Christian religion and the Federal
Constitution, and were deserving of death. In the South it
was taught that Northern society was founded on free-love
principles, and the text-books spoke of Northern "childless
wives," "old maids," and "divorced women" as constituting the female part of the population. The men of the
North were spoken of as cowardly, hypocritical, mercenary,
and meddlesome; it was taught and believed that one

Southern man could easily put six "Yankees" to flight, and that Northern men would never fight the aggressions of slavery if it came to blows. The Democratic party stood as the champion of slavery, and from a national became a sectional party, seeking the supremacy of the " institution," or, in the event of failure in that, a separation from the North by means of secession. The odium which it cast upon the workers for the confinement of slavery to its bounds as fixed by the terms of the Missouri Compromise had its effect and influence in the North, and many persons who really favored freedom were deterred by it from identifying themselves with the advocates of liberty.

Up to 1854 the abolition movement had accomplished little of practical benefit. Public sentiment was being slowly aroused—very slowly; the minister who preached the funeral sermon of John Brown in 1859 was driven from his charge. In the face of all the agitation and theory the slave-power constantly extended its prestige and influence. It had cause to be encouraged, and felt strong enough to undertake the removal of the last barrier which stood between it and the unsettled portion of the United States. In this spirit it triumphantly entered upon the repeal of the Missouri Compromise, and in the accomplishment of this purpose it stood in exultation on the ruins of the temporizing measures devised to prohibit the introduction of slaves into the Territories.

But it has often happened in this world that the exultant cry of victory and defiance was the voice that aroused the latent energies of a nation to a more desperate resistance. It proved so in this case. Theory and agitation had failed. It now came to blows in Kansas.

NOTE 1.—Rousseau, *The Social Contract;* article, SLAVERY.

NOTE 2.—Rousseau, *The Social Contract;* article, SLAVERY.

NOTE 3.—J. K. Ingram, in *Enc. Brit.;* article, SLAVERY, which the student should carefully read. Acknowledgment is here made for use of some of the ideas contained in it.

NOTE 4.—The property interests have always raised up defenders of wrongful acts against man and society. Thus, Rousseau's article on Slavery is principally a refutation of the contention of the writers of his time that slavery is justifiable. He says: "Grotius and others find in war another origin of the pretended right of slavery. The conqueror having, according to them, the right to kill the conquered, the latter can buy back his life at the expense of his liberty; an agreement the more legitimate as it turns to the profit of both. But it is clear that this pretended right to kill the conquered, results in no way from the state of war. From the fact alone, that men, living in their primitive independence, have not among themselves relations sufficiently permanent to constitute either the state of peace or war, they are not naturally enemies. It is the relation of *things* and not of *men* that constitutes war; and as it is impossible for war to arise from simple personal relations, but only from property relations, private war, or war between man and man, can exist neither in the state of nature, where there is no permanent property, nor in the social state, where all is under the authority of the laws."

NOTE 5.—This feature of the horrible results in the United States is now entering our literature. Mr. Opie Read's novel, "My Young Master," is founded upon such an incident. That many slave-owners sold their own children by slave mothers into the deepest degradation slavery could produce, is too well known to need elaboration or proof.

NOTE 6.—In Mr. Read's novel, "The Jucklins," the aristocratic old slaveholder is represented as refraining from killing Mr. Jucklin for defeating him in a wrestling bout only because there was present no spectator to witness his imaginary disgrace from having had "his back wallowed in the sand" by Mr. Jucklin, who was not a slave-owner.

NOTE 7.—Hume.

NOTE 8.—The Census of 1850 has the following:

"In Pennsylvania slavery was abolished in 1780. In New Jersey it was provisionally abolished in 1784; all children born of a slave after 1804 are made free in 1820. In Massachusetts it was declared after the Revolution that slavery was virtually abolished by the Constitution (1780). In 1784 and 1797, Connecticut provided for the gradual extinction of slavery. In Rhode Island, after 1784, no person could be *born* a slave. The Constitutions of Vermont and New Hampshire, respectively, abolished slavery. In New York it was provisionally abolished in 1799, twenty-eight years' ownership being allowed in slaves born after that date; and in 1817 it was enacted that slavery was not to exist after ten years, or 1827. The Ordinance of 1787 forbade slavery in the Territory Northwest of the Ohio river."

The above authoritative statement of the dates of the abolition of slavery in the Northern States effectually refutes the oft-repeated statement of Southern men, that the North, having found slavery unprofitable, sold her slaves to the South and immediately began a crusade for their emancipation.

———

NOTE 9.—The limits set for this paper will not permit us to discuss these various measures of the slave-power designed to retain or increase the prestige of slavery and slaveholders. Their full discussion belongs to the general history of the country. They are all briefly and excellently treated in the first volume of Greeley's "American Conflict."

———

NOTE 10.—"Let your emissaries cross the Potomac," writes the Rev. T. S. Witherspoon from Alabama to the *Emancipator*, "and I can promise you that their fate will be no less than Haman's."— *Greeley's "American Conflict," p. 128.*

———

NOTE 11.—At a public meeting convened in the *church* in the town of Clinton, Mississippi, September 5, 1833, it was—

"*Resolved*, That it is our decided opinion that any individual who dares to circulate, with a view to effectuate the designs of the Abolitionists, any of the incendiary tracts or newspapers now in the course of transmission to this country, is justly worthy, in the sight of God and man, of *immediate death;* and we doubt not that such would be the punishment of any such offender, in any part of the State of Mississippi where he may be found."

"The cry of the whole South should be *death*—instant DEATH—to the Abolitionist, wherever he is caught."—*Augusta* (Ga.) *Chronicle.*

"We can assure the Bostonians, one and all, who have embarked in the nefarious scheme of abolishing slavery at the South, that lashes will hereafter be spared to the backs of their emissaries. Let them send out their men to Louisiana; they will never return to tell their sufferings, but they shall expiate the crime of interfering with our domestic institutions by being BURNED AT THE STAKE."—*New Orleans True American.*

"Abolition editors in Slave States will not dare to avow their opinions. It would be instant DEATH to them."—*Missouri Argus.*

And Mr. Preston, of South Carolina, who once delivered a speech at Columbia in reference to a proposed railroad, in which he despondingly drew a forcible contrast between the energy, enterprise, knowledge and happiness of the North, and the inertia, indigence, and decay of the South, in the U. S. Senate afterward declared:

"Let an Abolitionist come within the borders of South Carolina, if we can catch him we will try him, and, notwithstanding all the interference of all the governments of the earth, including the Federal Government, we will HANG him."—*N. Y. Journal of Commerce, June 6, 1838.*

All this note is quoted from Greeley's "American Conflict," p. 128, notes 7 and 8.

NOTE 12.—"In 1835, a suspicion was aroused in Madison county, Mississippi, that a conspiracy for a slave insurrection existed. Five negroes were first hung; then five white men. The pamphlet put forth by their mob-murderers shows that there was no real evidence against any of them,—that their lives were sacrificed to a cowardly panic, which would not be appeased without bloodshed. The whites were hung at an hour's notice, protesting their innocence to the last. And this is but one case out of many such. In a panic of this kind, every non-slaveholder who ever said a kind word or did a humane act for a negro is a doomed man."—*Greeley's "American Conflict," p. 128, note 9.*

NOTE 13.—"From whose hands did this man receive fifty thousand dollars—improperly, if not illegally, taken from the public funds in Washington? When did he receive it?—and for what purpose?—and who was the arch-demagogue through whose agency the trans-

fer was made? He was an oligarchical member of the Cabinet under
Mr. Polk's administration in 1845, and the money was *used*—and
who can doubt *intended?*—for the express purpose of establishing
another negro-driving journal to support the tottering fortunes
of slavery. From the second volume of a valuable political work,
'by a Senator of thirty years,' we make the following pertinent
extract:

" 'The *Globe* was sold, and was paid for, and how? becomes a
question of public concern to answer; for it was paid out of public
money—those same $50,000 which were removed to the village
bank in the interior of Pennsylvania by a Treasury order on the
fourth of November, 1844. Three annual installments made the
payment, and the Treasury did not reclaim the money for these
three years; and, though traveling through tortuous channels, the
sharpsighted Mr. Rives traced the money back to its starting-point
from the deposit. Besides, Mr. Cameron, who had control of the
village bank, admitted before a committee of Congress, that he had
furnished money for the payments—an admission which the obliging
committee, on request, left out of their report. Mr. Robert J.
Walker was Secretary of the Treasury during these three years,
and the conviction was absolute, among the close observers of the
course of things, that he was the prime contriver and zealous man-
ager of the arrangements which displaced Mr. Blair and installed
Mr. Ritchie.'

"Thus, if we are to believe Mr. Benton, in his 'Thirty Years'
View,' and we are disposed to regard him as good authority, the
Washington *Union* was brought into existence under the peculiar
auspices of the ostensible editor of the Richmond *Enquirer*."—"*The
Impending Crisis*," *Helper, p. 104.*

———

Note 14.—"If the great founders of the Republic, Washington,
Jefferson, Henry, and others, could be reinvested with corporeal
life, and returned to the South, there is scarcely a slaveholder between the Potomac and the mouth of the Mississippi that would
not burn to pounce upon them with bludgeons, bowie-knives and
pistols! Yes, without adding another word, Washington would be
mobbed for what he has already said. Were Jefferson now employed as a professor in a Southern college, he would be dismissed
and driven from the State, perhaps murdered before he reached
the border. If Patrick Henry were a bookseller in Alabama, though
it might be demonstrated beyond the shadow of a doubt that he
never bought, sold, received, or presented any kind of literature
except Bibles and Testaments, he would first be subjected to the
ignominy of a coat of tar and feathers, and then limited to the

option of unceremonious expatriation or death."—*"The Impending Crisis," Helper, p. 188.*

NOTE 15.—Greeley's "American Conflict," p. 178. Samuel Hoar was sent by the Governor of Massachusetts to investigate the imprisonment of her sailors by South Carolina. These seamen were free negroes, and they were seized in the ports of South Carolina and sold into bondage in some instances, though they were usually imprisoned and fined and compelled to pay the costs of suits. Mr. Hoar was driven out of Charleston.

NOTE 16.—See Greeley's "American Conflict," p. 175.

NOTE 17.—"It may be painful, but nevertheless, profitable, to recur occasionally to the history of the past; to listen to the admonitions of experience, and learn lessons of wisdom from the effects and actions of those who have preceded us in the drama of human life. The records of former days show that at a period not very remote, Virginia stood preëminently the first commercial State in the Union; when her commerce exceeded in amount that of all the New England States combined; when the city of Norfolk owned more than one hundred trading-ships, and her direct foreign trade exceeded that of the city of New York, now the center of trade and the great emporium of North America. At the period of the War of Independence, the commerce of Virginia was four times larger than that of New York."—*Governor Wise, quoted by Helper in "The Impending Crisis," p. 16.*

NOTE 18.—"We want Bibles, brooms, buckets and books, and we go to the North; we want shoes, hats, handkerchiefs, umbrellas, and pocket-knives, and we go to the North; we want pens, ink, paper, wafers, and envelopes, and we go to the North; we want furniture, crockery, glassware and pianos, and we go North; we want toys, primers, school books, fashionable apparel, machinery, medicines, tombstones, and a thousand other things, and we go to the North for them all. Instead of keeping our money in circulation at home, by patronizing our own mechanics, manufacturers, and laborers, we send it all away to the North, and there it remains; it never falls into our hands again. . . .

"In infancy we are swaddled in Northern muslin; in childhood
we are humored with Northern gewgaws; in youth we are instructed out of Northern books; at the age of maturity we sow
our 'wild oats' on Northern soil; in middle life we exhaust our
wealth, energies and talents in the dishonorable vocation of en-
tailing our dependence on our children and our children's children,
and, to the neglect of our own interests and the interests of those
around us, in giving aid and succor to every department of Northern power; in the decline of life we remedy our eyesight with
Northern spectacles, and support our infirmities with Northern
canes; in old age we are drugged with Northern physic, and,
finally, when we die, our inanimate bodies, shrouded in Northern
cámbric, are stretched upon the bier, born to the grave in a Northern carriage, entombed with a Northern spade, and memorized with
a Northern slab."—*The Impending Crisis,*" Helper, *p. 22.*

From the same, p. 47:

"Food from the North, for man or for beast, or for both, is for
sale in every market in the South.   Even in the most insignificant
little villages in the interior of the slave States, where books,
newspapers and other mediums of intelligence are unknown, where
poor whites and the negroes are alike bowed down in heathenish
ignorance and barbarism, and where the news is received but once
a week, and then only in a Northern-built stage-coach, drawn by
horses in Northern harness, in charge of a driver dressed *cap-a-pie*
in Northern habiliments, and with a Northern whip in his hand,—
the agricultural products of the North, either crude, prepared,
pickled or preserved, are ever to be found."

In the same work, p. 90, Governor Wise is quoted as follows:

" Commerce has long ago spread her sails and sailed away from
you.   You have not, as yet, dug more than coal enough to warm
yourselves at your own hearths; you have set no tilt-hammers of
Vulcan to strike blows worthy of gods in your own iron-foundries;
you have not yet spun more than coarse cotton enough, in the way
of manufacture, to clothe your own slaves.   You have no commerce,
no mining, no manufactures.   You have relied alone on the single
power of agriculture, and *such agriculture!*   Your sedge-patches
outshine the sun.   Your inattention to your only source of wealth
has seared the very bosom of Mother Earth.   Instead of having to
feed cattle on a thousand hills, you have to chase a stump-tailed

steer through the sedge-patches to procure a tough beefsteak. The present condition of things has existed too long in Virginia. The landlord has skinned the tenant, and the tenant has skinned the land, until all have grown poor together."

NOTE 19.—"In the year 1836 or 1837 the Hon. Abbott Lawrence, of Boston, backed by his brother Amos and other millionaires of New England, went down to Richmond with the sole view of reconnoitering the manufacturing facilities of that place,—fully determined, if pleased with the water-power, to erect a large number of cotton-mills and machine-shops. He had been in the capital of Virginia only a day or two before he discovered, much to his gratification, that nature had shaped everything to his liking; and as he was a business man who transacted business in a business-like manner, he lost no time in making preliminary arrangements for the consummation of his noble purpose. . . .

"To the enterprising and moneyed descendant of the Pilgrim Fathers it was a matter of no little astonishment, that the immense water-power of Richmond had been so long neglected. He expressed his surprise to a number of Virginians, and was at a loss to know why they had not, long prior to the period of his visit amongst them, availed themselves of the powerful element that is eternally gushing and foaming over the falls of James river. Innocent man! He was utterly unconscious of the fact that he was 'interfering with the beloved institutions of the South,' and little was he prepared to withstand the terrible denunciations that were immediately showered on his head through the columns of the Richmond *Enquirer*. Few words will suffice to tell the sequel. That negro-worshipping sheet, whose hireling policy, for the last four-and-twenty years, has had to support the worthless black slave and his tyrannical master at the expense of the free white laborer, wrote down the enterprise! and the noble son of New England, abused, insulted and disgusted, quietly returned to Massachusetts, and there employed his capital in building up the cities of Lowell and Lawrence."—*"The Impending Crisis," Helper, p. 107.*

NOTE 20.—"In traversing that county, [Madison county, Alabama,] one will discover numerous farm-houses, once the abode of industrious and intelligent freemen, now occupied by slaves, or tenantless, deserted and dilapidated; he will observe fields, once

fertile, now unfenced, abandoned, and covered with those evil har-
bingers, fox-tail and broom-sedge; he will see the moss growing
on the mouldering walls of once thrifty villages, and will find
'one only master grasps the whole domain,' that once furnished
happy homes for a dozen white families. Indeed, a country in
its infancy, where fifty years ago scarce a forest tree had been
felled by the axe of the pioneer, is already exhibiting the painful
signs of senility and decay. The soil itself soon sickens and dies
beneath the unnatural tread of the slave.

"Such are the agricultural achievements of slave labor; such are
the results of 'the sum of all villainies.' The diabolical institution
subsists on its own flesh. At one time children are sold to procure
food for the parents, at another, parents are sold to procure food
for the children. Within its pestilential atmosphere, nothing suc-
ceeds; progress and prosperity are unknown; inanition and sloth-
fulness ensue; everything becomes dull, dismal and unprofitable;
wretchedness and desolation run riot throughout the land; an aspect
of most melancholy inactivity and dilapidation broods over every
city and town; ignorance and prejudice sit enthroned over the
minds of the people; usurping despots wield the sceptre of power;
everywhere, and in everything, between Delaware Bay and the Gulf
of Mexico, are the multitudinous evils of slavery apparent."—*"The
Impending Crisis," Helper, pp. 56, 57.*

NOTE 21.—Greeley's "American Conflict," p. 136.

NOTE 22.—"Oligarchical politicians are alone responsible for the
continuance of African slavery in the South. For purposes of self-
aggrandizement, they have kept learning and civilization from the
people; they have willfully misinterpreted the national compacts,
and have outraged their own consciences by declaring to their illiter-
ate constituents that the founders of the Republic were not Abolitionists."—*"The Impending Crisis." Helper, p. 189.*

NOTE 23.—Washington said in a letter to John F. Mercer, September 9, 1786:

"I never mean, unless some particular circumstances should compel me to it, to possess another slave by purchase, it being among
my *first wishes* to see some plan adopted by which slavery, in this
country, may be abolished by law."

General Washington made many similar expressions, and manumitted his slaves in his will.

In his Notes on Virginia, Jefferson says:

"With the morals of a people their industry is also destroyed; for, in a warm climate, no man will labor for himself who can make another labor for him. This is so true, that of the proprietors of slaves a very small proportion, indeed, are ever seen to labor. And can the liberties of a nation be thought secure, when we have removed their only firm basis—a conviction in the minds of the people that their liberties are the gift of God? that they are not to be violated but with His wrath? Indeed, I tremble for my country when I reflect that God is just; that His justice cannot sleep forever."

Mr. Jefferson uttered much more than this against slavery. Nothing stronger than the Declaration of Independence has ever been written, and the preamble to that instrument is a declaration for liberty.

Patrick Henry says:

"It would rejoice my very soul, that every one of my fellow-beings was emancipated. We ought to lament and deplore the necessity of holding our fellow-men in bondage. Believe me, I shall honor the Quakers for their noble efforts to abolish slavery."

John Randolph, of Roanoke, said:

"Sir, I envy neither the heart nor the head of that man from the North who rises here to defend slavery on principle."

He emancipated his slaves by will, in which he said: "I give to my slaves their freedom, to which my conscience tells me they are justly entitled."

Madison, Mason, Marshall, Bolling, Blair, Benton, and many other Southern patriots were against slavery. Franklin, Jay, and many of the most eminent statesmen of what were later called the free States were opposed to slavery in the convention which formed our Constitution.

NOTE 24.—His attitude was expressed thus: "The Federal Constitution is a covenant with death and an agreement with hell."

NOTE 25.—Read "The Rise and Progress of Abolition," in *The American Conflict*, by Greeley, Vol. I, p. 107, and following.

CHAPTER II.

THE POLITICAL BEGINNINGS OF KANSAS.

We cross the prairies as of old
  The fathers crossed the sea,
To make the West, as they the East,
  The homestead of the free.
We go to plant the common school
  On distant prairie swells,
And give the Sabbaths of the wilds
  The music of her bells.
Upbearing, like the ark of God,
  The Bible in our van,
We go to test the truth of God
  Against the fraud of man.
                    —*Whittier.*

The " Platte Country " was so called from some time perhaps as remote as the Missouri Compromise. It stretched from the Indian Territory and the Missouri river to the summit of the Rocky Mountains and to the borders of British America. The name came from the great river crossing it from west to east to add its turbid waters to the yellow flood of the Missouri.[1] It was in 1850 a vast plain covered with Indian tribes and buffalo—the home of wild men and wild animals. White men were prohibited from settling on this portion of the public domain, and the fairest and most fertile land in the West remained a waste. But, although without civilization, the land was well known. Great and ancient highways traveled these

(48)

boundless plains. One followed the Platte up to that depression in the great mountain-chain known as South Pass; here it divided, and separated into two ways. One of these followed western waters down to the Great Salt Lake Valley, and from thence across the burning sand-wastes, over plains of sage, cactus and grease-wood, up mountain ranges till the clouds were below, and down golden waters to the fair valleys of California. The other branch followed over rocky fastnesses, along and across deep and winding rivers, into wilderness wastes, over ragged and lava-scorched mountains to the green valley of the Willamette, in Oregon, and down the mighty Columbia to the shores of the Pacific ocean. The other "ancient way" was the "Old Santa Fé Trail," famous in romance and song, and leading from the mouth of the Kansas river across the plains and through the mountains to the land of the Montezumas. Along these plains highways rolled a commerce; the migration of the Mormons and the discovery of gold in California sent over them mighty streams of humanity.

By the Missouri Compromise the "Platte Country" was dedicated and set apart to human liberty; it was never to be polluted nor pressed by the foot of the slave. For this reason the Government, in the hands of the slave-owners, had removed it from the roll of lands upon which the people might enter and build homes. This removal was effected with plausibility; the land was assigned to tribes of eastern Indians, who held it by virtue of solemn treaties which guaranteed that neither they nor the tracts by them occupied should ever become part of any State or Territory to be organized by the United States. But so

—4

absurd became this policy of prohibition that even the Indians came to oppose it. In 1852 they began the agitation for the removal of restrictions which resulted in the formation of a provisional government for the country, which they called Nebraska. Clamor for the removal of the restrictions resulted, and the representatives of the provisional government knocked for admission to the halls of Congress.[2] The pressure of home-seekers upon the borders of the beautiful and forbidden land became tremendous. Public sentiment, led by the owners of the soil, was fast coming to demand that the country be opened to settlement. This sentiment was not confined to the free States; the people of some of the slave States, Missouri especially, were eager to have permission to establish themselves on the fair and fertile plains of Nebraska. On this account the provisional government received encouragement from that portion of the Missouri people reposing confidence in the leadership of Senator Benton. But as there was no available tract of country in that portion of the unsettled public domain surrendered to slavery to be opened to settlement to counterbalance the " Platte Country " should the restrictions to its settlement be removed, to allow its organization would be giving an advantage to freedom. By the Missouri Compromise this land rightfully belonged to the principles of freedom, and had been relinquished by the advocates of slavery thirty years before; but it was resolved to now make an effort to regain at least a portion of the domain then lost.

A new tenet had been recognized in the compromise of 1850; it permitted the people of a Territory applying for admission as a State to determine for themselves the nature of their institutions, and to legalize or prohibit slavery as they might choose. When the Nebraska question came up for discussion the slave-power contended that this principle abrogated the Missouri Compromise. The bills for the organization of Nebraska Territory were cast aside, and a bill providing for the formation of two Territories from the domain of the " Platte Country " was substituted for them. This bill declared the Missouri Compromise inoperative and void, and affirmed the application of the principle of the compromise of 1850 to the proposed Territories in explicit terms. The struggle was long and bitter, and no less so in Congress than in the country at large. The South was properly charged with bad faith, and the matter was discussed by every newspaper in the land—by citizens in private walks and in public assemblies. Ministers everywhere made it the subject of sermons—often objurgatory and vituperative in the North, always complimentary and commendatory in the South. But in the struggle the South had the advantage; she was perfectly united, and by seizing upon the personal ambitions and demagogical propensities of Northern politicians created and maintained a considerable sentiment in its favor in that part of our country where slavery was abhorred. She had looked forward to this very contingency, and fortified herself in the White House; Pierce was compelled to commit himself without reserve to the policy declared in the Kansas-Nebraska bill, in order to attain the Presidency.[3] It was with great satisfaction, therefore, that he approved the Kansas-Nebraska bill on the 30th day of May, 1854.

The result of this struggle was despondency in the North and exultation in the South. Slavery regarded the victory won as in fact a compromise on the same lines governing the admission of States into the Union in the early days of the Government, when equilibrium of Congressional representation was maintained by the admission of one slave and one free State at the same time.[4] On this principle two Territories were formed instead of one, and the South claimed the slave State—Kansas, and conceded the free State—Nebraska. The South was well equipped to enter the contest for the consummation of this design. On the east Kansas joined a slave State—Missouri. The western counties of Missouri contained a large population possessing many slaves, and an intense sentiment and desire for the extension of slavery into Kansas. This condition was largely relied upon in the formulation of the Kansas-Nebraska plan.[5] It was believed that the citizens of Missouri would at once migrate to the new Territory and seize all the choice lands before people from a greater distance could arrive. To facilitate this action the Government concluded secret treaties with the Indian tribes owning the land in the eastern portion of the Territory, wherein the greater part of the best land was to be at once opened to settlement; and the representatives of the slave-power in Missouri were apprised of the conclusion of these treaties long before their public proclamation. And other slave States were expected to contribute largely of their inhabitants with their slaves to form the population of the new Territory organized in the interest of slavery.

But, "the best-laid schemes o' mice and men gang aft a-gley." Missouri failed to meet the expectations entertained of her, because there was no pressing demand in

her western counties for land. These counties were yet
new, and the people had not more than accomplished the
subjection of the forest and prairie;[6] land was cheap, and
no great sum could be realized from its sale. When it
was known that people from the free States intended to
contest for Kansas, the people owning slaves in Missouri
became averse to jeopardizing their property by carrying
it to a Territory which might in the end destroy its value.
The institution proved too clumsy and too much of a
weight to be readily removed from States at a greater
distance.[7]

The despondency of the North was temporary, and disappeared after a brief period following the passage of the
Kansas-Nebraska bill. In New England this reaction
was largely sentimental.[8] In the free States of the Ohio
Valley it was intensely aggressive and practical. People
from Ohio, Pennsylvania and Indiana were in Kansas before the bill had finally passed.[9] When it was known that
it had become a law, people from western New York and
Pennsylvania, and from all the States made from the old
Northwest Territory, set their faces towards Kansas with
the avowed intention of building themselves homes and of
making the Territory a free State.[10] The people of Massachusetts turned their sentiment to practical use, and
other New England States followed the example. The
Emigrant Aid Company was formed to carry out the
policy announced by William H. Seward in the debate of
the bill in the United States Senate.[11] Eli Thayer was
the principal mover in this organization, which became a
potent factor in making Kansas a free State. It was
largely due to his efforts that the sentimental opposition

to the bill in New England was given some practical
direction and form.   Societies like that projected by him
were formed in other New England States, and, indeed,
in other parts of the North.   While it must be admitted
that they accomplished great good for Kansas and the
country, it is true that their organization first alarmed the
South, and many of the outrages perpetrated by the border
ruffians were inspired by their hostility to Northern emigrant aid societies.[12]   Similar organizations were formed
in the South in the interest of slavery; in Missouri it was
claimed that their organization was for the purpose of
counteracting those of the North; they were called " Blue
Lodges," " Social Bands," " Friends' Societies," and
" The Sons of the South." [13]

The result of the passage of the Kansas-Nebraska bill
was to localize for a time, and to transfer to Kansas, the
preliminary battle in the final contest between freedom
and slavery.   The forces on each side were stirred to effort.
The resources of each section were drawn upon to advance
respective interests and pave the way to ultimate victory,
of which the South was sanguine and the North hopeful.
In the actual conflict in Kansas, the South, flushed with
victory in Congress and animated with impatience of restraint, intolerance, and a fanatical but distorted faith
in the justice of her cause, was always the aggressor.   The
Northern emigrant was proclaimed an abolitionist, whatever his political faith or however tolerant his views.
No discriminations were made.   Abolitionists were denounced in Kansas, as they had been everywhere in the
South, as the enemies of society, religion, humanity, and
the Union.   Of rights they were supposed not to have any,

and they were to be accorded none in Kansas. Their lives were considered as forfeited here, as in the South, and the Pro-Slavery settlers were urged to destroy them. The partisans of freedom soon came to be called Free-State men; the advocates of slavery were known by various names: Pro-Slavery men, Law and Order men, and National Democrats. But the people of Kansas bestowed upon them the name, Border Ruffian.[14] Many of the more depraved characters among them came to glory in this term, but there were many good people in the slavery ranks, and they were opposed to violence at all times.[15] They were allowed little part in the formulation of the course in Kansas in the interest of slavery. Those in power and the great majority of those who came to Kansas were noisy, violent, aggressive, brutal and murderous from the very first. Some of the outrageous conduct of these slavery partisans is enumerated:

As early as the 6th of October, 1854, Westport sent a large body of men with arms, and banners decorated with strange devices and violent and threatening legends, to break up the Free-State settlement of Lawrence. In the most violent and horrible oaths possible of expression in the English language they ordered the "abolitionists" to strike their tents and leave the Territory. The settlers showed the "eyes and teeth" of courage, and the presumptuous invaders were so astonished at the exhibition of bravery in "Yankees" that they returned home swearing wicked oaths of what they would do when they returned at the end of a week with a larger force.[16]

The first elections were scenes of violence and disorder. Long lines of whisky-sodden ruffians[17] wound their sev-

eral ways about the prairies and along the streams of
Kansas, took armed possession of the polls and voting-
places, cast thousands of illegal votes, perjured themselves
by certifying to fraudulent election returns, and returned
in a drunken frenzy to their homes in Missouri. At
Leavenworth a Free-State election clerk named Wetherell
complained because a youth who said he was but nineteen
was allowed to vote, on the qualification of having a claim
in Kansas; he said he lived in Missouri. He was allowed
to cast nine votes for residents of Missouri who were not
present, but who, so the youth said, had claims in the
Territory. At this easy manner of exercising the rights
of suffrage Wetherell declared that the election was a
fraud. Charles Dunn was the chief ruffian present, and
hearing the remark of the clerk, seized him by the head,
dragged him from the building through the window with
great bodily injury, fell upon him, in company with other
ruffians, beat and kicked him in a shamefully brutal manner, and left him for dead. [18]

In the same city a vigilance committee was formed at
a meeting addressed by the Chief Justice of the Territory
on the 30th of April, 1855. The resolutions adopted
warned "all persons not to come to our peaceful firesides
to slander us, and sow the seeds of discord between the
master and the servant"; and the duty of the committee
was defined in the following explicit language: "All such
persons as shall by the expression of abolition sentiments
produce a disturbance to the quiet of the citizens or danger
to their domestic relations, shall be notified and made to
leave the Territory."

Mr. William Phillips, a lawyer, and by all reports a

brave and good citizen, lived at the time in Leavenworth, and soon became amenable to this power of the committee. A mob seized him and carried him to Weston, Mo. There one-half his head was shaved as were the heads of convicts in the dark ages; he was stripped of his raiment, tarred and feathered, ridden on a rail, had a halter put on his neck by which he was led to the block, and by a negro cried to the highest bidder and sold for one-fourth of one cent. He was allowed to return home, but was soon afterward murdered in his own house by a band of "law and order" men styling themselves "Territorial militia," and commanded by Frederick S. Emory; his sole offense was his refusal to leave the town of Leavenworth at the mob's bidding.[19]

One of the most brutal and wanton murders ever committed in the Territory was that of Rees P. Brown. He was a resident of Leavenworth county, and had been to the polls at the village of Easton to attend the election for State officers under the Topeka Constitution. As he and a number of other Free-State men were returning home they were met by Captain Charles Dunn, one of the most rabid ruffians that ever cursed the border. They were taken back to Easton and confined in a store; all but Brown were allowed to escape. A mob broke into the building in which Brown was confined and struck him several times in the face with a hatchet. The assault was made by one Gibson. He was thrown into a lumber wagon, where he remained for seven hours while his captors were drinking at a doggery, the weather being at the time bitterly cold. He was taken home and dragged from the wagon to the frozen ground; he was cast into

the cabin with the words, " Here is Brown! " He died
in about three hours, and the brutality he had suffered
made his wife a maniac.[20]

A Pro-Slavery man in Leavenworth made a bet that he
could in two hours bring in the scalp of an abolitionist. A
young German was just returning to town after having
taken his wife to visit her sister in Lawrence. The
ruffian shot him, and he fell from his carriage; then the
murderer scalped him and triumphantly returned with his
reeking trophy to claim his winning, which was a pair of
boots, against which he had bet six dollars. He was afterwards tried for murder, and acquitted! [21]

The paper of Stringfellow, published at Atchison, contained a standing notice that abolitionists would be
lynched if they dared to " pollute *our* soil."

But the *ne plus ultra* of ruffian outrage and villainy
was attained in the enactment of the infamous code known
as the Bogus Laws, by the Legislature fraudulently selected by the election at which the outrages before spoken
of occurred, and known in history as the Bogus Legislature. One of these statutes provided that any person
daring to discuss the question of the establishment of
slavery in Kansas, or "whether it exists or does not exist"
there, should be imprisoned at hard labor for at least two
years—the maximum term not fixed; it might be ninety-
nine years. By this code no man could serve on a jury
who was opposed to slavery. It contained many laws of
the same nature; and that certain indication of tyranny—
the appointment of all county and township officers by the
Legislature or executive—was fixed upon the people, who
were thus divested of the right of local self-government.[22]

Andrew H. Reeder, of Pennsylvania, was appointed the first Governor of the Territory; and his administration was one continuous struggle against the ruffians and minions of the slave-power for some semblance of right and justice for the people. His efforts in this direction were resented at Washington, and he was removed from office. He remained for a time in the Territory, and assisted in the founding of the Free-State party and became its first candidate for Delegate to Congress. He was defeated by fraud, and contested the election; the result was the appointment of a committee to investigate Kansas affairs. This committee was virtually driven from the Territory by the ruffians; but it formulated a report which contains more than a thousand printed pages of the outrages against liberty and the free people of Kansas. Reeder was forced to fly to escape assassination at the hands of the principal ruffian of Leavenworth county acting for the slave-power.[23]

Upon the removal of Reeder, Wilson Shannon was appointed Governor. His weakness and his cringing and obsequious sycophancy resulted in the outrages committed in the Wakarusa war, and, finally, in anarchy. The murder of Free-State men became so common that it ceased even to cause comment. Governor Shannon was himself compelled to seek safety from assassination in flight; he reported that dead bodies lay thickly all along all the Territorial highways.[24]

Thus, chaos, anarchy, confusion and disorder in Kansas resulted from the efforts of the Government to force human bondage upon the people. Nevertheless, emigrants from the free States continued to arrive. The foregoing description will serve to show to some degree the disordered and unsettled condition of society into which they came, and that their lives were forfeited the minute they set foot in Kansas. They were subjected to many indignities while passing through Missouri; and the pirates and ruffians there finally closed the Missouri river in the hope that they would thereby be deterred from attempting to reach the Territory. But these crusaders for freedom were made of sterner stuff. They turned to the north, and came into the Mecca of their faith by the way of Iowa and Nebraska.

There was in those days living in Ohio and New York a most remarkable family—that of John Brown. So important was the work of this family in the emancipation of the slaves of America, that a recent and eminent writer upon the subject assigns it the fourth place in the causes which resulted in their freedom. In the fall of 1854 five of the sons of John Brown determined to remove to Kansas to make themselves homes and assist in making it a free State. They were bred to rugged industry and self-reliance, and were inured to hardship, scant living, high thinking and right conduct before God and man. They came to labor, to till the soil, to erect houses, to plant and tend vineyards and orchards and to rear cattle,—to devote themselves to the peaceful pursuits of the farm. They brought with them their young fruit trees and grapevines, their plows and reaping-hooks, their tents and their cattle. They set out from the Western Reserve, in Ohio, where they then lived and where they had been born, in the fall of 1854, with their cattle, and got as far as Meredosia, Illinois. Here the brothers, Owen, Frederick and Salmon, remained to care for the cattle through the winter, and when spring came they drove them overland into Kansas.[25] The brothers, Jason and John, jr., came by steamer down the Ohio river and to St. Louis. At this point they and their families took passage on a boat bound for the Territory. It was crowded with people "mostly from the South, as was plainly indicated by their language and dress; while their drinking, profanity, and display of revolvers and bowie-knives—openly worn as a part of their make-up —clearly showed the class to which they belonged, and that their mission was to aid in establishing slavery in Kansas." Cholera appeared on the boat, and a number of passengers died; among them, Austin, the little son of Jason Brown. The brothers and their families went ashore at the panic-stricken town of Waverly, Missouri, at night, in a furious thunder-storm, to commit to the earth the body of their child; and without warning the boat cast off and continued her way without them.[26] They were left to make their way to Kansas City as best they could, and were compelled to complete their journey by stage.

These brothers arrived very early in the spring of 1855. If they were too late to see the ruffians come over from Missouri to carry the election, they arrived while that outrage was fresh in the minds of the people. They all selected claims some ten miles from Osawatomie, near that of their uncle, the Rev. S. L. Adair. Their farms did not adjoin, for claims were then selected with a view to secure some timber; but they were not far apart, and a circuit of two miles would have inclosed them all. They succeeded in raising something, though little, the first year.

But the political turmoil and the merciless persecutions of
the Free-State men raged during the summer. The usur-
pation of the government by the Missourians and their
enactment of the bogus laws could not be tamely submitted
to by a people loving liberty and coming from a country
where the laws were for all and obeyed by all. It was
generally agreed by the Free-State settlers that they could
not submit to all these laws. It was apparent that it was
intended that the laws should make it impossible for
Free-State people to remain in Kansas. As the newspapers along the border of Missouri were teeming with
threats and inflammatory articles, it was believed that
trouble would arise as soon as the crops ceased to engross
the attention of the people. The part of prudence demanded that the Free-State men be prepared to protect
themselves from assault. The Browns early identified
themselves with the movement to organize and make effective the anti-slavery forces in the Territory. On the 8th
of June, 1855, some of them attended the Free-State meeting in Lawrence, and John Brown, jr., was a member of
the committee on resolutions.[27] He and his brother Frederick were delegates to the Big Springs Convention, and
assisted there to form the Free-State party.[28]

Early in the summer John Brown, jr., wrote his father
the conditions existing in the Territory, and requested him
to procure arms for their defense and send them on to
Kansas.[29] John Brown was then living at North Elba,
New York. He attended an anti-slavery or abolition convention at Syracuse, in that State, in the latter part of
June. Here he made a "very fiery speech, during which
he said he had four sons in Kansas, and had three others

who were desirous of going there, to aid in fighting the battles of freedom. He could not consent to go unless armed, and he would like to arm all his sons; but his poverty prevented him from doing so." [30] It had not been his intention to go to Kansas. In a letter to his son John almost a year before he had said: " If you or any of my family are disposed to go to Kansas or Nebraska, with a view to help defeat *Satan* and his legions in that direction, I have not a word to say; *but I feel committed to operate in another part of the field.* If I were not so committed, I would be on my way this fall." [31] His attendance upon the Syracuse convention appears to have changed this determination; perhaps he met there persons with whom he was "committed" to labor in some different part of the field, and after discussion it was agreed that Kansas was as inviting and promising as any field for the time being need be. His appeal to the convention for arms and means to reach the Territory seems to have resulted to his satisfaction, for he wrote his wife: " I have reason to bless God that I came. I met with a most warm reception . . . a most hearty approval of my intention of arming my sons and other friends in Kansas." [32] Something more than sixty dollars was given him; and it is very probable that other and further contributions were sent him before he left New York for the Territory.

He set out for Kansas sometime in August, accompanied by his son-in-law, Henry Thompson. His son Oliver was then at Rockford, Illinois, and he was taken along, and wrote to his mother that he hoped to see them all in Kansas in a year or two. They wrote from Chicago that they had there purchased "a nice young horse for

$120, but have so much load that we shall have to walk a good deal—enough probably to supply ourselves with game." From a point in Scott county, Iowa, "about twenty miles west of the Mississippi," he wrote his wife that their load was heavy and they walked much. They fared "very well on crackers, herring, boiled eggs, prairie chicken, tea, and sometimes a little milk. Have three chickens now cooking for our breakfast. We shoot enough of them on the wing as we go along to supply us with fresh meat. Oliver succeeds in bringing them down quite as well as any of us." He further says: "We hope our money will not entirely fail us; but we shall not have any of account left when we get through." They expected "to go direct through Missouri." This letter contains the remarkable statement: "I think, *could I hope in any other way to answer the end of my being,* I would be quite content to be at North Elba." [33] He believed with his whole soul that God had appointed him to make war on slavery, and in no other way could he hope to answer the end of his being. To answer this call he surrendered the comforts of domestic happiness, the ease so much coveted by men of his age, anything like a competency for increasing years, and set forth on a journey long and toilsome, and in which he "walked much," to join a heroic band of freedom-loving men and women engaged then in fighting back the foul institution of human bondage threatening to engulf them on the plains of Kansas. In that sentence is the key and explanation of the character of John Brown.

They arrived at the "Brown settlement" on the 6th of October, and found all "more or less sick or feeble but Wealthy and Johnny." [34] The entire party had but *sixty cents* when they arrived. And—strange man, this Brown!—while anxious to battle to the death with the powers of slavery and darkness, and determined to shed blood if need be, and fully realizing that his own blood might be required, as well as that of his children, he was as sensitive to the touch of love and sympathy as is a mother to the cry of her babe. No mother ever carried more tenderness in her soul for her children than John Brown bore in his heart for suffering of every kind. His whole being responded to the grief of those who mourned. On this weary journey he remembered that his daughter-in-law had left the light of her life in an unmarked and lonely grave on a hill washed by the yellow tide of the Missouri. He turned aside to seek the lowly grave; he lifted from it the tiny body of his grandson, and carried it with him to the free land of Kansas to ·gladden the heart of her that wept.[35] All summer she had borne such grief as only a mother who has lost her child can feel. The parents had written: "We fully believe that Austin is happy with his Maker in another existence; and if there is to be a separation of friends after death, we pray God to keep us in the way of truth, and that we may so run our short course as to be able to enjoy his company again. Ellen feels so lonely and discontented here without Austin, that we shall go back to Akron next fall if she does not enjoy herself better." [36]

What manner of people are these Browns, old and young, to whom the world seems a sort of temporary stopping-place; who are continually seeking the sustaining arm of a higher power; who never fail to commend one another to God; who realize their weakness and ask

—5

strength only from Him who is able to give; who struggle in poverty to do the work a nation has neglected? Ah! these are questions which John Brown answered with his life on a scaffold in the beautiful mountains of Virginia!

NOTE 1.—*The American Conflict*, Greeley, p. 225.

NOTE 2.—*The Provisional Government of Nebraska Territory*, William E. Connelley, p. 17, and following.

NOTE 3.—*Memorial of S. N. Wood*, by his wife, p. 21. Also statement of Hannibal Hamlin. See *The Kansas Crusade*, Eli Thayer, p. 9.

NOTE 4.—"The repeal of the Compromise bill of 1820 by the passage of the Kansas-Nebraska Act of 1854, was, of itself, though not so specified or implied, a sort of compromise measure. The original act, as has been stated, provided for the organization of a single Territory, to be called Nebraska, which was to embrace all that section of country which constitutes the Territory of Kansas. The locality of the greater portion of Nebraska as thus designed; its ready access to immigration from the North; and its peculiar adaptation as respects both climate and soil, to free labor, rendered it certain of being received into the Union at an early day as a free State. The Southern politicians could not wisely and openly object to its organization upon this ground. Hence a more judicious policy, as it was less likely to meet with determined opposition and condemnation, was adopted. The substitute of Mr. Douglas, though it could not prevent the erection of a free State, would at least so far keep up the equality as to create another State, into which slavery would be introduced. By the proposition to erect two new Territories instead of one, as at first proposed, and to allow the inhabitants of each to determine for themselfes whether slavery should or should not be admitted, it was intended and so understood, that Nebraska should become a free State and Kansas a slave State. This was, beyond all question, the object and meaning of the Kansas-Nebraska bill of Mr. Douglas; and it was so regarded, as all its acts show, by the late Administration. This, in fact, is the only excuse, although by no means a sufficient one, that can be offered in extenuation of the outrages that have been committed against Free-State settlers. Many members of the Pro-Slavery party, believing it to have been a matter understood and fixed by certain contracting powers and the heads of the General Government, that Kansas was to become a slave State, in order to keep up an equilibrium of Northern and Southern sectional and political interests, conscientiously supposed that instead of its being a criminal offense, it was not only justifiable, but a virtue, to persecute, even to death, all Northern people who should enter the Territory with the disposition to defeat or thwart that object. All such were regarded as intruders, whom it was proper to remove at all hazards and by whatever means, however cruel or oppressive, that could be employed. This sentiment was not confined to Kansas and the adjoining State of Missouri, but was entertained by persons high in authority elsewhere, and especially at the seat of the Federal Government."—"*History of Kansas*," *John H. Gihon, pp. 27, 28.*

A meeting at Independence, Mo., resolved that "we ask only our rights as compromise, viz.: That we, the South, be permitted peaceably to possess Kansas, while the North, on same privilege, be permitted to possess Nebraska Territory."—"*History of the State of Kansas*," *A. T. Andreas, p. 83.*

The *Baltimore Sun*, June 28, 1854, said: "Abolitionists or Free-Soilers would do well not to stop in Kansas Territory, but keep on up the Missouri river until they reach Nebraska Territory, where they can peacefully make claims and establish their abolition and free-soil notions; for if they do, they will be respectfully notified that but one day's grace will be allowed for them to take up their bed and baggage and walk."—"*History of the State of Kansas*," *A. T. Andreas, p. 83.*

———

NOTE 5.—There was even a pro-slavery plan to annex the portion of Missouri known as the "Platte Purchase" to Kansas Territory.— "*Annals of Kansas*," *D. W. Wilder, p. 66.*

———

NOTE 6.—In fact, this had not yet been done. One township in

Jackson county was not subdivided until 1843; if there had been any pressing demand for land it would have been sectionized and sold prior to that date. It is true that there was much public land in the border counties of Missouri in even 1850. But the choice lands were selected and occupied long before. Much of the clamor for the opening of the "Platte Country" came from the vanguard of real civilization—frontier characters who would remain for a time and then depart to seek another new country. There was a great quantity of this human driftwood banked against the western State line of Missouri in 1854. It furnished the majority of the border ruffians.

NOTE 7.—The principal reason why the emigrant aid societies of the South made no better showing in sending slaveholding settlers to Kansas, was their poverty. They could secure no money. Alabama appropriated $25,000; whether any of this sum was ever paid is not known with certainty. The wealth of the South consisted largely of land and negroes; accumulations of money consequent upon commerce and manufactures did not exist. The people had no genius for the adroit handling of money in any enterprise where they met close competition. Missouri spent large sums, but not in an effective manner; she observed no system.

NOTE 8.—One of Eli Thayer's most effective arguments was, "that it was much better to *go* and *do* something for free labor than to stay at home and talk of manacles and auction-blocks and bloodhounds, while deploring the never-ending aggressions of slavery."—*"The Kansas Crusade," Eli Thayer, p. 31.*

NOTE 9.—"Early in May, 1854, the Barber brothers, Thomas W. and Oliver P., with Samuel Walker and Thomas M. Pearson, made a tour in the Territory with a view to settlement. They had all been 'boys together' in Franklin county, Pennsylvania, but the Barbers now lived in Indiana. They came to Westport, Missouri, by public conveyance. Here they hired a half-breed Indian to take them over the Territory with his team. They spent a night at 'Blue Jacket Crossing' on the Wakarusa, and passed over what was to be the site of Lawrence, passing up the spur of the hill south of where the University now stands. They went as far as Topeka, where there was an old-fashioned rope ferry; they then went across the prairies to Fort Leavenworth, and then back to their home. The Kansas-Nebraska bill passed while they were in the Territory. All four afterwards removed to Kansas, and were largly instrumental in inducing others to come."—"*A History of Lawrence, Kansas,*" *Rev. Richard Cordley, p. 3.*

NOTE 10.—"As soon as the land was thrown open to settlement 'squatters' came in from Missouri and from the Western and Northwestern States to secure claims. . . . Among the settlers who came into the county . . . in the spring and early summer of 1854, were J. W. Lunkins, of South Carolina, April 13; A. R. Hopper, May 9; Clark Stearns and William H. R. Lykins, May 26; A. B. and N. E. Wade, June 5; J. A. Wakefield, June 8; [he was a South Carolinian, but came to Kansas from Virginia, through Ohio, Indiana, and Illinois.—Wm. E. C.]; Calvin and Martin Adams, June 10; J. J. Eberhart, June 12; Bryce W. Miller, June 6; J. H. Harrison, June 14; H. S. and Paul C. Eberhart, June 15; S. N. Wood, June 24; Mr. Rolf, June 24; L. A. Largerquest, July 4; James F. Legate, July 5; William Lyon and Josiah Hutchinson, in July. On the Wakarusa, Joel K. Goodin settled in May, and William Breyman, July 18."—"*Douglas County,*" *in "History of the State of Kansas," A. T. Andreas, p. 308.*

"Then it is impossible to do justice to all the actors engaged. The movement that saved Kansas was of the people, rather than of the leaders. There were leaders, but they were leaders chiefly because they went before. They did not create the movement, nor the sentiment out of which it grew. The people moved toward Kansas of their own impulse. They did not go at the beck of any man. They followed certain men because they were going their way. If all the leaders had failed them they would have chosen others and gone on. They were moved by individual conviction and a common impulse. Men and women who have never been heard of displayed a spirit of self-sacrifice and heroism as worthy of remembrance as anything history records of noted names. No history can do honor to all who deserve it."—"*History of Lawrence,*" *Rev. Richard Cordley, p. iii, Preface.*

The above quotation from the excellent work of Dr. Cordley is the best statement of the cause actuating people to come to Kansas that has ever been written. It states the exact truth, and refutes completely the impression sought to be conveyed by Eli Thayer in his *The Kansas Crusade*, that the peopling of Kansas was largely the work of the Emigrant Aid Company. It is estimated that at the end of 1854 there were eight thousand Free-State settlers in Kansas. Of these, Mr. Thayer admits that but five hundred were on the rolls of the Emigrant Aid Company; but he impliedly and with remarkable procacity, claims them all. The claim that the Emigrant Aid Company either peopled or saved Kansas is preposterous and ridiculous. It was one of the many agencies that accomplished that great work. Its services were valuable; they have been and always will be recognized. Dr. Cordley leaves little to be said on this point.

For Mr. Thayer's claims, see his book, *The Kansas Crusade;* and for this particular matter, see page 54. The book is a very valuable contribution to Kansas history, but it is written with that pompous self-importance uppermost in the mind of the author, which detracts from candor.

NOTE 11.—The exact language is: "Come on, then, gentlemen of the slave States. Since there is no escaping your challenge, we accept it in the name of freedom. We will engage in competition for the virgin soil of Kansas, and God give the victory to the side which is stronger in numbers, as it is in right."

NOTE 12.—"The Pro-Slavery party fancied it saw in the immigration of these large Northern companies serious cause to apprehend the defeat of a measure that had occasioned great anxiety; been attended with many difficulties; which was of such momentous importance; and until now gave promise of certain and ultimate success. It therefore resolved, as a matter of safety and interest, not only to disperse those who had already entered the Territory, but to prevent, if possible, the admission of all others of similar character. To this end meetings were held in various parts of the Territory and in the border towns of Missouri, at which speeches were made and resolutions adopted of the most incendiary and inflammatory description. Some of them were so exceedingly violent and disgustingly profane, as to be unfit for publication. The tenor and spirit of them all was, that Kansas must be a slave State; that abolitionists—and this meant all Northern men not pledged to favor slavery extension—had no right to come there; and that all such should be driven from the Territory or destroyed.

"At one of these meetings held at Westport, Mo., in July, 1854, an association was formed, which adopted the following resolution:

"*Resolved*, That this association will, whenever called upon by any of the citizens of Kansas Territory, hold itself in readiness together and assist to remove any and all emigrants who go there under the auspices of the Northern emigrant aid societies;" etc., etc.—"*History of Kansas*," John H. Gihon, p. 29.

"The Platte County (Mo.) Self-Defensive Association was formed at Weston, Mo., July 29. Its objects were: (1) Expulsion of all free negroes from the country. (2) Traffic between whites and slaves forbidden. (3) Slaves not allowed to hire their own time. (4) Themselves, their honor and their purses, mutually pledged to bring to immediate punishment all *Abolitionists.*—"*History of the State of Kansas*," A. T. Andreas, p. 90.

NOTE 13.—The *Platte Argus* said:

"It is now time to sound the alarm. We know we speak the sentiments of some of the most distinguished statesmen of Missouri, when we advise that counter organizations be made both in Kansas and Missouri to thwart the reckless course of the abolitionists. We must meet them at their very threshold and scourge them back to their caverns of darkness. They have made the issue, and it is for us to meet and repel them."—"*History of Kansas Territory*," J. N. Holloway, p. 120.

NOTE 14.—"The *St. Louis Republican* says that B. F. Stringfellow knocked Governor Reeder down, at the Shawnee Mission, for having said that Stringfellow was a 'frontier ruffian' or 'border ruffian.' The expression soon becomes national."—"*Annals of Kansas*," D. W. Wilder, p. 66.

NOTE 15.—"The farmers, large landholders, capitalists, merchants and industrious artisans living in western Missouri, or emigrated to the new Territory, largely outnumbered the class above described. They were, many of them, slaveholders, and nearly all conscientiously, or from personal interest, favored the extension of slavery into the new Territory. Yet, they were high-minded, despised meanness, believed in fair play and law and order, and in living up to all contracts to the letter. Like Benton, they had had no hand nor heart in the recent abrogation of the old compromise, took no pride or satisfaction in it, and gave but lukewarm support to any lawless efforts to forestall the settlement of the Territory, or otherwise push hastily the advantages of the faithless abrogation." —*"History of the State of Kansas," A. T. Andreas, p. 90.*

Note 16.—*History of Kansas*, John H. Gihon, p. 30.

Note 17.—"A description of one of these will give the reader some idea of their general characteristics. Imagine a man standing in a pair of long boots, covered with dust and mud and drawn over his trousers, the latter made of coarse, fancy-colored cloth, well soiled; the handle of a large bowie-knife projecting from one or both boot-tops; a leathern belt buckled around his waist, on each side of which is fastened a large revolver; a red or blue shirt, with a heart, anchor, eagle or some other favorite device braided on the breast and back, over which is swung a rifle or carbine; a sword dangling by his side, and a chicken, goose or turkey feather sticking in the top of his hat; hair uncut and uncombed, covering his neck and shoulders; an unshaved face and unwashed hands. Imagine such a picture of humanity, who can swear any given number of oaths in any specified time, drink any quantity of bad whisky without getting drunk, and boast of having stolen a half-dozen horses and killed one or more abolitionists, and you will have a pretty fair conception of a border ruffian as he appears in Missouri and Kansas. He has, however, the happy faculty of assuming a very different aspect. Like other animals, he can shed his coat and change his colors. In the city of Washington he is quite another person. You will see him in the corridors of the first-class hotels—upon Pennsylvania Avenue—in the rotunda of the capitol, or the spacious halls of the White House, dressed in the finest broadcloths and in the extreme of fashion; his hair trimmed, his face smoothed and his hands cleansed; his manner gentle, kind and courteous; his whole deportment that of innocence, and his speech so smooth, studied and oily as to convince even the sagacious President himself that he is a veritable and polished gentleman, and obtain from the wise heads that form the cabinet the most important posts of trust, honor and emolument in the gift of the nation."—*"History of Kansas," John H. Gihon, p. 107.*

Note 18.—This differs from the account given by H. H. Johnson in his testimony before the committee to investigate the affairs of the Territory, as set out in its Report at page 973. I have followed the version given me by the Rev. J. B. McAfee, who was at that time a resident of Leavenworth, and saw the occurrence. Mr. McAfee is now a resident of Topeka, where he has lived for a great many years; he is a Lutheran minister, and one of the first citizens of the State in time of residence, intelligence, reliability, high standing, public spirit, and all that goes to constitute a Christian gentleman.

NOTE 19.—See the account of this outrageous affair in the *History of Kansas*, by John H. Gihon, p. 35. See also, "Leavenworth County," in *History of the State of Kansas*, A. T. Andreas, p. 425.

NOTE 20.—"The story of his brutal treatment is told by Cole McCrea, a neighbor of Captain Brown's, and whose wife was one of several kind friends who attempted to revive the injured man: 'They then [after the assault] tossed Brown into a lumber wagon and drove on to Merrill Smith's saloon, on Salt creek. The rough wagon, driven over hard, frozen ground, made the wounded man groan, when the ruffian kicked him in the face, neck and breast to make him keep still. Eli Moore, putting his foot to his cheek, twisted his neck so as to put a tobacco-spit into his wound, saying that would ease any d—d abolitionist. Thus abused and kept in the bed of the wagon some seven hours, they drove over to my cabin. Coming up so that the tail end of the wagon would come opposite the door, they flung it open, saying, "Here is Brown!" There being no one at the house but our wives and infant children, Charley Dunn and Pap Taylor undertook to bring him into the house. They first dragged him out of the wagon by the feet, letting his body fall at full length upon the hard frozen ground. The thud which the husband's body gave against the hard earth echoed in the faithful, loving heart of the wife, and she fell to the floor. Returning consciousness only found her a helpless maniac, and she so continued till my wife delivered her over to her brother at Chicago, who had come from Cass county, Mich., to receive her. The two ruffians then dragged Brown into the cabin as far as his knees. They then staggered and stumbled through the cabin, upsetting the water bucket. My wife could not drag the dying man further in, or close the door, that 18th of January night, one of the coldest ever known in Kansas.

The helpless women and children and dying man were left exposed till David Brown, a Tennesseean, came over from the adjoining claim. Captain Brown died about three hours after being brought home.' "— *"Leavenworth County," in "History of the State of Kansas," A. T. Andreas, p. 426.*

NOTE 21.—"One of the most heathenish (because so coolly premeditated, with no provocation whatever) occurred near the south line of the city [Leavenworth], on August 19. A Missouri ruffian named Fuget had made a bet of six dollars against a pair of boots, that in less than two hours he would bring into Leavenworth an abolitionist's scalp. Starting out on his inhuman errand he met a young man named Hoppe, who had just arrived from Illinois a few days ago, and was returning from Lawrence, where he had taken his wife to visit a sister. He was shot dead from his carriage by Fuget, who scalped his victim and left him in the road. He then carried the reeking scalp with him to the house of his cousin, Mrs. Todd, situated on the Lawrence road, about a mile from where the crime was committed!"—*"Leavenworth County," in "History of the State of Kansas," A. T. Andreas, p. 427.*

NOTE 22.—"John M. Clayton, United States Senator from the State of Delaware, afterwards referring to these laws, thus characterized them: 'Now, Sir, let me allude to that subject which is the great cause of all this discord between the two houses. The unjust, iniquitous, oppressive and infamous laws enacted by the Kansas Legislature, as it is called, ought to be repealed before we adjourn. . . . What are these laws? One of them sends a man to hard labor for not less than two years for daring to discuss the question whether slavery exists or does not exist in Kansas: not less than two years—it may be fifty; and if a man could live to be as old as Methuselah, it might be over nine hundred years. That act prohibits all freedom of discussion in Kansas, on the great subject directly referred to the exclusive decision of the people in that Territory; strikes down the liberty of the press, too; and is an act egregiously tyrannical as ever was attempted by any of the Stuarts, Tudors or Plantagenets of England,—and this Senate persists in declaring that we are not to repeal that!

"Sir, let us tender to the House of Representatives the repeal of that and of all other objectionable and infamous laws that were

passed by that Legislature. I include in this denunciation, without
any hesitation, those acts which prescribe that a man shall not
even practice law in the Territory unless he swears to support the
Fugitive Slave Law; that he shall not vote at any election, or be a
member of the Legislature, unless he swears to support the Fugitive
Slave Law; that he shall not hold any office of honor or trust, unless
he swears to support the Fugitive Slave Law; and you may as well
impose just such a test oath for any other and every other law.
. . . I will not go through the whole catalogue of the oppressive
laws of this Territory. I have done that before to-day. There are
others as bad as those to which I have now referred. . . . I
will not, on the other hand, ever degrade myself by standing for an
instant by those abominable and infamous laws which I denounced
here this morning. What I desire now is, that the Senate of the
United States shall wash its hands of all participation in these
iniquities, by repealing those laws."—*Quoted from "History of American Conspiracies," Orville J. Victor, p. 474.*

NOTE 23.—"During the year he was twice notified that he must
leave or hang, his only crime being that he was a Free-State man
and read the New York *Tribune* and similar papers. On June 5,
1856, the 'Law and Order' party held a meeting in Reese & Keith's
warehouse, in which violent and denunciatory speeches concerning
Free-State men were made by some and opposed by others. A 'committee of safety' of one hundred men was appointed, which appointed a sub-committee of six, whose duty was to notify Father
Gould, H. J. Adams and Joseph B. McAfee to 'leave or hang.' This
committee, consisting of Taylor, Todd, Murphy, Renick, Cook and
another, visited him with the notice, and also read to him a letter
he had written to Governor Reeder, which they had obtained when
their party had sacked Lawrence. The history of the letter is as
follows: The Pro-Slavery party had held a meeting, and at its close
he went near the house, and seeing a drunken Georgian whom he
knew, but to whom he was unknown, he walked up behind and said:
'Well, that was a good meeting.' The Georgian replied that it was.
He then said: "What was done about Governor Reeder?" To
which the Georgian answered: 'Charley Dunn has taken an oath that
shears shall not go upon his head, razor upon his face, nor whisky
down his throat until he has murdered Governor Reeder.' The man
supposed Mr. McAfee was one of their own men, but had failed to

hear what was said. Mr. McAfee went home and wrote a letter to Governor Reeder, as follows:

LEAVENWORTH, KANSAS, May 7, 1856.

Hon. A. H. Reeder, Lawrence, Kansas—MY DEAR GOVERNOR: I am credibly informed that Charles Dunn has just taken a solemn oath that shears shall not go upon his head, razor upon his face, nor whisky down his throat until he has murdered you clandestinely, or as Brutus did Cæsar in the Senate Chamber. Be on your guard. Vigilance is the mother of safety.

Yours respectfully,

J. B. McAFEE.

"He took this letter to William Phillips (afterwards murdered in Leavenworth), who sent it by his hired hand to Governor Reeder, the carrier swimming the Kaw river to deliver it. The Governor, instead of burning the letter, as he should have done, put it among his papers for future reference. This is the letter that was brought as an additional reason why he should be driven from the Territory."—*The sketch of Rev. J. B. McAfee, in "The United States Biographical Dictionary," Kansas Volume, p. 208.*

NOTE 24.—"While these parting ceremonies were being performed, a steamboat, bound down the river, and directly from Kansas, came alongside the Keystone. Ex-Governor Shannon was a passenger, who, upon learning the close proximity of Governor Geary, sought an immediate interview with him. The ex-Governor was greatly agitated. He had fled in haste and terror from the Territory, and seemed still to be laboring under an apprehension for his personal safety. His description of Kansas was suggestive of everything that is frightful and horrible. Its condition was deplorable in the extreme. The whole Territory was in a state of insurrection, and a destructive civil war was devastating the country. Murder ran rampant, and the roads were everywhere strewn with the bodies of slaughtered men. No language can exaggerate the awful picture that was drawn."—*"History of Kansas, John H. Gihon, p. 104.*

NOTE 25.—*Life and Letters of John Brown,* F. B. Sanborn, p. 189.

NOTE 26.—For a full account of the removal of the sons of John Brown to Kansas, see the statement of John Brown, jr., at page 188 and following, of *Life and Letters of John Brown,* F. B. Sanborn.

NOTE 27.—*Annals of Kansas*, D. W. Wilder, edition of 1886, p. 65.

NOTE 28.—*Reminiscences of Old John Brown*, G. W. Brown, p. 6.

NOTE 29.—In the account of the Syracuse convention written by John Brown to his wife and chi'dren he says: "John's two letters were introduced, and read with such effect by Gerrit Smith as to draw tears from the numerous eyes in the great collection of people present."— *"Life and Letters of John Brown," F. B. Sanborn, p. 194.*

NOTE 30.—*The Public Life of Captain John Brown*, James Redpath, p. 81.

NOTE 31.—*Life and Letters of John Brown*, F. B. Sanborn, p. 191.

NOTE 32.—This account is in his letter to his wife and children, which is published in *Life and Letters of John Brown*, F. B. Sanborn, p. 193.

NOTE 33.—See this letter published in *Life and Letters of John Brown*, F. B. Sanborn, pp. 199-200.

NOTE 34.—The wife and son of John Brown, jr.

NOTE 35.—See letter to his family, published in *Life and Letters of John Brown*, F. B. Sanborn, p. 201.

NOTE 36.—"I should have written you before, but since we laid little Austin in the grave I have not felt as if I could write." This quotation and the one in the text are taken from Jason Brown's letter, published in *Life and Letters of John Brown*, F. B. Sanborn, p. 197.

CHAPTER III.

THE BROWNS—A FAMILY OF PIONEERS.

The priest-like father reads the sacred page,
  How Abram was the friend of God on high;
Or, Moses bade eternal warfare wage
  With Amalek's ungracious progeny:
Or how the royal bard did groaning lie
  Beneath the stroke of Heaven's avenging ire:
Or Job's pathetic plaint, and wailing cry;
  Or rapt Isaiah's wild seraphic fire;
Or other holy seers that tune the sacred lyre.
        —*Burns's "The Cotter's Saturday Night."*

Peter Brown was an Englishman; he was a Puritan, and one of the Pilgrim Fathers who landed on Plymouth Rock, December 22d, 1620. In even that early age he was a crusader for political and religious liberty. He was by trade a carpenter, and of his life we know little more than has been already here told. But that he loved liberty and hated tyranny is fully established by his action in coming to America to brave the forces of the untamed wilderness on the bleak shores of rock-bound New England, when he might have remained in his native land in ease and peace had he chosen to conform outwardly to what his conscience condemned. That the evils under which he lay in his native land might be slowly reformed and finally corrected, was not enough for him. We see in the action of the Pilgrims in their migration to a primeval

(78)

land the uncompromising spirit which moved the old prophets to exhort those who had "not bowed the knee to Baal" to "come out of her, O my people."

Peter Brown, the Pilgrim, married; and to him was born in 1632 a son, called, also, Peter Brown.[1] The son married Mary Gillett, in 1658, and died in 1692, leaving four sons. The second son was named John, and he married Elizabeth Loomis in the year of his father's death. His second son was also named John; he married Mary Eggleston, and one of his sons, born November 4, 1728, was named John. This third John Brown married Hannah Owen in 1758; she was the daughter of John Owen, a native of Wales, who had sought broader opportunities and greater freedom in the New World. He was one of the first settlers of Windsor, Connecticut, where he was a good citizen and held as a man of worth and integrity to the end of life. The sons of John and Hannah (Owen) Brown were John, Frederick, Owen, and Abiel. In the war of the Revolution John Brown heeded the call of his country, and, disregarding his personal conveniences and interests, left the peace and quiet of private walks and joined the army of the patriots. He was chosen Captain of the trainband of West Simsbury, Connecticut, and sent to join the American army, then in New York. At the end of two months he was seized with a fatal illness and died in a barn, September 3, 1776, and was buried on the Highlands "near the western bank of East river." He, too, might have remained at home, a defender of accredited and established order, could he have reconciled his conscience to a course so unpatriotic and unjust; he could have been protected, and might have been carried to

England and there made the recipient of royal favors, as
others were. But he saw a duty and chose liberty for himself and others and resolved to battle for it as stoutly as
he might though hung for a traitor, as he would have been
had the cause failed and he had lived. He left a widow
and eleven children.

Owen Brown, the son of the Revolutionary hero, married Ruth Mills. She was a teacher, and came of illustrious ancestry, descending from a long line of God-fearing
men, ministers of the gospel, and Revolutionary soldiers.
The family was founded by Peter Mills,[2] an emigrant
from Holland to Connecticut, and was one of the first in
that stable, solid, patriotic, and enterprising commonwealth. Owen Brown was a tanner and shoemaker, and
lived at different places in Connecticut to the year 1805,
when he removed to Hudson, Ohio, in the Western Reserve.
This was in fact a New Connecticut, and no equal area of
our country has surpassed it in patriotic devotion to liberty
or enterprise in productive industry. It has stamped the
impress of its high purposes upon the civilization of the
entire West. This is the result of the just principles,
the upright lives, the rigid morality, and the uncompromising stand for the right and hostility to evil carried here
by the sons of old Connecticut to serve as foundations
for their institutions to be erected in the Western wilderness.

Owen Brown first came to the Western Reserve in 1804,
on a tour of observation, a journey preliminary to his
final removal. He made his way with his family, in 1805,
through Pennsylvania with an ox team. Hardships incident to pioneer life beset Owen Brown. His wife died

and he was subsequently married, and his second wife dying, he took a third. He had a large family. One of his sons, Salmon, "died in New Orleans with yellow fever. He was a lawyer, and editor of a French and English newspaper called the 'New Orleans Bee.' "

The remarkable things to be observed of Owen Brown are, the pure and exalted Christian life he led, and the principles and purposes he instilled into his children. He " became acquainted with the business people and *ministers* in all parts of the Western Reserve." In his own account of his life he says: " In 1807 (Feb. 13) Frederick, my sixth child, was born. I do not think of anything else to notice but the common blessings of health, peace, and prosperity, *for which I would ever acknowledge the goodness of God with thanksgiving.*" He was a man of strong attachments. Forty years after the death of his wife, Ruth, he writes: " These were days of affliction. The remembrance of this scene makes my heart bleed now." He was a home-lover: " I would say that the care of our families is the pleasantest and most useful business we can be in." The absence of a child caused him to suffer: "About this time my son Salmon was studying law in Pittsburg. I had great anxiety and many fears on his account." With Owen Brown the things of this life were counted as but dross: " I can say the loss or gain of property in a short time appears of but little consequence; they are momentary things, and will look very small in eternity." The justice of God as well as His mercy remained always before him: "January 29, 1832, my son Watson died, making a great breach in my family. He did not give evidence in health of being a Christian, but

—6

was in great anxiety of mind in his sickness; we sometimes hope he died in Christ." At the age of seventy-
eight he writes: "I have great reason for thanksgiving."
He was a lifelong abolitionist. In 1850 he wrote: "I am
an abolitionist.[3] I know we are not loved by many;
I have no confession to make for being one." Every
act of his life was ordered in the light he drew from the
Scriptures and his Christian experience. A few months
before his death he wrote his son John: "I feel as
though God was very merciful to keep such a great sinner
on probation so long. I ask all of you to pray more earnestly for the salvation of my soul than for the life of my
body, and that I may give myself and all I have up to
Christ, and honor him by a sacrifice of all we have."
His family remained unbroken, though widely scattered
and often invaded by death. He writes his son: "I consider all my children in Kansas as one family." He was
afflicted with stammering or a stoppage in his speech;
on this acount it was very painful to strangers to hear him
talk. But there was one place where this defect disappeared: in the services of the church, in his prayers, he
was eloquent from fervency, and "his tongue was loosed"
and he "spake with power." His life is fittingly described
in the words, "He walked in the fear and admonition
of the Lord."

To this humble and devout man who lived daily in the
sight of God and abased himself continually that his Master
might not refuse to exalt him, was born a son while he yet
lived in his native State of Connecticut. He notes this
in the simple annals of his life: "In 1800, May 9, John
was born, one hundred years after his great-grandfather."

This son was John Brown, afterwards the liberator of the lowly, despised, oppressed and enslaved, and the martyr for a more perfect Union. Some one has said that the first requisite of greatness is to be born right. Another has said that the first indication of genius in a man is manifested in the selection of his parents. Still another has said that the time to begin to educate a child is a hundred years before it is born. The biographer of a great man has said: " I do not think a great man ever lived who was not born of a strong, naturally intellectual, poetic and emotional mother." As much as John Brown owed to his father, he owed still more to his mother. She was a woman of superior intelligence, deep and profound religious convictions, emotional, and of great strength of character. Her husband wrote of her: "About this time I became acquainted with Ruth Mills (daughter of Rev. Gideon Mills), who was the choice of my affections ever after, though we were not married for more than two years. In March, 1793, we began to keep house; *and here was the beginning of days with me.*" [4] We have seen that she was descended from a Hollander who was early in Connecticut. The solid and enduring qualities of the Teuton were quickened and intensified in America, and enriched the character of the mother of John Brown. She died while he was yet a child, but his recollection of her was clear; and the memory of her justice as well as of her love remained to him a priceless heritage.[5] So complete was her influence over him and his love for her that he never ceased to feel her loss. In his " Life " written for the little son of George L. Stearns, he says: "At eight years old, John was left a motherless boy, which loss was complete and permanent, for notwithstanding his father again married to a sensible, intelligent, and on many accounts a very estimable woman, yet he never *adopted her in feeling,* but continued to pine after his own mother for years." In this brief autobiography he has described his youth and early manhood with a charming simplicity and faithfulness which no other can ever equal; and the reader is exhorted to read and study it.[6]

John Brown was taught from earliest childhood to "fear God and keep His commandments." He received no more education than fell to the lot of the average boy on the frontier, where schools were few and necessarily inferior. He acquired knowledge enough of mathematics to enable him to become a good surveyor of lands, and this vocation he followed at intervals for years. He was of a studious and reflective disposition. The books which he read were few, but the principles they inculcated were deeply pondered and became a part of his character; they were "Æsop's Fables," the " Life of Franklin," the " Pilgrim's Progress," the hymns of Dr. Watts, and above all, the Bible. Upon the teachings of this latter book he meditated both day and night; he was familiar with its every story and principle. He could recite many parts of it, and could readily turn to any portion referred to. He was particularly charmed with the beauties of the Old Testament; the stern old prophets denouncing the wickedness of the times had a peculiar fascination for him.

It has been shown that the Brown family have been pioneers in America for almost three centuries. They have been in the vanguard of advancing civilization in its march across the continent from sea to sea.[7] While

the frontier is always devoid of good schools, it possesses
facilities for education in the practical affairs of life
superior to those found in the elegant society of older communities. To develop sterling qualities of head and heart,
no other place equals the frontier of a progressive and
growing people. Here man must always grapple with
nature direct. Truth is not veiled with conventionalities,
and here shams cannot exist. Men stand before their
fellows uncovered and in their true characters. Crime
cannot be hidden nor virtue and worth concealed in a
frontier settlement. The few conventionalities indulged
are the simplest and those rendered most necessary by social
custom and the law. Heart touches heart and man knows
his fellow in every detail and relation of character; the
business and inclinations of one are known to all and are
usually the concern of all. All dealing and intercourse
between men become direct and personal. The somber
face of nature in winter, the lack of crowds and large
assemblies of men, and the absence of strangers and strange
things, all tend to develop the reflective faculties of the
mind and to induce melancholy. Melancholy is the child
of solitude, the parent of genius. Add to these influences
and agencies a poetic temperament and a fearful sense of
responsibility to a personal God "who numbers the hairs of
your head" and will demand a strict accounting "at that
day," and you have the environment that burned out the
dross and sent John Brown forth with a character purged
and refined as by fire.

The heroic age of any country is that in which man
meets and subdues the wilderness. Here in the subjection
of the forest and wild beast, confidence is obtained. Men

from this school expect to succeed; the overcoming of obstacles is the daily experience. Relations between men are
exhibited in their true light and are sharply defined. Merit
alone brings approval. The frontier is a social democracy
where nothing artificial or superfluous can exist. Men are
jealous of their rights and the rights of others, and are im-
patient of delays and restraints. Rude and exact justice is
demanded, and the manner of insuring it often shocks
the disciples of formal conventionalities. In matters of
character only the pure gold passes for anything; the false
is not tolerated, and it is usually requested to move on;
if it remains it is only by sufferance, and it must skulk
and cower and sink to depths of public scorn unknown in
more polite and well-ordered society.

In this school was John Brown reared and well learned.[8]
Other men of our country coming from this school were
Washington, Franklin, Sevier, Shelby, Jefferson, Jackson, Benton, Harrison, Corwin, Clay, Lincoln, and Lane.
In the establishment and maintenance of our Government
these men have been the friends and bulwarks of human
liberty. And our rank in the nations of the world and
our phenomenal advancement along all the lines of mental
and productive industry may be best accounted for by re-
membering that we are a nation of pioneers, and yet
attacking the primeval forest and plain with blade and
saw and share.

John Brown became a tanner, and worked in his father's
service as foreman of his establishment. He had not attained his majority when he married, as he says, "a remarkably plain, but neat, industrious and economical girl;

of excellent character, earnest piety, and good practical common-sense; about one year younger than himself." She was indeed all that he described her, and "by her mild, frank, and more than all else, by her very consistent conduct, acquired and ever while she lived maintained a most powerful and good influence over him. Her plain but kind admonitions generally had the right effect; without arousing his haughty obstinate temper." Her name was Dianthe Lusk, and he seems to have regarded her with the same deep affection held by his father for his mother, Ruth Mills Brown. Long after her death he said to his son, John, jr., "I feel sure that your mother is now with me and influencing me." Seven children were born to them.[9] After her death he married Mary Anne Day, daughter of Charles Day, of Whitehall, New York, but living at that time in Pennsylvania. Thirteen children blessed this marriage, but seven of them died in infancy and childhood.[10] She was the sheet-anchor of his hopes and the object of his anxious solicitude, the inspiration to exertion during the long years of his heroic battle against human bondage. She survived him more than twenty years, and died at the residence of her daughter in San Francisco, Cal.

John Brown was laboring at the vocations of both tanner and surveyor before his marriage. He lived in his own house, having employed a housekeeper, a widow named Lusk, who brought her daughter, Dianthe Lusk, who became his first wife, as we have seen. In 1825 he moved to Pennsylvania, settling near Randolph (now Richmond), where he remained for ten years. He served as postmaster here for some years, and carried on a large tannery. He took a leading part in the affairs of the community, and the neighborhood school was taught in a part of his huge log dwelling. He removed to Franklin Mills, Portage county, Ohio, in 1835. Here a speculation in village lots ruined him financially; he made an assignment and was discharged as a bankrupt, but afterwards paid much on the debts he was legally free from. Later he was an extensive sheep-farmer; and from this business became a member of the firm of Perkins & Brown, wool merchants, with warehouses at Springfield, Massachusetts, to which city he moved in 1846. He became an expert grader of wool,[11] and might have succeeded in his enterprise but for the attempt to dictate the price of wool to the New England manufacturers; this caused him to take a large cargo of wool to England in August, 1849, which was finally sold for much less than it would have brought in Springfield. He traveled considerably in Europe, and visited for critical inspection and study some of the most famous battlefields. He returned to Springfield in October. His reception by his partner was cordial, and he was urged to remain in business. He might have succeeded as a wool-factor, though he was not fitted by nature for a competitor in trade. And through all the years since 1837 he had another purpose in life than the accumulation of property: he had in that year dedicated his remaining years to an aggressive battle against slavery, and had ordered his life accordingly.

On August 1, 1846, the anniversary of the emancipation of slaves in the West Indies, Gerrit Smith offered to give one thousand acres of wild mountain land in the Adirondack Mountains of New York to such negroes as would

accept, clear and cultivate farms there.   The tracts were
limited to forty acres in size, and a few families accepted
them at once, though the severity of the climate and the
hardships of pioneer life made it a discouraging venture
for negroes.   In April, 1848, John Brown called upon
Smith and proposed to take one of the farms, go on it and
build a home, and become an example to the few negro
families then there and to those who might afterward come.
He explained that pioneer life was familiar to him, and
that he could be of much use and assistance to the colony
in teaching the best means of surmounting difficulties encountered in building homes in the wilderness.   There is
little doubt that he had other designs in mind, for he
had, when a resident in Pennsylvania, proposed to his
brother that they found some such colony as this now
projected by Smith.   The proposition was promptly accepted by Mr. Smith, and Brown secured one or more surveys, and the refusal of others.   Before the final settlement
of his wool business he removed a portion of his family to
North Elba, New York, where his home always remained,
and where he is buried.

Like his father, John Brown was a tender and affec-
tionate parent.   " Whenever he and I were alone, he never
failed to give me the best of advice, just as a true and
anxious mother would give a daughter," says Ruth.   " He
always seemed interested in my work.   .   .   .   When I
was learning to spin he always praised me, if he saw that I
was improving," she writes.   And again: " Father used to
hold all his children, while they were little, at night, and
sing his favorite songs."   She recorded the recollections
of her baptism: " The first recollection I have of father

was being carried through a piece of woods on Sunday,
to attend a meeting held at a neighbor's house. After we
had been at the house a little while, father and mother
stood up and held us, while the minister put water on our
faces. After we sat down, father wiped my face with a
brown silk handkerchief with yellow spots on it in dia-
mond shape. It seemed beautiful to me, and I thought
how good he was to wipe my face with that pretty handkerchief. He showed a great deal of tenderness in that
and other ways. He sometimes seemed very stern and
strict with me; yet his tenderness made me forget that
he was stern." He even accepted two-thirds of the punishment he felt due his son John, his sense of justice and
duty not permitting him to have any of it omitted.[12] Even
his daughters did not escape the rod; "He used to whip
me quite often for telling lies," one of them writes. His
affection for his children was very great; it caused him
to think of them constantly, and he was anxious on their
account. Ruth received a letter from him when she was
eighteen, from which we take the following:

"I will just tell you what questions exercise my mind
in regard to an absent daughter, and I will arrange them
somewhat in order as I feel most their importance.

"What feelings and motives govern her? In what
manner does she spend her time? Who are her associates?
How does she conduct in word and action? Is she improving generally? Is she provided with such things as she
needs, or is she in want? Does she enjoy herself, or is
she lonely and sad? Is she among real friends, or is she
disliked and despised?

"Such are some of the questions which arise in the
mind of a certain anxious father; and if you have a
satisfactory answer to them in your own mind, he can
rest satisfied."

She describes the sickness and death of her sister:

"The little babe took a violent cold that ended in quick consumption, and she died at the end of April, 1849. Father showed much tenderness in the care of the little sufferer. He spared no pains in doing all that medical skill could do for her, together with the tenderest care and nursing. The time that he could be at home was mostly spent in caring for her. He sat up nights to keep an even temperature in the room, and to relieve mother from the constant care which she had through the day. He used to walk with the child and sing to her so much that she soon learned his step. When she heard him come up the steps to the door, she would reach out her hands and cry for him to take her. When his business at the wool store crowded him so much that he did not have time to take her, he would steal around through the woodshed into the kitchen to eat his dinner, and not go into the dining-room, where she could see or hear him. I used to be charmed myself with his singing to her. He noticed a change in her one morning, and told us that she would not live through the day, and came home several times to see her. A little before noon he came home, and looked at her and said, ' She is almost gone.' She heard him speak, opened her eyes, and put up her little wasted hands with such a pleading look for him to take her that he lifted her from the cradle, with the pillows she was lying on, and carried her until she died. He was very calm, closed her eyes, folded her hands, and laid her in her cradle. When she was buried, father broke down completely, and sobbed like a child. It was very affecting to see him so overcome, when all the time before his great tender heart had tried to comfort our weary, sorrowing mother, and all of us." [13]

We give the private and domestic life of John Brown at some length that it may be fully known to the reader, on this account: a man is often best judged by the members of his own household. And if a man is strong with his neighbors or associates it may be taken as reasonably certain that his life is correct and his actions just. The first question asked when a man's character is a matter of inquiry, is, " What do the people of his home, his castle, think and say of him?" If at home he is strong in the affection and esteem of his family, friends, associates and neighbors, it is very sure that he is just.

In addition to the books enumerated as being the favorites of John Brown his daughter adds " Plutarch's Lives," " Life of Oliver Cromwell," and " Baxter's Saint's Everlasting Rest." She also mentions that greatest of all books, the Bible. He could, she says, repeat whole chapters and books from it. The stern and rigid righteousness of the old prophets was in accord with his own faith. He ordered his life by precepts taken from the Holy Word.[14] It has been said here that he sang well, and in his home he lifted his voice in song in the praise of God. His favorite hymns were, " Blow ye the trumpet, blow," " Why should we start, and fear to die," "Ah, lovely appearance of death!" His religion entered into his daily life. When a tanner he was very careful to see that his leather was perfectly dry before being offered for sale. His voice was daily lifted in supplication at the family altar. On the plains of Kansas he cried to God for help and guidance, and no meal was eaten in his camp until the blessing of heaven was invoked upon it.

Another feature of John Brown's life was his intense earnestness.[15] He early selected an object in life, or rather, it was selected by his training and the inherited tenden-

cies of his nature. He swore eternal war against slavery.
Following are his own words:

"During the war with England a circumstance occurred that in the end made him a most determined
Abolitionist, and led him to declare, or swear, eternal war
with Slavery. He was staying for a short time with a
very gentlemanly landlord, since a United States Marshal,
who held a slave boy near his own age, very active, intelligent, and good feeling, and to whom John was under considerable obligation for numerous little acts of kindness.
The master made a great pet of John: brought him to
table with his first company and friends; called their attention to every little smart thing he said or did, and to
the fact of his being more than a hundred miles 'from home
with a company of cattle alone; while the negro boy (who
was fully if not more than his equal) was badly clothed,
poorly fed and lodged in cold weather, and beaten before
his eyes with iron shovels or any other thing that came
first to hand. This brought John to reflect on the wretched,
hopeless condition of fatherless and motherless slave children; for such children have neither fathers nor mothers
to protect and provide for them. He sometimes would
raise the question, *Is God their Father?*"

Eternal war with slavery! This subject was never
absent from his mind; it abode with him; it glared in
upon him; it became a companion ever present. While
he toiled in the tan-yard, when he traced the lines of
tortuous surveys, in the care of his cattle, when he tended
his sheep in the starlit night, in the counting-house in
New England,—always and forever did this thing press
upon him for action. "The cry of the poor" he heard
ever appealing to him. About 1837 he assembled his
household and laid before them this burden of his heart.[16]
The time for action had come. In theory and practice

he had always been an abolitionist. But this was not
enough. Warfare was henceforth to be waged. His first
soldiers were to be members of his own house; if he was
strong at home he could not be weak anywhere. His
course met the perfect approval of his family. Three
of his sons (those old enough) consecrated themselves to
this work by prayer. In this service the father was seen
by his children to *kneel* for the *first* time, his uniform
attitude in prayer having previously been that of "standing with reverence before the throne." In a work so
mighty it was meet that it be commenced in humility
and in the strength of Him who turns to flight the armies
of aliens.

Defamers of John Brown have attempted to show that
he was a Garrisonian; nothing could be further from the
truth, but it would have been nothing to his discredit had
he been so. Garrison was not ten years old when John
Brown swore eternal war with slavery. John Brown followed no man; it was his intention and purpose to follow
God. He took counsel of no man in marking his line of
conduct. His father had become an enemy to slavery
when a mere child—in the war of the Revolution, while
his father was giving his life for liberty. The Brown
family were abolitionists of the Brown school exclusively.
If associated with others they were so only because others
followed—the Browns led. From the period of the enlistment of his family in his cause, preparation was made
against the time when they should be called to the field.
Frederick Douglass found the family living in severe plain-
ness at Springfield, although Brown's business was then
prospering.[17] Money saved to furnish a parlor was freely

given to purchase clothing for fugitive slaves at North Elba.[18] In Europe the ancient battlefields were examined, and the guerilla warfare of the world was studied to obtain a knowledge of strategy that would aid in this conflict that he had sworn.

Here, then, is a man who believes in himself before other men; who finds strength in his arm only in proportion as he feels that he finds favor with God; who is moved to tears at the unhappiness of his fellow-men in bonds; who, like Luther, could not if he would, turn from the appointed work; who consecrated his home a shrine to liberty; who made this shrine an altar, and like the great patriarch, offered his sons thereon; who asked nothing of any man he was not willing to freely give, no sacrifice he did not himself joyfully make; and who sealed with his blood the heroic faith in which he walked,—who received the crown of the martyr, and whose soul led the Nation as it marched to the higher plane of right, and liberty, and freedom for all.

Note 1.—"Peter Brown the Pilgrim had his home in Duxbury, not far from the hill where Miles Standish built his house, and where his monument is now seen."—"*John Brown and His Men,*" *Richard J. Hinton, p. 10.*

Note 2.—"The direct ancestor of John Brown's mother, Ruth Mills, of Simsbury, was a Protestant Hollander, Peter Van Huysenmuysen, who left the sturdy land when the Spanish Duke of Alva was harrying it. Settling in Connecticut, he built a mill and earned bread for his family. Hence the name Mills, under which the family passed into New England annals."—"*John Brown and His Men,*" *Richard J. Hinton, p. 11.*

NOTE 3.—"I wish to tell how long I have been one, and how I became so. I have no hatred to negroes. When a child four or five years old, one of our nearest neighbors had a slave that was brought from Guinea. In the year 1776 my father was called into the army at New York, and left his work undone. In August, our good neighbor Captain John Fast, of West Simsbury, let my mother have the labor of his slave to plow a few days. I used to go into the field with this slave,—called Sam,—and he used to carry me on his back, and I fell in love with him. He worked but a few days, and went home sick with the pleurisy, and died very suddenly. When told that he would die, he said he should go to Guinea, and wanted victuals put up for the journey. As I recollect, this was the first funeral I ever attended in the days of my youth. There were but three or four slaves in West Simsbury. In the year 1790, when I lived with the Rev. Jeremiah Hallock, the Rev. Samuel Hopkins, D. D., came from Newport, and I heard him talking with Mr. Hallock about slavery in Rhode Island, and he denounced it as a great sin. I think in the same summer Mr. Hallock had sent to him a sermon or pamphlet-book, written by the Rev. Jonathan Edwards, then at New Haven. I read it, and it denounced slavery as a great sin. From this time I was anti-slavery, as much as I be now."—*From Owen Brown's Account of his Life, published in "Life and Letters of John Brown," F. B. Sanborn, p. 10.*

———

NOTE 4.—This and the foregoing quotations concerning Owen Brown are from the narrative or sketch of his life written by himself, and published in *Life and Letters of John Brown*, F. B. Sanborn, p. 4 and following.

———

NOTE 5.—"I cannot tell you anything of the first four years of John's life worth mentioning, save that at that early age he was tempted by three large brass pins belonging to a girl who lived in the family, *and stole them.* In this he was detected by his mother, and after having a full day to think of the wrong, received from her a thorough whipping."—*John Brown's account of his life, written to the son of George L. Stearns, Esq.; quoted from "Life and Letters of John Brown," F. B. Sanborn, p. 12.*

———

NOTE 6.—It can be found in *Life and Letters of John Brown*, F. B. Sanborn; *John Brown and His Men*, Richard J. Hinton; and the *Life of Captain John Brown*, James Redpath.

NOTE 7.—Many of the Brown family now live in California, where they went many years ago.

NOTE 8.—"He did not go to Harvard. He was not fed on the pap that is there furnished. As he phrased it, 'I know no more grammar than one of your calves.' But he went to the University of the West, where he studied the science of Liberty; and, having taken his degrees, he finally commenced the public practice of humanity in Kansas. Such were his humanities—he would have left a Greek accent slanting the wrong way, and righted up a falling man."—*Henry D. Thoreau. Quoted from "Life of Captain John Brown," James Redpath, p. 27.*

NOTE 9.—"The children of his first marriage were born, married, and died as follows:

"John Brown, jr., born July 25, 1821, at Hudson, Ohio; married Wealthy C. Hotchkiss, July, 1847.

"Jason Brown, Jan. 19, 1823, at Hudson, Ohio; married Ellen Sherbondy, July, 1847.

"Owen Brown, Nov. 4, 1824, at Hudson (never married).

"Frederick Brown (1), Jan. 9, 1827, at Richmond, Pa.; died March 31, 1831.

"Ruth Brown, Feb. 18, 1829, at Richmond, Pa.; married Henry Thompson, Sept. 26, 1850.

"Frederick Brown (2), Dec. 31, 1830, at Richmond, Pa.; murdered at Osawatomie by Rev. Martin White, Aug. 30, 1856.

"An infant son, Aug. 7, 1832; was buried with his mother three days after his birth, at Richmond, Pa."—*"Life and Letters of John Brown," F. B. Sanborn, p. 35.*

NOTE 10.—"Children of John Brown and his wife Mary:

"Sarah Brown, born May 11, 1834, at Richmond, Pa.; died Sept. 23, 1843.

"Watson Brown, born Oct. 7, 1835, at Franklin, Ohio; married Isabella M. Thompson, Sept. 1856; killed at Harper's Ferry, Oct. 19, 1859.

"Salmon Brown, born Oct. 2, 1836, at Hudson, Ohio; married Abbie C. Hinckley, Oct. 15, 1857.

"Charles Brown, born Nov. 3, 1837, at Hudson, Ohio; died Sept. 11, 1843.

—7

"Oliver Brown, born March 9, 1839, at Franklin, Ohio; married Martha E. Brewster, April 7, 1858; killed at Harper's Ferry, Oct. 17, 1859.

"Peter Brown, born Dec. 7, 1840, at Hudson, Ohio; died Sept. 22, 1843.

"Austin Brown, born Sept. 14, 1842, at Richfield, Ohio; died Sept. 27, 1843.

"Anne Brown, born Dec. 23, 1843, at Richfield, Ohio.

"Amelia Brown, born June 22, 1845, at Akron, Ohio; died Oct. 30, 1846.

"Sarah Brown, born Sept. 11, 1846, at Akron, Ohio.

"Ellen Brown, born May 20, 1848, at Springfield, Mass.; died April 30, 1849.

"Infant son, born April 26, 1852, at Akron, Ohio; died May 17, 1852.

"Ellen Brown, born Sept. 25, 1854, at Akron, Ohio."—*Life and Letters of John Brown,*" F. B. *Sanborn, p. 43.*

———

NOTE 11.—"He was noted among the wool-dealers for the delicacy of his touch in sorting the different qualities and his skill in testing them when submitted to him. Give him three samples of wool,—one grown in Ohio, another in Vermont, and a third in Saxony,—and he would distinguish them from each other in the dark, by his sense of touch. Some Englishmen, during his sojourn abroad, put this power to the test in an amusing manner. One evening, in company with several English wool-dealers, each of whom had brought samples in his pocket, Brown was giving his opinion as to the best use to which certain grades and qualities should be put. One of the party very gravely drew a sample from his pocket, handed it to the Yankee farmer, and asked him what he would do with such wool as that. Brown took it, and had only to roll it between his fingers to know that it had not the minute hooks by which the fibers of wool are attached to each other. 'Gentlemen,' said he, 'if you have any machinery in England that will work up dog's hair, I advise you to put this into it.' The jocose Briton had sheared a poodle and brought the fleece with him; but the laugh went against him when Brown handed back his precious sample."— *"Life and Letters of John Brown,"* F. B. *Sanborn, p. 70.*

———

NOTE 12.—"My first apprenticeship to the tanning business consisted of a three-years course at grinding bark with a blind horse.

This, after months and years, became slightly monotonous. While the other children were out at play in the sunshine, where the birds were singing, I used to be tempted to let the old horse have a rather long rest, especially when father was absent from home; and I would then join the others at their play. This subjected me to frequent admonitions and to some corrections for 'eye-service,' as father termed it. I did not fully appreciate the importance of a good supply of ground bark, and on general principles I think my occupation was not well calculated to promote a habit of faithful industry. The old blind horse, unless ordered to stop, would, like Tennyson's Brook, 'go on forever,' and thus keep up the appearance of business; but the creaking of the hungry mill would betray my neglect, and then father, hearing this from below, would come up and stealthily pounce upon me while at a window looking upon outside attractions. He finally grew tired of these frequent slight admonitions for my laziness and other shortcomings, and concluded to adopt with me a sort of book-account, something like this:

John, Dr.,
  For disobeying mother....... 8 lashes.
  For unfaithfulness at work... 3 lashes.
  For telling a lie............. 8 lashes.

This account he showed me from time to time. On a certain Sunday morning he invited me to accompany him from the house to the tannery, saying that he had concluded it was time for a settlement. We went into the upper or finishing room, and after a long and tearful talk over my faults, he again showed me my account, which exhibited a fearful footing-up of *debits*. I had no credits or off-sets, and was of course bankrupt. I then paid about *one-third* of the debt, reckoned in strokes from a nicely prepared blue-beech switch, laid on 'masterly.' Then, to my utter astonishment, father stripped off his shirt, and, seating himself on a block, gave me the whip and bade me 'lay it on' to his bare back. I dared not refuse to obey, but at first I did not strike hard. 'Harder!' he said; 'harder, harder!' until he *received the balance of the account.* Small drops of blood showed on his back where the tip end of the tingling beech cut through. Thus ended the account and settlement, which was also my first practical illustration of the doctrine of the Atonement. I was then too obtuse to perceive how justice could be satisfied by inflicting penalty upon the back of the innocent instead of the guilty; but at that time I had not read the ponderous volumes of Jonathan Edwards's sermons which father owned."—"*Life and Letters of John Brown*," *F. B. Sanborn, pp. 92-93.*

NOTE 13.—The quotations from Ruth Brown are given from her statements in *Life and Letters of John Brown*, F. B. Sanborn.

NOTE 14.—"His favorite passages were these, as near as I can remember:

" 'Remember them that are in bonds as bound with them.'

" 'Whoso stoppeth his ear at the cry of the poor, he also shall cry himself, but shall not be heard.'

" 'He that hath a bountiful eye shall be blessed; for he giveth his bread to the poor.'

" 'A good name is rather to be chosen than great riches, and loving favor rather than silver and gold.'

" 'Whoso mocketh the poor, reproacheth his Maker; and he that is glad at calamities, shall not be unpunished.'

" 'He that hath pity upon the poor lendeth to the Lord, and that which he hath given will He pay to him again.'

" 'Give to him that asketh of thee, and from him that would borrow of thee turn not thou away.'

" 'A righteous man regardeth the life of his beast; but the tender mercies of the wicked are cruel.'

" 'Withhold not good from them to whom it is due, when it is in the power of thy hand to do it.'

" 'Except the Lord build the house, they labor in vain that build it; except the Lord keepeth the city, the watchman walketh in vain.'

" 'I hate vain thoughts, but thy law do I love.'

"The last chapter of Ecclesiastes was a favorite one, and on Fast-days and Thanksgivings he used very often to read the fifty-eighth chapter of Isaiah.

"When he would come home at night, tired out with labor, he would, before going to bed, ask some of the family to read chapters (as was his usual course night and morning); and would almost always say, 'Read one of David's Psalms.' "—*Life and Letters of John Brown*," *F. B. Sanborn, p. 39.*

. NOTE 15.—"I wish you to have some *definite plan.* Many seem to have none, and others never stick to any that they do form.

This was not the case with John. He followed up with *tenacity* whatever he set about so long as it answered his general purpose, and hence he rarely failed in some good degree to effect the things he undertook. This was so much the case that he *habitually expected to succeed* in his undertakings. With this feeling should be coupled the consciousness that our plans are right in themselves."— *"Life and Letters of John Brown," F. B. Sanborn, p. 16.*

NOTE 16.—Sanborn fixes this date. As early as 1834 he wrote a letter to his brother Frederick upon the subject of slavery, which the reader is requested to read. It is published in *Life and Letters of John Brown*, F. B. Sanborn, pp. 40, 41.

NOTE 17.—*Life and Letters of John Brown*, F. B. Sanborn, p. 66.

NOTE 18.—*Life and Letters of John Brown*, F. B. Sanborn, p. 100.

CHAPTER IV.

JOHN BROWN AND THE FUGITIVE SLAVE LAW.

"Awake the burning scorn!
  The vengeance long and deep,
That, till a better morn,
  Shall neither tire nor sleep!
Swear once again the vow,
  O freeman! dare to do!
God's will is ever NOW!—
  May His thy will renew! "

While the whole country acquiesced in that feature
of the Compromise of 1850 relating to fugitive slaves,
known as the Fugitive Slave Law, it was never satisfactory to the North. There were those harsh and overbear-
ing elements in it that made it seem as though the entire
North was harnessed to be driven in the disreputable interest of the haughty, triumphant and intolerant South.
But the country was at the time prosperous, and trade was
expanding. Business men everywhere hailed with delight
any measure which promised a settlement of the differ-
ences which had arisen between the two sections of the
country. This Compromise contained many provisions of
more consequence than the Fugitive Slave Law. One of
these was the principle which Senator Douglas embodied
in his Kansas-Nebraska Bill, and which became famous
as "squatter sovereignty." These provisions were lost to

(102)

view for the first years after the Compromise of 1850, because of the attention engrossed by the law for returning fugitive slaves to their masters.

The Fugitive Slave Law grew in disfavor in the North as the effects of its enforcement were observed. More slaves were seized and returned during the first year of its existence than had been carried back during the previous half century. Riots sometimes followed these seizures, caused by the brutality of the slave-hunters. The rewards and the opportunity to defraud the Government in the execution of the law enlisted the lowest and most desperate characters in the work of slave-hunting.[1] Kidnappers also developed under its provisions. Many negroes of the North, having either purchased their freedom or descended from free parents, had accumulated property and reared families. These were taken, often in the most brutal manner, and carried again to the South.[2] Sometimes their first intimation of the presence of kidnappers were blows which prostrated and disabled them.[3] Courts afforded them no protection. Indeed, it seemed that the courts were all in the interest of the man-stealers.[4] The victims were hurried South and sold again into bondage. Or perhaps they had been born of free parents in the North, and now found themselves as cruelly and remorselessly sold into slavery as had been their ancestors centuries before.[5]

Dissatisfaction with the law and its execution increased in the North. Humane men cried out against being made by enactment slave-hunters for the drivers and masters of the South. The fugitives were sometimes rescued, and the moral forces in the North became more and more antagonistic to the law. The "underground railway" was made more secure and rendered more effective. The best people sought opportunities to assist slaves to Canada; many free negroes removed there from fear of the kidnappers.

At that time John Brown had not fully settled his affairs in Springfield, Massachusetts, although his family were living in the Adirondacks. He was always outspoken against the Fugitive Slave Law. He favored resistance to it. Being always practical in his opposition to slavery in all its forms, he advised organized resistance to this tyrannical law which was so humiliating to every self-respecting man in the North. He believed that the white people could lend such aid and encouragement to the helpless and outraged negroes that they would resist the kidnappers who would sell them again into bondage. In this belief and for this purpose he organized the " United States League of Gileadites," the principles and purposes of which will fully appear in the following writings:

WORDS OF ADVICE.[1]

Branch of the United States League of Gileadites. Adopted January 15, 1851, as written and recommended by John Brown.

" UNION IS STRENGTH."

Nothing so charms the American people as personal bravery. Witness the case of Cinques, of everlasting memory, on board the "Amistad." The trial for life of one bold and to some extent successful man, for defending his rights in good earnest, would arouse more sympathy throughout the nation than the accumulated wrongs and sufferings of more than three millions of our submissive colored population. We need not mention the Greeks struggling against the oppressive Turks, the Poles against

Russia, nor the Hungarians against Austria and Russia combined, to prove this. *No jury can be found in the Northern States that would convict a man for defending his rights to the last extremity. This is well understood by Southern Congressmen, who insisted that the right of trial by jury should not be granted to the fugitive.* Colored people have ten times the number of fast friends among the whites than they suppose, and would have ten times the number they now have were they but half as much in earnest to secure their dearest rights as they are to ape the follies and extravagances of their white neighbors, and to indulge in idle show, in ease, and in luxury. Just think of the money expended by individuals in your behalf in the past twenty years! Think of the number who have been mobbed and imprisoned on your account! Have any of you seen the Branded Hand? Do you remember the names of Lovejoy and Torrey?

Should one of your number be arrested, you must collect together as quickly as possible, so as to outnumber your adversaries who are taking an active part against you. Let no able-bodied man appear on the ground unequipped, or with his weapons exposed to view: let that be understood beforehand. Your plans must be known only to yourself, and with the understanding that all traitors must die, wherever caught and proven guilty. " Whosoever is fearful or afraid, let him return and part early from Mount Gilead." (Judges, vii. 3; Deut. xx. 8.) Give all cowards an opportunity to show it on condition of holding their peace. *Do not delay one moment after you are ready; you will lose all your resolution if you do. Let the first blow be the signal for all to engage; and when engaged do not your work by halves, but make clean work with your enemies,—and be sure you meddle not with any others.* By going about your business quietly, you will get the job disposed of before the number that an uproar would bring together can collect; and you will have the **advan-**

tage of those who come out against you, for they will be
wholly unprepared with either equipments or matured
plans; all with them will be confusion and terror. Your
enemies will be slow to attack you after you have done up
the work nicely; and if they should, they will have to
encounter your white friends as well as you; for you may
safely calculate on a division of the whites, and may by
that means get an honorable parley.

Be firm, determined, and cool; but let it be understood
that you are not to be driven to desperation without making it an awful dear job to others as well as to you.
Give them to know distinctly that those who live in
wooden houses should not throw fire, and that you are
just as able to suffer as your white neighbors. *After effecting a rescue, if you are assailed, go into the houses of your
most prominent and influential white friends with your
wives; and that will effectually fasten upon them the suspicion of being connected with you, and will compel them
to make a common cause with you, whether they would
otherwise live up to their profession or not. This would
leave them no choice in the matter.* Some would doubtless prove themselves true to their own choice; others
would flinch. That would be taking them at their own
words. You may make a tumult in the court-room where
a trial is going on, by burning gunpowder freely in paper
packages, if you cannot think of any better way to create
a momentary alarm, and might possibly give one or more
of your enemies a hoist. But in such case the prisoner
will need to take the hint at once, and bestir himself; and
so should his friends improve the opportunity for a general rush.

A lasso might possibly be applied to a slave-catcher for
once with good effect. Hold on to your weapons, and
never be persuaded to leave them, part with them, or have
them far away from you. *Stand by one another and by
your friends, while a drop of blood remains; and be*

*hanged, if you must, but tell no tales out of school. Make
no confession.*

Union is strength. Without some well-digested arrangements nothing to any good purpose is likely to be
done, let the demand be never so great. Witness the case
of Hamlet and Long in New York, when there was no
well-defined plan of operations or suitable preparations
beforehand.

The desired end may be effectually secured by the means
proposed, namely, the enjoyment of our inalienable rights.

AGREEMENT.

As citizens of the United States of America, trusting
in a just and merciful God, whose spirit and all-powerful
aid we humbly implore, *we will ever be true to the flag
of our beloved country, always acting under it.* We, whose
names are hereunto affixed, do constitute ourselves a
branch of the United States League of Gileadites. That
we will provide ourselves at once with suitable implements,
and will aid those who do not possess the means, if any
such are disposed to join us. We invite every colored
person whose heart is engaged in the performance of our
business, whether male or female, old or young. The duty
of the aged, infirm, and young members of the League
shall be to give instant notice to all members in case of
an attack upon any of our people. We agree to have no
officers except a treasurer and secretary *pro tem.,* until
after some trial of courage and talent of able-bodied members shall enable us to elect officers from those who shall
have rendered the most important services. Nothing but
wisdom and undaunted courage, efficiency, and general
good conduct shall in any way influence us in electing
our officers.

RESOLUTIONS.

Resolutions of the Springfield Branch of the United States League of Gileadites. Prepared by John Brown, and adopted 15th January, 1851.

1. *Resolved,* That we, whose names are affixed, do constitute ourselves a Branch of the United States League, under the above name.

2. *Resolved,* That all business of this branch be conducted with the utmost quiet and good order; that we individually provide ourselves with suitable implements without delay; and that we will sufficiently aid those who do not possess the means, if any such are disposed to join us.

3. *Resolved,* That a committee of one or more discreet, influential men be appointed to collect the names of all colored persons whose heart is engaged for the performance of our business, whether male or female, whether old or young.

4. *Resolved,* That the appropriate duty of all aged, infirm, female, or youthful members of this Branch is to give instant notice to all other members of any attack upon the rights of our people, first informing all able-bodied men of this League or Branch, and next, all well-known friends of the colored people; and *that this information be confined to such alone,* that there may be as little excitement as possible, and no noise in so doing.

5. *Resolved,* That a committee of one or more discreet persons be appointed to ascertain the condition of colored persons in regard to implements, and to instruct others in regard to their conduct in any emergency.

6. *Resolved,* That no other officer than a *treasurer,* with a president and secretary *pro tem.,* be appointed by this Branch, until after some trial of the courage and talents of able-bodied members shall enable a majority of the members to elect their officers from those who *shall have rendered the most important services.*

7. *Resolved,* That, trusting in a just and merciful God,

whose *spirit* and *all-powerful aid* we humbly implore, we will most cheerfully and heartily support and obey such officers, when chosen as before; and that nothing but *wisdom, undaunted courage, efficiency,* and *general good conduct* shall in any degree influence our individual votes in case of such election.

8. *Resolved,* That a meeting of all the members of this Branch shall be immediately called for the purpose of electing officers (to be chosen by ballot) after the first trial *shall have been made* of the qualifications of individual members for such command, as before mentioned.

9. *Resolved,* That as citizens of the United States of America we will ever be found true to the flag of our beloved country, always acting under it.

This Branch consisted of forty-four members, all of whom signed the Agreement and Resolutions.

THE NEGRO SHOWN HIS ERRORS.

Some time before the organization of the United States League of Gileadites, Brown had undertaken to point out to negroes in the North their faults in their procedure against slavery. He believed in the use of tracts, and those short, sharp compositions which carried conviction and were unanswerable. To show the negroes their mistakes, that they might correct them, and be the better enabled to struggle effectively for their freedom, he wrote and published " Sambo's Mistakes," one of the quaintest and aptest of all his papers:

SAMBO'S MISTAKES.[7]

MESSRS. EDITORS,—Notwithstanding I may have committed a few mistakes in the course of a long life, like others of my colored brethren, yet you will perceive at a glance that I have always been remarkable for a seasonable discovery of my errors and quick perception of the true course. I propose to give you a few illustrations in this and the following chapters.

For instance, when I was a boy I learned to read; but instead of giving my attention to sacred and profane history, by which I might have become acquainted with the true character of God and of man; learned the true course for individuals, societies, and nations to pursue; stored my mind with an endless variety of rational and practical ideas; profited by the experience of millions of others of all ages; fitted myself for the most important stations in life, and fortified my mind with the best and wisest resolutions, and noblest sentiments and motives,—I have spent my whole life devouring silly novels and other miserable trash, such as most newspapers of the day and other popular writings are filled with; thereby unfitting myself for the relations of life, and acquiring a taste for nonsense and low wit, so that I have no relish for sober truth, useful knowledge, or practical wisdom. By this means I have passed through life without profit to myself or others, a mere blank on which nothing worth perusing is written. But I can see in a twink where I missed it.

Another error into which I fell in early life was the notion that chewing and smoking tobacco would make a man of me, but little inferior to some of the whites. The money I spent in this way would, with the interest of it, have enabled me to have relieved a great many sufferers, supplied me with a well-selected, interesting library, and paid for a good farm for the support and comfort of my old age; whereas I have now neither books, clothing, the satisfaction of having benefitted others, nor where to lay my hoary head. But I can see in a moment where I missed it.

Another of the few errors of my life is, that I have joined the Free Masons, Odd Fellows, Sons of Temperance, and a score of other secret societies, instead of seek-

ing the company of intelligent, wise, and good men, from
whom I might have learned much that would be interesting, instructive, and useful; and have in that way squandered a great amount of most precious time, and money
enough, sometimes in a single year, which if I had then
put the same out on interest and kept it so, would have
kept me always aboveboard, given me character and influence among men, or have enabled me to pursue some
respectable calling, so that I might employ others to their
benefit and improvement; but, as it is, I have always
been poor, in debt, and now obliged to travel about in
search of employment as a hostler, shoe-black, and fiddler.
But I retain all my quickness of perception; I can see
readily where I missed it.

II.

Another error of my riper years has been, that when
any meeting of colored people has been called to order to
consider of any important matter of general interest, I
have been so eager to display my spouting talents, and so
tenacious of some trifling theory or other that I have
adopted, that I have generally lost all sight of the business
in hand, consumed the time disputing about things of no
moment, and thereby defeated entirely many important
measures calculated to promote the general welfare; but
I am happy to say I can see in a minute where I missed it.

Another small error of my life (for I never committed great blunders) has been that I never would (for
the sake of the union in the furtherance of the most vital
interest of our race) yield any minor point of difference.
In this way I have always had to act with but a few, or
more frequently alone, and could accomplish nothing
worth living for; but I have one comfort,—I can see in a
minute where I missed it.

Another little fault which I have committed is, that
if anything another man has failed of coming up to my
standard, notwithstanding that he might possess many of

the most valuable traits, and be most admirably adapted to fill some one important post, I would reject him entirely, injure his influence, oppose his measures, and even glory in his defeats, while his intentions were good, and his plans well laid. But I have the great satisfaction of being able to say, without fear of contradiction, that I can see very quick where I missed it.

III.

Another small mistake which I have made is, that I could never bring myself to practice any present self-denial, although my theories have been excellent. For instance, I have bought expensive gay clothing, nice canes, watches, safety-chains, finger-rings, breastpins, and many other things of a like nature, thinking I might by that means distinguish myself from the vulgar, as some of the better class of whites do. I have always been of the foremost in getting up expensive parties, and running after fashionable amusements; have indulged my appetite freely whenever I had the means (and even with borrowed means); have patronized the dealers in nuts, candy, etc., freely, and have sometimes bought good suppers, and was always a regular customer at livery stables. By these, and many other means, I have been unable to benefit my suffering brethren, and am now but poorly able to keep my own soul and body together; but do not think me thoughtless or dull of apprehension, for I can see at once where I missed it.

Another trifling error of my life has been, that I have always expected to secure the favor of the whites by tamely submitting to every species of indignity, contempt, and wrong, instead of nobly resisting their brutal aggressions from principle, and taking my place as a man, and assuming the responsibilities of a man, a citizen, a husband, a father, a brother, a neighbor, a friend,—as God requires of every one (if his neighbor will allow him to do it); but I find that I get, for all my submission, about the same reward that the Southern slaveocrats render to the dough-faced statesmen of the North, for being bribed and browbeat and fooled and cheated, as the Whigs and Democrats love to be, and think themselves highly honored if they may be allowed to lick up the spittle of a Southerner. I say I get the same reward. But I am uncommon quick-sighted; I can see in a minute where I missed it.

Another little blunder which I made is, that while I have always been a most zealous Abolitionist, I have been constantly at war with my friends about certain religious tenets. I was first a Presbyterian, but could never think of acting with my Quaker friends, for they were the rankest heretics; and the Baptists would be in the water, and the Methodists denied the doctrine of the Election, etc. Of later years, since becoming enlightened by Garrison, Abby Kelly, and other really benevolent persons, I have been spending all my force on my friends who love the Sabbath, and have felt that all was at stake on that point; just as it has proved to be of late in France, in the abolition of slavery in their colonies. Now I cannot doubt, Messrs. Editors, notwithstanding I have been unsuccessful, that you will allow me full credit for my peculiar quick-sightedness. I can see in one second where I missed it.

NOTE 1.—"In one instance, a negro, near Edwardsville, Ills., who had been employed in the work of capturing several alleged fugitives, finally met a white man on the highway, presented a pistol, and arrested him as a runaway slave, for whom a reward of $200 had been offered. The white man happened, however, to be acquainted in Edwardsville, and was thus enabled to establish his right to himself."—*"The American Conflict," Horace Greeley, Vol. I, p. 218.*

NOTE 2.—"Of course, a law affording such facilities and tempta-

—8

tions to kidnapping was not allowed to pass unimproved by the numerous villains who regarded negroes as the natural and lawful prey of whites under all circumstances. *The Kentucky Yeoman,* a Democratic Pro-Slavery organ, once remarked that the work of arresting fugitives had become a regular business along the border line between the Slave and Free States, and that some of those engaged in it were not at all particular as to the previous slavery or freedom of those arrested. How could it be expected that they should be? In many instances, free colored girls were hired for household service at some point distant from that where they had previously resided, and were known; and, being thus unsuspectingly spirited away from all who could identify them, were hurried off into slavery. Sometimes, though not often, negroes were tempted by heavy bribes to betray their brethren into the hands of the slave-hunters. In one instance, a clerk in a dry-goods store in western New York, who was of full age, a member of a church, and had hitherto borne a respectable character, hired two colored boys to work for him in a hotel in Ohio, and on his way thither sold them as fugitive slaves to three Kentuckians, who appear to have believed his representations."—*"The American Conflict," Horace Greeley, Vol. I, p. 219.*

NOTE 3.—"The needless brutality with which these seizures were often made, tended to intensify the popular repugnance which they occasioned. In repeated instances, the first notice the alleged fugitive had of his peril was given him by a blow on the head, sometimes with a heavy club or stick of wood; and, being thus knocked down, he was carried, bleeding and insensible, before the facile commissioner, who made short work of identifying him, and earning his ten dollars, by remanding him into slavery. In Columbia, Pa., March, 1852, a negro named William Smith was seized as a fugitive by a Baltimore police officer, while working in a lumber-yard, and, attempting to escape, the officer drew a pistol and shot him dead. In Wilkesbarre, Pa., a deputy marshal and three or four Virginians suddenly came upon a nearly white mulatto waiter at a hotel, and, falling upon him from behind with a club, partially shackled him. He fought them off with the handcuff which they had secured to his right wrist, and covered with blood, rushed from the house and plunged into the Susquehanna, exclaiming: 'I will be drowned rather than taken alive!' He was pursued to the river-bank, and thence fired upon repeatedly, at a very short distance, as he stood in the water, up to his neck, until a ball entered his head, instantly covering his face with blood. The bystanders, who had by this time collected, were disgusted and indignant, and the hunters, fearing their interposition, retired for consultation. He thereupon came out of the water, apparently dying, and lay down on the shore. One of his pursuers remarked that 'dead niggers were not worth taking South.' His clothes having been torn off in the scuffle, some one brought a pair of pantaloons, and put them on him, and he was helped to his feet by a negro named Rex; on seeing which, the hunters returned and presented their revolvers, driving him again into the river, where he remained more than an hour, with only his head above the water. His claimants dared not come within his powerful grasp. As he afterward said, 'he would have died contented, could he have carried two or three of them down with him.' And the hunters were deterred or shamed by the spectators from further firing. Preparations being made to arrest them as rioters, they absconded; whereupon their victim waded some distance up the stream, and was soon after found by some women, lying flat on his face in a cornfield, insensible. He was then duly cared for, and his wounds dressed, which was the last that was seen of him."—*"The American Conflict," Horace Greeley, Vol. I, p. 216.*

NOTE 4.—"In one leading case, the court ruled, in effect, that the petitioner being young, and in bad health, and probably unadvised of the constitutional provision of that State making all its inhabitants free, 'is permitted to take Archy back to Mississippi.' An old lawyer dryly remarked, while all around were stigmatizing this decision as atrocious, that 'he thought it a very fair compromise, since it gave the law to the North and the negro to the South.'

"On Sunday, January 27, 1856, two slaves, with their wives and four children, escaped from Boone county, Ky., drove sixteen miles to Covington, and crossed to Cincinnati on the ice. They were missed before nightfall, and the master of five of them followed rapidly on horseback. After a few hours' inquiry, he traced them to the house of a negro named Kite, and, procuring the necessary warrants, with a marshal and assistants, proceeded thither on Monday. He summoned them to surrender. They refused. Whereupon the officers broke in the door, and were assailed with clubs and pistols by the desperate fugitives. Only one of the marshal's deputies was struck, and he not seriously injured; the negroes being disarmed before they could reload.

On a first survey of the premises they had captured, a horrible sight met the officers' eyes. In one corner of the room, a child nearly white lay bleeding to death, her throat cut from ear to ear. A scream from an adjoining room drew their attention thither, when a glance revealed a negro woman holding a knife dripping with gore over the heads of two children, who were crouched upon the floor, uttering cries of pain and terror. Wresting the knife from her hand, they discovered that the children were cut across the head and shoulders, but, though bleeding freely, not dangerously wounded. The woman proclaimed herself the mother of the dead child, as also of these, whom she desired to kill rather than see them returned to slavery. All were secured and taken to the marshal's office, where they sat quiet and dejected, answering all questions in monosyllables, or not answering at all. An excellent character was given the adults by their owners. The mother of the dead child, Margaret Garner, a dark mulatto, twenty-three years of age, seemed simply stupefied and dumb from excess of agony; but, on being complimented on the looks of her little boy beside her, quickly replied, 'You should have seen my little girl that—that—that died. *That* was the bird!' That girl was almost white, and of rare beauty. The mother alleged cruel treatment on the part of her master, and said she had resolved to kill all her children and then herself, in order to escape the horrors of slavery. A coroner's jury having rendered a verdict, in case of the dead child, that it was killed by its mother, Margaret Garner, with a knife, great efforts were made by the State authorities to hold her for trial on a charge of murder. All the adult slaves declared that they would go dancing to the gallows rather than be sent back to slavery. But Judges McLean and Leavitt, of the Federal Court, decided that they were in the custody of the U. S. Marshal, and could not be taken out of it by the *habeas corpus* of a State court, whether under a civil or criminal process; so they were all returned to slavery. The owner of Margaret pledged himself to hold her subject to a requisition from the Governor of Ohio to answer the charge of crime; but he failed to keep his promise, and sent her, with the rest of the fugitives, down the river for sale, where all trace of her was lost. The cost to the Federal Treasury of this single rendition was about $22,000, whereof at least $20,000 was shamefully squandered or embezzled, as $2,000 would have amply sufficed."—*"The American Conflict," Horace Greeley, Vol. I, p. 219.*

NOTE 5.—On the 2d of June, 1854—the repudiation of the Missouri compact having recently been consummated in the passage and Presidential approval of the Kansas-Nebraska bill—Anthony Burns having been adjudged a fugitive at Boston, President Pierce ordered the U. S. cutter Morris to take him from that city to life-long bondage in Virginia. The following spirited stanzas thereupon appeared (June 13th) in *The New York Tribune:*

HAIL TO THE STARS AND STRIPES.

Hail to the Stars and Stripes!
  The boastful flag all hail!
The tyrant trembles now,
  And at the sight grows pale;
The Old World groans in pain,
  And turns her eye to see,
Beyond the Western Main,
  The emblem of the Free.

Hail to the Stars and Stripes!
  Hope beams in every ray!
And, shining through the bars
  Of gloom, points out the way:
The Old World sees the light
  That shall her cell illume;
And shrinking back to night,
  Oppression reads her doom.

Hail to the Stars and Stripes!
  They float on every sea;
The crystal waves speed on
  The emblem of the Free!
Beneath the azure sky
  Of soft Italia's clime,
Or where Auroras die
  In solitude sublime.

All hail the flaunting Lie!
  The Stars grow pale and dim—
The Stripes are bloody scars,
  A lie the flaunting hymn!

It shields the pirate's deck,
    It binds a man in chains;
It yokes the captive's neck,
    And wipes the bloody stains.

Tear down the flaunting Lie!
    Half-mast the starry flag!
Insult no sunny sky
    With Hate's polluted rag!
Destroy it, ye who can!
    Deep sink it in the waves!
It bears a fellow-man
    To groan with fellow-slaves.

Awake the burning scorn!
    The vengeance long and deep,
That, till a better morn,
    Shall neither tire nor sleep!
Swear once again the vow,
    O, freeman! dare to do!
God's will is ever *now!*
    May His *thy* will renew!

Enfurl the boasted Lie!
    Till Freedom lives again,
To reign once more in truth
    Among untrammeled men!
Roll up the starry sheen—
    Conceal its bloody stains;
For in its folds are seen
    The stamp of rusting chains.

Be bold, ye heroes all!
    Spurn, spurn the flaunting Lie,
Till Peace and Truth, and Love
    Shall fill the bending sky;
Then, floating in the air,
    O'er hill, and dale, and sea,
'T will stand forever fair,
    The emblem of the Free!

—*"The American Conflict," Horace Greeley, Vol. I, p. 220.*

NOTE 6.—From *"Life and Letters of John Brown,"* F. B. Sanborn, pp. 124, 125, 126, 127.

NOTE 7.—From *"Life and Letters of John Brown,"* F. B. Sanborn, pp. 128, 129, 130, 131.

CHAPTER V.

FROM BIG SPRINGS TO POTTAWATOMIE.

Slavery, like the great Python
  Apollo slew;—bred in the slime
  Of earth;—whose birth was the first crime
  Against mankind, and that sublime
Iniquity of hell to dethrone

The rights of man, now crawling winds
  Herein in slimy, snaky fold:
  Or like the dragon great of old,
  On Thebes' rich plain in story told,
Great Cadmus slew, and wond'rous finds

That from his teeth sown in the earth,
  A race of men comes forth from clods,
  For civil strife; and whom the gods
  Turned man to man, barring all odds,
Against his equal man by birth.

Python and dragon both, with fierce
And bloody mouth, crawling it came;—
  Eyes that shot forth a burning flame
  Glared round for prey; and naught could tame
The gloated beast of hell, nor pierce

Its flinty scales, till it had fed
  And fattened on the blood and flesh
  Of Freedom's sons.
          —*Joel Moody's "The Song of Kansas."*

The bogus Legislature defined the issue for the Pro-
Slavery people and party of Kansas. This issue was

SLAVERY alone.[1]   In Kansas nothing else was to be known; anything which came in conflict with this issue was to be subordinated, no matter what its importance. The Free-State party was organized to meet and combat the issue made by the bogus Legislature. Up to this time there had been no concert of action by the opponents of slavery in Kansas. The Pro-Slavery party had acted in unison and for a single purpose from the beginning, and this gave it a great advantage in the opening conflict. Something of the spirit in which this action was manifested may be seen from the following expressions:

"We learn from a gentleman lately from the Territory of Kansas that a great many Missourians have already set their meg in that country, and are making arrangements to 'darken the atmosphere' with their negroes. This is right. Let every man that owns a negro go there and settle, and our Northern brethren will be compelled to hunt further north for a location."—*Liberty (Mo.) Democratic Platform, June 8, 1854.*

The same paper says, under date of June 27, 1854: "We are in favor of making Kansas a 'Slave State' if it should require half the citizens of Missouri, musket in hand, to emigrate there, and even sacrifice their lives in accomplishing so desirable an end."

And again it says: " Shall we allow such cut-throats and murderers as the people of Massachusetts are to settle in the Territory adjoining our own State? No! If popular opinion will not keep them back, we should see what virtue there is in the force of arms." [2]

This was the expression all along the border. The advantage of the Pro-Slavery party was the result of it.

The actions of the party up to and including the bogus Legislature plainly indicated that even the "Squatter Sovereignty" feature of the Kansas-Nebraska bill would not be tolerated, nor given any fair trial in Kansas. The penalty for enticing a slave away from his master was death. This Legislature believed that a law to make even the discussion of slavery in ordinary conversation a felony would be in their interest, and its enactment was seriously considered.[3]

To meet the sentiment for slavery in Missouri, and the issue forced upon Kansas by Missourians in the bogus Legislature, became the work of the Free-State men of the Territory. To prepare for this work, the Big Springs convention was called. This convention had its origin in a number of preliminary conventions held in Lawrence and elsewhere.[4] It was well attended, and representatives from all parts of the Territory were present. A platform of principles was drawn up and adopted; it demanded that Kansas be a free State.[5] Here, then, were the issues: Slavery alone, for the Pro-Slavery party; liberty and nothing else, for the Free-State party. These were the issues up to the Civil War—nothing else, in Kansas. All the invasions by Missourians, their election outrages and bogus Legislature and laws, all the campaigns for the enforcement of the bogus Territorial laws, all the murders and robberies by the ruffians, the Lecompton Constitution, and the aid of the Administration at Washington, were incidents in the battle waged by the slave-power for the supremacy of its issue. The "Topeka movement," Lane's Northern Armies, Black Jack, Fort Titus, Fort Saunders, Franklin, Hickory Point, and the Leavenworth Constitution, were incidents in the struggle of the Free-State party to make its issue victorious. It will be well to bear this always in mind; it is the key to Kansas Territorial history, and the fact that it is so has been overlooked by many writers on the subject.

If the Pro-Slavery party could enforce the bogus laws, their victory would be complete without aid of any other of the subordinate incidents. They were so framed that they could be obeyed only by adherents of slavery; and if obeyed by the people of the Territory, advocacy of free principles and a free State would disappear from Kansas. If the Free-State men remained in Kansas they were compelled to resist these tyrannical enactments. Their enforcement was the first step decided upon for the success of their issue by the Pro-Slavery men. Being in possession of the judiciary of the Territory and having all the offices and the coöperation of the Government, it seemed that the laws could not be successfully resisted by the Free-State party. But at the solicitation and instance of ex-Governor Reeder the Big Springs convention resolved to resist these infamous laws "to a bloody issue,"—a very unfortunate declaration for a party at so great a disadvantage as the Free-State party then was.[6] Reeder was angered by the treatment he had received from the bogus Legislature and the President, and acted from a spirit of revenge and retaliation, and in so doing brought indescribable woe to Free-State settlers. That the provocation under which the anti-slavery people lay was sufficient to justify the adoption of this resolution by their representatives, there is no doubt. But the more conservative leaders of the party would have devised some less dangerous way of evasion. The adoption of this resolution was the cause of war for " extermination, total and complete," by the Missourians a little later. The resolution did the Free-State cause much harm in Congress and in the East. In Kansas and Missouri it was regarded as a challenge to battle by the ruffians, and their supporters in the United States Senate took the same view. Nothing more unfortunate than this action of the convention could have befallen the Free-State party in Kansas, as was afterwards demonstrated by great cost of blood and treasure and untold hardship and suffering.

The Big Springs convention was held precisely one month before John Brown arrived in Kansas. We have seen that two of his sons were delegates to that gathering of patriots. On October 13, 1855, he wrote his family that he had "reached the place where the boys are located one week ago, late at night." He found the condition of his sons deplorable indeed. "No crops of hay or anything raised had been taken care of; with corn wasting by cattle and horses, without fences; and, I may add, without any meat; and Jason's folks without sugar, or any kind of breadstuffs but corn ground with great labor in a hand-mill about two miles off. . . . Some have had the ague, but lightly; but Jason and Oliver have had a hard time of it, and are yet feeble. . . . We have made but little progress; but we have made a little. We have got a shanty three logs high, chinked, and mudded, and roofed over with our tent, and a chimney so far advanced that we can keep a fire in it for Jason. . . . We have got their little crop of beans secured, which, together with johnnycake, mush and milk, pumpkins and

squashes, constitute our fare. Potatoes they have none of
any account; milk, beans, pumpkins, and squashes a very
moderate supply, just for the present use." [7] Their poor
success was largely due to the fact that little can be done
upon a prairie farm the first year. The thick, hard sod
is held firmly together by the heavy roots of the grass,
and is so firm and tenacious that its cultivation is profitless
and almost impossible. But by the second year the roots
have decayed, and the sod has fallen asunder; the field
is a bed of mellow loam, ready to yield immense crops.
The experience of the Browns was that of all settlers on
prairie farms, and was not a reason for discouragement.

Three weeks after the arrival of John Brown in Kansas,
Dow was murdered near the Hickory Point postoffice, in
Douglas county. This was the first of a series of events
which rapidly followed one another, and were seized upon
to serve as a pretext for the invasion of Kansas by the
Missourians "to enforce the laws,"—mark the purpose.
Thus early did the "bloody issue" resolution of the Big
Springs convention begin to bear fruit. This invasion
came to be known as the Wakarusa War or Shannon's
War.[8] In this war Brown and his sons took part. When
the rumors of the invasion spread over the Territory,
John Brown left Osawatomie and went to the locality
where dwelt his sons, some eight or ten miles distant.
He intended to go on to Lawrence to learn the true situa-
tion, but afterwards sent his son John. The younger
Brown had scarcely left the house when the courier from
Lawrence arrived to summon them to the defense of that
town at once.[9] No time was lost in obeying this order;
the father and four sons set out in the afternoon, and

after a march which continued all night and most of the
following forenoon, arrived in the threatened town Friday,
December 7, 1855.[10]   They found the negotiations between Governor Shannon, and the citizens of Lawrence
represented by Doctor Robinson and Colonel Lane,
under way. A company of militia was organized immediately after their arrival, of which they were made
members; the command of it was given to John Brown,
who was at once commissioned Captain by Doctor Robinson. It was composed of other new arrivals and some
men who had been for a few days in Lawrence. The neighbors of Thomas W. Barber and those having acted with
him in his labor in Lawrence were mustered into Brown's
company.

The war ended without any battle between the invaders
and the people of Kansas. John Brown was not well
pleased with what he first believed to be the terms of
the peace, but that he threatened to go out and fight the
Missourians against all orders is scarcely probable.[11]   He
left Lawrence believing that by the terms of the treaty
concluding the war the attempt to enforce the laws was
abandoned by Governor Shannon, and his account of the
matter shows that he was satisfied with what he was given
to understand were the conditions secured by the Free-
State men. He may have been misinformed or purposely
deceived. He says:

"After frequently calling on the leaders of the Free-
State men to come and have an interview with him, by
Governor Shannon, and after as often getting for an
answer that if he had any business to transact with anyone in Lawrence, to come and attend to it, he signified

his wish to come into the town, and an escort was sent to the invaders' camp to conduct him in. When there, the leading Free-State men, finding out his weakness, frailty, and consciousness of the awkward circumstances into which he had really got himself, took advantage of his cowardice and folly, and by means of that and the free use of whisky and some trickery succeeded in getting a written arrangement with him much to their own liking. He stipulated with them to order the Pro-Slavery men of Kansas home, and to proclaim to the Missouri invaders that they must quit the Territory without delay, and also give up General Pomeroy (a prisoner in their camp),— which was all done; he also recognizing the volunteers as the militia of Kansas, and empowering their officers to call them out whenever in their discretion the safety of Lawrence or other portions of the Territory might require it to be done. He (Governor Shannon) gave up all pretension of further attempt to enforce the enactments of the bogus Legislature, and retired, subject to the derision and scoffs of the Free-State men (into whose hands he had committed the welfare and protection of Kansas), and to the pity of some and the curses of others of the invading force.

"So ended this last Kansas invasion,—the Missourians returning with *flying colors,* after incurring heavy expenses, suffering great exposure, hardships, and privations, not having fought any battles, burned or destroyed any infant towns or Abolition presses; leaving the Free-State men organized and armed, and in full possession of the Territory; not having fulfilled any of all their dreadful threatenings, except to murder one *unarmed* man, and to commit some robberies and waste of property upon defenseless families, unfortunately within their power. We learn by their papers that they boast of a great victory over the Abolitionists."

It will be seen from a careful reading of the treaty that

Brown's understanding of it was incorrect. From whom he obtained his knowledge of it does not appear, for it was not published immediately. That he desired to fight, there is little doubt; that he would have advocated battle before the concession of any vital thing contended for, he evidently made plain. It may have been thought best to conceal for a few days the real terms, and claim more than was actually obtained from Governor Shannon; there were many Free-State men who would have insisted upon battle before yielding any semblance of submission to the bogus laws; especially was this the case after the murder of Barber, when they were restrained with difficulty.[12]

A study of all the acounts of the Wakarusa war makes it very certain that desire to arrest Branson and put him under bonds was only a pretense seized upon by the Pro-Slavery party to enable them to begin a war to force the Free-State people to obey the bogus laws.

John Brown and his sons returned to the Pottawatomie; there he was engaged during the winter in work upon the cabins of his sons, and in the erection of a house for his brother-in-law, Orson Day. He wrote, February 1, 1856, that Lawrence " is again threatened with an attack. Should that take place, we may be soon called upon to ' buckle on our armor,' which by the help of God we will do." He and Salmon made a trip to Missouri to buy corn, from whence they returned February 20th. There they heard that " Frank Pierce means to crush the men of Kansas, but I think he may find his hands full before it is all over." This rumor was not far wrong, as the whole slave-power was then making preparation to· enter Kansas and begin a vigorous campaign as soon as spring

opened. Buford was organizing in Alabama and South
Carolina. Mississippi was preparing to do her part in the
work. Jefferson Davis was committing the Administration to aid in this very purpose. It becomes necessary
for us to review these preparations for the invasion of
Kansas in the spring of 1856. It has been charged by
those who would disparage John Brown, that all the outrages committed upon the Free-State party and people
of Kansas after the killing of the Doyles and others by
John Brown and his company on the Pottawatomie were
the result of that act. Such writers charge that all the
trouble in Lawrence, all the troubles in southeastern Kansas, all the troubles at Leavenworth, Buford's march from
the South with his army for the subjugation of the Territory, the imprisonment of Doctor Robinson and others
for treason, the war of extermination, and finally the
Civil War, resulted from the bloody work at Dutch Henry's
Crossing.[13] If such were the truth it would be the highest
tribute to John Brown's judgment, for it would exalt that
event to the dignity of being the direct cause of the abolition of slavery in America. While that killing was one
of the great factors in making Kansas free, it cannot be
claimed the abolition of slavery grew directly out of it,
as one of the detractors from John Brown's fame would
have us believe. The campaign of the advocates of slavery in Kansas in the spring and summer of 1856 was the
result of elaborate preparation and long premeditation.

Of this period and the attitude of the South toward
Kansas after the Wakarusa war, we desire to cite as authority the *History of Lawrence,* by the Rev. Richard
Cordley. We have no authority in Kansas better than
that work:

"Though the settlers were not molested during this severe weather, they knew the quiet was only temporary. The opening of the spring would bring a renewal of hostilities. The hordes that had left Franklin so sullenly did not propose to drop the controversy. They saw they had made a mistake, and the Free-State men had profited by it. Next time they would plan more wisely. They would not be caught in court again without a case. All over Missouri and the South, preparations were going on to push the controversy to a successful issue for slavery. The shrewdest men in the land were planning together for the summer campaign. The general idea was to make it so uncomfortable for the Free-State men that they would flee the country, and so that others would not come.

"The line of attack was not hard to determine. The Free-State men occupied a position that was difficult to maintain. They knew that the Shawnee Legislature had been elected by Missouri votes. They pronounced its enactments an imposition and a fraud. They determined to ignore them, and as far as possible to nullify them or destroy their effect. The laws were of the most extreme pro-slavery type. They not only protected slave property, but punished all acts and expressions against slavery with great severity. They could not even discuss the subject without becoming liable to criminal prosecution. Their only course was to ignore these laws and practically nullify them. Then nobody would dare to bring any slaves into Kansas. If there were no slaves in Kansas, slavery would not really exist, even though the laws did recognize it. In two years there would be another election, and by that time the Free-State men felt they would be strong enough to take possession of all the machinery of government and shape the laws to suit themselves. If they could only keep things as they were till the next election, immigration from the North would do the rest.

"The Pro-Slavery people, on the other hand, strove to
—9

force an immediate issue. They laid their plans to compel the Free-State men to recognize the bogus laws, or else resist the officials charged with their enforcement. The problem of the Free-State men was to ignore the bogus laws and yet avoid a collision. They might suffer violence, but as far as possible they were to avoid doing violence. Above all, they were to avoid any collision with the authority of the United States.

"Another element entered into the problem, which must be mentioned that the whole situation may be understood. That element grew out of what has been referred to as the 'Topeka movement.' The Free-State policy had its negative side in the rejection of the bogus laws. It had its positive side in the adoption of the Topeka Constitution. During the autumn of 1855 the Free-State people held a constitutional convention at Topeka, which framed a State constitution. They then sent it to Congress and asked to be received into the Union as a State. The House of Representatives passed the bill admitting Kansas as a State, but the Senate rejected it. Thus the movement failed in Congress, but it was kept alive in Kansas as a rallying-point of defense. An election was held in January for State officers, and Dr. Robinson was elected Governor. The Legislature then chosen met in March and organized, and Governor Robinson sent in his message. No attempt was made, however, to put the State Government into operation. But the thought was to do this if the situation became intolerable. The occasion never came, and the Topeka government and constitution never went into effect.

"As spring opened, the policy of the Pro-Slavery men began to manifest itself. It was a deeply laid, shrewd scheme. It went on the assumption that the attitude of the Free-State men toward the bogus laws was rebellion, and that the actors in the Topeka Free-State movement were guilty of treason. They proposed to have the Free-

State leaders indicted for high crimes, and either have them arrested or compelled to flee from the Territory. This will give a general clue to the new line of attack, and will show the animus and purpose of the violent proceedings which followed."

The Constitutional Convention of the Free-State people met at Topeka October 23, 1855. The constitution formed there was adopted on the 15th of December by a vote of the people, which stood: In favor of the Constitution, 1,731; against the Constitution, 46.[14] This action of the Free-State men was taken as an additional act of hostility to the Territorial laws, and the Territorial authorities resented it accordingly. Although the Wakarusa treaty was supposed to be in force, neither side deceived itself with the belief that it had ended the conflict. On the 14th of November the convention at Leavenworth which formed the Law and Order party denounced the Topeka Constitutional Convention as treasonable, and after the constitution was adopted the members of the party were so profuse in threats that the Free-State men of Lawrence believed it necessary to form a secret league for the defense of the interests of the city and the party.[15] This was perfected in December, perhaps about the time of the holding of the convention to nominate State officers under the Topeka Constitution. It was the "Society of Danites"; sometimes called the " Regulators," and sometimes the " Defenders." [16] Lane, Robinson, Legate, and other Free-State leaders were at the head of this society. On the 12th of January a Free-State convention in Lawrence declared in favor of the establishment of the Free-State government at once; and on the 15th of the same month State officers under the Topeka Constitution were elected.[17]   While it is now known that it was never the serious intention to inaugurate a hostile government by the Free-State people, the Territorial authorities believed that an aggressive and conflicting government was to be immediately established.   The leaders of the Free-State party designed this " Topeka movement" to hold the anti-slavery forces together on the issue between the ideas contending for the supremacy, but most of the party believed with the Territorial authorities, that the Free-State government was to attempt to gain control of the affairs of the Territory.   This was to be accomplished through the admission of the Territory as a State.   On January 24th President Pierce sent a special message to Congress in which he indorsed the course of the bogus Legislature, and denounced the adoption of the Topeka Constitution and the election of officers thereunder as an act of revolution and rebellion.[18]   February 5, 1856, Governor Chase of Ohio recommended to the Legislature of that State that measures be taken to aid freedom in Kansas and fair play for its advocates.[19]   Henry Ward Beecher made his famous address in which he denominated a Sharps' rifle one of the moral agencies of the times.[20]   On the 6th of February the result of the Free-State election was proclaimed.   This was followed by the proclamation of President Pierce commanding "all persons engaged in unlawful combinations against the constituted authority of the Territory of Kansas, or of the United States, to disperse, and retire peaceably to their respective abodes." [21]   Very soon there came the promulgation of an order by Jefferson Davis, Secretary of War, authorizing Governor Shannon to use the United States troops to suppress "insurrectionary combinations," and "invasive aggression." [22] This latter term was to enable the Governor to turn back Free-State settlers, but was never construed to apply to the Missourians in favor of forcing slavery on the Territory, nor to Buford's men, who were coming with the avowed purpose of making war. On the 16th of February Secretary Marcy directed Governor Shannon to call on the officers of Fort Leavenworth and Fort Riley for troops for "the suppression of insurrectionary combinations, or armed resistance to the execution of the laws." [23]

These acts of the Administration were to counteract the movements of the Free-State men in resolving to resist the bogus laws and setting up the Free-State Government.[24] These were considered treason, and the United States courts for the Territory were not long in making this conclusion the law, in the promulgation of the "constructive-treason" theory. The South took alarm. Buford, of Alabama, proposed to give $20,000 toward the cost of leading an army into Kansas from the Southern States. The Legislature of his State appropriated $25,-000 for the same purpose. Other Southern States prepared to send men to contest for Southern rights. Virginia would send Colonel Wilkes; South Carolina commissioned Colonel Treadwell; Kentucky sent Captain Hampton; Florida dispatched Colonel Titus.[25] " 'We want money and armed men' was the perpetual cry, . . and it was heard all over the South." The response was all that it was hoped it would be.[26] The forces of the South were gathering to descend upon the plains of Kansas early in the spring of 1856. " The Eastern and

Northern States were continually warned that the war had hardly yet commenced, and that the next act in the drama would assume more terrible aspects than anything yet seen in the Territory." General Atchison had named the day of the meeting of the Free-State Legislature as the date of the attack of the Southern forces under the leadership of Missouri, as that act was held to come under the terms of the proclamations of the Administration as expressed in orders to Governor Shannon.[27] But the Free-State men were not to be frightened from their course by rumors and threats. The Legislature convened, and the course of the Free-State Government was clearly set forth in the message of Governor Robinson, and to this remarkably able paper was due the short respite enjoyed by the people of the Territory. Kansas had engrossed the attention of Congress, and a committee consisting of Congressman John Sherman of Ohio, M. A. Howard of Michigan and M. Oliver of Missouri was appointed to come to the Territory and investigate the outrages perpetrated by the ruffians in the early elections. April 18th this committee commenced its work by a session at Lecompton, and soon aroused the wrath of the Pro-Slavery party, both in Kansas and Missouri. The feeling against the members, against ex-Governor Reeder and against the Free-State people increased until the Republican members were driven from the Territory, and Mr. Reeder was forced to leave in disguise to escape assassination, as we have seen.

Buford's men began to arrive early in the spring.[28] They were quartered at different places in the Territory, supposed to be points from which they could most effect-

ually assist the Missouri invaders when they arrived.
They did not pretend to select claims and enter on the
work of building homes; they established themselves in
military camps, where they were drilled, and were sub-
sisted upon what could be seized from the Free-State
settlers. They were severe and often cruel and brutal in
their treatment of helpless and defenseless people who
opposed slavery. A large camp was established near Osawatomie, and their course there was one of outrage from
the first. They established intimate relations with the
most rabid Pro-Slavery settlers, and urged them to the
commission of horrible atrocities. The life of no Free-
State settler was safe in the vicinity of their camp. They
had an avowed object, and that was loudly proclaimed:
it was to make a slave State of Kansas, and to accomplish
this every means was to be utilized, fair or foul.

The hope of Kansas to turn this gathering horde from
her doors was in the arrival of settlers from the Northern
States as soon as the Missouri river was open to navigation in the spring of 1856. They were expected to come
armed with Sharps' rifles and ready to defend themselves
from outrage and robbery. But the forces of the South
took steps to prevent either men or arms from reaching
Kansas over the Missouri river route. The river was
blockaded and vessels were searched. Arms were seized,
and settlers turned back. Here was an unexpected blow
to the Free-State people, and their condition became critical in the extreme. The resources of the South were
organizing for invasion. The United States troops were at
the disposition of those demanding their extermination.
No means of defense could reach them by the usual route,

and a new way into the Territory could not be established by the way of Iowa and Nebraska for some months. It seemed that the Free-State settlers were at last at the mercy of their mortal enemies, and their condition desperate— almost hopeless. To add to their dangers, their leaders were arrested or forced to leave the Territory; and the offense charged against them was treason.

Having effectually isolated the Free-State men from their friends in the North and East and shut out the prospect of assistance from those sections, and having deprived them of their leaders, a cause was sought that would in some degree serve as an excuse for the invasion of the Territory. In this emergency Sheriff Jones was depended upon, and, as events demonstrated, the expectations entertained of him were fully realized. Mr. Jones took it upon himself to declare the Wakarusa treaty at an end, and came to Lawrence on the 19th of April, 1856, to arrest Samuel N. Wood for his complicity in the rescue of Branson. He effected his purpose, but his prisoner was enabled to escape by a diversion created by the citizens who witnessed the arrest. On the following Sunday Jones returned with some aids from Lecompton, and these not being considered sufficient for his object, he summoned several citizens who were on their way to church, to assist him. These were not to be so easily diverted from their then zeal for the cause of religion, very suddenly developed and intensified by the duty and service demanded by the sheriff. They gave no heed to his commands, and he, becoming exasperated, arrested another of the Branson rescuers, but one for whom he had no warrant. His efforts proving fruitless, he applied to Governor Shannon for

troops with which to effect the arrest of persons for whom
he had writs. These were furnished, and Jones again
appeared in Lawrence, on the 23d of April. With the
assistance of the detachment of soldiers he succeeded in
arresting those persons who had refused to obey his sum-
mons to aid him on the previous Sunday. These were put
into a tent and guarded. On the following night Charles
Lenhart, acting upon his own responsibility, shot Sheriff
Jones, inflicting a painful wound, but one not considered
dangerous. It was not known who did this deed, and the
people of Lawrence immediately assembled and disavowed
the act and condemned it; they also offered a reward of
$500 for the arrest and conviction of the criminal. This
was an unfortunate affair for the Free-State people generally and for the city of Lawrence particularly. It was
difficult of explanation, and was immediately seized upon
as the cause for the invasion of the Territory by the forces
organized for months previous for that very purpose. The
leaders spread reports of the death of Jones at the hands
of a Free-State mob or assassin, and the reports grew as
they were passed from ruffian to ruffian along the border.
Many Pro-Slavery Missourians were already in the Territory awaiting developments, having been placed there
by their leaders, who no doubt had some understanding
with Jones that he was to find them an excuse to attack
the settlers. In fact, there is little doubt that Jones was
having recourse to his old writs to exasperate the Free-
State men to some act that would bring on hostilities.
While Jones was disabled, his deputy, one Sam Salters,
an ignorant ruffian from South Carolina, was scouring
the country with United States soldiers at his heels and

arresting people on all kinds of charges.[29] The United States Marshal issued a proclamation May 11th calling on the "law-abiding" citizens of the Territory to assemble at Lecompton "in sufficient numbers for the execution of the laws." This was the authority under which the Missourians came from their hiding in the Delaware Reserve north of Lawrence, and again poured over the border from the western counties of that State. It is quite probable that Lawrence would have been so strongly manned and so well fortified and defended, had the leaders of the Free-State people there determined to battle for their town, that the ruffians would have been beaten off. They would have found some excuse for retiring, as they had in the Wakarusa war. But the policy of non-resistance was adopted, and couriers were sent out to turn back the patriotic men hastening to battle for the cause of right.

On the morning of the 21st of May, 1856, there were several hundred Missourians and ruffians from other Southern States in the vicinity of Lawrence. The Missourians were commanded by Senator Atchison, the Alabama forces were under Buford, and those from Florida under Titus.[30] Atchison had led his army in through the Delaware Reserve, on the north side of the Kansas river; Buford had his camp at Franklin, and Titus was in the vicinity of Lecompton. On the morning of the 21st these forces, together with the troops from the United States army, gathered on the hill south of Lawrence. The people had desired to defend themselves, but had been prevented by their committee of safety; then this committee had been discharged and a new one appointed. But the new was no better than the old. Every Kansan should read the letter sent to Donaldson by this craven committee; it may be seen in Phillips's "Conquest of Kansas," page 293. They offered to obey the Territorial laws passed by the bogus Legislature if the assembled forces would refrain from attacking the town. This act of the committee brought it into contempt with both the invaders and the citizens of Lawrence; it was designated the "Safety Valve," and was ever after the object of contempt and ridicule. The people did not generally wish a conflict with the United States troops, but some would have fought even them; almost all were in favor of resisting Jones and the "Territorial militia," as the Missourians and other invaders were called. Both the invaders and the troops were in close consultation with Governor Shannon, in whose office they met to discuss and arrange their plans of campaign. They had the approval of the Governor in all that was done. The forces of the United States pretended to be looking for persons upon whom to serve warrants; Jones and the invaders who were acting as his posse held orders from Chief Justice Lecompte to destroy the two newspapers of the town and the Free-State hotel, as they had been indicted under his "constructive-treason" doctrine and theory.

The Deputy Marshal first entered the town and made a few arrests. That he needed no troops to effect this was shown on the previous night, when he had been in Lawrence and made some arrests without any assistance and without molestation. When he had enacted his farce he withdrew, and Sheriff Jones entered with his horde of cutthroats. These worthies ran up various flags, and then proceeded with the work for which some of them had marched a thousand miles. The presses, type, paper-stock and fixtures of the printing-offices were destroyed. The Free-State hotel was first bombarded, and afterwards burned. Other buildings were burned, including the dwelling of Doctor Robinson, and the town was looted. As the shades of night fell the vandals departed by the red glare of the burning city, and weighted down with the booty obtained in its pillage.[31] Some of the Missourians returned home, but by far the greater number remained to assist the men of Buford, Titus and Treadwell in harrying the Free-State settlers and following up the work of the campaign planned the preceding winter, and so auspiciously begun at Lawrence.

The border papers were filled with exultation, and the ruffians were urged to continue the work. One paper said that nothing more would be done to the settlers if the ruffians were not further molested; but this was for effect in the East, where their allies, Davis and other members of the Administration, might need something to quiet the apprehensions of those not fully informed as to the situation in Kansas, and the designs of the slavery propagandists.

Following the sacking of Lawrence all semblance of order disappeared from the camps of the invaders, except that maintained among thieves. No secret was made of the fact that the conquest of the Territory had been decided upon. They were fortified in authority by the proclamations of the President and Jefferson Davis; the Governor had received from the Administration orders to assist in the work, and seemed anxious to do the bidding not only of Davis, but of the bloodiest ruffian on the plains

of Kansas.   For the Free-State settlers there was now no
protection.   Murder, anarchy, rapine—a reign of terror
surged around them.   It seemed that the boast of the
chivalry of the South, that the opponents to slavery in
Kansas should be exterminated, was on the point of fulfill-
ment.   But for the heroism and unconquerable will of one
man, this object of the South might have come to a consummation.

NOTE 1.—On the last day of the session of the bogus Legislature, the Speaker, Mr. Stringfellow (Mr. Anderson in the chair),
offered a preamble and one resolution which was adopted, and was
also adopted by the Council.   The resolution is as follows:

"*Be it resolved by the House of Representatives, the Council con-
curring therein,* That it is the duty of the Pro-Slavery party, the
Union-loving men of Kansas Territory, to know but one issue, slavery, and that any party making or attempting to make any other
is and should be held as an ally of abolitionism and disunion."—
House Journal, 1855, p. 380.

NOTE 2.—*History of the State of Kansas,* A. T. Andreas, p. 83.
The three quotations will be found on the same page of that work.

NOTE 3.—See *The Kansas Memorial,* p. 19, where the report of
the committee is quoted by Judge Usher in his address.   See also
the same work, p. 105, address of Colonel D. R. Anthony.

NOTE 4.—The best account of the movement leading up to the
Big Springs convention, and of the convention itself, will be found
in the *History of the State of Kansas,* A. T. Andreas, pp. 106, 107,
108, 109, 110.   All resolutions are there given in full, as is also
the platform.   (Twentieth Century Classics, No. 2, September, 1899,
page 53; article, "James Henry Lane.")

NOTE 5.—The first resolution of the platform declared: "That,
setting aside all minor issues of partisan politics, it is incumbent

upon us to proffer an organization calculated to recover our dearest rights, and into which Democrats and Whigs, native and naturalized citizens may freely come without sacrifice of their respective political creeds, but without forcing [them] as a test upon others. And that when we shall have achieved our political freedom, vindicated our rights of self-government, and come as an independent State upon the arena of the Union, where those issues may become vital where they are now dormant, it will be time enough to divide our organization by those tests, the importance of which we fully recognize in their appropriate sphere."

The third resolution declared: "That our true interests, socially, morally and pecuniarily, require that Kansas should be a free State; that free labor will best promote the happiness, the rapid population, the prosperity and the wealth of our people; that slave labor is a curse to the master and the community, if not the slave. That our country is unsuited to it, and that we will devote our energies as a party to exclude the institution and to secure for Kansas the constitution of a free State."—*"History of the State of Kansas," A. T. Andreas, pp. 108, 109.*

———

NOTE 6.—The convention appointed a "Committee on the late Legislature." Its report was adopted. One of the resolutions of the report is as follows:

"*Resolved,* That we will endure and submit to these laws no longer than the best interests of the Territory require, as the least of two evils, and *will resist them to a bloody issue* as soon as we ascertain that peaceable remedies shall fail, and forcible resistance shall furnish any reasonable prospect of success; and that, in the meantime, we recommend to our friends throughout the Territory, the organization and discipline of volunteer companies and the procurement and preparation of arms."—*"History of the State of Kansas," A. T. Andreas, p. 109.*

While the resolution declared no intention of immediate resistance to the bogus laws, it did recommend the purchase of arms, the formation and discipline of volunteer companies, and when taken with the avowed purpose of the individual Free-State leaders to resist the laws, the resolution indicated a clear intention of resistance. Other resolutions of the report declared that the laws had no binding force upon the citizens of the Territory, and that they were at liberty to resist and defy them should they choose to do so; that "we owe no allegiance or obedience to the tyrannical enactments of this spurious legislature; that their laws have no validity or binding force upon the people of Kansas."

NOTE 7.—Letter of John Brown to his family, November 2, 1855, in *Life and Letters of John Brown*, F. B. Sanborn, p. 203.

NOTE 8.—The best account of the war is that written by a newspaper correspondent, *The War in Kansas*, by G. Douglas Brewerton, pp. 137 to 351. The book contains a statement made by Governor Shannon; also statements of other parties. Mr. Brewerton visited and interviewed all the principal actors in the war, and printed what they had to say of it. It is one of the valuable and reliable books early written on Kansas.

NOTE 9.—Letter of John Brown to his family, December 16, 1855, in *Life and Letters of John Brown*, F. B. Sanborn, p. 217.

NOTE 10.—"It was near sunset, I should think about the 3d of December, when, in the distance, towards the south, a strange-looking object was seen approaching Lawrence. With many others I watched it. As it neared it proved to be the skeleton of a horse, covered with a poorly stuffed skin, wearily dragging a rather large one-horse lumber wagon. I think there were seven men standing in the box, which was made of wide, undressed, and weather-stained boards. Each man supported himself by a pole, of probably six to eight feet in length, surmounted with a bayonet. The poles were upright, and held in place at the sides of the box by leather loops nailed to the sides. Each man had a voltaic repeater strapped to his person, as also a short navy sword; at the same time supporting a musket at the position of 'order.' A formidable arsenal, well manned—all but the horse.

"As the party dismounted I grasped the hands of John and Frederick Brown, who introduced me to their father and brothers. Leaving the horse unhitched at the door, I took the whole family to the rooms of the Committee of Public Safety, and introduced them. On my suggestion a company of veterans was soon organized, and the command given to Old John Brown. . . . Here, at my suggestion, John Brown was first clothed with the title of Captain, conferred on him in the Wakarusa war by Governor Robinson, and approved by the Committee of Public Safety."—*Reminiscences of Old John Brown, G. W. Brown, M. D., pp. 7, 8.*

NOTE 11.—Redpath, in his *Life of Captain John Brown*, p. 88, gives an account of Brown's going with a number of other men to fight the ruffians. I find nothing to confirm this statement. As it was in violation of all orders under which Brown then served, I think it improbable that such an occurrence as is there described ever occurred.

NOTE 12.—In his account of the Wakarusa war John Brown makes no reference to any outspoken protest made by him to the treaty of peace, but it is probable that he made some such protest. It is possible, too, that he was then given to understand that more had been gained in the treaty by the Free-State men than was warranted by that instrument; it is evident that he returned home with an incorrect impression of the actual terms. G. W. Brown says:

"On the 10th the people were marshalled in front of the Free-State Hotel, from the steps of which Gov. Shannon made a short speech, in which he stated that matters had been unfortunately precipitated by their not understanding each other, and that he was glad to have a pacific termination of the affair. I think Gov. Robinson made a few remarks in the same direction. It was at this stage of procedure, when old John Brown mounted a piece of timber lying near the corner of the hotel, and began to harangue the crowd. He said the people of Missouri had come to Kansas to destroy Lawrence; that they had beleaguered the town for two weeks, threatening its destruction; that they came for blood; that he believed, 'Without the shedding of blood there is no remission'; and asked for volunteers to go under his command, and attack the Pro-Slavery camp stationed near Franklin, some four miles from Lawrence.

"Listening to his speech to this point, I made my way to the room of the Committee of Public Safety, where others came immediately, leaving the Captain trying to excite insubordination. Col. G. W. Smith was instructed by the committee to place him under arrest, and detain him in custody until the excitement should cease. Col. Smith made his way directly to the Captain, took him by the arm, and requested to speak with him. Leading the Captain away, the storm that he was inciting was soon at an end."—*"Reminiscences of Old John Brown," G. W. Brown, M. D., p. 8.*

There is much of improbability in this account. G. W. Brown was always a bitter enemy of John Brown. His book is one of the most unfair, and malicious in spirit, ever written. It is only an effort to defame the character of John Brown. G. W. Brown was the editor and proprietor of the *Herald of Freedom*, published at Lawrence. He was always accused of being in Kansas for the sole purpose of making money. He would issue one weekly edition of his paper for home reading; this was very mild, and often supposed to be as much in favor of the ruffians as of the Free-State settlers. Then he would rewrite the editorial page of the paper, and make his editorials conform to the most patriotic spirit of the free North. This edition he would mail to New England, where he was seeking patronage under guise of aiding the Free-State cause. Among the number who have told me this I will only mention E. P. Harris, Esq., long a compositor on the paper, and now one of the foremost printers and proof-readers in America; also Mr. Frank A. Root, of Topeka, who was a compositor for Brown. Mr. Root was with the Overland Stage Line in the interest of the Government for many years, and is one of the most respected citizens of the State. At the Old Settlers' Meeting at Bismarck Grove, September 15th and 16th, 1879, Brown tried to get a number of his former compositors to join him in a reunion, but his efforts were unsuccessful.

Senator Ingalls says of the statement that John Brown, jr., became insane because of the killing of the Doyles, Wilkinson and Sherman:

"These statements are made upon the testimony of G. W. Brown, in the 'Herald of Freedom,' in 1859. The witness may be competent, but he is not disinterested. He sustains the same relation to the anti-slavery men of '56 that Judas Iscariot did to the disciples, and is as well qualified to write their history as Judas Iscariot would be to revise the New Testament."

For his course in Kansas he was unmercifully criticized by many Free-State people, among them John Brown. He was called "Gusty Windy" Brown by others, who held him in contempt. The Emigrant Aid Company loaned him $2,000 after his paper was destroyed; and it will be noticed that he takes the same position in regard to John Brown that is held by Eli Thayer, from whom he secured the money.

In this relation we make the following quotation from an article written by William H. Carruth, of the Kansas University, in Kansas Historical Collections, Volume VI, page 90, and following: "Of the Free-State papers at Lawrence, one openly and constantly antagonized the movements and policy of the Aid Company, while the *Herald*

—10

of Freedom, which was equipped by money borrowed from the company, *considered it policy for a time to deny all connection with the New England propagandists.* . . . The proprietor of the *Herald of Freedom* repaid the loan of $2,000 in Territorial scrip,* which was never redeemed." It was quite a favor for Mr. Thayer to accept worthless "Territorial scrip" in payment of this loan. The relation established by this transaction continued through the life of Mr. Thayer. And Mr. Thayer was one of the very first assailants of John Brown. He used every means at his command to induce others to attack him.

That John Brown protested against the terms of the treaty, there is no doubt; and perhaps then it was that he was deceived as to what had been conceded by each side. That there was any attempt to arrest him, in the state in which the men were after Barber was murdered, there is no probability; it was with much difficulty that the men were restrained. They would not have suffered the arrest of anyone for wishing to fight. The commanders, knowing this, would not have attempted it.

"Mr. E. A. Coleman writes me: 'When Lawrence was besieged, we sent runners to all parts of the Territory, calling on every settler. We met at Lawrence. Robinson was commander-in-chief; I was on his staff, appointed of course by the commander. We had gathered to the number of about two hundred and fifty, all told. The ruffians were gathered at Franklin, four miles east, with four or five hundred men. We were not well armed, all of us,—at the same time being somewhat afraid of getting into trouble with the General Government. Robinson sent to Shannon, at Lecompton, to come down and see if something could not be done to prevent bloodshed. He came; we all knew his weakness. We had plenty of brandy, parleyed with him until he was drunk, and then he agreed to get the ruffians to go home,—which he did by telling them *we* had agreed to obey all the laws, which was a *lie.* As soon as Brown heard what had been done, he came with his sons into our council room, the maddest man I ever saw. He told Robinson that what he had done was all a farce; that in less than six months the Missourians would find out the deception, and things would be worse than they were that day (and so it was); that he came up to help them fight, but if that was the

---

* This was scrip issued by the Executive Committee under the " Topeka movement," always absolutely worthless.

way Robinson meant to do, not to send for him again.' Mr. Foster,
of Osawatomie, meeting Brown on his return from Lawrence, asked
him about Robinson and Lane. 'They are both men without principle,' said Brown; 'but when worst comes to worst, Lane will
fight,—there *is no fight in Robinson.*' "—*"Life and Letters of John
Brown,"* F. B. Sanborn, p. 220.

"Captain Brown got up to address the people, but a desire was
manifested to prevent his speaking. Amidst some little disturbance,
he demanded to know what the terms were. If he understood
Governor Shannon's speech, something had been conceded, and he
conveyed the idea that the Territorial laws were to be observed.
Those laws they denounced and spit upon, and would never obey—no!
Here the speaker was interrupted by the almost universal cry, 'No!
No! Down with the bogus laws!—lead us down to fight first!'
Seeing a young revolution on the tapis, the influential men assured
the people that there had been no concession. They had yielded
nothing. They had surrendered nothing to the usurping Legislature.
With these assurances the people were satisfied, and withdrew. At
that time it was determined to keep the treaty secret, but before
many days it was sufficiently public."—*"The Conquest of Kansas,"
William A. Phillips, p. 222.*

This is perhaps exactly what did occur. It has in it the ring of
truth and bears the air of probability.

————

NOTE 13.—In *Reminiscences of Old John Brown,* G. W. Brown,
p. 27, he is attempting to show that all the evils that came upon
the Union from 1856 to 1865 were the result of the killing of the
ruffians at Dutch Henry's Crossing. According to G. W. Brown,
slavery was only an incident, and if John Brown had never been
born there would have been no trouble about the matter!

————

NOTE 14.—*Annals of Kansas,* D. W. Wilder, p. 90.

————

NOTE 15.—For a full account of the formation of the " Law and
Order" party, see *History of the State of Kansas,* A. T. Andreas, pp.
114, 115. The resolutions are there set out.

————

NOTE 16.—*Annals of Kansas,* D. W. Wilder, p. 91. Also, *John*

Brown and his Men, Richard J. Hinton, p. 697. See also, John Brown MSS. in the library of the State Historical Society, Topeka.

NOTE 17.—See corresponding dates in *Annals of Kansas,* D. W. Wilder.

NOTE 18.—*Annals of Kansas,* D. W. Wilder, p. 108. *History of the State of Kansas,* A. T. Andreas, p. 122.

NOTE 19.—*Annals of Kansas,* D. W. Wilder, p. 109.

NOTE 20.—*Annals of Kansas,* D. W. Wilder, p. 109.

NOTE 21.—February 11, 1856. The proclamation is given in full at page 124, *History of the State of Kansas,* A. T. Andreas.

NOTE 22.—February 15, 1856. *Annals of Kansas,* D. W. Wilder, p. 109.

NOTE 23.—*Annals of Kansas,* D. W. Wilder, p. 110.

NOTE 24.—"Every act of the Free-State party was turned into treason by their [the ruffians'] Iago-like coloring, and Dr. Robinson, the newly elected Free-State Governor, figured as the embodiment of a conspiracy against law and order, which had its ramifications all over the New England States."—*"Tuttle's History of Kansas,"* *p. 288.*

NOTE 25.—*Tuttle's History of Kansas,* p. 290.

NOTE 26.—*Tuttle's History of Kansas,* p. 291. Senator Atchison's address to the South is there quoted from at length. He said the year could not pass without fierce civil war, and that there was to be no more pacification. "It was no longer scenting the battle from afar off; the troops were already in the field, the perfume of powder filled the air, Southern chivalry was in the saddle."

NOTE 27.—"Rumors often exaggerated and painfully indefinite were continually being half revealed about deep-laid plots to surprise the little settlement, and leave it a smoking ruin, are combining a carnival and a massacre within its walls. Well-known Pro-Slavery leaders came to Lawrence in hot haste, held whispered consultations with their adherents, and were off, for all that could be known, to carry out some nefarious scheme already concocted for the destruction of the Free-State party. The press in the border counties continually breathed fire and sword, and there was no means of ascertaining at what instant the customary braggadocio might cover the sinister movement long anticipated. Messengers had long since assured the ever-wary authorities of Lawrence that stores were being collected on the border, and none could doubt their eventual destination. Civilized nations do not commence hostilities until there has been first a declaration of war, but there could be no surety when the fatal blow would come from an enemy that declared war every second. The assault must come; on that point there was no difference of opinion, but when, where and how, were the momentous anxieties of the troubled citizens. A camisado was the event most dreaded, and men hated the thought of being surprised in their beds by an enemy so relentless as the foes across the border."—*"Tuttle's History of Kansas," p. 295.*

NOTE 28.—"In the spring of 1856 Missouri received a fresh supply of active allies. Col. Buford, a Southern adventurer from Alabama, brought up the Missouri river, in April, a regiment of young men, from Alabama, and Carolina and Georgia. These adventurers were armed, and came in military companies. They came for the avowed purpose of making Kansas a slave State,—by violence, if necessary,—and returning after this had been acomplished. Many of them were poor young men, but well connected; dependent members of the decaying Southern aristocracy,—a numerous class, who can be dispensed with by the South unless in case of servile war. But the larger portion of these carpet-bag adventurers were reckless characters, from the vilest purlieus of society; men who had been robbers and gambling loafers, and whose lawless character well suited them for the task they were to perform. As an illustration, these gentry robbed Buford himself of a considerable sum of money while coming up the river; and they got into disgrace, even among the Missourians they were called to aid, by their depredations.

"Shortly after their arrival in Kansas City, Mo., they were drawn up in military array, in a sort of review. Here speeches were delivered about their mission to conquer Kansas for slavery; and

Buford, in order to give his expedition a specious appearance at the East, made a prayer *to them,* which was an odd mixture of hypocrisy and blasphemy. These men were called to sign a pledge and give an oath that they would not leave Kansas until it was made a slave State; that they would be ready to fight for 'Southern rights' when called upon, and that they should never vote anything but the Pro-Slavery ticket, and should be subject to the direction of their leaders, etc. There was also a business contract between them, the terms of which, as promulgated in Kansas City, gave great dissatisfaction, the young adventurers declaring them different and less favorable than the promises by which they had been lured from their homes." —*"The Conquest of Kansas," William A. Phillips, p. 265.*

NOTE 29.—"As Sheriff Jones was unable to attend to his duties, his deputy, Sam Salters, undertook the arduous duties devolving, in the progress of 'law and order,' on the sheriff of Douglas county. With a party of dragoons at his heels, he rode backward and forward over the county, making, or trying to make, or pretending he wished to make, arrests. One lady ordered him not to come into her house, and threw some scalding water on him when he tried to do so. Some of the men whom he declared that he wished to arrest, had to leave their homes, and sleep in thickets and in prairies, to avoid his legal persecutions. Armed bands of the Southerners now began to come into the Territory, and not only Salters but all the Territorial officials were soon in full communion with them. As citizens were often molested and stopped by these persons, the following is a pass given by this redoubtable Sam Salters to a law-and-order man, who found it necessary to travel:

" '*Let this man pass i no him* two be a *Law* and abidin Sittisen.
  (Signed)   SAMUEL SALTERS,
                      depy sherf.' "

—*"The Conquest of Kansas," William A. Phillips, p. 267.*

NOTE 30.—A band of Buford's men captured a Mr. Miller, from South Carolina, but then a Free-State man:

" Mr. Miller was originally from South Carolina; and, as he had ventured to be a Free-State man in Kansas, they made up what they were pleased to consider a court from among their own number, and, placing Mr. Miller before it, tried him for treason to South Carolina. After a hard effort, some of the Carolinians who knew him, and felt friendly, contrived to prevent his being hung, although he was found guilty. He got off after losing his horse and money."—*"The Conquest of Kansas," William A. Phillips, p. 283.*

This was Mr. Josiah Miller, editor of the *Kansas Free-State*, in Lawrence. His paper was destroyed when Lawrence was sacked, May 21st, 1856, and never revived.

NOTE 31.—The best account of the troubles leading up to the sacking of Lawrence will be found in *The Conquest of Kansas*, by William A. Phillips, pp. 265 to 309, inclusive. It is among the best authorities we have on this period. *Kansas: Its Interior and Exterior Life*, by Mrs. Sara T. D. Robinson, is one of the best authorities ever prepared of the events of this time. Mrs. Robinson is the widow of the late Governor Charles Robinson, of Lawrence; was a resident of that city at the time, and saw what she records: there can be no higher authority. *History of the State of Kansas*, A. T. Andreas, and *Tuttle's History of Kansas*, are good authorities. *History of Kansas*, John H. Gihon, has valuable documents. The library of the Kansas Historical Society, Topeka, has a great accumulation of papers and documents pertaining to this period.

CHAPTER VI.

WAR ON THE POTTAWATOMIE—PRELIMINARY.

Then Slavery's champions these words
    Proclaim: "Come, direful War, and whet
    Thy sword; and let no freeman set
    His foot on Kansas soil,—forget
That he is man, ye ruffian hordes!

"Let bogus votes and bogus laws
    Stand as the will of God! Drive out
    The villain cursed who talks about
    The 'Higher Law!' Let him not spout
His treason here! The righteous cause

"Of slavery is recognized
    By the first law of man and God;—
    Kansas we own, and on her sod
    Shall stand no man, unless he nod
To our great *Truth*, and be baptized

"And taken into fellowship
    With all the dear, beloved ones
    Who are not classed with Freedom's sons.
    Give to Northern men solid tons
Of iron hail! and then let slip

"The dogs of War! Let no church ope
    The door to him who cannot pray
    For Slavery's cause! Let no man stay
    On Kansas soil, who casts a ray
Of heavenly light on sinking hope."

Brave Kansas! Now thy bitter hour
Comes like a gale of piercing woe,—
And where fair Freedom stands, the foe
Unsheaths his sword. Her friends bend low
The neck beneath usurping power.
—Joel Moody's "The Song of Kansas."

We come now to consider the most important work of
John Brown in Kansas. It is the principal point of attack
by those who seek to detract from the fame of the hero and
martyr.   It has been said by those more interested in
exalting names of his contemporaries than in preserving
the truth of history, that John Brown, without provocation,
deliberately, and with malice aforethought, went to the
peaceful vales of the Pottawatomie and there took five
peaceable, harmless, Christian men from their peaceful
homes and their families, and, carrying them away, hewed
them to pieces with broad claymores and remorselessly
and fiendishly mutilated their bodies after death.   If this
were true, it would indeed be a just cause for condemnation.   There could be nothing offered in justification; and
if I believed that history did in any manner substantiate
this charge, I would drop my pen here, or continue its
use to execrate the diabolical crime.

But justice demands that any historical character be
judged by the times in which he lived. He cannot justly
be tried by conditions existing in any other age, nor by
those existing in any other part of the country in which
he lived than the scene of his acts.   A few men have done
John Brown the injustice to try him by the conditions
existing to-day.   Others have tried him by the conditions
existing in his own time in New England, where no danger

ever threatened anyone and where the sect of non-resistants
has ever been of great influence. Various causes can be
justly assigned for this injustice to John Brown's memory
and his character. They lie deep in human nature, and
are political jealousies and the desire of incompetent persons to exalt their own names at the expense of the fame
of any and all persons engaged in the same cause.[1]

In a former chapter we have set out some of the conditions found in Kansas in the year 1856, when the war on
the Pottawatomie raged. It will be necessary to be more
specific, that the reader may have a clear comprehension of
all the conditions under which John Brown acted. We
have seen Free-State men murdered for pastime and as the
result of wagers.[2] We have seen them hacked in the face
with hatchets and flung dying into their cabins in a manner so inhuman that their wives were made maniacs. We
have seen a town sacked because it would not sanction
slavery. We have seen the ruffians of Kansas upheld and
assisted by the President of the United States. We have
seen the infamous doctrine of "constructive treason" orig-
inated for the purpose of forcing Free-State men to for-
swear themselves and subscribe to the most diabolical code
ever devised by tyranny and oppression; and under this
doctrine we have seen patriotic men indicted, torn from
their families and immured in vermin-infested prisons to
be tried for their lives.[3] We have seen Free-State women
and children harried and outraged by remorseless ruffians.
We have seen all these things, but still the record is not
complete. New England people can never comprehend
the fact that such things were suffered here by the brave
men and women who stood continuously in the presence

of death that liberty might survive. The patriot pioneers have always said to me: We could never make the people in the East comprehend our situation; they believed the most conservative accounts of the revelry in blood indulged by the ruffians overdrawn. Let us look a little deeper into the affairs of Kansas in the year of 1856.

Buford established one of his camps south of the Pottawatomie, and near the settlement in which John Brown and his sons lived.[4] In this settlement there were many Free-State men, but not a majority of them. This settlement was in the western part of what is now Miami county and the eastern part of Franklin county. The streams are clear and deep, and timber along their courses was plentiful; and as claims were selected in the early settlement of the Territory for their timber, this part of Kansas was early seized by the Missourians. The present town of Paola was a stronghold of slavery. For virulence and intolerance the Pro-Slavery settlers of this region were the equals of those in any part of the Territory. Here were the Miami, Wea, Peoria and other fragmentary Indian tribes with just enough of civilization to make suitable allies for the cruel and ignorant ruffians who came to make a slave State of Kansas or assist Davis, Hunter and others to make it a part of the Southern Confederacy.[5] If such a thing were possible, the Pro-Slavery settlers in this part of the Territory were more ignorant and sodden than in any other portion. The present counties of Linn, Bourbon, Anderson, Franklin and Miami were seized by a class of "poor whites" owning few slaves, but more fanatical and unreasonable in support of slavery than the slave-masters themselves. They brought their bloodhounds with them from Tennessee and Mississippi, and came to do the bidding of the slave-owners as blindly and unquestioningly as they had in the country from whence they came, where they were regarded as so degraded that they were not subject to the laws. What a blessing to those fair counties that freedom prevailed and made it possible for patriotic and civilized people to build them into integral parts of a glorious free State! But it must be remembered that in 1856 these Pro-Slavery "poor whites" were largely in possession of them; and the Free-State settlers were yet weak in numbers.

On the 16th of April John Brown, John Brown, jr., O. V. Dayton, Richard Mendenhall, Charles A. Foster, David Baldwin,[6] and others of the settlement, met and resolved to not pay the taxes levied under the authority of the bogus laws. For this act they were soon afterwards indicted by the United States courts as conspirators, under the constructive-treason theory of Judge Lecompte, Chief Justice of the Territory.[7] James F. Legate has preserved a picture of the Grand Jury of that court; he says: "What a sweet-scented jury it was! There were seventeen members, and at least fifteen bottles of whisky in the room all the time." These jurymen were of the class described as committing such acts as "the sacking of Free-State towns—the burning of Free-State houses—the *ravishing* and *branding* of Free-State women, and *turning them and their helpless children naked upon the prairies*—the murders of Free-State men and shocking mutilations of their dead bodies."[8] These acts were common then in the Territory, and were some of those believed in New England as improbable and impossible of execution by man; and they were impossible in New England—but not in Kansas. The mobbing, tarring and feathering of Rev. Pardee Butler at Atchison and the turning him adrift upon the Missouri river occurred on the 30th of April. Early in May some of Buford's men camped on Washington and Coal creeks, along the Santa Fé Trail, and "were not only committing depredations upon the property of the settlers, but were intercepting, robbing and imprisoning travelers on the public thoroughfares, and threatening to attack the towns." [9] On the 19th of May they murdered a young Free-State man named Jones, at a store near Blanton's Bridge. On the following day another Free-State man, a young gentleman recently from New York, was shot in a cowardly and wanton manner in the public highway about one and one-half miles from Lawrence. The retreat from the sacking of Lawrence was marked by the pillaging of houses, "stealing horses, and violating the persons of defenseless women." [10] "There are hundreds of well-authenticated accounts of the cruelties practiced by this horde of ruffians, some of them too shocking and disgusting to relate, or to be accredited, if told. The tears and shrieks of terrified women, folded in their foul embrace, failed to touch a chord of mercy in their brutal hearts, and the mutilated bodies of murdered men, hanging upon trees, or left to rot upon the prairies or in the deep ravines, or furnish food for vultures and wild beasts, told frightful stories of brutal ferocity from which the wildest savages might have shrunk with horror." [11]

These ruffians were joined in their robberies and murders by the Pro-Slavery settlers, and even by the Territorial officials. Governor Geary describes them as "bands of armed ruffians and brigands whose sole aim and end is assassination and robbery." " These men," he continues, "have robbed and driven from their homes unoffending citizens; have fired upon and killed others in their own dwellings; and stolen horses and property under the pretense of employing them in the public service. They have seized persons who had committed no offense, and after stripping them of all their valuables, placed them on steamers, and sent them out of the Territory. Some of these bands, who have thus violated their rights and privileges, and shamefully and shockingly misused and abused the oldest inhabitants of the Territory, who had settled here with their wives and children, are strangers from distant States, who have no interest in, nor care for the welfare of Kansas, and contemplate remaining here only so long as opportunities for mischief and plunder exist.

" In isolated or country places, no man's life is safe. The roads are filled with armed robbers, and murders for mere plunder are of daily occurrence. Almost every farmhouse is deserted, and no traveler has the temerity to venture upon the highway without an escort." [12]

The chief centers of these ruffians were Leavenworth and Lecompton—towns sunk by them to the lowest degree of depravity. Dr. Gihon says: " Lecompton is situated on the south side of the Kansas river, about fifty miles from its junction with the Missouri, and forty miles in a southwesterly direction from Leavenworth City, upon as inconvenient and inappropriate a site for a town as any in the Territory; it being on a bend of the river, difficult of access, and several miles beyond any of the principal thoroughfares. It was chosen simply for speculative purposes. An Indian 'floating claim' of a section of land was purchased by a company of prominent Pro-Slavery men, who found it easy to induce the Legislative Assembly to adopt it for the location of the capital, by distributing among the members, supreme judges, the governor, secretary of the Territory, and others in authority, a goodly number of town lots, upon the rapid sale of which each expected to realize a handsome income. It contained, at the time of Governor Geary's arrival, some twenty or more houses, the majority of which were employed as groggeries of the lowest description. In fact, its general moral condition was debased to a lamentable degree. It was the residence of the celebrated Sheriff Jones (who is one of the leading members of the town association), and the resort of horse-thieves and ruffians of the most desperate character. Its drinking saloons were infested by these characters, where drunkenness, gambling, fighting, and all sorts of crimes were indulged in with entire impunity. It was and is emphatically a border-ruffian town, in which no man could utter opinions adverse to negro slavery without placing his life in jeopardy." [13]

These brigands and murderers can be well described by repeating the boast of one Robert S. Kelly, one of their leading men in the Territory, who declared that he could never die happy until he had killed an abolitionist. " If," said he, " I can't kill a man, I'll kill a woman; and if I can't kill a woman, I'll kill a child." [14] On the 21st of June, an Indian agent, named Gay, was traveling in the vicinity of Westport, and was stopped by a party of Buford's men, who asked him if he was in favor of making Kansas a free State. He promptly answered in the affirmative, and was instantly shot dead. Such was the only crime for which this soul was hurried into the eternal world." [15]

The foregoing will serve to give some idea of the general condition of the Territory in the spring and early summer of 1856. This condition was the result of the campaign commenced immediately after the Wakarusa war; we have seen the preparations made for this campaign all over the South and in the cabinet of the President. The active operations against the Free-State men began with the arrival of the bands under Buford. We will now see what were the conditions existing on the Pottawatomie.

Henry Sherman had been in the Territory for some years. He was at first a laborer for John T. Jones, or "Ottawa" Jones, as he was called. Jones was an educated Ottawa Indian and a minister; he is universally spoken of as a good man. Sherman finally went into business for himself. He squatted on a claim where the military road crossed the Pottawatomie, and his place soon came to be known as Dutch Henry's Crossing. It was agreed by all that his character was bad; his principal occupation was getting his brand upon the cattle of Indians and others. He was a giant in stature, drunken and quarrelsome, and finally lost his life for the outrageous course he adopted towards the wife of a Free-State settler. He was in favor of slavery only because he saw in its adherents kindred spirits to his own, and the opportunity to carry on his questionable business if slavery should succeed. As a matter of principle he cared no more for slavery than any other institution; he supported it because it gave him the opportunity to gratify the basest of inclinations and propensities. His brother, William Sherman, was much such a man, but without the ability of Henry; he was younger, just as drunken, a little more reckless because of the confidence he had in the ability of his brother to defend and protect him and his known willingness to do so.[16] Allen Wilkinson found a congenial companion in Henry Sherman, and in the first rush for claims he seized one adjoining that of " Dutch Henry," and a little below the Crossing. In the first election for members of the Legislature he was chosen to the bogus Legislature by fraudulent votes from Missouri and while yet a resident of that State. In this execrable body he was one of the most servile, obsequious, abject and sycophantic tools of the slave-power in the whole assembly.[17] He was made a great *fanfaron,* boaster, and jack-pudding by the service he had rendered slavery there, and seeing that he who became the vilest was given political preferment he aspired to the leadership of his precious constituency. Such men are always the tools of others without knowing it; "Dutch Henry" was the man upon whom the slave leaders relied. Wilkinson supposed it was himself, and to retain the high position he supposed he had won he was ever foremost in the outrages perpetrated upon Free-State settlers. The Doyle family were from Tennessee; they were of that class considered too low in the social and moral scales to be amenable to law.[18] Though detested and despised, and by slavery reduced to a level below the negro, they believed in the vile system and were ready to commit any outrage suggested by its advocates. They had lived in the South by patrolling plantations and spying on the actions of slaves; they brought their bloodhounds to Kansas with

—11

them, and were located in this settlement to hunt down
and turn back fugitive and runaway slaves. They were
the abject tools of Henry Sherman, and had a miserable
and squalid cabin on a branch of Mosquito creek, directly
north of that of Wilkinson, and less than a mile away,
although on the opposite side of the river.[19] Here with
their bloodhounds they spied on the actions of the Free-
State settlers and reported to Wilkinson and Sherman,
and after the arrival of Buford's men were in constant
communication with them. They lost their bloodhounds
in trying to capture a Free-State man who had been
through their reports notified to leave the Territory. He
fled before Buford's Georgians and the Doyles, and when
the hounds came up with him he took refuge in the river;
the dogs followed him there, but were not so dangerous in
the water. He caught them one by one and stabbed and
drowned them all, and escaped to Leavenworth, where he
had friends who protected him; and he was there when he
heard of the death of the Doyles.[20] Man does not descend
any lower in the scale of humanity than the point reached
by the Doyle family. There are things told of them too
vile to write, and long years of inquiry lead me to believe
them true.

The nearest camp of Buford's men was that of a company of Georgians, about four miles away. "Dutch
Henry" kept liquor, and his place was the congregating
point for the Pro-Slavery men and the Georgians. It was
the headquarters of this band, the center from which intelligence of the best localities for stealing cattle and
horses and other supplies was supplied. The Shermans,
Wilkinson and the Doyles spent much time in the camp

of their friends, and kept them informed of the arrival of Free-State families, who came in greater numbers in 1855 and the spring of 1856 than did those of the Pro-Slavery party. In the spring of 1855 Henry Sherman had warned two Germans that they might expect the fate of a Vermont man who had been hanged a short time before, but rescued before death.[21]

The Browns, and the Shermans and their protégés soon came into conflict. Frederick Brown interfered in behalf of a woman against whom one of the Shermans had designs.[22] The Browns did not drink whisky nor steal cattle—and this was enough to turn the ruffians against them. While there had been no public outbreak in the settlement against the Free-State men, the reinforcement of the Pro-Slavery men by the arrival of the Georgians was an event of a nature to create anxiety in the minds of the Browns. Wishing to ascertain what might come from this location of Buford's men in their midst, John Brown took his surveying instruments and ran a line through their camp; he knew that only Pro-Slavery surveyors were employed, and that the ignorant Georgians would believe him one of the Government surveyors without asking questions. He found that the death or expulsion of himself and sons and other Free-State people had been decided upon, and evidently through the information supplied by the Shermans, Wilkinson, and the Doyles.[23] One of Brown's neighbors said in 1885: "The Browns were hunted as we hunt wolves to-day; and because they undertook to protect themselves they are called cold-blooded murderers,—merely because they 'had the dare,' and were contented to live and die as God intended them to. Brown

was a Bible-man,—he believed it all; and though I am
not, I give him credit for being honest, and the most consistent so-called Christian I have ever met. Brown and
his sons had claims, and worked them, as I did mine,
when these devils were not prowling about, killing a man
now and then, stealing our stock and running them off to
Missouri." [24]

When Sheriff Jones stirred the caldron of border-
ruffianism to find a pretext for the attack so elaborately
prepared for by the South, the Free-State men of Kansas
determined to again assist the people of Lawrence to beat
back the invaders. John Brown, jr., was Captain of the
" Pottawatomie Rifles," and these were held in readiness
to march on very short notice. The Browns were summoned to the defense of Lawrence on the 22d of May,
"and every man (eight in all) except Orson, turned out;
he staying with the women and children to take care of the
cattle." They went in two companies, John Brown, jr.,
going with his company, which was joined by two other
companies on the road; he was elected to command the
combined force, but probably this was a temporary con-
solidation, intended to remain effective during the campaign then being entered upon. In the second company
of the Brown family were John Brown, his sons Owen,
Frederick, Salmon, Oliver, and Henry Thompson, his son-
in-law. He speaks of these as "the other six," saying,
"the other six were a little company by ourselves." [25] On
the way to Lawrence they learned that it had been destroyed on the 21st, the day before they had received orders to march to its defense. The forces halted, and it
was decided not to proceed to Lawrence, but to await

further orders before either advancing or returning home. The camp was pitched on Ottawa creek, on the claim of Captain Shore. John Brown favored continuing the march to Lawrence; this might have been done had not a courier arrived to say that the town was short of food, and that the people had submitted to the sacking of the town without any attempt at resistance. The halt was made on the evening of the day upon which the march began—May 22d.

On the following day, in the forenoon, a messenger arrived in the camp with intelligence which caused John Brown to return to the Pottawatomie with his company.

When the Free-State men on the Pottawatomie heard that Lawrence was threatened, and before they had received any formal notice that their services might be needed, they had made preparations to render what assistance they could to their neighbors and fellow-sufferers. All the lead that could be procured was cast into bullets, and the guns were put in as good condition as possible. The only store at which lead could be obtained in the settlement was at the little establishment near Dutch Henry's Crossing, kept by an old gentleman from Michigan, a Free-State man named Morse. He seems to have been a widower with a family of little children. He was a harmless and inoffensive old gentleman, very timid, and too old to take part in the protective arrangements made by the settlers. He had engaged in the vocation of tradesman for the purpose of procuring a living for his motherless children, the oldest of whom was about twelve. He supposed his age and his expressed intention to devote himself to his business exclusively would afford him protection. He dealt in such things as the condition of the settlers rendered most profitable—groceries, and lead and gunpowder. Frederick Brown had bought some thirty pounds of lead of him, and this had been used in getting ready to go to Lawrence, should it become necessary. He was questioned about the use to which the lead was to be put, as he carried it by the home of the Shermans, where the Doyles and others were congregated; he made no secret of the purpose of its purchase.[26]

A company from Missouri was expected to come into the Free-State settlement on the Pottawatomie and attack the settlers there; this was a part of the general plan to move against the Free-State settlers and enforce obedience to the bogus laws and subdue the spirit of resistance manifest. When the Free-State companies went to the aid of Lawrence the Pottawatomie settlement was left without any means of self-protection. Such a time would naturally be seized upon in which to strike the contemplated blow, by the Missourians and their ruffian allies, the Shermans, Doyles, the Georgians and the other companies of Buford then in the doomed settlement or hanging on its outskirts. And the invaders were to do much more than make an attack upon the Pottawatomie; they were to do for this part of the Territory what Sheriff Jones and Donaldson were to accomplish at and about Lawrence. The blow was to be a little later, and to be coöperated in by the invaders from about Lawrence, if found necessary; many of these invading bands did march to the vicinity of the Pottawatomie settlements after Lawrence was sacked. The active work of the campaign was commenced as soon as the "Pottawatomie Rifles" marched out to aid Lawrence. The Pro-Slavery men, under the lead of William

Sherman,—Henry Sherman being in Missouri at the time, and probably to bring in invaders,—took a rope and repaired to the store of Mr. Morse to hang him.[27]   They told him to leave by eleven o'clock, after being persuaded to spare his life. At eleven o'clock they returned, much under the influence of whisky, and attempted to kill the old gentleman with an axe. He was saved by the pleadings and tears of his children, but was warned to be gone by sundown, and that there would be no further trifling with him; if found he would be killed at once. Notices were prepared and delivered to Free-State settlers warning them to leave in three days, and threatening them with death if found there after that time. These notices were written with red ink and had a skull-and-crossbones rudely drawn upon them.[28]   They went to the families of the Browns and threatened to burn their cabins over their heads, and when prevailed upon to spare their lives ordered them to leave, and after the women had found a yoke of cattle and hitched them to the cart, they were allowed to put into this rude conveyance their children and a few valuables and go to the home of the Rev. S. L. Adair. The ruffians went to the houses of two German settlers who favored the Free-State cause, warned them to leave, and burned their houses. One of these, that of Theodore Weiner, contained a considerable stock of goods. Weiner fled to the company of men who had gone to the assistance of Lawrence.[29]

This is a brief statement of the actual conditions which confronted the Free-State settlers on the Pottawatomie immediately after the departure of the militia to fight for Lawrence. We have not enumerated all the outrages committed, as it is not necessary to go into greater detail. Other actions of the ruffians were as rabid and reprehensi-

ble as those set down here.   Some wives fled to overtake
their husbands in the companies marching to the relief
of Lawrence.   The country was terrorized by the Pro-
Slavery men under orders from the Shermans.   The notices given the Free-State families made it plain that they
were to be murdered if they were found there on the night
of the day mentioned in them.   The ruffians were moving
upon them from Missouri and from their camps in the
vicinity; Cooke arrived from Bates county, Missouri, on
Tuesday, the 27th, with a considerable force.   Their defenders were away to battle for liberty in another part of
the Territory.   The only thing to be done was to send word
for them to return.   The settlers put a young man on a
horse, and directed him to overtake the forces marching
away and urge that some help be sent back to protect their
own homes.   All this is clear and undisputed.

This, then, was the condition on the Pottawatomie on
the night of May 22d.   Helpless women and children had
been turned out of their own houses under threats of death,
and their houses burned to ashes; they had sought what
refuge they could find.   They and those of whom they
asked shelter and protection bore red notices that their
lives were forfeited if they were found there three days
later.   The sacred calling of the ministry of the gospel
afforded no protection.[30]   The people could almost see the
camps of the ruffians by the light of their burning cabins.
If help could not be had they must depart from their
homes and carry with them what they could.   But where
could they go?   Missouri was on the east and the desert
of raw prairies on the west.   To them it seemed that they
were in the power of the ruffians, and that there was little
hope of escape.[31]

NOTE 1.—Read chapter VIII of *Kansas: The Prelude to the War for the Union*, Leverett W. Spring. Observe how he insists that all the troubles of Kansas in 1856, after this event, were the results of it. Perhaps he knew no better; but that he was mistaken he admits by the position he takes in his article in *Lippincott's Magazine*, January, 1883. Mr. Spring's book is not considered authority in Kansas, although it seems to fare better away from home; Rhodes and Burgess seems to believe it the principal work in existence that treats of Kansas affairs: they may mention other works incidentally, but with them Spring, only, seems authority and worthy of credit.

The reader is requested to take notice of the malicious spirit and ghoulish satisfaction with which he introduces quotations from Andrew Johnson and others who were never within five hundred miles of the scene of the occurrence. He makes the stories told by Territorial officials, the families of the bereaved persons, and the conclusions of Mr. Oliver, the Democratic member of the Congressional Investigation Committee, tell his story. He introduces testimony before the Strickler Commission, and endeavors to make it appear that John Brown assisted to loot a store. The language says nothing of the kind. It says the robbery was committed by part of John Brown's company, or a part of the company that was commanded by John Brown. And as to this testimony, it may be well to remark here, that so unreliable has it been considered by all the Legislatures since it was taken, that no effective action has ever been had upon it. Every person who ever investigated these claims in any impartial spirit believes them to be at least ten times as much as they should be, and none of them doubt that many of them are wholly fraudulent. One of Mr. Spring's Kansas friends reduced one item of his claim from $10,000 to $500. There were hundreds of communications of truthful and prominent persons who fought for freedom in Kansas on file in the library of the Historical Society concerning these killings on the Pottawatomie. But Mr. Spring ignored them all, and chose to give the version made up for political effect by the enemies of Kansas,—the very men who had planned to exterminate the Free-State people of Kansas and were at the very moment the blow was struck by Brown planning to massacre the families of those who had gone in defense of Lawrence; who had driven wives and children from home and burned their houses on the very day the company set out. Mr. Spring knew these things, and still he mentioned them not. These are the facts; students can form their own conclusions.

Spring was professor of English Literature in the University of Kansas. In the University Governor Robinson had great influence to the day of his death. The people of Kansas generally believed that Spring wrote to please Governor Robinson; that belief prevails to this day. The book espoused the cause of Robinson in his quarrels with John Brown, General Lane, and other eminent Kansans. It attempted to make plain that the Free-State men were much at fault in the struggle for freedom; it exalted and praised the ruffians who invaded our borders. The storm of indignation which arose in every part of the State blew Spring back to Massachusetts.

One of the most scathing criticisms of his work, and the one which led the attack and set the press upon it in every town, was written by Honorable Daniel W. Wilder, author of *The Annals of Kansas*, one of the greatest historical works in America. Mr. Wilder is a graduate of Harvard College, was long Auditor of the State of Kansas, and has edited our greatest newspapers with credit and ability. When Spring's book appeared, Wilder was editor of the *Topeka Daily Commonwealth*. He wrote the following criticism, which appeared in that paper, Saturday, October 10th, 1885. It is accepted in Kansas as the most correct and just estimate of the work ever written, and is now the verdict of Kansas upon the book:

"THE PREACHER'S BOOK.

"There is a preacher in Lawrence named L. W. Spring, who is a 'professor' in the State University. Kansas does not know him and he does not know Kansas, but he has written a book to tell us who we are and who are our neighbors. He has met Charles Robinson and Robinson's wife. They have talked to the preacher, after giving him a dinner at the railroad farm, and Spring has squatted in a corner and copied their words like a craven menial. His book is called 'Kansas'; the word 'history' does not appear on the title-page, and yet it is probably supposed to be a history by the poor fool who wrote the manuscript. He says he is 'professor *in* English literature in the University of Kansas,' but has not gone into the language far enough to write good English. He attempts on every page and in every sentence to glorify himself and his learning—a silly sophomore, who does not know that simplicity is strength. The book will not attract the stranger who attempts to read it; the vanity of the author and his unnatural style will soon repel and disgust any sensible man. It can take no place in literature, because the preacher can't write. He only knows men as he has learned about them in the prayer-meetings or in sermons; and nobody is ever candid with a bandbox preacher. Spring knows nothing about men in action, in affairs, as business men, soldiers, or legislators. While other men are in the midst of the struggle for life, this preacher has been eating frosted cake at some afternoon tea party in the presence of a half-dozen women, who secretly laugh at him, and give him more cake and green tea.

"The only histories that have any value are those written by men who know men; who have met and fought with them. The sewing-society man is never seriously talked to or even answered by any man of sense. Gibbon, Grote, Macaulay, and our own Grant and Blaine write well because they have something to say. You cannot paint your portraits until you have seen faces. But this dapper little fool was just the man for Robinson to catch up and dictate to. How Charley must have laughed after every interview! 'The ass will write down everything that I give him!'

"And here it is all printed. How Charles Robinson made Kansas; Robinson's wisdom; Robinson's courage; Robinson's diplomacy! Kansas does not appear to have had any people—none worth mentioning. The name of Kansas should be blotted from the map and Robinson take its place. In the index Robinson is the longest title. And yet Robinson has had little to do with the early or late history of Kansas. He is a man of hates, grudges, revenges. Such men cannot become leaders; they do not inspire confidence. Robinson has never been a leader in Kansas, and this book will only serve the purpose of reviving all the ugly facts in his crooked history.

"This book is the work of a defamer. The most glorious struggle for freedom made on American soil since the day of '76 was fought and won here, on these prairies; won not only for Kansas, but for the United States, for black as well as white, for all mankind. The lovers of liberty all over the world looked to us, helped us; it was a fight for the rights of man.

"And yet this sniveling idiot, who lives in a closet, goes through three hundred pages of 'history' and never once sniffs a breath of freedom. Lies about Jim Lane and John Brown and almost every man who did brave work here. He speaks fairly, we believe, of Col. Sam Walker, a man worthy of all praise, but probably he does so because Sam still lives, and in Lawrence, and would slap the fool's chops if he lied about him.

"According to Spring, the Kansas Jawhawkers and Red Legs were worse men than Quantrill's band. He sympathizes with our enemies all through his book. He copies with approval the apologies of the Pro-Slavery officials and tells with relish some story about a Republican or Free-State horse-thief. He assassinates Major Plumb for not accomplishing an impossibility; of course Plumb has not been consulted, and has been given no chance to tell what the facts were. But Judge Lecompte is permitted, in 1885, to construe and explain

his decisions of 1856. Governor Denver's cock-and-bull story about
the Leavenworth Constitution bill is treated as veritable history.
In speaking of the brave, honorable and truthful Col. Montgomery,
he is classed with the border horse-thieves. Jennison's name does not
appear in the book. Colonel Hoyt is mentioned incidentally with the
other thieves. Matters of no importance whatever are treated at
length, while historical events of enduring interest are not even
alluded to. If this book, from the pen of a college professor, were
introduced into our schools, the children would get the notion that
Jim Lane and John Brown were worse men than the gangs of
Quantrill and the James Boys.

"The book is an insult to Kansas—a slap in the face by a stranger.
The writer is not a fit person to teach our children. Ingalls—who of
course is not mentioned in the book—replied to Robinson's other
preacher in the *North American Review*. We shall hear from him
and Plumb, and all the early Kansans, in regard to this detestable
job of a hired interloper, and some Kansas man will write a Kansas
history, while the stray copies of this book will be burned in bonfires,
as were burned the Bogus Laws years ago."

NOTE 2.—Reference was made in a former note to the action of
one Fuget, in Leavenworth. We give here another account:

"Individual instances of barbarity continued to occur almost daily.
In one instance, a man belonging to General Atchison's camp made
a bet of six dollars against a pair of boots, that he would go out
and return with an Abolitionist's scalp within two hours. He went
forth on horseback. Before he had gone two miles from Leavenworth on the road to Lawrence, he met Mr. Hopps, driving a buggy.
Mr. Hopps was a gentleman of high respectability, who had come
with his wife, a few days previously, to join her brother, the Rev.
Mr. Nute, of Boston, who had for some time been laboring as a minister in Lawrence. The ruffian asked Mr. Hopps where he came from.
He replied, he was last from Lawrence. Enough! The ruffian drew
his revolver, and shot him through the head. As the body fell from
the chaise, he dismounted, took his knife, scalped his victim, and then
returned to Leavenworth, where, having won his boots, he paraded
the streets with the bleeding scalp of the murdered man stuck upon
a pole. Eight days later, when the widow, who had been left at
Lawrence sick, was brought down by the Rev. Mr. Nute, in the hope
of recovering the body of the murdered husband, the whole party,
consisting of about twenty persons in five wagons, was seized, robbed
of all they had, and placed in confinement. One was shot the next
day for attempting to escape. The widow and one or two others
were allowed to depart by steamer, but penniless. A German, in-
cautiously condemning the outrage, was shot; and another saved his
life only by precipitate flight."—*"Kansas," by Thomas H. Gladstone,
London, 1857, p. 279.*

See, also, Historical Note No. 44, *The Song of Kansas,* Joel Moody. *Border-Ruffian Troubles in Kansas,* Letters by Judge L. D. Bailey, published by Charles R. Green, Lyndon, Kansas, has important material; for this incident, see p. 22.

NOTE 3.—The Chief Justice, one Lecompte, charged his jury as follows:

"This Territory was organized by an act of Congress, and so far its authority is from the United States. It has a Legislature elected in pursuance of that organic act. This Legislature, being an instrument of Congress by which it governs the Territory, has passed laws. These laws, therefore, are of United States authority and making; and all that *resist these laws resist the power and authority of the United States, and are therefore guilty of high treason.* Now, gentlemen, if you find that any persons have resisted these laws, then you must, under your oaths, find bills against them for high treason. If you find that *no such resistance has been made,* but that combinations have been formed for the purpose of resisting them, and individuals of influence and notoriety have been aiding and abetting in such combinations, *then must you still find* bills for constructive treason."—*"Life and Letters of John Brown," F. B. Sanborn, p. 231.*

NOTE 4.—In the private collection of William Elsey Connelley, of Topeka, is the only letter written by Buford known to be in existence in Kansas. It is as follows:

St. Louis, Apl. '56.

Dear Sir

I desire to settle a portion of my company on the Wyandott reserve provided that tribe will freely consent to my doing so, but not otherwise. & I would select for that purpose only orderly good citizens—among them blacksmiths, carpenters brick & stone masons physicians school teachers agricultural laborers &c &c—and any of them who become obnoxious to *the Indians* I would have removed—with such settlers under such an arrangement I think both parties would be benefitted—and especially would it aid your views in building up your city of Wyandotte which by the way seems the place endowed by nature for the great town of the territory—

I hope to see you soon & confer more fully with you in relation to this matter. Very respectfully yr obt Sevt

J. BUFORD

Col Wm Walker
 of Wyandotte city
 at Kansas city.

NOTE 5.—"The following letter from James M. Mason, of Virginia, to the then Secretary of War, Jefferson Davis, explains itself:

" 'SELMA, NEAR WINCHESTER, VA., Sept. 30, 1856.

" 'MY DEAR SIR: I have a letter from Wise, of the 27th, full of spirit. He says that the governments of North Carolina, South Carolina and Louisiana have already agreed to rendezvous at Raleigh, and others will,—this in your most private ear. He says, further, that he had officially requested you to exchange with Virginia, on fair terms of difference, percussion for flint muskets. I don't know the usage or power of the Department in such cases, but if it can be done, even by liberal construction, I hope you will accede. Was there not an appropriation at the last session for converting flint into percussion arms? If so, would it not furnish good reason for extending such facilities to the States? Virginia probably has more arms than the other Southern States, and would divide, in case of need. In a letter yesterday to a committee in South Carolina, I gave it as my judgment, in the event of Frémont's election, the South should not pause, but proceed at once to 'immediate, absolute and eternal separation.' So I am a candidate for the first halter.

" 'Wise says his accounts from Philadelphia are cheering for Old Buck in Pennsylvania. I hope they be not delusive.

'"*Vale et Salute,*

(Signed)   " 'J. M. MASON.

" 'Colonel Davis.' "—*"History of American Conspiracies,"* Orville J. Victor, p. 520.

This is one of the men—already an avowed traitor for almost four years—who was so anxious concerning and so instrumental in having John Brown hanged for "treason." All these traitorous years he had been representing Virginia in the United States Senate, and under oath to support the Constitution of the United States. About this time Stringfellow's paper in Atchison said: "For we confidently *hope that the last national Congress may meet in Washington on the first Monday in December next; and we prophecy* with firm conviction that the time will verify our words." The same editor gives an account of the celebration of the return of the ruffians from the campaign against Free-State men, a little later:

"At the head of the table hung the 'blood-red flag,' with the lone star, and the motto of 'Southern Rights' on the one side, and 'South Carolina' on the other. The same flag that first floated on the rifle-pits of the abolitionist at Lawrence, and on the hotel of the same place, in triumph, now hung over the heads of the noble soldiers who bore it so bravely through that exciting war.

"The following are among the toasts drank:

" 'Disunion: by secession or otherwise—a beacon of hope to an oppressed people, and the surest remedy for Southern wrongs.' (Enthusiastic cheers.)

" 'The city of Atchison: may she, before the close of the year '57, be the capital of a Southern republic.' (Cheers.)

" 'The distribution of public lands: one hundred and sixty acres to every Pro-Slavery settler, and to every Abolitionist six feet by two.' "

For a fuller account of this feast, see *The Conquest of Kansas*, William A. Phillips, p. 411.

It must be remembered that these sentiments were uttered openly by the "Law and Order" party, who were then murdering Free-State men for resisting the bogus laws. Were villainy and treason ever carried to greater extent and length? The sentiment, disunion the surest remedy for Southern wrongs, had been acted upon for more than thirty years. The South had ascertained that the North would submit to great injustice before consenting to any act that would endanger the life of the nation. The loyalty of the North had been counted upon to counteract the discontent of the people at the continued advance and aggression of the slave-power.

NOTE 6.—"Mr. David Baldwin selected land near John Pingry in the fall of 1834, and in April of the next year he and William Baldwin settled there. They thought it a very wild place, for they would sometimes stand in their cabin door and shoot the deer that were browsing on the trees which had been cut down to keep them from falling on the house. David Baldwin opened a blacksmith and gunsmith shop that year (1835), which were the first shops of the kind in the county. The Indians were frequent travelers there then. David Baldwin was a true pioneer—an active and very useful man. As a Christian, he was a Methodist local preacher; as a mechanic, he was a blacksmith and cabinet-maker; and as a pioneer, a farmer, good bee-tree and deer hunter. He afterwards emigrated to Kansas, where he served under the famous John Brown."—*"History of Jay County, Indiana," M. W. Montgomery, pp. 94, 95.*

NOTE 7.—*Life and Letters of John Brown*, F. B. Sanborn, p. 228.

NOTE 8.—*History of Kansas*, John H. Gihon, p. 75.

NOTE 9.—*History of Kansas*, John H. Gihon, p. 78.

NOTE 10.—*History of Kansas*, John H. Gihon, p. 85.

NOTE 11.—*History of Kansas*, John H. Gihon, p. 91.

NOTE 12.—*History of Kansas*, John H. Gihon, p. 121. This description was written in September following the war on the Pottawatomie, but Governor Geary had only just arrived. It is a good description of the conditions that had prevailed all the time after the arrival of Buford's men, the previous April.

NOTE 13.—*History of Kansas*, John H. Gihon, p. 122.

NOTE 14.—*History of Kansas*, John H. Gihon, p. 131.

NOTE 15.—*History of Kansas*, John H. Gihon, p. 91.

NOTE 16.—For a description and character of the Shermans, see *Life and Letters of John Brown*, F. B. Sanborn, pp. 230, 253, 255, 265, 323, 331. No viler or more brutal characters ever lived in any country.

NOTE 17.—"In the first invasion of Kansas, one Hon. Allen Wilkinson, who would not move to Kansas, was elected a member of the Legislature by some gentlemen who came into Kansas to assist in voting. After he was elected he was earnest in getting a bill through the Legislature which would result in hanging John Brown, before he knew him. Long before John Brown got to Kansas, Wilkinson had assisted in the passage of a law more rigid towards 'abolitionists' than any statesman before him had ever succeeded in engrafting upon the slave code. Mr. Wilkinson, the statesman, settled on the Pottawatomie. John Brown, the tanner and wool merchant, settled in his neighborhood. Mr. Wilkinson got tired of the delays of his own law, and notified Mr. Brown that he did not want him in that community. John Brown had brought some cows there, and did not like to go away and leave his cows and other property, and having some apprehension of evil, and preferring not to be transformed into a 'reprisal' (to change the élite of the University to the vernacular of the border ruffian) 'got the drop' on Wilkinson and his gentle friends, and made 'reprisals' of them."—*Hon. John Speer, in a paper in the John Brown Documents in the library of the State Historical Society.*

Note 18.—Young E. Allison, in *Southern Bivouac*, Vol. II, No. 9, February, 1887. Mr. Allison there describes the "poor white trash" of the slave-infested districts of the South, and endeavors to make it apply to the free men of Appalachian America who fought for liberty and the preservation of the Union, and who, by doing so, earned the undying hatred of the old slave-owners and their descendants. The recent attempt to disfranchise the Kentucky Republicans through the Goebel election law is only a manifestation of this hatred.

Note 19.—Communicated to me by Montgomery Shore, one of the associates of John Brown, and a member of the company of Free-State men commanded by Captain S. T. Shore, his brother. Mr. Shore is a resident of Wyandotte county, where I have known him for almost twenty years, and where he was my personal and political friend. He is a man noted for integrity and worth of character, and is honored by his neighbors and held in high esteem by all who know him. He gave me much valuable information of the early days in Kansas. He was in the battle of Black Jack, and knew all the settlers on the Pottawatomie at the time of the war there. He worked for "Ottawa" Jones for some two years, but not steadily; he was held in high esteem by Mr. Jones.

Note 20.—This circumstance was related to me by Mr. Edwin R. Partridge, of Topeka. He escaped from the dogs in the manner I have described. Mr. Partridge is one of the first settlers in the State. In 1844, when the great flood swept down the Missouri and the Kaw, he was camped on the site of the cemetery, east of Topeka. He was a member of an expedition to carry supplies and reinforcements to California to Frémont. Mr. Partridge was an associate of John Brown, and lived in the Pottawatomie settlement. George and William Partridge were his cousins.

Note 21.—*Life and Letters of John Brown*, F. B. Sanborn, p. 254.

Note 22.—Charles A. Foster, in *Life and Letters of John Brown*, F. B. Sanborn, p. 256, note. He says:

"In the spring of 1856 William Sherman had taken a fancy to the daughter of one of his Free-State neighbors, and had been refused by her. The next time he met her he used the most vile and insulting

—12

language toward her, in the midst of which Frederick Brown appeared and was besought for protection, which was readily granted. Sherman then drew his knife, and, speaking to the young woman, said: 'The day is soon coming when all the damned Abolitionists will be driven out or hanged; we are not going to make any half-way work about it; and as for you, Miss, you shall either marry me or I'll drive this knife to the hilt until I find your life.' Frederick Brown quietly warned Sherman that if he attempted any violence he would be taken care of; when, with an oath and threat, Sherman left them."

NOTE 23.—It is quite possible that there were two of these surveying expeditions, or that John Brown obtained information from both the camp of Georgians and also from the Pro-Slavery settlers, by personating a Government surveyor. Read all the accounts of this matter in the works of Sanborn and Hinton. One of the accounts by Sanborn is as follows:

"Brown, without consulting any one, determined to visit their camp and ascertain their plans. He therefore took his tripod, chain, and other surveying implements, and with one of his younger sons started for the camp. Just before reaching the place he stuck his tripod, sighted a line through the center of the camp, and then with his son began 'chaining' the distance. The Southern men supposed him to be a Government surveyor (in those times, of course, Pro-Slavery), and were very free in telling him their plans. They were going over to Pottawatomie creek to drive off all the Free-State men; and there was a settlement of Browns on North Middle creek, who had some of the finest stock,—these also they would 'clean out,' as well as the Dutch settlement between the two rivers. Thy were asked who had given them information about the Browns, etc., and who was directing them about the country; and without any hesitation the Shermans, Doyles, Wilkinson, George Wilson, and others were named. In the midst of the talk these men walked into the camp, as Mr. Foster says, and were received with manifestations of pleasure. A few days after, the camp was moved over to Pottawatomie creek, and the men began stealing horses, arms, etc. This had been going on for some weeks when the attack upon Lawrence was made in May."

The Dutch settlement named in the above "was the neighborhood where Benjamin, Bondi, and Weiner had settled, and where the valuable warehouse of Weiner was afterwards burned. The Doyles and Wilkinson were not far off, and the Shermans at Dutch Henry's Crossing were between the 'Dutch settlement' and Buford's camp."— *"Life and Letters of John Brown," F. B. Sanborn, p. 230.*

Mr. E. A. Coleman made the following statement:

"Brown replied: . . . 'Mr. Coleman, I will tell you all about it, and you can judge whether I did wrong or not. I had heard that these men were coming to the cabin that my son and I were staying in' (I think he said the next Wednesday night) 'to set fire to it and shoot us as we ran out. Now, that was not proof enough for me; but I thought I would satisfy myself, and if they had committed murder in their hearts I would be justified in killing them. I was an old surveyor, so I disguised myself, took two men to carry the chain, and a flagman. The lines not being run, I knew that as soon as they saw me they would come out to find out where their lines would come.' And taking a book from his pocket he said: 'Here is what every man said that was killed. I ran my lines close to each man's house. The first man that came out said: "Is that my line, sir?" I replied: "I cannot tell; I am running test lines." I then said to him: "You have a fine country here: great pity there are so many Abolitionists in it." "Yes, but by God we will soon clean them all out," he said. I kept looking through my instrument, making motions to the flagman to move either way, and at the same time I wrote every word they said; then I said: "I hear that there are some bad men about here by the name of Brown." "Yes, there are, but next Wednesday night we will kill them." So I ran the lines by each one of their houses, and I took down every word, and here it is word for word for each one.' "—*The Kansas Memorial, pp. 196-7.*

NOTE 24.—*Life and Letters of John Brown,*" F. B. Sanborn, p. 260, note.

On the same page, in a note, is given the account rendered by John Brown, jr., of the first surveying expedition. He says:

"Father took his surveyor's compass, and with him four of my brothers—Owen, Frederick, Salmon, and Oliver—as chain-carriers, ax-man, and marker, and found a section line on which, on following, led through the camp of these men. The Georgians indulged in the utmost freedom of expression. One of them, who appeared to be the leader of the company, said: 'We've come here to stay. We won't make no war on them as minds their own business; but all the Abolitionists, such as them damned Browns over there, we're going to whip, drive out, or kill,—any way to get shut of them, by God.' The elder Doyle was already there among them, having come from the Pottawatomie, a distance of nine miles, to show them the best fords of the river and creek."

NOTE 25.—*Life and Letters of John Brown,* F. B. Sanborn, p. 236.

NOTE 26.—The full account of the outrages inflicted upon Mr. Morse can be found in the statement made by George Grant; this statement is published in *Life and Letters of John Brown,* F. B. Sanborn, pp. 255, 256.

NOTE 27.—This information of the whereabouts of "Dutch Henry" at this time was given me by Rev. J. G. Pratt, at the Old Settlers' First Annual Picnic (Wyandotte county), held at Chelsea Park, in Kansas City, Kansas, June 17th, 1896. Mr. Pratt came to Kansas as a missionary to the Shawnees, in 1837, and has lived here almost continuously since. The year after he came first, the Missionary Board sent out a young lady from North Yarmouth, Maine, to assist in the Mission school. This young lady afterwards married John T. Jones, or "Ottawa" Jones, the educated Indian and Christian gentleman for whom Henry Sherman afterwards worked when he first came to Kansas. Mr. Jones and Mr. Pratt were ever intimate, warm and confidential friends. Mr. Jones often gave Mr. Pratt the account of this affair, and he always justified John Brown.

NOTE 28.—Judge W. A. Johnson, of Garnett, Kansas, one of the Justices of the State Court of Visitation, author of the *History of Anderson County*, and one of the first settlers in Kansas, both in point of time and of legal attainments and also of high and honorable standing, has one of these notices, and has described it to me; but it was mislaid and he could not find it in time to send it to me that a copy of it might be printed here.

NOTE 29.—"When the parting of the two companies took place, which I have previously related, John Brown and his party started for home. The first place they struck was the cabin of his son-in-law, which he found empty; next John Brown, jr.'s, which he also found empty. A neighbor informed him that the houses had been visited by the party from Pottawatomie, who had threatened to burn them over their heads. The women, being alarmed, found a yoke of cattle, yoked them to a cart, put their valuables into it with the children, and drove down to Mr. Adair's house, where we found them upon our return. The party, leaving Middle creek, proceeded on their way to Pottawatomie. Coming in sight of where Weiner's house should be, they found it burned, with a small stock of goods which it contained. A little farther on they found the house of August Bondi also burned, and he soon after appearing told them it was the party who that night were killed, together with 'Dutch Henry' and Judge Wilson, who had done the work."—*"John Brown and His Men,"* Richard J. Hinton, p. 693.

This is the statement of Major H. H. Williams, who was the messenger sent by the Grants and other Free-State settlers to bring help from the companies on the way to Lawrence. He afterwards married one of the daughters of Mr. Grant. He says that it was the report that Judge Wilson was marked for death by Brown's company, but being a member of a world-wide secret fraternity, was warned in time to flee and escape.

NOTE 30.—"I have heard the notorious Henry Sherman ('Dutch Henry' as he was called), declare under oath, that he would rather kill that old man who wore spectacles, that lived on the hill (meaning the Rev. David Baldwin, now living in Garnett, Anderson county), than to kill a rattlesnake, and believed he would be doing the country service."—*James Hanway, in a MS. in the John Brown Documents in the library of the State Historical Society.*

NOTE 31.—As tending to still further show the conditions existing in the settlement on the Pottawatomie, a more lengthy quotation will be made here from the MS. of Judge Hanway, referred to in the preceding note. He says:

"In reading history, we must, to understand it aright, not judge of acts and circumstances by the standard of *our day*, but by the times in which they transpired; or in the language of Mr. Froude, the historian, 'The equity of history requires that men be tried by the standard of their time.' This is the true measure of justice.

"A few days after the destruction of the Free-State Hotel at Lawrence, and the destruction of the two printing-presses, in the month of May,'56, the *Border Times*, published in Westport, Missouri, after giving a short statement of the pillage and destruction of Lawrence, comments thus: it says, '*This is right, nuisances should be suppres[s]ed,*' and then [urges] the Pro-Slavery party of the Territory '*to drive [out] and exterminate every black-hearted abolitionist, and drive them from the Territory.*'

"This paper was circulated in the Territory, and obtaining a copy of it, I copied its remarks into my scrap-book. There it is; ponder it well, for it came from the party who called themselves 'the law and order party.' Here then is evidence that orders from headquarters were to exterminate and drive out all the 'black-hearted abolitionists.' The result of such advice was, that Doyle and his sons called on a man who kept a small store, near the crossing of the creek, of the name of Morse, and told him to pack up his goods, move off his claim, and make his exit from the Territory within five days, or they would kill him. His offense consisted in selling some lead to the party who had left in defense of Lawrence. (This circumstance was taken to old John Brown while in camp on Ottawa creek.) Morse objected to obey the orders of these ruffians, and remained. A few days after the tragedy he was arrested by the United States Marshal, but as there was no evidence against him he was set at liberty.

"The Shermans repeatedly made threats to shoot and exterminate Free-State men, and when the news of the fall of Lawrence was received one of the Shermans it is said raised a red flag, which was the sign that the war was commenced, and they would do their part. This fact I received from a trustworthy person, who was also ordered to leave the Territory. Other Free-State families had been notified to leave by the Shermans, in five days. . . .

"Wilkinson, the postmaster, and member of the bogus Legislature from this district, frequently made threats of burning and killing, etc. He was a violent party man, and his wife remarked to Dr. R. Gillpatrick, who was the first person who called at the house of Wilkinson after he had been killed,—said that she had frequently urged him to be more quiet and moderate in his language, but she added, he would not regard her advice. These deluded men had doubtless concluded that as Lawrence had been sacked and burned, that the Free-State party was annihilated; that the war of extermination was to be followed up, as the *Border Times,* of Westport, had promulgated the orders to be carried out. There was, however, nothing new in this program,—it was only carrying out the policy of the Pro-Slavery leaders of the previous year.

"General Whitfield, in a speech on accepting the nomination for Congress before the convention, thus speaks: 'If you place upon me the responsibility of the formation of a platform, you may rest certain that the enemy will be met on the square, with only two issues, "slavery or no slavery." We can recognize but two parties in the Territory—the Pro-Slavery and the Anti-Slavery parties. If the citizens of Kansas want to live in this community *in peace and feel at home, they must become Pro-Slavery men;* but if they want to live with gangs of thieves and robbers, they must go with the abolition party. There can be no third party—no more than two issues— slavery or no slavery, in Kansas Territory.'

"Dr. Stringfellow remarked, 'the laws must be executed,' and said that by executing the laws passed by the Legislature, *every free-soiler who had any respect would be driven from the Territory, for no man with the spirit of a gentleman would stay in a country where the expression of his opinion was forbidden by legal enactments.'* He of course referred to the 12th section of the bogus slave code, which provides that the promulgation of abolition or free-soil opinions is to be punished by two years' imprisonment with hard labor in the penitentiary.

"Dr. Stringfellow, after one of his marauding expeditions through Kansas, writes an article in the *Squatter Sovereign:* 'Home again. After a campaign of over two weeks in the Territory, we have been subject to the arduous duties of a soldier's life, we have returned to our home to resume our long-neglected business. We are still of the opinion that the two parties cannot exist in the Territory. We hope our friends in this portion of Kansas who have been subjects of many insults and injuries from these Northern harpies will *no longer suffer them to remain in their midst.* Treat them as you would the midnight assassin, for they are no less, and whenever they are seen with arms in their hands, let the crack of your rifle be the only salutation they receive from you. . . . Kansas, deprived of the aid hitherto received from the Southern allies, would prove an easy prey to the rapacious thieves of the North. We can tell the impertinent scoundrel of the *Tribune,* that they may exhaust an ocean of ink, their emigration aid societies spend their millions and billions, their representatives in Congress spout their heretical theories till doomsday, and his excellency Franklin Pierce appoint abolitionists after free-soilers as our governors; yet we will continue to *tar and feather, drown, lynch and hang every white-livered abolitionist, who dares to pollute our soil.'* . . .

"Is it surprising that the ignorant and deluded followers of the slave-power, like the Doyles, Wilkinson, and Shermans, should attempt to carry out the advice which their leaders announced was necessary to establish slavery in the Territory? There cannot be a reasonable doubt that Brown and his party took the border ruffians at their word, and considered it his duty to strike *first;* a mere question of time."

"The *Border Times* (of Westport, Mo.) did issue an extra on the morning of the 23d, the day John Brown was notified of the intention of driving out or executing the Free-State settlers on the Pottawatomie. This 'war extra' contained a false statement that a Mr. Cox, with his wife, had been shot at, as well as other persons near Franklin, and goes on to say: 'Fish's Abolition hotel may meet with an accident. All nuisances should be abolished.' Paschal Fish was an educated Shawnee Indian; never had been an abolitionist; was a humane, good man,—a preacher of the Methodist Church, and therefore a dangerous character, because he would not aid in murdering and driving out Free-State people.

"Recollect, on the 21st Lawrence had been sacked and robbed, two printing-presses destroyed, and the hotel and other property burned. This 'war extra' goes on to say: 'There should be no mistake in this matter; our *Missouri friends must understand that this is but the beginnig of the end. We want you still,* and if our citizens are to be shot at simply because they are true to Southern principles [in burning hotels and printing-offices, and murdering abolitionists] in the streets of Lawrence, in open day, and that, too, within four-

and-twenty hours of receiving *such a bitter lesson as the Pro-Slavery men* taught them on the 21st instant, we have but one resource left, and that is to *level Lawrence*, and, if necessary, *every other abolition settlement in Kansas, with the ground.* We pity the women and children on whom this unhappy state of affairs falls, *but the responsibility must rests with the fanatics* who preached Sharps' rifles and armed resistance to the laws.

" '*Come, then;* we call upon every *true-hearted Pro-Slavery man* and Son of the South, to come up and help us.'

"Bear in mind, reader, this was a Pro-Slavery paper *in Missouri,* calling on '*Mississippians*' and '*Sons of the South,*' but one day before *John Brown executed the Pro-Slavery men, to overrun all Kansas, burn all her towns and murder her people,* and in much sympathy saying that the women and children must share their fate. The probabilities are, and the facts tend all that way, that this 'extra' had not only reached their leaders, Wilkinson, and William Sherman, . . . but that John Brown had also seen it, and that in pursuance of it the notice was sent to John T. Grant, that they must leave or die. Brown, getting that notice, made prompt work. Instead of John T. Grant, Townsley, Judge Hanway and John Brown hanging on trees, the executioners who had given the notice were themselves executed.

"At this very time the women and children at Lawrence were subsisting on cracked corn and cracked wheat, ground but not bolted, in the little mills for cracking corn for cattle, and in many instances broken with a hammer on the poll of an axe. If these brutal men of Missouri could threaten anything worse than this, what could it be?"—*Hon. John Speer, in The Home Journal, Lawrence, December 18, 1879.*

CHAPTER VII.

WAR ON THE POTTAWATOMIE—*COUP DE MAÎTRE.*

The raven croaks!
The black cloud is low over the thane's castle;
The eagle screams—he rides on its bosom.
Scream not, gray rider of the sable cloud,
Thy banquet is prepared!
The maidens of Valhalla look forth,
The race of Hengist will send them guests.
Shake your black tresses, maidens of Valhalla,
And strike your loud timbrels for joy!
Many a haughty step bends to your halls,
Many a helmèd head.
Dark sits the evening upon the thane's castle,
The black clouds gather round;
Shrink not then from your doom, sons of the sword!
Let your blades drink blood like wine;
Feast ye in the banquet of slaughter,
By the light of the blazing halls!
Strong be your swords while your blood is warm,
And spare neither for pity nor fear,
For vengeance hath but an hour.
—*Sir Walter Scott.*

Governor Robinson thus defines Eli Thayer's theory of freedom in Kansas:

"Eli Thayer, as he has often said, looked upon the struggle in Kansas as the entering-wedge in the conflict for the overthrow of slavery in the nation. Freedom once planted in Kansas would spread east and south in accordance with the popular sovereignty of the Kansas-Nebraska bill, till not a slave should be found in any State. This

(185)

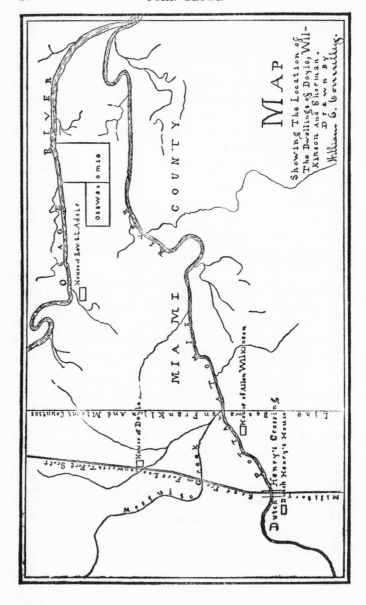

was the view of the agents of the Aid Company and many others who came to Kansas from the North and East."

This theory, as stated by Mr. Thayer's most devoted friend and closest confidant, was: Make Kansas a free State without any regard to the slave question as it affects the country at large,—without any regard to the *right* or *wrong* of slavery,—then the beauties of freedom and its advantages, as exemplified in Kansas under the squatter features of the Douglas bill, will so impress and appeal to the slave States that they will voluntarily abolish the slave system and give freedom to the slaves. As freedom was to "spread east and south," it is supposed that Missouri was counted upon as the first convert to this "epidemic" theory of freedom, and, no doubt, Arkansas was to become the second. This theory was to "spread" until not a slave was left in "any State."

It may be well affirmed that if a whimsical, impracticable, and foolish vagary was ever promulgated on earth it was this. This squatter feature had always remained to the Southern States. Mr. Thayer would have us believe that no State was empowered to free the slaves it contained until the Douglas bill became a law. But the truth is, any State could have liberated its slaves at any time, if it had desired to do so. Slavery rested upon the sentiment of the people of the South quite as much as it rested upon legal enactments; in fact, there could have been no enactments without the existence first of the sentiment. And the whole South had seen the rapid progress of the North under freedom, and the decadence of the South under slavery; but public sentiment there had increased for slavery until its aggressions had upset the solemn compact of the

nation and created the conditions existing at the very time
of the promulgation of Thayer's ridiculous "epidemic"
theory. He seemed to forget that Missouri, the first State
into which his theory was to "spread," bordered on two
free States, Illinois and Iowa: Illinois had been a free
State and Missouri a slave State for more than thirty
years. The Free-State men who encountered these same
Missourians on the plains of Kansas could discover no
sentiment in them in favor of Mr. Thayer's theory. Their
favorite theory was the extermination of Free-State men!
—the nationalization of slavery! But Governor Robinson
very properly and correctly says that there existed an element in Kansas who held to this preposterous theory.[1]

It was very fortunate for the settlers on the Pottawatomie, and in fact for all the Free-State men of Kansas,
that there were no men in the camp on Middle Ottawa
creek on the 23d of May who were believers in so trans-
parent an absurdity. These men had guns in their hands.
They were practical, common-sense men. They had not
gotten beyond the impression that when their country was
invaded by whisky-sodden ruffians, armed, loudly proclaiming their intention to exterminate Free-State people,—in
this extremity these men had somehow gotten the idea that
they were in duty bound to defend their families and homes
as best they could. They may have been mistaken, and in
fact we are often told by the non-resistants that they *were
wrong;* but they had their wives and children on an exposed and dangerous frontier, and they were threatened
with death by as relentless and brutal foes as ever carried
desolation and rapine into a border-land. These Free-State
men in camp on the Middle Ottawa creek were mistaken to

that degree that they imagined they were justified in trying
to defend their homes and make some effort to turn back the
hordes of invasion!   Actual occurrences and experiences
made impressions upon them, strange as it may seem!   If
a man burned a house, they were foolish enough to believe
he meant mischief!   If he came with a blood-red notice
to warn a family to move away by a certain day on pain of
death, they mistrusted that he might mean harm!   And
when he went to cabins where were wives and children of
men on the road to defend Lawrence and threatened murder, driving mothers and children to seek safety in flight
after terrorizing them with the avowed intention of burning the cabins over their heads, and even outrage, these
men felt that there was danger which called upon them to
take some steps to defend their families!   But they were
only plain men, intent upon having some share of their
rights if they had to fight for them; and having, also, some
idea, mistaken or otherwise, that duty demanded that they
defend their families with their lives, and if in doing so
they killed some ruffian they might be justified in the eyes
of all right-thinking men!

The message carried by Mr. Williams to the camp on
Middle Ottawa creek was not sent to any particular person
or commander; it was a statement of conditions and
an appeal for help.[2]   John Brown heard the message delivered.   He immediately declared: "I will attend to those
fellows."[3]   He called for volunteers to return with him to
the Pottawatomie.   His son, John Brown, jr., objected to
the separation of the men at that time, but as many as were
required to make an investigation were readily secured.
It has often been asked why the whole company did not

return, if there was danger to the Pottawatomie settlements. There was but a portion of the company from that
particular settlement. And Judge Hanway says that it
had been determined to proceed, and rescue Doctor Robinson, as it was expected that he would be brought by
a certain route to Lecompton.[4] It was learned later that
he was taken over a different road. Then, it was not
known just what would be necessary in the settlement when
John Brown left the camp. And the camp was but a few
hours' ride from the Pottawatomie, and from it reinforcements could be speedily obtained. Again, as they were
not to go on to Lawrence, they would perhaps all return to
their homes in a day or two, and arrive in time to prevent
the expulsion of the Free-State settlers on the following
Wednesday.[5] Whatever the reason, it is nowhere set
down that they remained away because they supposed no
danger threatened.

The party which left the camp on Middle Ottawa creek
to return to the Pottawatomie consisted of John Brown
and his sons Frederick, Owen, Watson and Oliver, and his
son-in-law Henry Thompson, Theodore Weiner, and James
Townsley,—eight. It was soon known in the camp that
Brown had raised a company to return to the Pottawatomie
in response to the appeal for protection, and to take such
action as might be required by the conditions found existing there when the company arrived. Some were requested
to go, and told what would be done should necessity require
it, who declined to go. Indeed no secret was made of the
intentions of the company, nor of the purpose for which
it was to return in advance of the company of enlisted
"Rifles." The men who remained in camp helped to grind

the swords of those who returned. When the little party
moved out to go in the defense of home and family, three
cheers were given by the men who remained, and the commander of the company says all knew that a blow of retaliation was to be struck.[6] The departure was open, public,
amid the cheers of companions in arms, in nowise secret,
with no intention that it should be so. All the party except
Theodore Weiner rode in the wagon of James Townsley.
Weiner rode his own gray pony. It seems that he was not
a member of the Pottawatomie Rifles, but that he had fled
to the camp the previous day, after having received his
notice to quit the Territory. It is claimed by some that
his store had been burned by the Doyles and others, and
that he had been obliged to fly for his life, but the preponderance of the evidence says that Captain Pate burned
his store a few days later. The Doyles only delivered the
notice, and accompanied it with dire threats of what would
follow its disregard.

The only evidence we have of the party's having been
seen on the road is contained in a letter written by Colonel
James Blood, twenty-three years after the occurrence.[7] He
was a very timid man, and was slipping into Lawrence by
a roundabout way to escape the ruffians. He says he met
the party a few miles north of Dutch Henry's Crossing.
The letter contains many curious and strange statements,
contradictory of what is now known to be true, and insist-
ing upon what is known to be false. A mile north of Dutch
Henry's Crossing the party went into camp in the woods
between deep ravines. What happened in this camp for
the next twenty-four hours is set out in Townsley's statement. If he had not made several statements, no two

alike—all different—our knowledge of the actions of the
party at this point might be easily gained, and be very
satisfactory after we had obtained it. In his later statements Townsley maintains that the party remained inactive
here all the night and following day, trying to induce him
to point out *all* the Pro-Slavery men in the settlements on
the Pottawatomie, so that they might "sweep the creek,"
and destroy them indiscriminately. He remained obdurate, and the expedition could do nothing until the following night, when he agreed to point out only a stipulated
number of the ruffians; and then the work was done,—
the Pro-Slavery men killed. This is preposterous, when
it is remembered that John Brown knew the location of
the Pro-Slavery settlers quite as well as Townsley.[8] And
it is disproved by what actually occurred. Brown had no
intention of "sweeping the creek." He only sought the
guilty; and two Pro-Slavery men who were captured were
returned to their homes unharmed, because they satisfied
Brown that they had no part in the outrages inflicted, and
no intention to join in those contemplated. If Brown
had desired or intended to kill indiscriminately, he would
never have spared these men who were found so near the
house of Henry Sherman and where he found William
Sherman. In one of his statements Townsley says he did
not point out other persons to be killed, because it was too
near daylight when those who were killed had been disposed of. Other men of the party have left statements
of what occurred in the camp and in the settlement on the
24th of May. They are entitled to as much credit as
Townsley, especially since his stories do not always agree.
The many contradictory statements make it difficult to

reach a satisfactory determination. The most that can be said is, that what did actually take place in the camp of Brown and his party on the night of the 23d and the following day must for the present remain a matter of conjecture, with the absolute certainty that it was not spent as Townsley says in his last statements that it was occupied. All that Townsley was invited to join the party for was to carry them in his wagon—nothing else. Every member of the party knew the settlement as well as Townsley knew it. Let us endeavor to account for the day—May 24th— from what reliable evidence we have.

It is maintained by almost all the early writers on Kansas history—those who were here at the time and should have known—that these men had a trial. The known circumstances tend to confirm their statements. That some inquiry or investigation was conducted by Brown during the day of the 24th of May, is quite possible, even probable. Brown told Governor George A. Crawford, "that the death of those Pro-Slavery men had been determined upon at a meeting of the Free-State settlers the day before; that he was present at the meeting, and, I think, presided, and that the executioners were then and there appointed." Governor Crawford was a man of remarkably clear comprehension and vivid recollection, and there is no doubt that John Brown told him precisely what he has recorded.[9] Gihon, the private secretary of Governor Geary, says: "These five men were seized and disarmed, a sort of trial was had, and in conformity with the sentence passed, were shot in cold blood. This was doubtless an act of retaliation for the work done but a few days before at Lawrence." Holloway, in his history, says:

—13

" Pro-Slavery men in the region of Osawatomie had for some time been very impudent, bold and threatening. The spirit of extermination which incited the destroyers of Lawrence and which had been breathing its threats along the border all spring, at once seized the Pro-Slavery men of that section. . . . When the men about Osawatomie were absent at Lawrence, their Pro-Slavery neighbors visited their defenseless families, insulted and notified them to leave the country, and threatened, in case they did not observe this order, to kill them all. . . . On the return of Captain John Brown, junior, and his company, and learning of the deep-laid plots of assassination, a council was held near Osawatomie, at which the question of taking the field and engaging in actual hostilities was discussed, of which Captain John Brown, senior, warmly advocated the affirmative. The majority of the company, on its being put to a vote, deciding against him, he stepped out from the ranks, and with sword upraised, called upon all who were willing to begin the 'war in earnest' to follow him. About eight responded, and with them he left the camp of his son, to begin his memorable career. Proceeding up the Marais des Cygnes a short distance, he halted his men, and there, in the still and deep-tangled woods, held a council. Exactly what was said is not known. But Brown soon infused in his followers his own spirit of determination and hostility to slavery. At this council it was determined whenever any demonstration towards executing the plot to massacre Free-State men should be made, that certain parties should be killed on the spot."

Redpath says:

"A meeting of the intended victims was held; and it was determined that on the first indication of the massacre, the Doyles,—a father and two sons,—Wilkinson, and Sherman should be seized, tried by lynch law, and

summarily killed. . . . On the night of the 24th of May,
the Doyles, Wilkinson, and Sherman were seized, tried,
and slain. This act was precipitated by a brutal assault
committed during the forenoon on a Free-State man at the
store of Sherman, in which the Doyles were the principal
and most ruffianly participators. These wretches, on the
same day, called at the house of the Browns; and, both
in words and by acts, offered the grossest indignities to a
daughter and daughter-in-law of the old man. As they
went away, they said, 'Tell your men that if they don't
leave right off, we'll come back to-morrow and kill them.'
They added, in language too vile for publication, that the
women would then suffer the worst brutalities."

Tuttle's History of Kansas thus portrays this feature
of the event:

" In addition to this instance of wanton cruelty, the
Missouri settlers about Osawatomie availed themselves of
the absence of the free-soil fighting men, to visit and insult their wives and families, giving them orders to quit
the Territory on pain of death. There may have been no
deliberate intention back of all these threats, but there is
abundant reason to be found in the tactics of the party
elsewhere for the assumption that every Free-State settler
would have been compelled to vacate his lot, if he could
not defend it with his own right arm. . . . The belief
was common that the whole settlement, and the Browns
more particularly, would be destroyed by an act of sim-
ultaneous assassination, and there were very few that
wished to sit calmly down and wait for the consummation.
A council of war was held, and 'Old John' advocated war
on the instant. The majority inclined to bide the course
of events, waiting for reinforcements and watching the
enemy closely, but a small minority of nine, including the
leader, declared for the arbitrament of the sword. It is
not easy for us to determine which policy was the best.

The younger Browns were not among those who followed the more impetuous leader, but the men who had chosen the more eventful career were soon heard from. The little army of observation determined, upon mature consultation, that certain men who were the leading spirits of the Pro-Slavery section, and had made themselves peculiarly conspicuous by their evil deeds during the Lawrence invasion, should be held responsible for the actions of their party, and if any indication appeared that the scheme of murder was to be prosecuted, they should be destroyed *instanter,* as a precautionary measure."

The other early writers almost all declare that the men had a trial. There are mistakes in the works of the writers, and some of their errors are contained in the quotations given; they appear when the statements are compared with what we now know to be the truth. The writers were not in possession of all the facts. But there is unanimity on the point that the men had a sort of trial. All the circumstances that have come to light in later years confirm this view. It is not contended that this was any regular trial by a competent legal tribunal. It was only a sort of inquiry into the danger the families were in; the evidence was believed to be sufficient to warrant the killing of those afterward slain, and they were killed accordingly.

Brown told Mr. E. A. Coleman: "I had heard these men were coming to the cabin that my son and I were staying in" (I think he said the next Wednesday night) "to set fire to it and shoot us as we ran out. Now that was not proof enough for me." He then described to Coleman and his wife how he disguised himself, took his surveying implements and ran lines by the houses of each of these men, recording in a book what each man said of the contemplated course towards the Free-State settlers. He found that the death of the Browns "next Wednesday night" had been fully determined upon. And no doubt he found true all that he had heard at the camp on Middle Ottawa creek.[10] Anyone reading Mr. Coleman's statement of the surveying expedition and the statements of others concerning the running of the lines through the camp of Buford's men, must conclude that there were two surveying parties engaged in by John Brown. In that to the camp he depended for his safety upon the fact that he was a surveyor. In the one Mr. Coleman describes he *disguised himself,* probably because he was to meet and talk to men who knew him well. That John Brown, and perhaps the others of his party, were engaged upon that day in finding out for themselves the exact conditions then and there existing, it is most reasonable to believe. The mere message to the camp by the settlers was not "proof enough" for him; he must be convinced by his own investigations that they "had committed murder in their hearts." Having informed himself thoroughly of the intention of the Shermans and their tools, he reported to a meeting of the settlers assembled for the purpose of determining what should be done. At this meeting the situation was reviewed, the execution of the guilty parties determined upon, and the executioners appointed. This is what the statements of Governor Crawford and Mr. Coleman establish. These statements are founded upon what Brown himself said, and in each instance he avowed the killing and his own participation in it, and assumed his full share of the guilt, if guilt there was; and as Governor Robinson says he did not base his reasons for this act on

self-defense, he could have no object in making any mis-
statement of these preliminary and minor affairs.   All
the circumstances point to a day spent in investigation into
affairs; John Brown said it was; he said the sentence
of death was passed in the meeting of settlers.   It is true
that he was an interested party, testifying in his own
behalf.   But his testimony should be as good as that of
Townsley, who told at least three different stories of the
expedition, and was also an interested party, speaking in
his own interest.   And this view is still further confirmed
by what Brown told Colonel Samuel Walker, of Lawrence.
They went to the Nebraska line to escort into Kansas
Lane's Army of the North.   We give Mr. Walker's statement at length as recorded in Sanborn's Life of Brown:

"Then Walker said he would take him back under escort,
with Brown's help; and they started so, with twenty or
thirty men, and Brown among them.   When they camped
for the night, Brown, according to his custom, went
away to sleep by himself; and Walker describes him as
sitting bolt upright on his saddle, with his back against a
tree, his horse 'lariated' to the saddle-peak, and Brown
asleep with his rifle across his knees.   At early dawn
Walker went up to waken Brown, and as he touched him on
the shoulder Brown sprang up 'quick as a cat,' leveled,
cocked, and discharged his piece, which Walker threw up
with his hand in time to escape death; but the bullet grazed
his shoulder.   'That shows how quick he was; but he was
frightened afterward, when he saw it was I he had fired
at.   Then,' said Walker, 'as we rode along together, Brown
was in a sort of study; and I said to him, "Captain Brown,
I would n't have your thoughts for anything in the world."
Brown said, "I suppose you are thinking about the Pottawatomie affair."   Said I, "Yes."   Then he stopped and
looked at me and said, "Captain Walker, I saw that whole

thing, but I did not strike a blow. *I take the responsibility of it; but there were men who advised doing it, and afterward failed to justify it,"'* meaning, as Walker supposed, Lane and Robinson. Walker now believes Brown, and cannot think that Townsley's statement about Brown's shooting Doyle through the head is correct; 'for Brown would never tell me what was not true, and would not deny to me anything he had really done.' "

Brown may have meant that Lane and Robinson advised and failed to justify the Pottawatomie killings, but we believe he meant to say here that some of the settlers in the vicinity advised the action and afterwards failed to justify it. But we recur to our former conclusion, that what did actually take place in the Pottawatomie settlement on the 24th day of May is not clear—is not established beyond doubt, and is a matter of conjecture. That the day was not spent in idle and fruitless argument with Townsley to overcome his scruples as to the *number* of men to be killed, we may well believe.[11]   John Brown, as Governor Robinson has well said, did not rely entirely upon self-defense for his justification. But that he might well have rested his cause upon this ground, we now know.[12] He also knew it. But in meting out justice to these guilty parties he looked beyond the matter of self-defense. It was a blow for Kansas, then prostrate and bleeding. And above all, it was a thrust at slavery, and time proved that it was one of a very serious nature to that institution.

As to the number slain and the manner in which the men were killed, we are not left in doubt.[13]   Those who were released by the party, as well as the widows of Doyle and Wilkinson, made affidavits in which their recollections are preserved; and the statements of Townsley confirm

much they said, and they are evidently in the main true.[14]
The Doyles were the first to meet death. Mrs. Doyle
testified that Brown's party arrived at her house about
eleven o'clock on Saturday night, the 24th day of May.
The name of her husband was James P. Doyle; those of
her slain sons were William and Drury. William was
"about" twenty-two years of age, and Drury was "about"
twenty, she said. The Doyles were of that class of poor
whites that never know the precise and exact ages of their
children. They determine the dates by some event that
occurred about the time of their births, such as being more
brutally intoxicated than usual, or shooting a neighbor
or his ox or his dog, or the "high water," or "the overflow,"
or being chased from a community for petty thieving. So,
the sons were "about" twenty-two and twenty respectively,
as Mrs. Doyle said.[15]

John Brown and his sons Owen, Watson and Oliver, and
his son-in-law, went to the house and brought out Doyle and
his two sons. They were taken a short distance down the
road towards the Crossing and there killed with swords.
The son, William, attempted to escape by running away,
but was soon overtaken and cut down.[16] Townsley says that
John Brown shot "the old man" Doyle in the forehead
with his pistol; this has always been denied by the other
members of the company. John Brown said to Captain
Walker, "I saw the whole thing, but I did not strike a
blow." He commanded the company, and the ruffians were
all executed by his direction; there was absolutely no reason why he should deny killing anyone if he had "struck
a blow." Mrs. Doyle says she heard two shots here, and
also a "wild whoop." There is much contradiction in the

evidence concerning the number of shots fired by the party during the killing. Townsley says one was fired here by Brown. This does not agree with what Mrs. Doyle said. Townsley keeps in the background any work he may have done, and says he was always one of those left on guard. By his own statement, he was not where he could see who did the killing. Others of the party say they heard a shot below them while they were at Harris's house, and that they did not know what the shot meant. Those in the house say they heard a cap burst; they evidently heard no shot, and believe that the cap was exploded as a signal for the others to leave the house where they had been left as guards and return to their leader.[17]

It was past midnight when the party arrived at the house of Allen Wilkinson. His wife was sick with measles. He seems to have been suspicious, and to have manifested a strong disposition to not come out when summoned. The party forced him to open the door. His wife entreated for him, but he was marched away and swiftly and silently slain with swords. His body was dragged from the road and left.[18] Brown and his party of swift and terrible vengeance went noiselessly in search of the Shermans.

In his statement Townsley says that the party went from the house of Wilkinson to that of the Shermans. Here, according to him, two persons were brought out and questioned; afterwards they were taken back to the house and not molested further. He says that when they were returned, William Sherman ("Dutch Bill") was brought out, taken to the river, and slain with swords.[19] A Mr. James Harris made an affidavit for Mr. Oliver, of the Congressional Committee of Investigation, in which he says that William Sherman was taken from his house. He was living near the house of "Dutch Henry." William Sherman and two others were staying overnight with him.[20] He says William Sherman was taken out, after the others had been taken out and brought back by Brown and his men, and did not return; and that at about ten o'clock the following morning he found Sherman lying in the creek, dead, his skull having been split with some weapon. There are many other discrepancies in the statement of Townsley, and they become apparent when it is examined with the affidavits of the Doyles, Mrs. Wilkinson and Mr. Harris. There are still more to be found, and many of them irreconcilable, when examined with the statements of the other members of the body of men who did the killing on the Pottawatomie. The Pro-Slavery affidavits agree in saying that the party represented themselves as a portion of the "Northern Army," and searched for and carried away arms and ammunition, as well as saddles. One of the party took a pony and other horses belonging to Henry Sherman.

The fact that Townsley believed William Sherman was taken from the house of " Dutch Henry," when in fact he was not, goes far to disprove his statement that he was to "point out the Pro-Slavery settlers" so that the creek might be "swept." It might be said that he was to do this "pointing out" in the vicinity of his own home, but he gives us the impression that John Brown originally depended upon him to do the guiding that was to "sweep the creek." Townsley doubtless tells much truth, but it is plain, that from some motive, he did not tell all the truth.

In his first statement, or one of the first, he says the party were going from house to house in his wagon when the killing was done, or at least leaves us to infer that. "They then wanted Mr. T. to drive them to another place, but it was now late at night, and he declined to take them any farther." [21] This is the only statement in the first of Townsley's "confessions" about any refusal to obey orders, and completely disposes of the statement in his last "confession" that this refusal was made on the first night when he would not consent to kill *all* the Pro-Slavery settlers, but did afterwards consent to kill *some* of them. The facetious Mr. Spring remarks that "his theological education had evidently been neglected."

In one of his statements, the one upon which most reliance is placed, Townsley says that from the house of Henry Sherman the party returned to the camp, where he had left his team. They remained here in camp until the afternoon of the following day, when they set out to return to the camp of the military company on Middle Ottawa creek, arriving there about midnight. All the evidence is agreed that no prisoner was carried to their camp by the party who did the killing. Harris says that the two men taken first from his house were brought back and remained with him, leaving the next morning. In 1880 one James Christian wrote a sensational letter in which he made a bid for notoriety. It will perhaps result in all the distinction he hoped to gain, but of a dishonorable, disreputable, and infamous variety. He says one of these young men was taken from the house of Mr. Harris; that he was detained until the next morning in the camp of Brown, and that when John Brown raised his hands to ask a blessing upon their breakfast they were stained with the dried blood of his victims. This statement is improbable in itself. It is disproved by all the evidence on both sides. It bears all the marks of being manufactured out of whole cloth. It is made by a man who says another man gave him the information from which he writes, a short time before he was killed by the Browns, twenty-four years before the letter was written. The statement made in this letter is wholly disproved by the affidavit of Harris and by all of Townsley's statements.[22]

There has been much controversy as to whether John Brown himself killed any one of these men on the Pottawatomie or not. Townsley says he shot the "old man" Doyle with his pistol. The affidavits of the Doyles say that the elder Doyle had the mark of a pistol-ball on his forehead. John Brown told many persons that he killed no man at Pottawatomie, but never denied his full measure of responsibility for the killing of them all. It is a matter of little importance, for he commanded the party which did the killing, and if the killing was a crime he was guilty of the blood of each and every one of the slain.

The charge has been persistently made that John Brown and his men wantonly and fiendishly mutilated the dead bodies of the persons killed. This charge has been made by the bitter personal enemies of Brown. It will be remembered that the men were killed with short heavy swords at night. The victims evidently tried to ward off the blows with their hands and arms, and as they were wholly unprotected the swords severed fingers, hands, and possibly arms. No blow was struck after death came to the misguided men.[23] This is expressly stated by Townsley. In some of the works prepared for the purpose of defaming the memory of John Brown the last statement of Townsley is published at length, but that portion of it which says the bodies were not intentionally mutilated and were not struck after death, is omitted, as is also that portion saying that the killing was a benefit to the Free-State cause. After this omission is made concerning the mutilation, the works in question go on and insist that the bodies were mutilated after death.

When John Brown turned from the settlement toward his camp on Sunday morning, five men lay prone and stark on the Pottawatomie. They had whetted a sword for the Free-State settlers. John Brown turned this red blade against those who had taken it in hand. It was a new departure in the warfare in Kansas—a startling revelation at which the Pro-Slavery forces stood aghast. Champions of freedom could no longer be murdered with impunity by ruffian hordes. Henceforth men were to defend their families and their homes; here was notice of it; let him who dared to do so violate or disregard it,—he did it at his peril. It was notice to the Pro-Slavery men who had roamed bloody-handed through the Free-State settlements that "he who takes up the sword must die by the sword." These five dead men lay there, a warning to the advocates of the issue made in the bogus Legislature, that a new factor had entered the contest in opposition to their barbarous dogma. This new factor was on the side of those who stood for the other issue in Kansas Territory. It was an assertion·that the Free-State men were entitled to life, liberty, freedom of conscience, the protection of the Constitution, and equality before the law—FREEDOM.

Could these dead men have spoken on that Sunday morning in May on the Pottawatomie, they would have plainly said to their misguided brethren and fellow-ruffians: "You invoked the sword; the people of Kansas submitted long and patiently while we mercilessly wielded it. The bones of her people whiten on the prairies; we have given their flesh as a prey to the fowls of the air, to the wolf and her whelps. The wild winds chant their requiem. Widows and orphans wail in cabin homes. Outraged maidens implore death and entreat the grave to hide their shame. Their Christian forbearance and their fortitude have been our marvel; we believed them weak and courageless. In the dawn of this Sabbath, with fixed and glassy eyes that see not we look up to the pure stars, and with tongues that are forever stilled and speak not we proclaim to you that we have stood for a lie. We have devoted our energies to the establishment of a crime against humanity. We forfeited our lives in the interest of a barbarous cause—one that is reactionary and against all law, human and divine, and opposed to human nature itself. The winter storm, the gentle rain of spring, the summer sunshine, and the glorious colorings of autumn will pass over us, and battles rage around us, but we shall heed them not. But to us it is now given to say to you that liberty and freedom must reign in all this land, after having been baptized in blood and consecrated anew on the plains of Kansas."

NOTE 1.—It is not meant to disparage Mr. Thayer's labor for Kansas. He rendered us good service in our days of trouble and peril; and those days were days of peril for freedom in all **America.** Mr. Thayer did his duty, and did it well and to our satisfaction; **we** are grateful for it; as a people we have never failed to acknowledge our debt of gratitude, and we never shall. He possessed a genius for the work be performed, and perhaps did his work better than another could; he was the right man in the right place. He possessed organizing power, and had the confidence of the people of New England who so freely and nobly poured out their wealth in aid of Kansas and free institutions. What is to be condemned in Mr. Thayer's book is the assumption in it that he did *all* the work that made Kansas free—his taking credit for everything successfully done here. What he did was, as we said, only his duty.; he did that in a spirit of self-sacrifice that makes him immortal here and elsewhere. That should be the sum of his claims, but it is not. After a careful reading of Mr. Thayer's book one must come to the conclusion that after the war was over he was enabled to see what had been successful in Kansas and what had been unsuccessful; and then, with effrontery unparalleled, claimed all the successful efforts as his own, or as the outgrowth of his scheme, and left all the failures to the rest of mankind. This is more in the spirit and pompous tone of the book than in specific claim, though there is much of that. Now, Kansas would have been made free had there been no Eli Thayer and no Emigrant Aid Company. It might have been in longer time, and in more suffering; although the organization of the Emigrant Aid Company enraged the South more than any other one thing, and many of the crimes committed against Kansas were inspired by hatred of it. Slavery would have been thrown off without the martyrdom of John Brown, and if John Brown had never been born. But Kansas *was* made free by the assistance of Eli Thayer, as well as by that of John Brown; and slavery *was* abolished by the assistance of John Brown as well as by that of Eli Thayer, though Thayer contributed much less towards the result than did Brown. The fate of universal freedom has never been in the keeping of any one man. Progress and advancement are inherent in mankind, and while many reactionary movements impede and hamper them, the work never stops for a moment. Carlyle has well said that nothing else than justice *can* survive in this world.

Neither is it intended here to detract from any State in the work of making Kansas free. Senator Ingalls says that Kansas is the

child of Massachusetts, and so she is—a little; she is much more
the child of the Ohio Valley. This is so patent to all who make
even a cursory investigation of the subject, that no argument is
necessary to establish it. In the convention which formed the present
State Constitution, in 1859, there were two members from Massachusetts, and only eleven from all New England. There were five
members from Kentucky, six from Indiana, six from Pennsylvania,
and fourteen from Ohio. Concerning the population of that period,
I quote from D. W. Wilder's "The Story of Kansas," in the *Kansas
Historical Collections*, Volume 6, page 336, and following:

"By the United States census taken in June, 1860, Kansas had a
population of 107,206. Of these persons 94,515 were born in the
United States; 12,691 were born in foreign countries. The census
reports give the States in which the 94,515 natives were born.
During the last forty years Ohio has led in great generals—Grant,
Sheridan, Sherman; in presidents, and in many other ways,—but she
took her first great championship in coming to Kansas Territory.
By that census Ohio stands No. 1, with 11,617 natives in Kansas
in 1860. Missouri follows with 11,356. Then come the babies born
in Kansas itself, 10,997. Gen. James H. Lane helped to put next
Indiana, with 9,945. Lincoln next sends from Illinois, 9,367. His
native State is No. 6: Kentucky, 6,556. Then comes Franklin's
Pennsylvania, 6,463. Horace Greeley's *Tribune* makes New York
6,331. No. 9 is our neighbor, Iowa, 4,008. Kansas is sometimes
called, from the States of Indiana, Illinois, and Iowa, the State of the
three I's. Most folks are satisfied with two.

"I have named 76,640 out of the 94,515, leaving 17,875 for the
other States, and someone is beginning to say, 'I thought this was a
New England State,' and 'Where is the Emigrant Aid Company?'
From the days of the agitation against slavery and its extension,
in which New England took a prominent part—it was the home of
Garrison, Phillips, Sumner, Parker, Emerson, Lowell, and Whittier—
down to this day, New England has often been called the mother
of Kansas. Exceedingly few persons ever examine a census report.

"The last State above cited is Iowa, with 4,008 natives in Kansas
when the Territory was six years old. The six New England States
then had 4,208 natives in Kansas. State No. 10 is Virginia, with
3,487 natives here. Virginia then included West Virginia. Most
of these immigrants were probably in favor of making Kansas a
free State.

"There was then no railroad across Missouri. But nearly all of
the States that contributed largely to Kansas in the early and
later years were connected with us by river navigation. These
States were Pennsylvania, Ohio, Virginia, Kentucky, Tennessee,
Indiana, Illinois, Arkansas, Missouri, and Iowa. These States and
their rivers made Kansas. These States with their poor men who

wanted homes in a free State, with free schools, made Kansas free. I will add a few names to that census list. No. 11 is Tennessee, 2,569; No. 12, Wisconsin, 1,351; No. 13, Massachusetts, 1,282; No. 14, North Carolina, 1,234; No. 15, Michigan, 1,137; No. 16, Vermont, 902; No. 17, Maine, 728; No. 18, Connecticut, 650; No. 19, Maryland, 620; No. 20, New Jersey, 499.

"The story is told. You see that the new State, farther south than any other free State, was settled by the North. Missouri, her nearest neighbor, was settled by the South. Kansas broke all precedents; its people could not have been free without standing up to shoot and to be shot at. Slavery was a wild beast, and had to be killed. John Brown understood this fact more completely than any other Kansan."

Kansas claims, and justly claims, to have drawn by her struggle for freedom, great men and minds from all the free States and from some of the slave States. These were quickened and ground to sharpness here, and the result is the most metropolitan and aggressive State in America. And the honor of having contributed to make her free is great—too great for any one man to have more than his just share; justice demands that he have that, and that he have no more.

NOTE 2.—Mr. H. H. Williams claims to have carried this message. See *John Brown and His Men*, Richard J. Hinton, p. 691. Townsley says that he always understood that one of the sons of Mr. Grant carried this message. Mr. Sanborn says that it was Grant, but in a note mentions that others are said to have carried it.

NOTE 3.—See Spring's *"Kansas,"* p. 143.

NOTE 4.—"The following day we camped at Palmyra. We had heard of the arrest of Governor Robinson, and our object was to rescue him if they brought him by the Santa Fé road to Lecompton."—*Statement of James Hanway, in "Life and Letters of John Brown," F. B. Sanborn, p. 258.*

NOTE 5.—It was known that the situation was desperate on the Pottawatomie, and that desperate measures would have to be adopted to save the settlers there. No one doubted that death would be meted out to some, but to how many, when, and how, was not known. That John Brown would do this killing with this

—14

company was also known, for he informed several people that that was his purpose, and invited them to go with him. But just what course would be pursued was not known until after the arrival of the party in the troubled district.

NOTE 6.—"We aided him in his outfit, and I assisted in the sharpening of his cutlasses. James Townsley, who resided near Pottawatomie creek, *volunteered* to return with his team, *and offered to point out the abodes of such as he thought should be disposed of.* No man of our entire number could fail to understand that a retaliatory blow would fall; yet when father and his little band departed, they were saluted by all our men with a rousing cheer."—*John Brown, jr., in "Life and Letters of John Brown," F. B. Sanborn, p. 264.*

NOTE 7.—Colonel Blood says:

"In the spring of 1856, I went east on business, leaving my family in Lawrence. I was in New Hampshire, when I learned that the border ruffians were gathering, under ruffianly Federal officers, to destroy Lawrence. I immediately started for home, arriving at Kansas City, I think on the 21st of May, 1856. I could find no way of getting to Lawrence, direct, but hired a close hack to take me, with two or three friends (one of them was J. F. Bliss, now residing at Oskaloosa), to Osawatoosa. We instructed the driver to say to anyone who might halt us, that he was taking some men to Pleasant Hill, Missouri. We drove south through Westport, and the parties halting us appeared to be satisfied with the reply of the driver. We stayed that night at a farm-house in Missouri, a short distance south of Westport. The next day, the 22d, we took dinner with Baptiste Peoria, where Paola now stands, and arrived at Osawatomie in the afternoon. . . . It was nearly sundown that afternoon when, between Pottawatomie creek and Middle creek, and but a few miles from the Doyle settlement, I saw a party of men coming from the west and going towards Pottawatomie creek. As we approached each other I could see the gleam of the sun's rays reflected from the moving gun-barrels of the party in the wagon. When within perhaps 100 yards they stopped, and a man rose up in the wagon and cried 'Halt!' I immediately recognized old John Brown, and stated who I was, calling him by name. I was then allowed to approach the party. There were in the wagon John Brown, and, to the best of my recollection, four of his sons, his son-in-law, and a man driving the team whom I did not know, making seven in the wagon. There was also a man on horseback; I think his name was Wymer, or Winer.

"The party appeared to be fully armed with rifles, revolvers, knives or swords. I think some of them at least had a peculiar instrument, something like a Scotch claymore, or a short, very heavy broadsword. John Brown had presented me with one of the same kind, while at Lawrence, during the Wakarusa war, in the fall of 1855.

"I talked with the old man for some time. I believe he was the only one of the party who spoke. He stated that they had left Captain John Brown, jr., with the Pottawatomie company, in camp near Palmyra. He informed me that Lawrence had been sacked and burned, and that a number of leading Free-State men had been taken prisoners. He seemed very indignant that there had been no resistance; that Lawrence was not defended; and denounced the members of the committee and leading Free-State men as cowards, or worse. His manner was wild and frenzied, and the whole party watched with excited eagerness every word and motion of the old man. Finally, as I left them, he requested me not to mention the fact that I had met them, as they were on a *secret expedition*, and did not want anyone to know that they were in that neighborhood. . . .

"I sincerely believed that it was the work of insane men. Their halting at that distance a solitary traveler, who was apparently unarmed, and upon the open prairie where they could see for miles around, seemed to me evidence of insanity. *Certainly that number of so well-armed men could not fear an assault and capture, or that they were in any immediate danger. I noticed that while we were in conversation the boys watched every look and gesture of the old man—keeping their guns in their hands ready for instant action.*"

Strange statements! No one else has left any statement of John Brown's becoming "frenzied." Colonel Washington told Governor Wise that Brown was the coolest man he ever saw under fire. He may have had good cause to denounce the committee, for it is recorded that the men who had gathered at Lawrence to defend the town left in disgust when the committee announced that no resistance was to be made. (See twentieth chapter of *The Conquest of Kansas*, by Phillips.) If there is any reliance at all to be placed in this letter, it convicts Townsley of lying. Blood says that Brown announced to him that they were on a *secret expedition*. Townsley says he did not know the nature of the expedition, whether it was secret or not, until Brown made it known to him in camp that night. The letter contains what was known at the time of writing to be a very erroneous statement. It says that Brown's son, John Brown, jr., became insane, when, *on the afternoon of the 24th,* "news was received of the massacre," and that he "was taken home the next day a maniac." It says, "We heard of the massacre of the

Doyles, Wilkinson, and Sherman, on the Pottawatomie, *on the night of the 23d."* The killing was in fact done on the night of the 24th, after John Brown, jr., was made insane from hearing of it! Upon such contradictory and unreliable, not to say flimsy and untrustworthy, productions is the defamation of John Brown based. Colonel Blood may have met this party as he says, but his letter bears many evidences of having been written to incorporate and set out the theories of the people engaged at that time in a bitter attack upon Brown.

Colonel Blood's statement concerning the action of the men in keeping their guns ready for instant action would indicate that he had frightened the party! No other Kansan ever saw Brown scared. To Colonel Blood belongs the honor of being the only man who ever frightened John Brown! And Colonel Blood had slipped down through Missouri pretending to be on his way to Pleasant Hill, and was now making his way into Lawrence by the back door for fear of meeting Missourians, and John Brown had seven armed men with him. Truly, the brave Colonel must have presented the very personification of courage and daring on his fleet steed as he skimmed over the prairies north of the Pottawatomie!

NOTE 8.—John Brown, jr., says in a preceding note that Townsley volunteered to return and point out the homes of such as he thought should be disposed of. But John Brown was familiar with the people of the settlement, and knew where they lived. One of his characteristics was the power to go anywhere at any time of night and not lose his way. It has always seemed to me improbable that John Brown took anyone to show him where his neighbors lived; he certainly knew this for himself. He had spent the winter there, and had built a cabin for his relative, Orson Day. In a new country people do not stand much on formalities; they come to know each other quickly and without formal introductions. It was certainly useless to carry a man along to perform this service; all our knowledge of Brown leads us to believe that he was quick to locate names and places. Mr. Coleman, in his address at Bismarck, says so. Notwithstanding the statement of Townsley to the contrary, it is plain that he was sought because he had a wagon and team, and that he went along because he believed he ought to go, for his family was there, and in fact he gives this latter as his reason in one of his statements; or because he was informed that there was to be fighting, and he desired to have a hand in it.

NOTE 9.—This letter is published in *Reminiscences of Old John Brown*, G. W. Brown, M. D., p. 67.

NOTE 10.—*Kansas Memorial*, p. 196.

NOTE 11.—James Townsley says in his last statement: "About noon the next day, the 23d, old John Brown came to me and said he had just received information that trouble was expected on the Pottawatomie, and wanted to know if I would take my team and take him and his boys back so they could keep watch of what was going on. I told him I would do so. . . . After my team was fed and the party had taken supper, John Brown told me for the first time what he proposed to do. He said he wanted me to pilot the company up to the forks of the creek, some five or six miles above, into the neighborhood where I lived, and show him where all the Pro-Slavery men resided; that he proposed to sweep the creek as he came down of all the Pro-Slavery men living on it. I positively refused to do it. He insisted upon it, but when he found that I would not go he decided to postpone the expedition until the following night. I then wanted to take my team and go home, but he would not let me do so, and said I should remain with them. We remained in camp that night and all the next day."— *"Kansas: Its Interior and Exterior Life,"* Sara T. D. Robinson, edition of 1899, p. 408, Appendix.

NOTE 12.—Governor Robinson's letter to the *Topeka Commonwealth*, and quoted by James Hanway in a letter to the *Kansas Daily Tribune*. I have not been able to find either of these letters. I found a part of each in the *Hanway Scrap Books*, in the library of the State Historical Society.

NOTE 13.—"It was the expressed intention of Brown to execute Dutch Henry also, but he was not found at home. He also hoped to find George Wilson, Probate Judge of Anderson county, there, and intended, if he did, to kill him too. Wilson had been notifying Free-State men to leave the Territory. I had received such a notice from him myself."—*"Reminiscences of Old John Brown,"* *G. W. Brown, M. D., p. 73.*

This is a part of the statement of James Townsley, which is given there in full. This quotation, and also that portion stating that the bodies were not mutilated after death, as well as other statements favorable to Brown, are omitted from the "confession" of Townsley in some recent Lawrence, Kansas, publications.

NOTE 14.—"We then crossed the Pottawatomie and came to the house of Henry Sherman, generally known as Dutch Henry. Here John Brown and the party, excepting Frederick Brown, Winer, and myself, who were left on the outside a short distance from the door, went into the house and brought out one or two persons, talked with them some time, and took them in again. They afterwards brought out William Sherman, Dutch Henry's brother, marched him down into the Pottawatomie creek, where he was slain with swords by Brown's two youngest sons, and left lying in the creek."— *Townsley's Statement, in "Reminiscences of Old John Brown," G. W. Brown, M. D., p. 73.*

NOTE 15.—The ages are given here for the reason that Governor Robinson in his *The Kansas Conflict,* p. 276, uses the expression, "five men and boys."

NOTE 16.—"We were all in bed, when we heard some persons come into the yard and rap at the door and call for Mr. Doyle, my husband. This was about 11 o'clock on Saturday night of the 24th of May last. My husband got up and went to the door. Those outside inquired for Mr. Wilkson, and where he lived. My husband told them that he would tell them. Mr. Doyle, my husband, opened the door, and several came into the house, and said they were from the army. My husband was a Pro-Slavery man. They told my husband that he and the boys must surrender,—they were their prisoners. These men were armed with pistols and large knives. They first took my husband out of the house, then they took two of my sons—the two oldest ones, William and Drury—out, and then took my husband and these two boys, William and Drury, away. My son John was spared, because I asked them in tears to spare him. In a short time afterwards I heard the report of pistols. I heard two reports, after which I heard moaning, as if a person was dying;

then I heard a wild whoop."—*From Affidavit of Mahala Doyle, in "Report of the Special Committee appointed to Investigate the Troubles in Kansas," p. 1193.*

"The old man Doyle and his sons were ordered to come out. This order they did not immediately obey, the old man being heard instead to call for his gun. At this moment Henry Thompson threw into the house some rolls or balls of hay in which during the day wet gunpowder had been mixed, setting fire to them as he threw them in. This strategem had the desired effect."—*Townsley's first Statement, in "History of the State of Kansas," A. T. Andreas, p. 604, under "Franklin County."*

———

NOTE 17.—In his last two statements Townsley says that the killing was done with the swords, to avoid alarming the neighbors by discharging firearms. Then, why kill the first man with a pistol?

———

NOTE 18.—"On the 25th of May last, somewhere between the hours of midnight and daybreak, cannot say exactly at what hour, after all had retired to bed, we were disturbed by the barking of the dog. I was sick with the measles, and woke up Mr. Wilkinson, and asked if he 'heard the noise, and what it meant?' He said it was only some one passing about, and soon after was again asleep. It was not long before the dog raged and barked furiously, awakening me once more; pretty soon I heard footsteps as of men approaching; saw one pass by the window, and some one knocked at the door. I asked, 'Who is that?' No one answered. I awoke my husband, who asked, 'Who is that?' Some one replied, 'I want you to tell me the way to Dutch Henry's.' He commenced to tell them, and they said to him, 'Come out and show us.' He wanted to go, but I would not let him; he then told them it was difficult to find his clothes, and could tell them as well without going out of doors. The men out of doors, after that, stepped back, and I thought I could hear them whispering; but they immediately returned, and, as they approached, one of them asked my husband, 'Are you a Northern armist?' He said, 'I am.' I understood the answer to mean that my husband was opposed to the Northern or Free-Soil party. I cannot say that I understood the question. My husband was a Pro-Slavery man, and was a member of the Territorial Legislature held at Shawnee Mission.

"When my husband said, 'I am,' one of them said, 'You are our

prisoner. Do you surrender?' He said, 'Gentlemen, I do.' They said, 'Open the door.' Mr. Wilkinson told them to wait till he made a light; and they replied, 'If you don't, we will open it for you.' He opened the door against my wishes, and four men came in, and my husband was told to put on his clothes, and they asked him if there were not more men about; they searched for arms, and took a gun and powder-flask, all the weapons that was about the house."
—*From the Affidavit of Louisa Jane Wilkinson, in "Report of the Special Committee appointed to Investigate the Troubles in Kansas," pp. 1197, 1198.*

This affidavit further recites that Mrs. Wilkinson was sick, and requested that her husband be allowed to remain with her, and finding that her wish was not to be granted, she told him to get ready and go with them; she saw him no more alive.

"The company then proceeded down Mosquito creek, to the house of Allen Wilkinson. Here the old man Brown, three of his sons, and son-in-law, as at the Doyle residence, went to the door and ordered Wilkinson to come out, leaving Frederick Brown, Winer and myself standing in the road east of the house. Wilkinson was taken and marched some distance south of his house and slain in the road, with a short sword, by one of the younger Browns. After he was killed his body was dragged out to one side and left."—*Last Statement of Townsley, in "Reminiscences of Old John Brown," G. W Brown, M. D., p. 73.*

NOTE 19.—See Note No. 14, of this chapter.

NOTE 20.—"On last Sunday morning, about two o'clock, (the 25th of May last,) whilst my wife and child and myself were in bed in the house where we lived, we were aroused by a company of men who said they belonged to the Northern army, and who were each armed with a saber and two revolvers, two of whom I recognized, namely, a Mr. Brown, whose given name I do not remember, commonly known by the appellation of 'old man Brown,' and his son, Owen Brown. They came in the house and approached the bedside where we were lying, and ordered us, together with three other men who were in the same house with me, to surrender; that the Northern army was upon us, and it would be no use for us to resist. The names of those other three men who were then in my house with me

are, William Sherman, John S. Whiteman; the other man I did not
know. They were stopping with me that night. They had bought
a cow from Henry Sherman, and intended to go home the next morning. When they came up to the bed, some had drawn sabers in their
hands, and some revolvers. They then took into their possession
two rifles and a bowie-knife, which I had there in the room—there
was but one room in my house—and afterwards ransacked the whole
establishment in search of ammunition. They then took one of these
three men, who were staying in my house, out. (This was the man
whose name I did not know.) He came back. They then took me
out, and asked me if there were any more men about the place. I
told them there were not. They searched the place, but found none
others but we four. They asked me where Henry Sherman was.
Henry Sherman was a brother to William Sherman. I told them
that he was out on the plains in search of some cattle which he had
lost. [It will be observed that Harris says, "I *told* them that he
was out on the plains," etc. Not even in this affidavit does he say
that Henry Sherman was actually on the plains in search of cattle.
Dutch Henry may have been on the plains, but it was not to look for
cattle; he was preparing for a search for Free-State men when the
ruffians should return from sacking Lawrence, and their allies from
Missouri should arrive.] They then asked if I had ever taken any
hand in aiding Pro-Slavery men in coming to the Territory of Kansas, or had ever taken any hand in the last troubles at Lawrence,
and asked me whether I had ever done the Free-State party any
harm or ever intended to do that party any harm; they asked what
made me live at such a place. I then answered that I could get
higher wages there than anywhere else. They asked me if there
were any bridles or saddles about the premises. I told them there
was one saddle, which they took, and they also took possession of
Henry Sherman's horse, which I had at my place, and made me
saddle him. They then said if I would answer no to all the questions
which they had asked me, they would let me loose. Old Mr. Brown
and his son then went into the house with me. The other three men,
Mr. William Sherman, Mr. Whiteman, and the stranger were in the
house all this time. After old man Brown and his son went into the
house with me, old man Brown asked Mr. Sherman to go out with
him, and Mr. Sherman then went out with old Mr. Brown, and
another man came into the house in Brown's place. I heard noth-

ing more for about fifteen minutes. Two of the Northern army, as
they styled themselves, stayed in with us until we heard a cap
burst, and then these two men left. That morning about ten o'clock
I found William Sherman dead in the creek near my house. I was
looking for Mr. Sherman. As he had not come back, I thought he
had been murdered. I took Mr. William Sherman out of the creek
and examined him. Mr. Whiteman was with me. Sherman's skull
was split open in two places, and some of his brains was washed out
by the water. A large hole was cut in his breast, and his left hand
was cut off except a little piece of skin on one side. We buried him.

(Signed)   JAMES HARRIS."

For this affidavit, see *Report of the Special Committee appointed
to Investigate the Troubles in Kansas*, pp. 1195-96-97.

This affidavit disposes of the allegations of one Christian, that
prisoners were taken. None were taken. It also refutes the statement of Mr. Townsley, that it was the purpose to kill Pro-Slavery
men indiscriminately. No such purpose was ever entertained. Here
were four Pro-Slavery men; only the one, having been convicted of
outrages and intention of future outrages, was harmed. This fact
tends to a confirmation of what Brown told Governor Crawford
and Mr. Coleman, viz., that only such men as had been tried and
found guilty were killed.

———

NOTE 21.—This statement was made by Hon. Johnson Clark, of
Miami county, Kansas, and published in the *United States Bio-
graphical Dictionary*. It was published, also, in the *Lawrence Home
Journal*, Nov. 20, 1879. It may be found in *Reminiscences of Old
John Brown*, G. W. Brown, M. D., p. 59.

———

NOTE 22.—This letter is published in *Kansas: Its Interior and
Exterior Life*, Sara T. D. Robinson, p. 413, edition of 1899, Appendix.

———

NOTE 23.—"I desire to say here, that it is not true that there was
any intentional mutilation of the bodies after they were killed.
They were slain as quickly as possible and left, and whatever gashes
they received were inflicted in the process of cutting them down
with swords. I understand that the killing was done with these
swords so as to avoid alarming the neighborhood by the discharge
of firearms."—*Townsley's Statement, in "Reminiscences of Old John
Brown," G. W. Brown, M. D., p. 73.*

CHAPTER VIII.

WAR ON THE POTTAWATOMIE—DETERMINATION.

————

*The web of our life is of a mingled yarn, good and ill together:
our virtues would be proud, if our faults whipped them not; and our
crimes would despair, if they were not cherished by our virtues.—
Shakespeare's "All's Well that Ends Well."*

From the very day after the men were killed on the
Pottawatomie there was never any doubt in the vicinity
as to who had killed them. The members of the party never
made a secret of the matter, nor of their participation in
the killing. John Brown always declared that they were
killed by his order, but said he had not killed any of them
himself. It remains for us to inquire into the effects of
this act upon—(1) the settlers of the Pottawatomie; (2)
upon the Free-State cause in Kansas; (3) upon the cause
of general abolition.

The party left the vicinity of Dutch Henry's Crossing
on the afternoon of Sunday, and arrived at the camp of
the company under the command of John Brown, jr., near
the house of Ottawa Jones, about midnight. The company had come to this point on the return to their homes.
John Brown, jr., had been to Lawrence in the meantime,
taking with him a number of his company. Upon his return he had seized two slaves belonging to a Missourian
living near Palmyra. These slaves he carried to the camp
of his men, to be disposed of as they might decide. The

company were in favor of returning them to their master, who had fled to Missouri. The slaves were given to a courier, who was ordered to overtake the master and deliver them to him; this he did, and was rewarded for so doing, the master giving him a sidesaddle. This incident caused some opposition to John Brown, jr., and the opposition increasing, he resigned his command on Monday morning, May 26th. The company voted for a new commander; the candidates were H. H. Williams and James Townsley, Williams being elected. The company then broke camp and returned to their homes.[1]

G. W. Brown says that John Brown, jr., remained insane much of the following summer on account of the action of his father on the Pottawatomie.[2] There are many of his letters in existence, some of them written at that time, and they do not reveal insanity. He was, soon after his return home, arrested upon an indictment charging conspiracy to resist the bogus laws, and upon this charge was imprisoned at Lecompton. He was made insane by being driven before a body of armed Pro-Slavery men a whole day in June while bound with chains.

On the 27th of May, Tuesday following the Saturday upon which the men were killed, a meeting of the settlers on the Pottawatomie condemned the killing. Their first resolution declared, " That we will from this time lay aside all sectional and political feelings and act together as men of reason and common-sense, determined to oppose all men who are so ultra in their views as to denounce men of opposite opinions." In their second resolution they expressed their intention "to stay at home during these exciting times and protect, and, if possible, restore the peace and harmony of the neighborhood." The last resolution said, "That we pledge ourselves, individually and collectively, to prevent a recurrence of a similar tragedy, and to ferret out and hand over to the criminal authorities the perpetrators for punishment." [3]

This meeting seems to have been more in the nature of a precautionary measure than of a determined effort to apprehend John Brown and his men.[4] In fact, neither party regarded it as affording any guaranty of protection. For a short time there were armed incursions into the neighborhood from Missouri and other parts of the Territory. The headquarters of these were at Paola, and they ranged the country in search of those against whom the courts had found indictments for resistance to the bogus laws—a continuation of the campaign so recently concluded against Lawrence.[5] There is little doubt that the killing of Wilkinson and others directed the attention of the Pro-Slavery men to the Pottawatomie settlements, and that they overran them for a short time. But this did not continue long; the "law and order" settlers left in great numbers, and returned to Missouri and other slave States. In order to make the Pottawatomie killings the cause for all the woes which afterwards fell upon Kansas, some writers of Kansas Territorial history assert that the sacking of Lawrence was a great victory for the Free-State party, and the end of the Territorial troubles; and that these troubles would not have again revived if the Pottawatomie affair had not occurred.[6] I have searched diligently for some confirmation of this strange conclusion, but can find none. I find no evidence that Buford was withdrawn from the Territory, and none that it was contemplated that he should withdraw. None of his camps were abandoned, but all of them were strengthened. Some of the Missourians returned home, but remained only long enough to replenish their supply of whisky and dispose of the plunder carried from their defeat (?) at Lawrence! I have failed to find any order for the release of Governor Robinson and other Free-State treason prisoners! On the contrary, I find that the work of increasing their number went persistently on. Officers scoured the Territory, not to apprehend the men who had killed the ruffians on the Pottawatomie, but to capture men for whom they had warrants for resistance to the bogus laws.[7] The campaign for which such elaborate preparations had been made in the previous winter, and which had threatened to break over the border since March, continued, and continued all summer, and would have continued all summer if the men on the Pottawatomie had never been killed. There is some evidence that the Pro-Slavery forces used the incident in Missouri to inflame the people and get them to rally to the work determined upon, but this seems not to have been very successful. War extras of newspapers were thrown into steamboats, but the people of Missouri needed nothing of this kind to whet them for the campaign; they had made preparation for it for months, and they intended to prosecute it until the bogus laws were triumphant or the last Free-State man was driven from the Territory or exterminated. And they were too well acquainted with the characters killed to shed any false and sentimental tears over their fate. They regarded the matter in its true light, and as an incident of the war, and would have respected the Free-State men more and have departed to their homes much sooner if this resistance had manifested itself earlier and over larger areas. They were waging war, and expected that others would wage war against them.

Let us examine the record to some extent for the results of the Pottawatomie killings. We will first introduce Mr. Townsley, who continued to live in that locality for more than thirty years. Mr. Clark, in writing down Townsley's first statement or "confession," says: "On May 24, 1855, William Sherman called at the house of John T. Grant, a Free-State man from New York, and there, in anger and in liquor, told the Grant family that they (the Pro-Slavery men) intended to drive out the Free-State men from Pottawatomie creek and other parts of Kansas. This alarmed Grant, and he sent his son George to the camp of John Brown, who was at that time on Ottawa creek, some twenty-five miles northwest. Upon arriving in camp, young Grant told John Brown the condition of things in his neighborhood, and the trouble anticipated if help was not had immediately. And here it is proper to state that news had come from Kansas City that Buford had organized and armed a large force of Georgia immigrants, and was about to march upon Kansas. The news had also arrived that Lawrence was in ashes, and that our Free-State Governor, Robinson, was a prisoner in the hands of Pro-Slavery 'border ruffians,' at Leavenworth. *In brief, it was a time of terror so appalling that it was felt that the destiny of Kansas was trembling in the balance, and its fate about to be decided.*" [8] This is the testimony of Mr. Clark, put as a preface to the statement of Townsley.

In Townsley's second extensive statement he says: " I

did not then approve of the killing of those men. . . . In after-years my opinion changed as to the wisdom of the massacre. *I became, and am, satisfied that it resulted in good to the Free-State cause, and was especially beneficial to the Free-State settlers on Pottawatomie creek. The Pro-Slavery men were dreadfully terrified, and large numbers of them soon left the Territory.* It was afterwards said that one Free-State man could scare a company of them." In his last statement he uses exactly the same language.[9]

Colonel Samuel F. Tappan says:

" In the summer of 1856 I was at Leavenworth as clerk of the Congressional Committee investigating Free-State affairs. A reign of terror prevailed. Free-State men, women and children were forcibly driven from their homes, put upon steamers, and sent down the river. Free-State men were arrested by a mob of Buford men, and imprisoned in the basement of a warehouse. Miles Moore, M. J. Parrott, Charles Robinson, Judge Wakefield, and others, were also held as prisoners in the city. This continued until one afternoon the *Herald* (General Eastin, editor) published an extra about six inches long—giving an account of the horrible murder by John Brown, of Wilkinson and six [four] others, on Pottawatomie creek, southeastern Kansas. This put a stop to further demands upon Free-State men, and they were all soon after released. The Buford men remained quiet, no longer appearing in the street under arms. In a few days I took passage in [a] mail-coach for Lawrence, with S. C. Smith. Mr. Weibling, who had been a prisoner, drove the team. Judge Wakefield, having been released, was also on the coach, and we drove to Lawrence without further trouble." [10]

We give the statement of John B. Manes: " I came to Kansas in 1854. I worked for the Shermans in the sum-

mer of 1855. Have often heard them say that the d—d
Yankees on the Pottawatomie ought to have and would
have their d—d throats cut.

"While Weiner was absent at the defense of Lawrence,
Mr. Benjamin, who was Weiner's partner in a store on
Mosquito Branch, was warned to leave in five days, or have
his store, himself and his family burned. The old man
Doyle and William Sherman were the men who warned
him to leave. The Grant family was warned to leave in
the same limit of time, and on pain of murder and destruction of property if they refused to heed the warning. At
the time of the warning William Sherman flourished a
bowie-knife, and threatened to cut the d—d Yankee heart
out of Mary Grant, the daughter of the Grant referred to
in Townsley's testimony. Other Free-State people were
warned to leave on penalty of death if they remained, and
the time was about up, these men being killed before the
expiration of the 'five days.'

"I was but a boy of 13 or 14 at this time, but know what
there occurred as well as anyone could know who didn't
see all that was done and hear all that was said, as indeed
no one person could. Being a boy, I was often sent on
errands when it was thought older people could not go
without being murdered by 'border ruffians'; and at this
time of dread, when even my nearest kindred dared not
move abroad without danger of being assaulted or killed,
I would not be likely to forget what was generally believed
to be the danger surrounding those who were in favor of
a free State.

"I know that my father was knocked down for having
a *New York Tribune* in his pocket. I know that my
father's house and brother-in-law's store were burned to
ashes. I know there was a reign of terror, of which those
men who were killed were the authors; and I am surprised that anyone should believe that the killing of those
men was without excuse. Were the Free-State men to

—15

abandon Kansas? Were they to fold their arms in martyrdom at the end of five days? Or were they to slay their
would-be murderers before the fifth day arrived? Which
of these?" [11]

It has often been said that these settlers who stood in
the shadow of death on the Pottawatomie should have appealed to courts. This was the cry of the impracticables
and non-resistants in John Brown's day, and was later
heard in New England, chiefly through the efforts of Eli
Thayer, and in the Administrative circles of the Government, and wherever the enemies of Kansas as a free State
did then congregate. This was so manifestly absurd and
ridiculous that Emerson gave it his attention: " In this
country for the last few years the Government has been
the chief obstruction to the common weal. Who doubts
that Kansas would have been very well settled if the
United States had let it alone? The Government armed
and led the ruffians against the poor farmers. . . .
In the free States we give a sniveling support to slavery.
The judges give cowardly interpretations to the law, in
direct opposition to the known foundation of all law,—that
every immoral statute is void. And here, of Kansas, the
President says, 'Let the complainants go to the courts';
though he knows that when the poor plundered farmer
comes to the court, *he finds the ringleader who has robbed
him dismounting from his own horse, and unbuckling his
knife to sit as his judge.*" [12]

Charles Robinson was the Free-State Governor of Kansas at the time these men were killed by John Brown on
the Pottawatomie. Having the interests of the Free-State
men of Kansas in his charge, and it being his business to
know the conditions everywhere prevailing, he bestowed

upon John Brown the highest praise and most flattering panegyrics. In 1878 he said: " I never had much doubt that Captain Brown was the author of the blow at Pottawatomie, *for the reason that he was the only man who comprehended the situation and saw the absolute necessity of some such blow, and had the nerve to strike it."* [13]

Sanborn quotes Colonel Samuel Walker:

"Colonel Walker, of Lawrence, in quoting to me Brown's saying in August, 1882,—'the Pottawatomie execution was a just act, and did good,'—added: 'I must say he told the truth. It did a great deal of good by terrifying the Missourians. I heard Governor Robinson say this himself in his speech at Osawatomie in 1877; he said he rejoiced in it then, though it put his own life in danger,—for he [Robinson] was a prisoner at Lecompton [Leavenworth] when Brown killed the men at Pottawatomie." [14]

We again quote from Sanborn:

"At a public meeting held in Lawrence, Dec. 19, 1859, (according to the newspaper reports at the time,) the citizens passed resolutions concerning the Pottawatomie executions, declaring 'that according to the ordinary rules of war said transaction was not unjustifiable, but that it was performed from the sad necessity which existed at that time to defend the lives and liberties of the settlers in that region.' This resolution was supported by Charles Robinson, who said that he had always believed that John Brown was connected with that movement. Indeed, he believed Brown had told him so, or to that effect; and when he first heard of the massacre, he thought it was about right. A war of extermination was in prospect, and it was as well for Free-State men to kill Pro-Slavery men, as for Pro-Slavery men to kill Free-State men." [15]

In 1877 the people of the Pottawatomie settlements, being proud of the part their ancestors took in the battle which made Kansas free, and desiring to commemorate their heroic deeds, joined with the survivors of those battles in the erection of a monument to those who fell in the great cause. This monument was built at Osawatomie, where it now stands, and was dedicated August 30, 1877.[16] It was fitting that the old Free-State Governor, the Hon. Charles Robinson, under whose direction the struggle was carried on, should preside over the ceremonies of dedication, and he did. He delivered two addresses upon the occasion, one at the monument and one to an audience of citizens who came to pay him honor at the residence where he was a guest, in Paola, the county seat of the county in which the monument was erected. He said:

" This is an occasion of no ordinary merit, being for no less an object than to honor and keep fresh the memory of those who freely offered their lives for their fellow-men. We are told that 'scarcely for a righteous man will one die, yet peradventure for a good man some would dare to die'; but the men whose death we commemorate this day, cheerfully offered themselves a sacrifice for strangers and a despised race. They were men of convictions, though death stared them in the face. They were cordial haters of oppression, and would fight injustice wherever found; if framed into law, then they would fight the law; if upheld and enforced by government, then government must be resisted. They were of Revolutionary stock, and held that when a long train of abuses had put the people under absolute despotism, it was right and duty to throw off such government and provide guards for future security. The soul of John Brown was the inspiration of the Union armies in the emancipation war, and will be the inspiration of all men in the present and distant future who may re-

volt against tyranny and oppression; because he dared to
be a traitor to the government that he might be loyal to
humanity. To the superficial observer, John Brown was
a failure. So was Jesus of Nazareth. Both suffered
ignominious death as traitors to the government, yet one
is now hailed as the savior of the world from sin, and
the other of a race from bondage." [17]

August Bondi was a resident of the " Dutch settlement"
on the Pottawatomie at the time. This settlement had in-
curred the enmity of the Shermans, Wilkinson, and the
Doyles, because it was composed of men who desired that
Kansas should be a free State. In this settlement was
the store of Weiner and Benjamin, which the ruffians
burned. Mr. Bondi says: "At 9 o'clock that evening
(22d) a messenger from Pottawatomie creek arrived and
reported that the Pro-Slavery men there (Wilkinson,
Doyle and sons, William and Dutch Henry Sherman)
had gone from house to house of Free-State men and
threatened that shortly the Missourians would be there
and make a clean sweep of them, and at many places
where the men were absent grossly insulted their wives
and daughters." [18]

General Jo. O. Shelby, of Missouri, was a great ad-
mirer of John Brown, and often referred to his brave acts
in the border wars in Kansas and to his heroic death in
Virginia. He delighted to tell " how Captain Pate captured John Brown at Black Jack," and this he could tell
in an inimitable manner that would "set the table in a
roar." General Shelby was one of the bravest and most
chivalrous of soldiers, and could appreciate bravery in
another, even though an enemy. He said of John Brown:

"I knew him well. I freighted with him in Kansas, and I fought him in Kansas. I knew him thoroughly, and I tell you a braver or more gallant man never breathed. It is all a mistake to say John Brown was a coward."

"Do you think he murdered people as charged?"

"Why, of course he did, but it was simply a measure of retaliation. He didn't have any the best of us. We killed and John Brown killed; there was no difference on that score." [19]

Hon. James F. Legate was one of the first settlers in Kansas. He had settled in Douglas county before Lawrence was founded. No man in Kansas ever knew the conditions existing here in the Territorial days better than Mr. Legate knows them. He wrote the following in December, 1879:

"Out of the history being written by George W. Brown, a trial is made to make of John Brown a murderer rather than a martyr.

"Hatred must have its full share in the promptings of such a history. We believe old John Brown planned the killing of Wilkinson, Sherman and the Doyles, and perhaps was one of the actors in the drama. But if that be true, he was not a murderer, for it was the sacrificing of human life for the advancement of a great cause.

"Wilkinson was especially a bad man, and the leader of the Doyles and others in raids against the Free-State men. The Georgia company had built a fort just below or south of there, and murder and robbery and arson was their daily avocation. Wilkinson, Sherman and the Doyles were parties to all their crimes. These men were scouts and spies of the Georgians. The Georgians were planning to murder the whole Free-State settlement in the neighborhood of Osawatomie, and would have executed their plans but for this interposition. Brown knew it, and the Free-State men throughout the Territory knew it. But it was hard to explain to the Eastern, moral people why it was necessary to take such steps, and it never was explained, denounced or justified.

" But the result of that deed was peace in the Territory. Before this time, the Pro-Slavery settlers were active participants in the Pro-Slavery raids in the Territory; they justified the deeds of the Pro-Slavery ruffians, but after that, even the Pro-Slavery men were active in their opposition to the atrocities of the border ruffians, and did their full share in stopping them. It made those Southerners, who were committing all manner of depredations, feel that their lives were not secure and that they must measure their conduct by the exigencies of the times, and they were less offensive. It emboldened the Free-State men to assert their rights, and in asserting their rights they won a victory for freedom.

"John Brown planned the taking of the lives of these men in the interest of peace and freedom, and if he executed the plan himself he was a *hero*, not a *murderer.*" [20]

In relation to the part played by the Blue Lodges of Missouri in the preparation of the campaign to be waged against Kansas in the spring of 1856, we quote S. N. Wood, one of the first settlers in Douglas county. He was a member of an anti-slavery organization there early in June. He was a prominent actor in the stirring times of Territorial days, and the object of much hatred by Missourians. He says:

" The Blue Lodges of Missouri and Kansas were secret organizations, whose members swore, on peril of their lives, to make a slave State of Kansas. In the fall of 1855 they became very active and strong; and one of the members, whose conscience revolted against murder even in the interest of slavery, revealed the fact that a new policy had been agreed upon: Free-State men were to be killed privately—struck down, one to-day in one place, one tomorrow in another, until no Free-State man would feel safe. This put every man on his guard." [21]

Judge James Hanway was a resident in the settlement on the Pottawatomie. He was a member of the company called the "Pottawatomie Rifles," of which John Brown, jr., was captain. He was a man of good mind, and did much for the intellectual development of Kansas. He was a just man and a good citizen. He was a member of the convention which formed the present State Constitution. His ability and integrity were everywhere recognized, and his attainments were great. He was one of the men invited to go with the party under John Brown to the Pottawatomie. He refused, and tried to induce the company to wait until all could return together.[22] He knew that the company left the camp with the avowed purpose of killing some of the ruffians on the Pottawatomie, should conditions there be found as represented. He often declared that James Harris told him that when John Brown and his men came into his house in search of the ruffians, his wife supposed they were the men from Missouri come to expel or murder the Free-State settlers. It is also said that she arose and commenced to prepare something for them to eat, under the impression that they were the expected Missouri ruffians. Judge Hanway always said that the account that Harris gave of the affair to his neighbors was very different from that contained in his affidavit.[23] Judge Hanway says, further:

"I was informed by one of the party of eight who left our camp on Ottawa creek, May 22, 1856, to visit the

Pottawatomie, what their object and purposes were. I protested, and begged them to desist. Of course my plea availed nothing. After the dreadful affair had taken place, and after a full investigation of the whole matter, I, like many others, modified my opinion. Good men and kind-hearted women in 1856 differed in regard to this affair, in which John Brown and his party were the leading actors. John Brown justified it, and thought it a necessity; others differed from him then, as they do now. I have had an excellent opportunity to investigate the matter, and, like others of the early settlers, was finally forced to the conclusion that the Pottawatomie 'massacre,' as it is called, prevented the ruffian hordes from carrying out their programme of expelling the Free-State men from this portion of the Territory of Kansas. It was this view of the case which reconciled the minds of the settlers on the Pottawatomie. They would whisper to one another: 'It was fortunate for us; for God only knows what our fate and condition would have been, if old John Brown had not driven terror and consternation into the ranks of the Pro-Slavery party.' " [24]

In a communication to Judge Adams, Secretary of the State Historical Society, February 1, 1878, Judge Hanway says:

" So far as public opinion in the neighborhood where the affair took place is concerned, I believe I may state that the *first* news of the event produced such a shock that public opinion was considerable divided; but after the whole circumstances became better known, there was a reaction of public opinion; and the Free-State settlers who had claims on the creek considered that Capt. Brown and his party of eight had performed a justifiable act, which saved their homes and dwellings from threatened raids of the Pro-Slavery party." [25]

We have seen that Mrs. Harris was aware that ruffians from Missouri were expected to arrive to aid the Pro-Slavery settlers in their work of expelling the Free-State families on the Pottawatomie. There is no doubt that Mrs. Wilkinson had been apprised also that such was the plan being matured for the ejection of the Free-State neighbors around her. Sanborn says:

" Mrs. Wilkinson, an unfortunate woman who had tried in vain to keep her husband from engaging in the outrages against their Free-State neighbors, was visited early in the morning after the executions, by Dr. Gillpatrick and Mr. Grant, two Free-State men, who went to her house (which was the postoffice) to get their mail. They found the poor woman weeping, and saying that a party of men had been to the house during the night and taken her husband out; she had heard that morning that Mr. Doyle had been killed within the night, and she was afraid that her husband had been killed also. Among other reasons she gave for fearing this, he had said to her the night before that there was going to be an attack made upon the Free-State men, and that by the next Saturday night there would not be a Free-State settler left on the creek. These, she said, were his last words to her the night before as they were going to sleep." [26]

Professor Spring was particularly unjust to Brown in his history of Kansas. But later, he made a modification of his views, and says:

"The Dutch Henry's Crossing of 1882 is a paradise of rural peace and happiness. Here quiet and security seem to have reached their utmost limit. The Pottawatomie—half limpid, with slighter mixtures of discoloring mud than any Kansas stream that I have seen—winds languidly between beautifully shaded banks towards the Marais des

Cygnes.   The vast fields of corn and wheat, with their
picturesque borders of orange hedge, lie mapped upon the
rolling prairie in every direction,—

> " 'As quietly as spots of sky
>   Among the evening clouds.'

"The Dutch Henry's Crossing of 1856 stands in an-
tithesis to all this Arcadian repose.   Then there was no
law but force, no rule but violence, in the Territory of
Kansas.   A veritable reign of terror was inaugurated.
Marauders were prowling about, in whose eyes nothing
was sacred that stood in the way of their passions.   The
opposing factions into whose hands the question of slavery
or no slavery for Kansas had fallen, hunted each other like
wolves.   Pistol-shots and sword-slits were the prevailing
style of argument." [27]

We shall see later that he finally gained a correct estimate of the results of the descent of John Brown upon the
ruffians of the Pottawatomie.

The outrages on the Grant family have been spoken of,
but a more specific statement will be given:

"My father, John T. Grant, came from Oneida county,
N. Y., and settled on Pottawatomie creek, in 1854.   We
were near neighbors of the Shermans, of the Doyles, and of
Wilkinson, who were afterwards killed.   There was a company of Georgia Border Ruffians encamped on the Marais
des Cygnes, about four miles away from us, who had been
committing outrages upon the Free-State people; and these
Pro-Slavery men were in constant communication with
them.   They had a courier who went backward and forward carrying messages.   When we heard on the Pottawatomie that the Border Ruffians were threatening Lawrence,
and the Free-State wanted help, we immediately began to
prepare to go their assistance.   Frederick Brown, son of
John Brown, went to a store at Dutch Henry's Crossing,
kept by a Mr. Morse, from Michigan, known as old Squire

Morse, a quiet, inoffensive old Free-State man, living there
with his two boys, and bought some bars of lead,—say
twenty or thirty pounds. He brought the lead to my
father's house on Sunday morning, and my brother Henry
C. Grant and my sister Mary spent the whole day in
running Sharps' and other rifle bullets for the company.
As Frederick Brown was bringing this lead to our house,
he passed Henry Sherman's house, and several Pro-
Slavery men, among them Doyle and his two sons, William
Sherman, and others, were sitting on a fence, and inquired
what he was going to do with it. He told them he was going to run it into bullets for Free-State guns. They
were apparently much incensed at his reply, as they knew
that the Free-State company was then preparing to go to
Lawrence. The next morning, after the company had
started to go to Lawrence, a number of Pro-Slavery
men—Wilkinson, Doyle, and his two sons, and William Sherman, known as ' Dutch Bill '—took a rope
and went to old Squire Morse's house, and said they
were going to hang him for selling the lead to the
Free-State men. They frightened the old man ter-
ribly; but told him he must leave the country before eleven o'clock, or they would hang him. They then
left and went to the Shermans' and went to drinking.
About eleven o'clock a portion of them, half drunk, went
back to Mr. Morse's, and were going to kill him with an
axe. His little boys—one was only nine years old—set
up a violent crying, and begged for their father's life.
They finally gave him until sundown to leave. He left
everything, and came at once to our house. He was nearly
frightened to death. He came to our house carrying a
blanket and leading his little boy by the hand. When
night came he was so afraid that he would not stay in the
house, but went outdoors and slept on the prairie in the
grass. For a few days he lay about in the brush, most of
the time getting his meals at our house. He was then taken
violently ill and died in a very short time. Dr. Gillpat-

rick attended him during his brief illness, and said his death was directly caused by the fright and excitement of that terrible day when he was driven from his store. The only thing they had against Mr. Morse was his selling the lead, and this he had previously bought of Henry Sherman, who had brought it from Kansas City. While the Free-State company was gone to Lawrence, Henry Sherman came to my father's house and said: 'We have ordered old Morse out of the country, and he has got to go, and a good many others of the Free-State families have got to go.' The general feeling among the Free-State people was one of terror while the company was gone, as we did not know at what moment the Georgia ruffians might come in and drive us all out." [28]

As tending to show that Brown was justifiable, I give additional instances—among them some further quotations from the writings of Judge Hanway and Governor Robinson:

" It was thought that the effect of the Pottawatomie affair would be disastrous to the settlers who had taken up their quarters in this locality. For a few weeks it looked ominous. I spent most of my time in the brush. The settlement was overrun by the 'law and order men,' who took every man prisoner whom they came across, 'jay-hawked' horses and saddles, and even, in several cases, work-cattle; but after these raids ceased, the Pro-Slavery element became willing to bury the hatchet and live in peace. The most ultra of those who had been leaders left the Territory, only to return at periods to burn the house of some obnoxious Free-State man. The Pottawatomie affair sent a terror into the Pro-Slavery ranks, and those who remained on the creek were as desirous of peace as any class of the community." [29]

As a note to the foregoing, Mr. Sanborn has the following:

"As to the wisdom of John Brown's general policy of brave resistance and stern retaliation, the sagacious Judge Hanway says: 'In the early Kansas troubles I considered the extreme measures which he adopted as not the best under the circumstances. We were weak, and cut off, as it were, from our friends. Our most bitter enemies received their support from an adjoining State. We were not in a condition to resist by force the power of the Border Ruffians, backed and supported as they were by the Administration at Washington. Events afterwards proved that the most desperate remedies, as in the Pottawatomie affair, were best. In place of being the forerunner of additional strife and turmoil, the result proved it was a peace measure.' Charles Robinson, in an article written for the 'Kansas Magazine' many years ago, said of the executions by Brown: 'They had the effect of a clap of thunder from a clear sky. The slave men stood aghast. The officials were frightened at this new move on the part of the supposed subdued free men. This was a warfare they were not prepared to wage, as of the *bona fide* settlers there were four free men to one slave man.'"

The Pottawatomie executions were the work of John Brown. No meeting of outraged citizens to condemn murderers to death would have been held on the Pottawatomie had not John Brown left the camp of the Free-State company on Middle Ottawa creek and returned to the settlements at Dutch Henry's Crossing. Whether he killed any with his own hand is of no consequence so far as responsibility is concerned. Each one of the eight, whatever his part in the actual work, stood upon precisely the same ground. John Brown never denied his participation in this foray, and he always avowed his responsibility for it. The utmost of his denial was that he had not killed anyone with his own hand. "Captain Brown, did you

kill those five men on the Pottawatomie, or did you not?"
asked Mrs. Coleman. "I did not; but I do not pretend
to say they were not killed by my order; and in doing so
I believe I was doing God's service," he replied without
hesitation. So he always said. This avowal was in the
summer of 1856, and but a short time after the killing.
This was always known in Kansas to be the position of
John Brown; that he killed those men with his company
there was never the slightest doubt. The denials attributed
to him are the work of Mr. Redpath, principally, and
always did Brown an injustice; they were made without
his knowledge or consent.

Had not John Brown killed the ruffians on the Pottawatomie, the campaign against the Free-State men for
the enforcement of the bogus laws would have been successful. The Free-State men held for treason would have
been killed or sentenced to long terms of imprisonment
in Federal prisons. Liberty would have been trampled
down by ruthless barbarians and washed into the earth
by the blood of martyrs for her cause. Slavery, with legal
mien and hypocritical face, "but ending foul, in many a
scaly fold," would have encircled Kansas in fatal coils.
If freedom's cause had failed in Kansas, the conflict
would have been delayed and a future generation would
have been compelled to battle with greater difficulties.
Who sees no more in this raid on the Pottawatomie than
the mere protection of a few families, (though as a matter
of justification, that was for it a sufficient cause,) has read
the history of his country in vain. While it was indeed
that, it was primarily much more than that: it was a blow.
against slavery in America. It was the opportunity long

sought by John Brown. For this purpose he came to Kansas. Compromise with crime was, in his eyes, a crime. If slavery was a curse, it was the duty of men everywhere to attack it. Many of the leaders of Kansas were in favor of dissimulation. Their opposition must be carried forward while they rendered a passive submission to the powers they were battling against. Attacks must be covertly made, so that if need be they could be effectively disavowed. This double-dealing was scorned by John Brown. He saw evil standing as a menace to humanity. His duty was clear to him; his resolution was, Let others do as they may; in God's name I will battle against it as best I can; I should be joined by all men, but if I must fight alone, then be it so. The old truism, that a man should be true to duty though he stand alone, was exemplified by John Brown on the Pottawatomie. He came from that field confirmed in his own belief that he was chosen of God to battle against the foul institution that threatened his country and oppressed humanity. His fame spread abroad, and for a season the campaign against freedom in Kansas was diverted from its purpose and turned against John Brown; and at this he rejoiced.

The following is a quotation from Professor Spring:

"It may be that this modern Mr. Valiant for Truth was a fanatic. I am not disturbed by that word. Every great cause has so fascinated some men—so taken possession of their souls, subduing, inspiring, harnessing them to its service, so bounding their visions by its horizon—that they have been indifferent to other questions and interests. The passion of liberty enslaved John Brown. In his judgment, violence alone could save the day; violence was the charmed weapon for the impending contest; and the bloody instrument which he seized did not break in his hand. I recall a sentence in Oliver Cromwell's dispatch announcing the storming and massacre of Drogheda, which is at once a declaration of Brown's motive and prophecy of his hope when he lifted his hand against the cabins on the Pottawatomie: 'Truly, I believe this *bitterness* will save much effusion of blood, through the goodness of God!'

" Was the fanatic's expectation realized? Did the event approve his sagacity? I think there is but one answer to questions like these. After all, the fanatic was wiser than the philosopher. The effect of his retaliatory policy, in checking outrages, in bringing to a pause the depredations of bandits, in staying the proposed execution of Free-State prisoners, was marvelous. The raid upon Dutch Henry's Crossing is not least among the deeds that saved Kansas to liberty." [30]

In the February, 1884, *North American Review,* Senator John J. Ingalls said:

" Judge Hanway, before quoted, says:

" ' I did not know of a settler of '56 but what regarded it as amongst the most fortunate events in the history of Kansas. It saved the lives of the Free-State men on the Creek, and those who did the act were looked upon as deliverers.'

"One of the most eminent of the Free-State leaders, who is still living, writes:

" ' He was the only man who comprehended the situation, and saw the absolute necessity for some such blow, and had the nerve to strike it.'

"Another prominent actor writes:

" ' I wish to say right here about the Pottawatomie Creek massacre, which has been the theme of so much magazine literature, that at the time it occurred it was approved by myself and hundreds of others, including the most prominent of the leaders amongst the Free-State

—16

men. It was one of the stern, merciless necessities of the times. The night it was done I was but a few miles away on guard, to protect from destruction the homes of Free-State men and their families, who had been notified by these men and their allies to leave within a limited time or forfeit their lives and property. The women and children dared not sleep in the houses, and were hid away in the thickets. Something had to be done, and the avenger appeared, and the doomed men perished,—they who had doomed others.'

" It was the 'blood and iron' prescription of Bismarck. The pro-slavery butchers of Kansas and their Missouri confederates learned that it was no longer safe to kill. They discovered, at last, that nothing is so unprofitable as injustice. They started from the guilty dream to find before them, silent and tardy, but inexorable and relentless, with uplifted blade, the awful apparition of vengeance and retribution."

I cannot close this chapter in any more suitable manner than by adding the testimony of the most eminent historian who has ever written of Kansas, D. W. Wilder, author of the "Annals of Kansas":

" MAY 24–25.—James P. Doyle and his two sons, and William Sherman and Allen Wilkinson (a member of the Bogus Legislature), all Pro-Slavery, taken from their homes at night and murdered. They lived on the Pottawatomie, in Franklin county. Capt. John Brown led the party that did the deed. No other act spread such consternation among the ruffians, or contributed so powerfully to make Kansas free. Hitherto, murder had been an exclusive Southern privilege. The Yankee could 'argue' and make speeches; he did not dare to kill anybody. Blood sprinkles all the pages of history."

NOTE 1.—*Life and Letters of John Brown*, F. B. Sanborn, pp. 273, 274.

———

NOTE 2.—As showing the feeling of the Free-State men towards G. W. Brown, I quote from Webb Scrap Book No. 17, library of the State Historical Society, Topeka:

"G. W. Brown had his press—*The Herald of Freedom*—destroyed by a mob from Missouri, who were acting in the capacity of a *posse comitatus*. He himself was arrested and imprisoned in the camp before Lecompton, on the charge of high treason or some similar misdemeanor. Terrified for his life, he became a traitor. Bought by Administration gold, he continues one."

November 30, 1879, the *Lawrence Journal* quoted from the St. *Joseph Herald* the following: "Geo. W. Brown is the same liar and mercenary politician that he was twenty years ago, and the *Lawrence Journal* is hardly to be excused for publishing his venom. Brown hates the cause and the men that he betrayed. He is not trying to write history, but to make a rogues' gallery of the Kansas pioneers."

Governor Robinson said of G. W. Brown: "He would crawl on his belly to Jerusalem to save his miserable neck." (See The Webb Scrap Book No. 17.)

———

Document No. 2966, Brown Collection, library State Historical Society, Topeka, says:

"Thayer has published letters from G. W. Brown! *You know his reputation* as well as I. It was current report at the time that he *courted arrest*. He was despised both by Pro-Slavery and Free-State men—a man without character or influence, and in order to get notoriety and in high company with the state prisoners submitted to arrest by a negro *slave*. Bah!"

The foregoing paper was written by William H. Ambrose, Esq., Greeley, Kansas.

In 1857, Mr. James H. Holmes wrote of G. W. Brown:

"Governor Walker comes to town frequently, and stops at the *Herald of Freedom* office, in secret conclave with G. W. Brown. When you come here (if you should), you can judge for yourself."— *"Life and Letters of John Brown," F. B. Sanborn, p. 395.*

———

John Brown himself wrote of G. W. Brown: "I believe all honest, sensible Free-State men in Kansas consider George Washington Brown's *Herald of Freedom* one of the most mischievous, traitorous publications in the whole country."—*Life and Letters of John Brown,*" *F. B. Sanborn, p. 476.*

NOTE 3.—These resolutions are given in full in *The Kansas Conflict,* Charles Robinson, p. 275.

NOTE 4.—The Free-State men said in public that they condemned the act, and privately they commended it and owed their lives to it. To strangers and the public they said they would search out the offenders; among themselves they whispered that John Brown had saved their lives by striking down the ruffians on the Pottawatomie.

NOTE 5.—A little later Jefferson Davis wrote to General Smith:

"The President has directed me to say to you that you are authorized from time to time to make requisitions upon the Governor for such militia force as you may require to enable you to suppress the insurrection against the government of the Territory of Kansas. Should you not be able to derive from the military of Kansas an adequate force for the purpose, you will derive such additional number of militia as may be necessary from the States of Illinois and Kentucky. . . . The position of the insurgents is that *of open rebellion against the laws and constitutional authorities,* with such manifestation of purpose to spread devastation over the land as no longer justifies further hesitation or indulgence."—*Quoted from "Life and Letters of John Brown," F. B. Sanborn, p. 284.*

NOTE 6.—"This decisive victory over the Slave-State party was achieved May 21, 1856, and to all appearance was final."—*The Kansas Conflict, Charles Robinson, p. 265.*

Governor Robinson does not give so great prominence to the effects of the Pottawatomie affair as is ascribed to it by G. W. Brown. But he enumerates in his book all the invasions of the following summer, and then says: "All these movements resulted from the massacre." It took Governor Robinson more than twenty years to find that out, for at the dedication of the Brown Monument at Osawatomie, twenty-one years later, he said that Brown stood next to Jesus Christ. As he was the Free-State Governor, he should have known what did and what did not injure the Free-State cause in Kansas; and he should have made some progress in that discovery in twenty-one years! If John Brown's actions in May, 1856, were detrimental to the cause of freedom in Kansas, Governor Robinson should have discovered it in *one* year, or *two* years, or *three* years; at least, long before *twenty-one* years. No other man has ascribed to John Brown so great praise as did Governor Robinson upon that occasion. Unfortunately for his conclusion that the sacking of Lawrence was a great Free-State victory and the end of the war— the dawn of peace in Kansas—we have the testimony of men who saw the transactions of that summer. The records they made of these events were not for the purpose of condemning the course of anyone in Kansas, nor were they designed to establish the reputation of anyone for statesmanship. They are numerous and conclusive. One of the most trustworthy was made by Thomas H. Gladstone, who was a passenger on the boat that carried Governor Robinson from Kansas City to Leavenworth on the night of the 22d of May, 1856. He says:

"In the morning, like my fellow-travelers, I was early astir. My Western companions, accustomed to frequent potations, seemed already sobered down by their few hours' rest. If less boisterously demonstrative, however, in relation to 'Yankee Abolitionists' than in the night, the change was only to an animosity of a more calculating and determined character. News of fresh strife had been received during the night. 'Extras' of the different journals, in the form of printers' slips, containing the latest intelligence, were put on board and largely circulated. These invariably contained distorted accounts of the events of the hour, and appeals of the most inflammatory character. As they were read aloud to the eager listeners, they gave occasion to renew determination to 'fight the nigger-worshipping crew to the last drop of blood.' One 'extra' I obtained, issued by the *Border Times* at Westport, in which the outrages at Lawrence were announced beneath the heading, "THE KANSAS BALL OPENED—WAR IN EARNEST.' In another, a Lecompton paper, the narrative was headed, 'LAWRENCE TAKEN—GLORIOUS TRIUMPH OF THE LAW AND ORDER PARTY OVER FANATICISM IN KANSAS.' When cold-blooded murder, which has left behind its destitution, widowhood and orphanage, comes to be regarded by journalists as the mere opening of a ball and a ground for exultation, it is not to be wondered at that the men who perpetrated these deeds were eager to acquire fresh glory in the achievement of further 'triumphs.' "—*"Kansas," by Thomas H. Gladstone, p. 42.*

NOTE 7.—G. W. Brown, in his *Reminiscences of Old John Brown*, page 12, gives a harrowing account of how Marshal Donaldson came into the pen where were the treason prisoners and informed them that all the "rangers," "tigers," thieves, thugs, and cut-throats in Missouri and Kansas had resolved to break into the prison, which was an old and crazy brick shed or small house, and hang them in retaliation for the deaths of the Doyles and others. The doughty Marshall assures them that as they are *all* Odd Fellows, *Masons*, etc., he will save them, and that he had enlisted all the Territorial officers to help, even the Governor and the Judges! Of course it is to be understood that only the fact that they belonged to these secret orders saved them; had they been ordinary people they would have suffered a horrible death. It is not supposed that a governor, or even judges, will fight to save common people from mob violence, and perhaps no such Governor as was Shannon could have been induced to do so. And Judge Lecompte, who, by the way, lived at Leavenworth, and must have marched a long way to mount guard, could not be expected to do so. But we are told that these would have been unavailing had not Donaldson enlisted all the members of the secret orders he could find to reinforce the Governor and Judges, and with these "he hoped to save them." Such stuff as this is written in G. W. Brown's book under pretense of correcting history! Even Professor Spring admits that John Brown's work on the Pottawatomie *saved* the treason prisoners from death, and no one can accuse Spring of willingly saying anything in favor of Brown. See his article in *Lippincott's Magazine*, January, 1883. But the really pathetic part of this story is to be found on page 23 of G. W. Brown's book. There he pictures the ruffians under guise of the "better class of citizens," when they find they cannot save Governor Robinson from the mob in Leavenworth, as breaking into tears and weeping like children "as one by one they took him by the hand and bade him farewell"! This is, I suppose, one of the most pathetic and tear-producing incidents in all history! Governor Robinson has left us no such incident in his writings, but as Brown wrote to correct history, we must believe it! He says an "eye-witness" told him about it, but very discreetly forgets to set down the name of this person who witnessed the most remarkable manifestation of grief to be found in all the annals of Kansas history. With all of Governor Robinson's hatred of John Brown, he did not descend to the ridiculous in any descriptions of him or the scenes he caused.

What occurred in Leavenworth upon this occasion is fully described by Thomas H. Gladstone, in his "Kansas." Mr. Gladstone was at the time in the city, and saw what he describes. His book is one of the most reliable and valuable contributions to Kansas history:

"At the same moment came the news from Washington of the outrage committed in the Senate chamber upon the person of Mr. Sumner. I well remember the effect this had upon many, who concluded that the rule of force and violence had been fairly inaugurated even in the highest places of the land, and was no longer restricted to the lawless inhabitants of the frontier. Bands of armed men under military command paraded the streets of Leavenworth; others guarded the points of egress from the city. They held lists in their hands, containing the names of Free-State men, whom they made rapid work of seizing and placing in confinement. The Committee of Investigation, although holding appointments from Congress, found itself compelled to interrupt its sittings. Every hour brought intelligence of some fresh deed of violence or wrong."—*"Kansas," by Thomas H. Gladstone, p. 275.*

Why is it not possible that this same intelligence caused the danger to the prisoners at Lecompton and the scene described by G. W. Brown, if any such scene ever occurred?

NOTE 8.—Johnson Clark's statement, in *Reminiscences of Old John Brown,* G. W. Brown, M. D., p. 59, and following.

NOTE 9.—The second statement can be found in the *History of the State of Kansas,* A. T. Andreas, under head of " Franklin County." The last statement can be found in the *Reminiscences of Old John Brown,* G. W. Brown, M. D., p. 72, and following.

NOTE 10.—*John Brown and His Men,* Richard J. Hinton, p. 91. Colonel Hinton further says, on the same page:

"So much is certain. The men who were slain represented the worst elements arrayed in behalf of slavery, and engaged in harrying the Free-State settlers; the results of the deed were immediately and permanently beneficial, and the most of those who have since defamed and assailed the name and fame of John Brown under pretense of being shocked by the Pottawatomie tragedy, were conspicuous in earlier days in eulogizing the man they now assail. It is an act not to be judged by soft 'lutings of my lady's chamber,' or the usual conventionalities of peaceful periods. Those who are shocked always at the shedding of blood will shudder when reading the story. Those who comprehend that evolution includes cataclysm as well as continuity, will realize the nature of the forces in issue, and decide as their own conception of events and their righteousness may determine. Those who lived through those titanic days, and stood for freedom, will have no doubt in ranging themselves. For John Brown himself, no one who understands the conditions then existing will offer apology or excuse. The act done proved to be a potential one in the winning of free institutions for Kansas. And that is what they have to deal with. John Brown always declared that the people of Kansas would surely sustain and justify the deed done on the 24th of May, 1856. The marble statue erected in his honor at Osawatomie is in evidence of the faith that was in him. For himself, while never acknowledging participation in the Pottawatomie slaying, he never denied it either. He always declared, however, that, as he avowed a belief in its righteousness, he could not, therefore, avoid a personal responsibility for the deed. This has been the attitude of every honorable Free-State man in Kansas. To avoid now would be cowardice indeed. Time has lifted the shadows, but it has not dulled the memory."

NOTE 11.—*Garnett Plaindealer.* Quoted by the *Lawrence Journal,* January 22, 1880. Files 920–B, 81, library State Historical Society, Topeka.

NOTE 12.—Quoted from *Life and Letters of John Brown,* F. B. Sanborn, p. 500.

NOTE 13.—*Life and Letters of John Brown,* F B. Sanborn, p. 171.

NOTE 14.—*Life and Letters of John Brown,* F. B. Sanborn, p. 280.

NOTE 15.—*Life and Letters of John Brown,* F. B. Sanborn, p. 281.

NOTE 16.—The inscription to John Brown is as follows:

THIS INSCRIPTION IS ALSO IN COMMEMORATION OF THE
HEROISM OF CAPTAIN JOHN BROWN, WHO COM-
MANDED AT THE BATTLE OF OSAWATOMIE,
AUGUST 30, 1856, WHO DIED AND CON-
QUERED AMERICAN SLAVERY AT
CHARLESTON, VIRGINIA,
DECEMBER 2, 1859.

NOTE 17.—In justice to Governor Robinson's memory I must say that he afterwards changed his opinion of the value of the services rendered Kansas and humanity by John Brown. He became the most bitter of all the defamers of Brown's memory. He attacked not only Brown, but all his family, and accused them of being liars for thirty years. He accused Brown of going to the gallows with a lie on his lips. He attributed all the sufferings borne by the Free-State people in Kansas in the summer of 1856 to Brown's raid on the Pottawatomie. He gave as his reason for this change the confession of Townsley. Now, as Townsley said that the slaying of those men on the Pottawatomie was a benefit to the Free-State cause, and to the settlers around Dutch Henry's Crossing, the position taken by Governor Robinson in relation to that part of Brown's work must have been caused by something else. It is very strange that Governor Robinson did not ascertain for more than twenty years that Brown's work on the Pottawatomie injured the Free-State cause. Townsley's statement may have been sufficient cause for him to change his estimate of Brown's humanity, of the justice or injustice of the motives governing Brown's actions; but it could not possibly furnish any pretext for a change of opinion as to whether or not his work on the Pottawatomie injured or did not injure the Free-State cause in Kansas. If it injured that cause the injury should have been apparent at once, and Governor Robinson, as the head of the Free-State movement, should have denounced it and Brown then and there. But he said for many years that Brown's work was beneficial to the Free-State cause, and when Brown left Kansas in September, 1856, he carried letters commending his work in Kansas, and these letters were from Governor Robinson. If Governor Robinson knew that Brown's work in Kansas had injured the Free-State cause, and knowing this, gave him letters saying that this work was beneficial, then he is as much to be condemned as is Brown; and if he gave such letters under such conditions, all that he says of Brown can justly be said of Robinson. Governor Robinson says he is convinced no violence was done on the Pottawatomie and none was contemplated. In this conclusion he ignores the statements of all the Free-State men living there at the time. This quiet and peaceful condition of the Pottawatomie, which existed only in Robinson's mind, is assigned as a reason for his change.

But the truth of the matter is that John Brown's work in Kansas was of as much or even more benefit to the Free-State cause than that of any other single individual who fought for freedom here. John Brown did not save Kansas any more than Eli Thayer, or Charles Robinson, or James H. Lane, or any one of the very great number of others who saved it. But like the distinguished men named, he did his duty here, and did *all* his duty; he did not agree with any of the men named in the policy to be pursued; he was in advance of them, and in advance of the men of his generation. He was the pioneer in whose broad and well-marked trail-way the nation marched to a higher plane of liberty a few years later. Governor Robinson was right when he said the soul of John Brown was the inspiration of the armies of the North fighting to save the Union; and his soul is now the inspiration of all the oppressed of Europe struggling for some share of their liberty.

If Governor Robinson came to honestly believe that John Brown was a wicked man and a murderer, and that he was a great detriment to the cause he was trying to forward, then it was his duty to change his opinion of him and his work. He says this is the case. He assigns his reasons for the change, and gives his causes. They were no doubt sufficient to satisfy and convince Governor Robinson. But a later generation will claim for itself the right to examine these same causes, and determine whether the verdict rendered by Governor Robinson was just or unjust. And a later generation will decide for itself whether Governor Robinson was right for the first twenty-one years after the work of Brown and wrong in his estimate after that period, or *vice versa*.

It has been the condition here in Kansas for twenty years, that if any writer said anything in favor of John Brown or General Lane he was immediately attacked by the friends of Governor Robinson. Or if Governor Robinson's acts were criticized the writer was immediately accused of not appreciating the services of the great first Governor. And the same conditions have existed in regard to other men—Montgomery, and many others. Their friends forget that these men, one and all, were in the service of the people. They forget that the acts of these men are a proper subject for criticism and comment. There was great rivalry between the politicians for the highest place. They became bitter personal enemies, and had followers and partisans as bitter as themselves. Every weakness of each was mercilessly exposed. The intense feeling then engendered has existed to this time, but, happily, it is now passing rapidly away. The old quarrels and feuds between leaders interest us no more except as they enable us to get at the truth of motive and action. We see in all these men champions of freedom who fought and sacrificed and died for our liberties. They are all immortal, and with their hates, grudges, feuds, political aspirations, party affilia-tions, disappointments or successes in seeking office, we have nothing to do unless these help us in some way to get at a right understand-ing of facts vital to the history of Kansas.

NOTE 18.—*Topeka Commonwealth*, Saturday, February 16, 1884.

NOTE 19.—*Topeka Commonwealth*, Saturday, February 16, 1884.

NOTE 20.—This statement is a clipping from the *Leavenworth Weekly Press*, of which Clarke and Legate were publishers at the time. The clipping is in the files of the newspaper clippings concerning John Brown, in the library of the State Historical Society, but only "December 11," is there preserved as the date. It was probably in 1879, and as the files of the paper are preserved in the library of the Society the date can be ascertained.

NOTE 21.—*Memorial of S. N. Wood*, Mrs. Margaret L. Wood, p. 41.

NOTE 22.—*Life and Letters of John Brown*, F. B. Sanborn, p. 280.

NOTE 23.—*Life and Letters of John Brown*, F. B. Sanborn, p. 266.

NOTE 24.—*Life and Letters of John Brown*, F. B. Sanborn, p. 280.

NOTE 25.—Documents relating to John Brown, in library of the State Historical Society, Topeka.

NOTE 26.—*Life and Letters of John Brown*, F. B. Sanborn, p. 266.

NOTE 27.—In *Lippincott's Magazine*, January, 1883.

NOTE 28.—*Life and Letters of John Brown*, F. B. Sanborn, pp. 255-6.

NOTE 29.—*Life and Letters of John Brown*, F. B. Sanborn, p. 331.

NOTE 30.—In *Lippincott's Magazine*, January, 1883.

CHAPTER IX.

THE BATTLE OF BLACK JACK.

Thankless, too, for peace,
Secure from actual warfare, we have loved
To swell the warwhoop, passionate for war!
Alas! for ages ignorant of all
Its ghastlier workings, (famine or blue plague,
Battle, or siege, or flight through wintry snows,)
We, this whole people, have been clamorous
For war and bloodshed. —*Coleridge.*

John Brown and the company who were with him on the Pottawatomie returned with the "Pottawatomie Rifles" after they had disbanded in the camp at the house of Ottawa Jones. The eight men remained together, and at the crossing of Middle creek they separated from the main body of returning soldiers and went to the cabin of John Brown, jr., which was deserted and solitary, the family having been driven away by the Doyles and others. They remained here one night, and with guard set; the following night they went to the cabin of Jason Brown, which was also deserted and lonely. Here they remained a few days, and maintained a guard all the time; and were joined by August Bondi and another, believed by Townsley to have been Benjamin L. Cochran. They were ready to go to the assistance of any Free-State family or community. They were poorly armed; Captain Brown had a sword and a heavy revolver. His sons were armed with

(252)

revolvers, the heavy swords that had done such fearful execution on the Pottawatomie, and old obsolete rifles of
small bore.[1]   Townsley bore an old musket, Weiner a
"double-barreled" gun, and Bondi an old-fashioned flint-
lock musket.

John Brown, jr., and Jason Brown went to the residence
of their uncle, the Rev. S. L. Adair, where they found their
families, on their return from the expedition to aid Lawrence.   But as they did not want to subject Mr. Adair to
danger on their account, they determined to go to some
camp of United States troops and surrender themselves.
This conclusion was reached after they were informed
that a posse was seeking them with warrants for conspiracy against the bogus laws or for treason.   There was
a command of United States troops at the house of Ottawa
Jones, and Jason set out to reach it and deliver himself
up.   He was on foot, and in crossing the prairies he met
a company of Pro-Slavery men under command of Rev.
Martin White; here he expected to be killed.   He marched
backward in the road for some distance, all the time with
his bosom bared and avowing that he was an abolitionist.
The ruffians were slowly advancing upon him, and finally
told him that he would not then be killed.   He was carried
to Paola, where Judge Cato had been located for some time,
intending to hold a term of court.   The charge against him
was conspiracy, and he narrowly escaped lynching.   He
was imprisoned and well guarded, but as the town was full
of Buford's men and Pro-Slavery Missourians, he expected
to be killed, and had been driven by their brutality to the
verge of despair, and cared little whether he was murdered
or not.   John Brown, jr., was taken by Captain Pate and

the United States Marshal, at the house of his uncle, on the 28th of May, and was also taken to Paola.

John Brown, hearing that his sons were captured and in Paola, sent his relative, Horace Day, a mere boy, with a note to the people of Paola, which said simply that he was aware that two of his sons were held there as prisoners. This brief note threw the town into consternation. Midnight alarms were frequent thereafter, and the prisoners were shifted about from place to place in order that they might not be rescued; and in these uneasy and troubled perambulations the prisoners were left sometimes to care for themselves while the invincible guards betook themselves to the brush until the danger from "Old Brown" was past. There were times, too, when the ruffians crowded about with uplifted knives to slay them.[2] John Brown, jr., had been spending the nights in the woods, deeply anxious for the safety of his family. His uncle says he was suffering from a temporary insanity while at his house. When it was determined to remove the prisoners to Lecompton, Captain Walker bound the arms of John Brown, jr., so tightly that he was in great pain; he was made to trot before the horses in the hot sun for nine miles. The bonds were not removed for twenty-seven hours; all circulation of the blood was stopped and his arms were fearfully swollen; when the chains were taken off the skin clung to them, and the marks so made remained with him to the grave. He was a maniac for some days; he was seized with a dangerous illness and his life was despaired of for a time, but he finally recovered.[3]

The settlers of Prairie City were threatened by the ruffians in that vicinity. They sent O. A. Carpenter to

THE BATTLE OF BLACK JACK

search out John Brown and request him to come to their protection; and such a message was never sent to John Brown in vain. He agreed to go, and at dusk set out for the troubled district, which he reached on the morning of May 27th; he went into camp in a deep wood, where he could be reached with great difficulty by an enemy and with considerable trouble by his friends.[4] He devoted his time to searching for the marauders, but they were wary and not easily found. A large camp of Buford's men were stationed at the house of one La Hay, on the Wakarusa, and spent their time between their camp and the house of Colonel Titus and a Mr. Clark; they were preying upon the Free-State settlers, and it was evident that they would join any band of Missourians who might invade the settlement. The settlers kept a close watch upon these precious rogues, and more than once came into collision with them as they were prowling about for plunder and bent on murder in the interest of slavery.

H. Clay Pate was a Virginian.[5] He seems to have been a man of some education; he was a graduate of some college, and, like many wiser men, supposed that the world was breathlessly waiting for his graduation in expectation that he would at once give it a thorough overhauling, and remedy all its ills, and especially the ills that slavery was falling into from the scoundrels in the North who called themselves abolitionists. In his peregrinations toward the setting sun he stopped a season in Cincinnati. Here he published a book of reminiscences, which the world treated with much indifference; he also entered journalism, where he had some pecuniary success. But as slavery cried out for champions beyond Missouri he chafed under restraint, and finally breaking through hindrances and subordinate alliances he continued his perambulations, and halted on the border of Kansas Territory. He seized upon Westport, and there devoted himself to journalism and war. He raised a company of ruffians, almost all Missourians, and had himself elected Captain. This company was mustered in as "Shannon's Sharp-Shooters." As they were poor marksmen, it is supposed that the word "sharp" in their official designation was meant to indicate that they were "men of intelligence who could shoot," or that it might indicate that "they could shoot men of intelligence"; but on this point there is much doubt, and we are left altogether to the resources of conjecture.* This company was made a part of the Kansas militia, under some authority of the bogus laws. Pate had it at the sacking of Lawrence, where he distinguished himself by riding rapidly about upon a horse decked in trappings such as might delight an Indian warrior; there were ribbons attached to mane and tail, and the wind carried them out as gay streamers. He was jealous of the unsavory reputation of the Kickapoo Rangers, and strove to do some service to the cause dear to the ruffian heart which would place him upon the same footing enjoyed by that band of cut-throats.[6] After the town of Lawrence was sacked he tarried in the Territory, and was in no hurry to return to Missouri. His headquarters were at Lecompton, but he remained here but a short time. Phillips says he burned the house and store of Weiner, in the Pottawatomie settlements. If this be true he must have gone directly from Lawrence to the vicinity of Dutch Henry's Crossing. Sanborn says that he re-

* This is General Jo. O. Shelby's characterization of this band.

mained at Lecompton until the 25th, when, hearing of the
killing of the Doyles and others, he resolved to capture
John Brown. The fact that the *Lecompton Union* announced his departure, but made no reference to his desire
to capture Brown, but gave as his mission that explanation
furnished by his lieutenant, one Brockett, "We are going
down to the southern part of the Territory expecting to see
rattlesnakes and abolitionists, and shall take our guns
along," makes it probable that Pate departed before the
25th, and before the raid on the Pottawatomie by John
Brown. He pretended to be a deputy United States Marshal, and may have been one in fact. He was at Paola
when the sons of John Brown arrived as prisoners, and indeed captured John Brown, jr., at the house of Mr. Adair.
He took to the prairies, declaring that he would capture
Old John Brown, and the robberies he committed upon
Free-State men in this mission caused the men of the
Prairie City region to seek the aid of Brown.

Pate and his company left the United States troops on
Middle Ottawa creek on Saturday, the 31st day of May,
and marched to the Santa Fé road, near Hickory Point,
in Douglas county. That night he camped on the prairie
near the ravines which formed a small stream called
Black Jack, from the abundance of scrub-oak of that
name which grew about it. He was much discouraged
that he had not found John Brown, and began to fear
that he might not be able to find him at all. But not to
entirely fail in their objects, they went, as soon as it was
dark, to Palmyra, which town they attacked and plundered. They took some Free-State men prisoners, and one
of these being a preacher, he was outrageously treated.

—17

A funnel was placed in his mouth and through it a bountiful supply of ruffian whisky was poured down his throat.
The predatory expedition to Palmyra on Saturday night
was not satisfactory, and it was renewed on Sunday morning. They brought a wagon, which they filled with the
goods of the village storekeeper, after destroying much
that they could not carry away. This only whetted their
appetites. In the afternoon they expressed their intention
to go to the little town of Prairie City and pillage it.
It is said that Pate tried to dissuade them, but was unsuccessful; six of them rode away to accomplish this object. The people had gathered to hear the Gospel
preached, among them some twenty men; and in true
Western-frontier fashion, they had carried with them
their guns, for the minister had been captured the previous night and released. They mistrusted that it might
devolve upon them to do battle against the visible as well
as the invisible powers of darkness and allies of the devil,
and their guns were always in ready reach. Services were
almost closed when the guard rushed in and cried:

" The Missourians—the Missourians are coming! "

The congregation immediately dispersed and surrounded
the four ruffians who came in first; the two who were following at a little distance in the rear, seeing how the
matter was likely to turn out, wheeled their horses and galloped away and escaped, though they were fired at.[7]

As soon as Captain Shore was informed of the presence
of the enemy he began to collect his men. Captain Brown
was notified that the invaders were in the vicinity in force;
he and Captain Shore spent Sunday looking for their
camp, which was concealed in the clumps of bushes grow-

ing in the ravines. They returned to Prairie City at daylight on Monday morning, and there met two scouts who
had just returned from the head of Black Jack, and who
gave them information which enabled them to find Pate's
camp.[8] Captain Shore had collected nineteen of his company, and Captain Brown had nine men. The Free-
State forces numbered thirty men. Captains Shore and
Brown led these forces against the camp of Pate. It was
well chosen for defense, and had a breastwork of wagons
in front; in the rear it was protected by a deep ravine in
which grew timber, and beyond this was a quagmire filled
with high grass and swamp-bushes. Captain Brown led
his men up to the head of the ravine, and directed Captain Shore to get into the lower part of the ravine where
his men would have protection, and from which both
parties could fire at Pate while they were out of range
of the guns of each other. Captain Brown gained his
position, but Captain Shore was not so successful. Being
challenged by Pate, he formed his men on the prairie and
delivered a volley, which was returned at once by the
Missourians. The fight continued some ten minutes, when
Pate retreated from his breastwork of wagons to the ravine. He was here protected from the fire of Captain
Shore, whose position became untenable. His men retreated some distance up the hill, where they were out of
range. Captain Shore then went to the line of Brown,
where he remained through much of the action, and some
of his men went with him. Brown's position was a good
one, and several of the Missourians were wounded. Ammunition was low in the Free-State ranks, and some men
were sent away to secure more. Runners were sent, among

them Captain Shore, to Captain J. B. Abbott, to request him to bring his men and help in the work of defeating Pate.[9]

After the firing had continued about three hours, Captain Brown directed some of his men to shoot at the horses belonging to Pate's forces. He went to Shore's men and had them do the same. The Missourians began to slip down the ravine until they were out of range, and then make a dash for their horses; they would mount, one by one, and gallop away. Frederick Brown mounted his horse and galloped around the camp, shouting to imaginary reinforcements to hurry up. Captain Pate saw no hope of being able to escape, and sent out a flag of truce. Captain Brown inquired of the bearer if he was the Captain of the company, and when assured that he was not, ordered a Mr. Lymer, a Free-State prisoner who had been sent with the flag of truce, to return and call the commander.

It is said that a Mr. James carried the flag of truce; and some claim that it was Lieutenant Brockett. Whoever the man, he remained with Captain Brown while Mr. Lymer returned for Captain Pate, who, now that his flag of truce served no better purpose than to summon him to face a grim and relentless foe in conference, reluctantly and with misgivings as to the result, came forth. Upon being asked whether he had a proposition to make, he hesitated, and said he believed he had not. Captain Brown cut into his explanation that he was a Deputy United States Marshal, and said he wanted to hear no more about that. " I know *exactly* what you are, sir. I have a proposition to make to you—that is, *your unconditional surrender.*"

As Captain Brown held a large revolver in close proximity to Pate's head, there was little to be expected from duplicity.[10] Brown ordered his men to go to the mouth of the ravine to prevent the escape of the Missourians, while he went to their camp with their Captain. Brockett objected to surrender, and talked defiantly, but Brown demanded of Pate that he order Brockett and his men to lay down their arms and surrender, and as the large revolver was thrust a little nearer, Pate ordered them to comply. This they did. Twenty-two Pro-Slavery men surrendered to nine Free-State men. The losses of Captain Pate were as follows: twenty-one surrendered; wounded and escaped, twenty-seven. Perhaps others escaped before the battle closed; all the wounded except two escaped. The Free-State men captured a large quantity of arms and ammunition, and recovered much property the marauders had stolen from the settlers; some of the plunder taken from Lawrence when it was sacked was recovered. The four wagons were fairly well loaded with provisions.[11] In his account of the battle, written for the *Missouri Republican,* Pate said: " I was taken prisoner under a flag of truce. I had no alternative but to submit or to run and be shot. I went to take old Brown and old Brown took me."

The arms of the Missourians were taken from them, and they were marched to John Brown's camp. Just as the file of captives were starting under guard, Captain Abbott came up with reinforcements, some fifty men. So Captain Pate could not have escaped had he even known that John Brown and his men had remaining but one round of ammunition when the demand for the surrender was made.[12] Pate and his command were marched to Brown's camp on Middle Ottawa creek, where they were kept as prisoners. An agreement was here made between Captains' Brown and Shore and Pate and Brockett that prisoners should be exchanged. John Brown, jr., and Jason Brown, who were yet in the camp of the United States dragoons near the house of Ottawa Jones, were to be given up for the release of Pate and Brockett; and other prisoners were to be exchanged on equal terms.[13]

In the Territorial days of Kansas it was always the duty of the Governor to aid the ruffian forces in every conceivable way, and this duty was generally cheerfully performed. No sooner had Governor Shannon been informed that Pate had not only failed to capture John Brown but had been himself captured, than he issued a proclamation ordering all armed bands to disperse and retire to their homes. Colonel Sumner was directed to go to the vicinity of the late battle and release the "Shannon Sharp-Shooters" from the iron grip of Old John Brown. It was well known that had Pate been successful in his enterprise, no proclamation would have been issued. This proclamation was not issued until after the Pro-Slavery men had been attacked at Franklin, on the night of June 4th, although it was dated the same day. Colonel Sumner was ordered to defend Franklin and the house of a Pro-Slavery man who sheltered a company of Buford's men. But the attack frightened the ruffians and Franklin was not continued as one of their bases, and not so used for some time.

When the news of the capture of Pate reached Missouri, Whitfield left Westport in haste, on the evening of the 2d of June, to succor and relieve that worthy. He had three

companies of Missourians under him, each numbering
seventy men, all well equipped and armed. He was accompanied by "General" Reid, who was a candidate for
Congress in some Missouri district. They went into camp
on Bull creek, some twelve miles east of Palmyra. Other
Pro-Slavery parties gathered, and some of them camped
on the same field made gory by the heroism of Captain
Pate! On the 5th of June Colonel Sumner went to John
Brown's camp and released Pate and his men, and restored
to them their arms and horses. He prevailed upon Captain Brown and Captain Shore to disband their forces;
this he accomplished by assuring them that the forces
under Whitfield and Reid should return to Missouri at
once. This they agreed to do, and a part of their force did
so return; but by far the larger portion of the men had
not had any opportunity to steal from Free-State men, and
as plunder was always one of the strong inducements for
the invasion of Kansas, these men could not be so easily
turned back. They had murdered only one Free-State
man, and this was another reason why they could not be
induced to return; some town must be pillaged and more
than one "abolitionist" killed before they would feel warranted in returning from an expedition of which so much
was expected. Pate agreed to return to Missouri, but
failed to do so; and it is said that he and his men participated in the trial of Jacob Cantrel for "treason to Missouri," of which he was convicted and for which he was
shot. In all the orders to the Free-State men to disperse,
the United States troops warned them that they must
obey the bogus laws or leave the Territory. Indeed, this
was the cause of the invasions; resistance to the bogus

laws was the foundation upon which all the outrages committed upon the Free-State men by the Pro-Slavery Missourians in the summer of 1856 were built.

On the 6th of June Whitfield set out on his return to Missouri, but not until he had seen Pate, Reid, Jenigan and Bell start to Osawatomie with one hundred and seventy men. The Free-State forces having been disbanded, there could be no effective resistance at Osawatomie. The ruffians were led to the town by a spy who had been sent in the day before, and who pretended to be sick and had received good treatment. They pillaged dwellings and business houses alike. Trunks, drawers, boxes, desks and wardrobes were broken and ransacked. Rings were torn from the fingers of the women, as well as from their ears; clothing and even furniture were loaded on their horses to be carried away to Missouri. Whisky was seized and swallowed while the crusaders for slavery raged and threatened. Some of them tore the clothing from women and children, and an eminent writer of that time says that "they ought to have had a petticoat apiece as trophies." I close this chapter with a quotation from this writer: [14]

"Having got all the plunder they wanted, they were anxious to be off.

"'Hurry, hurry!' they said to each other. 'These d—d abolitionists are somewhere not far off, and will be down on us the first thing we know.' They accordingly retreated from the ill-fated town as rapidly and unmolested as they had entered it, carrying their booty with them.

"When they got to their camp the company divided. Half of them started immediately back for Westport, and the remainder moved off and camped on the lower part of Bull creek, some eight miles from Osawatomie. There they had an adventure.

"As might be expected, they kept a sharp lookout for abolitionists. Two days after sacking the city of Osawatomié, a couple of their own number had been on a scout, and on their return to camp, while near it, fired off their guns. The guard in that direction gave the alarm, fired his gun in the direction of the two men, and cried at the top of his lungs, ' The abolitionists are coming!—the abolitionists are coming!' Whereupon the whole camp got into a panic, and, without taking time to pack up their effects, started off at the run. There were some horses harnessed to wagons; these were hurriedly taken out, and off the whole party went in a helter-skelter race, outrivaling John Gilpin's. Once or twice one of their number would discharge a pistol or a gun behind him, as a warning to abolitionists to keep off, which had the effect of keeping up the fear of the retreating party.

" They never stopped till they got to Battiesville [Paola], an Indian station among the Weas. The Indian storekeeper, seeing a band of wild-looking fellows galloping up, with arms in their hands, and looking very terrible from fear and excitement, closed his door, and, in spite of all their entreaties, would not let them in.

" ' The abolitionists are coming!—we want to come in and defend the place!'

" The Indian happened to be a Pro-Slavery Indian, but he was moderately suspicious of the appearance of these ' law and order' men; so he grunted,

" 'Abolitionists, heap bad!—no come!'

" ' Yes, they *are* coming!' yelled a score of anxious voices. 'G—d blast ye! let us in! They'll be here in a minute!'

" 'Come in to-morrow, maybe,' was the cautious answer.

" Time was pressing. There were two or three unoccupied log houses close at hand; so they made a virtue of necessity and got into them. The chinking was driven out for portholes, and the doors barricaded; meanwhile two of the best-mounted were dispatched in hot haste to

Missouri,—one to Jackson, and the other to Cass county,—telling their friends to come up quick, for the abolitionists with great force were besieging them in Battiesville, and that they would endeavor to *hold out till they could come.*

"A party of men did start to the rescue, and more would have gone if these had not returned and reported it a hoax. This masterly retreat was a standing joke amongst the border ruffians in that quarter, who taunted their comrades about their 'holding out against the abolitionists.' " [15]

NOTE 1.—"The swords used were not sabers exactly, but weapons made like the Roman short-sword, of which six or eight had been given to Brown in Akron, Ohio, just before he went to Kansas, by General Bierce of that city, who took them from an old armory there. They had been the swords of an artillery company, then disbanded, which General Bierce had something to do with, and there were also some guns and old bayonets among these arms. The bayonets would not fit any guns the Kansas people had; and so in December, 1855, when the Browns went up to defend Lawrence for the first time, they fastened some of them on sticks, and intended to use them in defending breastworks. They were thrown loosely 'into the bed of the wagon,'—not set up about it for parade, as some have said. There were also some curved swords among these Akron arms."—*"Life and Letters of John Brown," F. B. Sanborn, p. 264, note.*

NOTE 2.—In the library of the State Historical Society, in the John Brown Collection, there is a long statement made by Jason Brown, April 2, 1884, to F. G. Adams, at that time Secretary of the Society. The statement was made in Topeka, and fully covers the captivity of Jason Brown and John Brown, jr., and is one of the very valuable papers in relation to this period of Kansas history, although there are some inaccuracies and minor errors in it, such as will always be found in a paper prepared exclusively from memory after the lapse of so great a time after the events described.

NOTE 3.—That John Brown, jr., was insane for some time, there is no question; perhaps he was partially insane before he was captured, but this was from the effects of anxiety for his family, loss of sleep, and exposure. This was a slight form of insanity or nervous derangement incident to the hardships to which he had been subjected. It was much aggravated by the brutal treatment he received at the hands of his captors. It did not entirely disappear for some time.

NOTE 4.—"Brown started at once, Saturday evening, April [May] 30, with about a dozen men, among whom was his son Salmon, now a resident of Salem, Ore., from whom this story was obtained, and who had already lost considerable sleep, so that he was not in good condition for an all-night march. He rode a skittish, ugly little mule, on which were piled all the blankets. Young Brown was unable to keep awake, so every time the mule gave a sudden start he rolled off.

"Just south of Toy [Ottawa] Jones's place was a lane, half a mile long, through which it was necessary to pass. With a view of capturing Brown and his party, 200 soldiers had camped in this lane. Suddenly Salmon Brown was awakened by his brother Fred, who was an exceptionally fine horseman, talking to a soldier, who said to him, 'Hold on, there, or you will get shot!' For a moment Fred continued to talk, then made a sudden dash through the camp-fire, followed by his party in single file. The movement was so sudden and unexpected that no one was shot. As soon as the camp was passed, Salmon Brown looked back, and saw the road crowded with suddenly awakened soldiers, who were yet unable to realize what had happened. Fatigue was such, however, that he soon fell asleep again and fell from his mule."—*W. G. Steel, in Portland Oregonian.*

NOTE 5.—"Pate, by birth a Virginian, first sought to find fame and fortune in the city of Cincinnati. He published 'a thin volume of collegiate sketches,' and 'several pointless, bombastically written stories,' which, we are told, 'was embellished with the author's portrait and autograph.' He failed to get readers or even favorable reviewers, although he sought to make genial critics by entering into sanctums 'armed with a cowhide and revolver.' Not even by his next effort, 'a large engraved portrait of himself,' could the hungerer after literary reputation find satisfaction.

"He then sought fame as a journalist, and again was preëminently unsuccessful. As a parasite of the Protestant demagogue, Gavazzi, he gained in pocket, but lost in caste; and what he earned in purse he again squandered in publication—in a new and equally fruitless effort to win a literary reputation without the intellect to found it on, or the moral character to dignify and support it. 'He had a signboard on his door, inscribed, H. Clay Pate, Author'; but as Heaven had not written this inscription on his forehead, the sign in due time disappeared, and 'the author' with it.

"He hurried to the borders to seek notoriety as a champion of the South. He determined at first to be distinguished with his pen; but, surpassed on every hand as a journalist and writer, he next sought the ever-flying phantom of fame with sword in hand, and on the tented field."—*"Life of Captain John Brown," James Redpath, p. 121.*

"Captain Pate, however, pretended to be an officer under Marshal Donaldson. Quite likely they belonged to the 'militia,' as they had the United States arms belonging to the Territory; but most of them, like their gallant captain, lived in Missouri. Captain Pate is a Virginian by birth. He is a good-looking fellow, and a man of intelligence. He has been engaged as an editor in Cincinnati, and has acted as the Kansas correspondent of the *Missouri Republican;* for which he provided Pro-Slavery versions of the occurrences in Kansas, he residing in western Missouri. He is a violent Pro-Slavery man, and has been engaged in the lawless inroads on the Territory ever since he has lived in the Missouri border. He was at the sacking of Lawrence, and distinguished himself chiefly by riding about on a fine horse, he being decorated with ribbons. It would be impossible to speak highly of the moral character of a man who has participated so actively in the outrages on an intelligent and moral people. He has the bearing of a gentleman, but is either the tool of a corrupt system, or is a very corrupt man."—*"The Conquest of Kansas," William A. Phillips, p. 331.*

There is some question as to whether it was Captain Pate or his horse that was decorated with ribbons. Phillips says it was Pate; some of the pioneers who saw him at the time say it was the horse; others say both horse and man. The ribbons were plundered from the Lawrence people, and the incident is of no importance, except to show the foppery and vanity of Captain Pate.

NOTE 6.—There were some Wyandot Indians in the company of

Captain Pate. They lived in what is now Wyandotte county. Irvin P. Long was with Pate at the battle of Black Jack. When the battle became desperate, Pate sent him to Missouri to summon Whitfield. Long was a brave man, and had served through the Mexican War; he was in the regiment commanded by the late Colonel W. P. Overton, of Kansas City, Kansas.

MacLean, the chief clerk in the office of the Surveyor-General, was also in this company. He borrowed a rifle from Matthew Mudeater, a Wyandot, and during the battle shot at John Brown three times with it. He declared that he took deliberate aim, but could not kill him. He knew the gun was a good one, for he had used it before. He was a good shot, and his failure made him believe that Brown was specially protected by God, and miraculously saved from death. This rifle was brought from Ohio by Jared Dawson, a Wyandot. When I was in the Indian Territory some years ago, I learned these facts from the Wyandot Indians. The gun still remained in the family of Mr. Mudeater, and his youngest son, Alfred Mudeater, Esq., gave it to me to present to the Wyandotte County Historical Society. As the Society had no suitable place to preserve the valuable relic, I left it in the care of Mrs. Lillian Walker Hale, the gifted writer, who is a Wyandot; she is to retain it until the Society has proper facilities for preserving it, when she is to turn it over to the secretary or president of the Society.

MacLean was one of the men who stole away, mounted his horse, and fled. His failure to kill John Brown discouraged him; he often spoke of this incident in the years that followed. It is not known whether he was then in the service of the Surveyor-General or not.

———

NOTE 7.—"The other men were merely taken prisoners of war. One of them, however, had come very near getting his quietus. A son of Dr. Graham, a boy of about eleven years, seized his father's double-barreled gun at the first alarm, and hurried out to the fence, the Missourians, who were thus all taken aback, being immediately outside of it. The daring boy, with his Irish blood up, went within three rods of them, and, poking his gun over the fence, took deliberate aim at one of the men, and would have fired the next moment,— for Bub was not enlightened in the mysterious 'articles of war,'— when a Free-State man put aside his gun, and said,

"'Bub, what are you doing?'

"'Going to shoot that fellow.'

" 'You mustn't.'

"Bub shook his head and began to put up his gun again, muttering,
" 'He's on pap's horse.'

"Bub remembered that his 'pap' was then a prisoner in the enemy's
camp, if not killed, and he felt that important interests were devolving on him, and must not be neglected. The names of three of the
men taken were Forman, Luck, and Hamilton."—*The Conquest of
Kansas," William A. Phillips, p. 366.*

NOTE 8.—"About 2 o'clock in the morning they reached a point,
probably half a mile from Palmyra, and camped. Sometime during
the night several of Pate's men raided the village, and left it terror-
stricken. When Brown arrived in the morning he found the people
shouting and praying to discount a camp-meeting. This disgusted
his son Salmon, who remembered that he and his party had made
a forced march in the night to defend these people, only to find
them a lot of cowards, who should stop praying and prepare for a
fight. About 10 o'clock six men were seen to come out of a ravine
and start for the village. Instantly the shouting ceased, and 'bang!
bang!' rang out from the houses, and young Brown concluded that
the people had quit shouting and had gone to shooting at an oppor-
tune time. Two men laid close to their horses' necks, put spurs and
got away, but Brown's sons, Salmon and Oliver, brought in the
other four, one of whom, an unusually large man, was said to be
very cruel. When he learned that Brown was on his way to inter-
cept Pate, he ridiculed the idea, and said 1,000 men could not dislodge
him. 'Well,' replied Brown, 'we will have the fun of trying.'

"Pate was camped about five miles from Palmyra, and Brown
knew the two men who escaped would warn him of an intended
attack. He knew, too, how thoroughly they were armed, drilled and
intrenched, but hoped to make a night attack. With that idea in
view, he left Palmyra late Sunday afternoon with thirty men, and
reached the neighborhood of Black Jack springs after dark. Not
being acquainted with the vicinity, he was unable to locate Pate, so
camped on the side of a ridge about half a mile from the springs.
Just at daylight one of Pate's sentinels fired on him from the top
of the ridge, and ran for camp, just beyond."—*W. G. Steel, in
Portland Oregonian.*

NOTE 9.—"Brown sent Captain Shore with fifteen men to a
piece of sloping ground, in full view of Pate, and about 150 yards

distant, while he ran with the remaining force to a point, partly
sheltered by high grass and a ridge, within seventy-five yards of
Pate's position in a ravine. Fred Brown was left in charge of the
horses and camp. Pate's men ran in all directions to get their horses
in safe quarters, and a deadly fire was poured in on them. A few
well-directed shots brought them to their senses, and sent them to
the ravine. Brown had them under a cross-fire, and used his advantage. Salmon Brown says of it: 'Alongside of me laid a man by
the name of Carpenter, who would imitate the sound of bullets as
they passed over his head, then shout to Pate's men to do better
shooting. They took his advice, for every moment they came a
little closer. By-and-by Carpenter's right shoulder was exposed,
when loading his gun, and a bullet struck it. We would load our
guns lying down, rise above the grass to fire, then fall to the ground
again. Now and then a man would rush from the ravine to his horse,
and make a break for Missouri. Our own men continued to find
more attractive spots elsewhere, until, at noon, there were but seven
of us left. Before noon Fred became restless, mounted a horse, and
rode back and forth on the ridge, flourishing his saber, until Pate's
men, who were unable to hit him, imagined that he held reserves.
Father finally gave orders to open fire on Pate's horses, which we
did, killing all of them in just about a minute. This seemed to
bring Pate to his senses, and to thoroughly discourage his men, who
realized that their means of retreat to Missouri were cut off. Immediately afterwards we saw a man coming out of a ravine frantically
waving a white flag on a ramrod. He proved to be an Englishman
and a friend of ours whom Pate had captured. Father refused to
receive his message, but told him to go back and send the captain
himself. Pate came at once, and commenced to explain that he was
there to enforce Territorial laws. Father cut him short with the
expression, "If that is all you have to say, I want an unconditional
surrender, and I'll have it." Turning to us he said, "Boys, you go
round to the mouth of the ravine and I will go back with Captain
Pate." We took a circuitous route, and ran to the ravine as rapidly
as possible, arriving about as soon as father and Pate. We found
Lieutenant Brockett, a Virginian, weighing about 180 pounds, in
charge. He was a regular tiger. He had his men in the form of a
crescent, with only their heads and shoulders in view, and guns
drawn on us. Our seven guns were leveled on them at once, with
the muzzles of the two sides about six or eight feet apart.

" 'Father said to Brockett, "Tell your men to lay down their arms."
Father looked savage enough, and so did Brockett, who replied, "If
our captain says so I'll do it, but not by your d—n orders; and I
don't believe he is d—d coward enough to do it." With that he
ordered his men to take aim at us. Just at this point my brother
Oliver, a tall, stout lad of 17, shouted, "Boys, there's a rifle I'm going
to have," referring to the magnificent one held by Brockett. I
touched him with my elbow and said, in an undertone, "You had
better wait until you get it." The instant Brockett gave the order
to take aim on us, Pate said to his men, "Well, boys, lay down your
guns a minute until we talk it over." Brockett swore like a pirate
when the order was given, but his men laid down their arms, keeping their hands on them, however. Brockett held on to his gun, and,
as Oliver took hold of it, showed signs of resistance, until I placed
my six-shooter at his head and said slowly and quietly, "Let go;
let go," which he did very reluctantly. He resisted in the same
manner when his sword was taken. This sword is the one exhibited
at the World's Fair by H. N. Rust, of Pasadena, Cal. It was the
work of only an instant until their guns were stacked and we had
absolute possession. They seemed to have no idea of our audacity.
The moment our possession seemed complete we were startled to see
a long line of horsemen coming towards us at full gallop and horses
covered with foam. It looked pretty scaly for a time, but, as we
prepared for a second attack, we were delighted to discover that
they were friends. Early in the morning Captain Abbott heard the
firing, knew that a fight was under way, and started out to secure
help. About noon he returned with 100 men, but the fight was
over. . . . In casting up our accounts we found we had three
men shot, nineteen deserted, one detailed to guard camp, and seven
at the surrender, as follows: Captain John Brown, Owen Brown,
Oliver Brown, Salmon Brown, Charles Keiser, a Mr. Bondi, and a
Mr. Hill. Pate had seventeen shot, thirteen deserted, and thirty-
two captured. During the fight I noticed a puff of smoke issue from
a tent, now and then, and I fired into it several times without effect.
Afterwards I learned that a ministerial friend of ours had been captured, securely bound and laid at right angles to us, on the inside
of the tent. A hole was cut in the tent just above him, while behind
him lay one of Pate's men, shooting at us from this improvised
breastworks.' "—*W. G. Steel, in Portland Oregonian.*

This is an interview with Salmon Brown, who lived at that time
in Salem, Oregon.

NOTE 10.—"As they drew near the line, where Pate's Lieutenant Brockett was in command, Brown called upon him also to surrender. He hesitated, seeing the great apparent superiority of his force over Brown's. Quick as thought, Brown placed his pistol at Pate's head, and cried in a terrible voice, 'Give the order!' The Virginian yielded, and bade his men lay down their arms, which they sullenly did."—*"Life and Letters of John Brown," F. B. Sanborn, p. 300.*

NOTE 11.—John Brown's account of the battle is as follows:

"We were out all night, but could find nothing of them until about six o'clock next morning, when we prepared to attack them at once, leaving Frederick and one of Captain Shore's men to guard the horses. As I was much older than Captain Shore, the principal direction of the fight devolved on me. We got to within about a mile of their camp before being discovered by their scouts, and then moved at a brisk pace, Captain Shore and men forming our left and my company the right. When within about sixty rods of the enemy, Captain Shore's men halted by mistake in a very exposed situation, and continued to fire, both his men and the enemy being armed with Sharps' rifles. My company had no long-shooters. We (my company) did not fire a gun until we gained the rear of a bank, about fifteen or twenty rods to the right of the enemy, where we commenced, and soon compelled them to hide in a ravine. Captain Shore, after getting one man wounded, and exhausting his ammunition, came with part of his men to the right of my position, much discouraged. The balance of his men, including the one wounded, had left the ground. Five of Captain Shore's men came boldly down and joined my company, and all but one man (wounded) helped to maintain the fight until it was over. I was obliged to give my consent that he should go after more help, when all his men left but eight, four of whom I persuaded to remain in a secure position, and there busied one of them in shooting the horses and mules of the enemy, which served for a show of fight. After the firing had continued for some two or three hours, Captain Pate with twenty-three men, two badly wounded, laid down their arms to nine men, myself included,—four of Captain Shore's men and four of my own. One of my men (Henry Thompson) was badly wounded, and after continuing his firing for an hour longer was obliged to quit the ground. Three others of my company (but none of my family) had gone off. Salmon was dreadfully wounded by accident, soon after the fight.

—18

"I ought to have said that Captain Shore and his men stood their ground nobly in their unfortunate but mistaken position during the early part of the fight. I ought to say further, that a Captain Abbott, being some miles distant with a company, came onward promptly to sustain us, but could not reach us till the fight was over."—*Letter of John Brown to his family, in "Life and Letters of John Brown," F. B. Sanborn, pp. 238, 239.*

NOTE 12.—Governor Robinson, in an attempt to belittle Brown and his services at Black Jack, misstates facts. He says:

"Pate's company was encountered at Black Jack on the 2d of June by about thirty Free-State men, and, after exchanging shots several hours from the ravines and tall grass, Pate, seeing Captain Abbott with his company approaching to reinforce the Free-State men, surrendered. No serious harm was done."—*"The Kansas Conflict," Charles Robinson, p. 294.*

He does not even mention that Captains Brown and Shore were present! He attributes the surrender of Pate to the approach of Captain Abbott! All the evidence says that Captain Abbott arrived after the battle was over and the surrender of Pate and his men had taken place. Townsley, whom Governor Robinson loved to quote (in part), says:

"In the afternoon, after we camped in the woods near Captain Shore's, we moved up to Prairie City. We picketed our horses and laid down not over one hundred yards from the store. About the middle of the afternoon six of Pate's men came riding into town, four of whom we captured and held as prisoners. During the afternoon Captain Shore raised a company of about thirty men, and in the evening we started in pursuit of Pate. The next morning before daylight we obtained information that he was camped at Black Jack point, and we moved forward with about twenty-four men to attack him. When within a mile of Pate's forces we all dismounted, left seven men in charge of the horses, and, with seventeen men, made the attack. In about fifteen minutes we drove them into the ravine. The fight continued about three hours, when Pate surrendered. About the time we got the captured arms loaded into the wagons ready to move, Major Abbott's company came up."

No one but Governor Robinson has ever attributed the surrender of Pate to the approach of Captain Abbott. All the old authorities agree on this point. What a pity that Governor Robinson should mar a valuable historical work to gratify his grudges and hates toward the men who labored with him to make Kansas free!

Townsley mentions nothing of any help in the capture of the

four of Pate's party on Sunday, but says they were captured by Brown's men. I followed Colonel Phillips, in his *The Conquest of Kansas*. There is a conflict in the evidence, and as the incident was unimportant when considered as to *who* captured them, I did not make an exhaustive search for authorities. Mr. Steel, before quoted, would seem to agree with Townsley.

———

NOTE 13.—This agreement was signed in duplicate. It is in the handwriting of Lieutenant Brockett. Both the original and duplicate copies are in the library of the State Historical Society. A copy of it may be found in *The Life and Letters of John Brown*, F. B. Sanborn, p. 240, note. There is some reference to it in a note on page 300 of Mr. Sanborn's work.

John Brown made a report of this battle to the authorities at Lawrence, and the original of this report, in Brown's handwriting, is in the Library of the State Historical Society. There is much there also, in addition. The old and reliable first works on Kansas affairs, the authorities upon whom all historians must to a great degree depend, have much concerning the battle of Black Jack. There is much also in Mr. Sanborn's book that we have no space to even mention.

———

NOTE 14.—"In their investigations they entered the house where the press was, but happening to fall in with a case of excellent brandy and some wine, they proceeded to help themselves pretty freely to these 'anti-abolition' articles. After drinking freely, they concluded that no 'abolition' press could be in a place where there was so good brandy. In fact, that is one way the border ruffians have of judging whether a man is 'sound on the goose.' A person who does not drink is voted an 'abolitionist' at once, without further testimony; and the presence of liquor, especially good liquor and an abundance of it, is considered as a sure symptom, infallibly tending to 'law and order.' "—*"The Conquest of Kansas," William A. Phillips, p. 374.*

———

NOTE 15.—*The Conquest of Kansas*, William A. Phillips, pp. 375, 376. See also the same work, page 368, for the authority for the statement that United States troops demanded submission to the bogus laws.

CHAPTER X.

WOODSON'S WAR OF EXTERMINATION—1856.

Bethink thee, Gordon,
Our death-feud was not like the household fire,
Which the poor peasant hides among its embers,
To smoulder on, and wait a time for waking.
Ours was the conflagration of the forest,
Which, in its fury, spares nor sprout nor stem,
Hoar oak, nor sapling—not to be extinguished,
Till Heaven, in mercy, sends down all her waters;
But, once subdued, its flame is quench'd forever;
And spring shall hide the track of devastation,
With foliage and with flowers.
—*Sir Walter Scott.*

Some of the emigrant aid societies were founded upon the old colonization principle, that money should be made in the settlement of a new country. This was not the only object of those corporations, but was one of the paramount considerations. Not a few New England people refused to come to Kansas under their auspices when the plans to obtain town lots and other property were made known; they chose rather to endure greater sacrifices, and carry to Kansas the true spirit of liberty, which required no hope of pecuniary reward, but was moved by right conscience. These people came to fight for the liberties they enjoyed at home; with them property interests were subordinated. If Kansas could not be a free State, property in her bounds would be to them of little value, for they could not re-

(276)

main to foster and to care for it. These people believed in
defending their lives with weapons; they supposed that
all law sanctioned defense of wives and babes when the
blood-stained fangs of wolfish barbarians gnashed at the
doors of their dwellings. They were not moved to compro-
mises and subterfuges in the interest of property. They
expected no dividends except those paid by an approving
conscience; they believed that when Kansas was once
free, with slavery blotted from the books of all America,
industrial and intellectual development such as the world
had not before witnessed would follow. They did not
want Kansas a free State with the South, or even what
is now Colorado and all the West and Northwest, slave
States. They believed that Kansas was the field on which
the question of slavery should be settled—settled finally
and forever. And they were right.*

The battle of Black Jack, while insignificant in itself,
was important in this respect,—it was the first field in
the Kansas struggle where the free men cast aside the tram-
mels of property interests and marched out to make war
upon any and all who came to fight for the establishment
or maintenance of the institution of slavery. Men have
only been great as they placed all upon the altar and staked

* "Mr. Thayer's plan was an epitome of Yankee characteristics — thrift, and devotion to principle. He did not propose to win Kansas with hirelings, but to show the
natural aggressiveness of the Yankee an outlet for his energy at once honorable and
profitable. And thus, also, the company he proposed was not to be a charitable labor
entirely, as religious missionary societies mostly are; but he asked, Why is it worse
for a company to make money by extending Christianity, or suppressing slavery, than
by making cotton cloth? The company which he planned was intended to be an investment company, giving and taking advantages with those whom it induced to go to
Kansas, *and incidentally crippling slavery*. . . . While the Aid Company must be
credited for something of the high tone of the New England emigrants, it is a common
error to suppose that these emigrants came to Kansas expecting to win martyrs'
crowns. I have questioned many of them as to their motives, and the uniform answer
has been: 'We went to Kansas to better our condition, *incidentally expecting to make
it a free State*. We knew we took some risks; but if we had foreseen the struggles and
hardships we actually underwent, we never should have gone.'"—*William H. Carruth's*
"*The New England Emigrant Aid Company as an Investment Society*," *in The Kansas
Historical Collection, Vol. VI, p. 90.*

their very lives in the hazard. If anything at all is reserved, it is as fatal to noble purpose as was the hiding of a portion to Ananias and Sapphira. Peoples have been great only as they had a strong faith in God and were actuated by a deep and single motive to live and act up to the highest conceptions of His law. All history teaches this—in fact, it teaches only this. " In this God's-world, with its wild-whirling eddies and mad foam-oceans, where men and nations perish as if without law, and judgment for an unjust thing is sternly delayed, dost thou think there is therefore no justice? It is what the fool hath said in his heart. It is what the wise, in all times, were wise because they denied, and knew forever not to be. I tell thee again, there is nothing else but justice. One strong thing I find here below: the just thing, the true thing. My friend, if thou hadst all the artillery of Woolwich trundling at thy back in support of an unjust thing; and infinite bonfires visibly waiting ahead of thee, to blaze centuries long for thy victory on behalf of it,—I would advise thee to call halt, and fling down thy baton, and say, 'In God's name, No!' Thy 'success'? Poor devil, what will thy success amount to? If the thing is unjust, thou hast not succeeded; no, not though bonfires blazed from North to South, and bells rang, and editors wrote leading articles, and the just thing lay trampled out of sight, to all mortal eyes an abolished and annihilated thing. Success? In a few years thou wilt be dead and dark,—all cold, eyeless, deaf; no blaze of bonfires, ding-dong of bells or leading articles visible or audible to thee again at all forever: What kind of success is that!—It is true, all goes by

approximation in this world; with any not insupportable
approximation we must be patient. There is a noble Conservatism as well as an ignoble. Would to Heaven, for
the sake of Conservatism itself, the noble alone were left,
and the ignoble, by some kind severe hand, were ruthlessly
lopped away, forbidden evermore to show itself! For it
is the right and noble alone that will have victory in this
struggle; the rest is wholly an obstruction, a postponement
and fearful imperilment of the victory. Towards an
eternal centre of right and nobleness, and of that only, is
all this confusion tending. We already know whither
it is all tending; what will have the victory, and what
will have none! The Heaviest will reach the center. The
Heaviest, sinking through complex fluctuating media and
vortices, has its deflections, its obstructions, nay, at times
its resiliences, its reboundings; whereupon some block-
head shall be heard jubilating, ' See, your Heaviest as-
cends!'—but at all moments it is moving centreward,
fast as is convenient for it; sinking, sinking; and, by
laws older than the World, old as the Maker's first Plan of
the World, it has to arrive there. The *dust* of controversy,
what is it but the *falsehood* flying off from all manner of
conflicting true forces, and making such a loud dust-whirl-
wind,—that so the truths alone may remain, and embrace
brother-like in some true resulting force! It is ever so.
Savage fighting Heptarchies: their fighting is an ascer-
tainment, who has the right to rule over whom; that out
of such waste-bickering Saxondom a peaceful coöperating
England may arise. Seek through this Universe; if with
other than owl's eyes, thou wilt find nothing nourished
there, nothing kept in life, but what has right to nourish-

ment and life. The rest, look at it with other than owl's
eyes, is not living; is all dying, all as good as dead!
Justice was ordained from the foundations of the world;
and will last with the world and longer." [1]

With these old Puritanical doctrines was John Brown
deeply imbued,—not from Creed-books and Faith-confes-
sions, but from an absorbing contemplation of righteousness and the principles of liberty. Great men are the
result of evolution. First principles of justice and humanity lay hold upon them; they demand that some great
reform be consummated—be accomplished; for in the
progress of the world, evil institutions grow to such pro-
portions as to seriously menace the good. These men
are allowed to see but one great underlying principle;
and the strange thing in this world is, that this great
right-principle has had to be consecrated anew and dyed
in the blood of those who proclaimed it before it was visible to mankind. John Brown was aware of that; it
nerved his arm and strengthened his heart when making
what seemed so hopeless and uneven a battle in the scrub-
bush in the ravines of Black Jack. The United States
troops might wrest from him the fruits of his victory, and,
while retaining under the bogus laws the prisoners they
had, release, arm and set on the path to pillage and arson
those so lately taken from it by him, but there remained
the example of resistance to cut-throats; and this example
was not lost on the free men of Kansas. It marked a
new era in the struggle for freedom. Kansas men saw
that those who fought for their rights and the lives of
wives and children were held in more respect and were
accorded more protection than those who preached non-

resistance in the interest of property preservation. These men had the example of Pomeroy and others, who surrendered Lawrence without even a show of resistance, hoping to save the city in a fawning sycophancy and a hypocritical pretension that they would in future not fail to render allegiance to the bogus laws. These Free-State men, who had now resolved to fight for their lives and for their wives and children, remembered that all the humility of leaders did not save the good people of Lawrence from outrage and their fair city from pillage. Free-State men have told me with what scorn and contempt Pomeroy and others were regarded in New England when the people heard that instead of using a cannon donated by them for the defense of Lawrence, they had handed it over to the enemy to be used in battering down Free-State institutions! They have also described to me how the same people pointed with pride to the first defense of Lawrence, when Robinson, Lane and Brown stationed their men like a wall to turn back the ruffians; and how they deplored the absence of these heroes when the hordes again compassed it, bent on its destruction. This first resistance openly made in Kansas to the minions of the slave-power and the current issue that the bogus laws must be obeyed, strengthened John Brown and encouraged him to still fight and hope. It also aroused the Missourians, for it revealed a new phase in the conflict. Whitfield, summoned by Long, the courier sent by Pate, hastened to the field. He was turned out of the Territory by the mild remonstrances of the United States military, but sent his men to destroy and plunder Osawatomie before he departed.

Lane had been sent East by the leaders of the Free-State

men. He was in Washington for some time in the interest
of the Topeka Constitution. That instrument was presented to the United States Senate by Mr. Cass, on the
24th of March. Lane traveled extensively over the Eastern States, speaking to the people and describing the true
conditions in Kansas. In this work he arrived in Chicago
on the 31st of May, 1856; his speech here was one of the
greatest ever delivered in behalf of Kansas, and was followed by a remarkable demonstration in favor of the patriots who were struggling for freedom. In all his addresses Lane urged people to go to Kansas, and largely to
his efforts was due the remarkable immigration that poured
into the Territory in the summer and fall of that year.
Many of these were known as "Lane's Army of the
North," and in the succeeding years did valiant service
in the cause of liberty.

Governor Robinson had been ordered East also, but
being delayed by affairs demanding his attention in the
interest of the Free-State people, he could not leave the
Territory before the closing of the Missouri river to the
people opposed to slavery. He was arrested by ruffians
and returned to Kansas, and her people lost his valuable
services for some four months while he was closely guarded
and held prisoner under a charge of high treason.

John Brown remained in the vicinity of Osawatomie.
He was at Topeka when the Free-State Legislature was
dispersed, and no doubt he believed that the United States
troops should be resisted when they interfered with matters which did not concern their true functions. And it
is probable that he would have made such resistance at
Topeka if he had but been in command of a sufficient

force. He returned to the Pottawatomie and raised a company of Free-State men for the defense of the settlers and for striking a blow at slavery if occasion favored. The "Articles of Enlistment and By-Laws" of this company are preserved, and reveal to us the spirit in which all of John Brown's warfare against slavery was made:

"KANSAS TERRITORY, A. D. 1856.
"1. THE COVENANT.

"We whose names are found on these and the next following pages do hereby enlist ourselves to serve in the Free-State cause under John Brown as Commander; during the full period of time affixed to our names respectively, and we severally pledge our word and sacred honor to said Commander; and to each other, that during the time for which we have enlisted we will faithfully and punctually perform our duty (in such capacity or place as may be assigned to us by a majority of all the votes of those associated with us: or of the companies to which we may belong as the case may be) as a regular volunteer force for the maintenance of the rights & liberties of the Free-State citizens of Kansas: and we further agree; that as individuals we will conform to the *by Laws of this Organization* & that *we will insist* on their regular & punctual *enforcement* as a first & last duty: and in short that we will observe & maintain a strict & thorough Military discipline at all times until our term of service expires."

To this Covenant are subscribed the names of thirty-five men, with the dates of their enlistment; these dates extend from August 22 to September 16. Among these men were many that were leading citizens of the State for a quarter of a century after its admission. Many of the by-laws are quaint and odd, but they show that morality was considered a part of "thorough Military discipline." And the company was a democracy; its internal affairs were regulated and determined by vote, and offenders were to have trial "by a jury of Twelve." Article XIV provided that, "All uncivil, ungentlemanly, profane, vulgar talk or conversation shall be discountenanced." It is followed by another declaring that, "All acts of petty theft needless waste of property of the members or of Citizens is hereby declared disorderly: together with all uncivil, or unkind treatment of Citizens or of prisoners." Humane treatment of prisoners was made obligatory: " *No person* after having first surrendered himself a prisoner shall be *put to death:* or *subjected to corporeal punishment,* without *first* having had the benefit of an impartial trial." The use of liquor was prohibited: " The ordinary use or introduction into camp of any intoxicating liquor, *as a beverage:* is hereby declared disorderly." [2]

The organization of this company was after his return from Nebraska with Lane's Army of the North. Soon after the Legislature was dispersed, Brown took his son-in-law, Thompson, who was wounded at Black Jack, to Iowa to remain with friends there until he recovered. All Kansas waited for the coming of Lane's Army; the people saw their hope of deliverance in the patriotic army moving slowly through Iowa to pass into Kansas to fight for freedom. Brown was anxious to welcome this host of liberty-loving people. We shall get a view of him as he passed along.

Among the good men in Kansas in those days was Samuel J. Reader. He lived then near Indianola, in Shawnee county, a town which disappeared long since. Mr. Reader still resides near the old townsite, and is one of the most respected citizens of the State, a man of great intelligence, and proficient in stenography and drawing. He kept a journal through all the Territorial period, and this record is one of the most valuable within my knowledge. I have been accorded the privilege of examining it, and I make a few extracts from it:

" TUESDAY MORNING, July 29th.—I had been sleeping in the stable loft, with a double-barreled shotgun at my side, guarding our team from predatory lovers of horse-flesh. When I returned to the house in the morning, I was told that 'Kickapoo Stephens' had been there a few minutes before, to notify us that a party of Free-State men were at the house of Mr. Fouts, in Kansopolis—about two miles east, or northeast, of where we lived. The object of the party was to march north to the Nebraska line, with the expectation of meeting and escorting into Kansas a Free-State emigrant train, and guard it from possible molestation by the 'Kickapoo Rangers'—a most lawless and bloodthirsty band of border ruffians. It was also reported that Jim Lane was coming with the train; and that he had expressed the wish to have some of the genuine 'Kansas boys' with him when he crossed the line, into our Territory. . . . There was but a single baggage wagon. A very tall young man seemed to have charge of it. Some of the boys were calling him 'Handsome Hunter.' But Hunter seemed to take it all in good part, and talked back to them, in a drawling, good-natured tone of voice. 'Captain Whipple' was a name I heard more frequently than any other. I was not long in finding out who was the owner of that cognomen. He was a large, burly man; about six feet tall, good-sized head and face, short neck, deep-chested; arms and shoulders full and muscular; and would certainly pull down the scale at 200 pounds. His countenance was pleasant, but firm. He had a way of compressing his lips while speaking, that seemed a little peculiar. He wore no beard. Complexion clear and fresh; eyes dark gray, and not large; dark-brown hair; large, straight nose, and correspondingly large jaw and chin. At first I thought him a trifle too *fat;* but when I afterwards saw him walk, I discovered that what I had taken for adipose tissue was simply *brawn.* He wore a gray cloth cap on his head, while a summer vest partly concealed his cotton shirt. About his waist was buckled a dress sword; and on his shoulder he carried—not a Sharps' rifle—but a double-barreled shotgun. This was Captain Whipple as I first saw him.[3]

" There was a small party of mounted men. One was our guide—Dr. Root. He was a large, fleshy man; jolly, and affable. Another was Captain Sam Walker, of Lawrence. He seemed to have command of the mounted men. His face was stolid and determined—the very opposite of Dr. Root's. Capt. Mitchell rode with his party, although he commanded none of the infantry companies.

" CAMP ON PONY CREEK, K. T., Sunday, August 3d, 1856.—When I stepped up the opposite bank, I came face to face with two men. They had a covered wagon, drawn by a single yoke of oxen. One was a young man, somewhat above the ordinary height; the other, quite old. Both were walking, and both were dusty, and travel-stained. The team was stopped, and the old man inquired of me: 'Do you belong to a Free-State party, in camp near by?' I replied that I did. 'Where is your camp?' I pointed in its direction, and told him how he could find it. I was about to continue on my way, when he detained me, by remarking: 'Your coming has caused a good deal of excitement among the Pro-Slavery men living on the road.' I said nothing, and he continued: 'They didn't mind talking with us about it, as we are surveyors.' He motioned with his hand toward the wagon. I looked, and noticed for the first time a surveyor's chain hanging partly over the front end-board of the wagon. Just behind was a compass and

tripod, standing up, under the wagon cover. It struck me
that he might possibly be Pro-Slavery himself, but for-
tunately I gave no outward expression to the thought. He
was talkative—almost garrulous. I answered his direct
questions, but ventured to make no remarks myself. I had
been cautioned, only a day or two before, to be very careful what I said to men living along our line of march.
The ox team naturally led me to suppose that these men
were settlers in the immediate neighborhood. 'Where do
you live?' he asked. 'Indianola.' 'O yes! I know. It is
a hard place, and has got a very bad reputation. I have
heard of it.' I ventured no reply. 'Have you ever been
in a fight?' he next inquired. 'No.' 'Well,' he continued,
'you may possibly see some fighting, soon.' I was silent,
but all attention. 'If you ever *do* get in a battle, always
remember to aim *low*. You will be apt to over-shoot at
first.' I told him I would remember, and perhaps I
smiled a little, for he added: 'Maybe you think me a
little free in offering advice; but I am somewhat older
than you, and that ought to be taken in account.' He said
this gravely and pleasantly. The younger man, behind
him, was looking at me, with a broad grin on his face.
I was a little puzzled. The old man continued in pretty
much the same strain, for some time longer; but I find
it impossible to recollect it with any degree of accuracy.
The young man had not a word to say, but seemed vastly
amused at something. We separated. They forded the
creek, and went in the direction of camp, while I continued my hunt. I shot nothing, and soon returned. I
met one of our boys, and told him I had seen an old man
inquiring the way to camp. 'Yes,—and do you know who
it was?' I told him that I did not. 'Well,' he continued,
'that was old John Brown; we are to break camp, and
move farther on.' My delight and astonishment were
about equal. Even at that early date, John Brown was a
very noted man, and was trusted and esteemed by all who
held anti-slavery views. I felt it an honor and a pleasure

to have seen and conversed with so prominent a leader. One thing, however, has always puzzled me: why should the old man have spent any of his time talking to a youth, and a perfect stranger? It is possible, my being a resident of Indianola excited his interest, as he might have considered an armed Free-State man from such a noted 'Pro-Slavery hole' an anomaly and a curiosity. But whatever his motive, I shall always remember this little episode with pride and pleasure.

" Between three and four o'clock we formed in marching column, and started forward at a swinging pace. We were all well rested, and a little tired of staying in camp. We had been on the road perhaps an hour or more, when some one in front shouted, 'There he is!' Sure enough, it was Brown. Just ahead of us we saw the dingy old wagon-cover, and the two men, and the oxen, plodding slowly onward. Our step was increased to 'quick time'; and as we passed the old man, on either side of the road, we rent the air with cheers. If John Brown ever delighted in the praises of men, his pleasure must have been gratified, as he walked along, enveloped in our shouting column. But I fear he looked upon such things as vainglorious, for if he responded by word or act, I failed to see or hear it. In passing I looked at him closely. He was rather tall, and lean, with a tanned, weather-beaten aspect in general. He looked like a rough, hard-working old farmer; and I had known several such, who pretty closely resembled Brown in many respects. He appeared to be unarmed; but very likely had shooting-irons inside the wagon. His face was shaven, and he wore a cotton shirt, partly covered by a vest. His hat was well worn, and his general appearance, dilapidated, dusty, and soiled. He turned from his ox team and glanced at our party from time to time as we were passing him. No doubt it was a pleasing sight to him to see men in armed opposition to the Slave-Power. None of us were probably aware that John Brown's most ardent wish was for a sectional war between the North and the South—that slavery might die. We supposed his only aim—like our own—was to make Kansas a free State. *We* proposed to lop one limb only from the deadly 'Upas tree'—*he* would lay the ax at the root.

"We made no pause in our march, and rapidly left John Brown and his outfit in our rear. At the top of the next ridge I glanced backward, and looked again at that homely, humble figure, following in our wake at a snail's pace. What man among us could then have predicted that in a little more than three years he would shake this American republic from center to circumference?

"NEMAHA FALLS, N. T., Monday, August 4th, 1856.— I was loitering about camp, when I heard some one cry out, 'Here comes Brown!' I ran to the road with the rest of the men, and saw a horseman coming from the south. It was he. Where he got his horse, I never learned. Very likely he had borrowed the animal from some Free-State settler in the neighborhood. Several of our men stepped out into the road, and hailed the old man. He stopped immediately, and seemed very willing to talk. I think our principal spokesman was Wilmarth. 'Do you find a great deal of surveying to do?' he inquired of Brown. 'Yes, now and then I pick up a job,' replied the old man, with a perfectly grave face. We scanned him closely. His appearance was anything but military. He looked round-shouldered and awkward as he sat on his horse; and his resemblance to an old farmer, that one can see almost any day, was more striking than ever. 'Do you survey for Government?' was the next question. 'No. I am not exactly in that line. My surveying is strictly for private parties.' I watched him closely as he said this. There was not the vestige of a smile, and the tone of his voice seemed to indicate 'the words of truth and soberness.' He could hardly have failed seeing our scarcely concealed merriment; but his own face was long as the moral law.

—19

Our spokesman was equally grave, and plied Brown with
many and various questions, but utterly failed in getting
the old man to admit his object in coming, or even his
own identity. Judging from this conversation, my impression is that when he visited our camp the day before
he had not openly announced himself as Old Osawatomie
Brown, but had been recognized by some of our men who
had seen him before. Brown waited patiently until the
questioner was through, and then continued his journey
north. Of course he knew that we were not ignorant of
who he was; but from policy or force of habit, chose to
assume the appearance of a stranger. At the time, I
supposed be was indulging in a bit of dry humor. But
after-events have proved that even at this time his gray
head was teeming with revolutionary schemes, that would
have fairly taken our breath away had he divulged them
to us. 'The pear was not ripe.'

" NEMAHA, NEBRASKA TERRITORY, Thursday, August
7th, 1856.—It was a nice, warm morning, and we were
astir at an early hour. We answered to roll-call, and
were about ready to start, when Col. Dickey came over to
us and read a paper of instructions from his superiors.
There it was in black and white, that armed men should
not escort the train when it crossed the line into Kansas.
Some heated discussion followed. Dickey urged us to put
our arms in the wagons, and as soon as we were across
the line we could take them back again. Other men
joined the Colonel, and expostulated with our obdurate
commander. But it availed nothing. Captain Whipple
was standing a few feet in front of our line, and not
three paces from where I stood. A horseman rode up in
front of him. I looked up. It was Old Osawatomie
Brown. He addressed himself earnestly to Whipple.

" ' Do as they wish. This train is to enter Kansas
as a peaceable emigrant train. It will never do to have
it escorted by armed men. As soon as we are across the
line, there will be no objection to your retaking your

arms. Let us all stay together. Your services may be needed.'

"He said considerably more to the same effect. Capt. Whipple said but little in reply. He was striking the ground at his feet with the point of his sword, during most of the conversation. He looked obstinate, and sullen—something like a big school-boy when taken to task by his teacher.

"'Perhaps,' added Brown, 'you don't know me; you don't know who I am?'

"'Yes, I do,' exclaimed Whipple; 'I know who you are, well enough; but all the same, we are not going to part with our arms. We came armed, and we're going back armed.'

"I was somewhat surprised to learn by this conversation that Brown and Whipple were strangers to each other. Almost within reach of my arm, stood and spoke to one another for the first time these two self-sacrificing martyrs, whose futures were so tragically blended together,—John Brown, and Aaron Dwight Stevens. Both to battle bravely and hopelessly; both to be stricken down with seemingly mortal wounds, and both to perish on the Slaveholder's scaffold. Brown saw that further entreaty would be useless. He turned, and rode away. It was the last time I ever saw 'Old John Brown of Osawatomie.'"

Lane and Brown left the Army of the North and came in advance to make arrangements for the beginning of an aggressive campaign for the recovery of the ground lost in the campaign against Kansas Free-State men relentlessly prosecuted by the "Law and Order" party in the Territory and Missouri since the early spring. Lane had not seen Kansas since March. He had made a brilliant campaign in the Northern and Eastern States in the interest of Kansas. He had largely contributed in this way

to the assembling of the army which was marching into
Kansas to seek for homes, and who were determined that
these homes should be in a free State. The coming of
Lane's army carried dismay to the Missourians. On the
16th of August their leaders issued a call to arms which
showed their anxiety and apprehension:

"To the Public: It has been our duty to keep correctly and fully advised of the movements of the Abolitionists. We know that since Lane commenced his march
the Abolitionists in the Territory have been engaged in
stealing horses to mount his men, and in organizing and
preparing immediately on their arrival to carry out their
avowed purpose of expelling or exterminating every pro-
slavery settler. We have seen them daily become more
daring as Lane's party advanced. We have endeavored to
prepare our friends to the end, which was foreseen, and
which we now have to announce—Lane's men have arrived!—Civil war has begun!"

After the sacking of Osawatomie the Georgians near
that town became bold, and their thieving and plundering
became unbearable. A small force of Free-State men
assembled and attacked them. Although in a fortified
camp, and out-numbering their assailants, they were
routed and fled to Fort Saunders, several miles south-
west of Lawrence. Here Buford's Colonel Treadwell was
in command, and it was one of the most dangerous and
troublesome posts held by the ruffians. Major D. S. Hoyt,
of Lawrence, desired to obtain information which would
enable the Free-State men to make a successful attack
upon this point. It was a dangerous undertaking, and he
was urged to relinquish his design; but he was a brave
man, and believed he could safely accomplish it. Some

accounts say he carried a flag of truce. John Armstrong, Esq., of Topeka, whose account of this affair I have followed, assures me that he stopped at the fort, pretending that he was going to attend to some business in the little town of Marion, four miles beyond. He believed that no one would recognize him, and went into the fort and asked for a drink of water. After looking the fort over thoroughly he departed. There was a man there who had worked on the ferry at Lawrence; he recognized Hoyt at once, and when he was gone he gave it as his opinion that he was a spy and should be shot. Two men were detailed to do this. They followed Hoyt, and came up with him about a mile and a half on his way to Marion. They shot him, and after burning his face with some corrosive substance, buried him near the road. According to all rules of war, Hoyt had forfeited his life the moment he entered the fort in the capacity of a spy, but his death justly enraged the Free-State men, and they determined to attack the Buford camp at Franklin.[4] The assault was made on the evening of the 12th of August, and was directed by Lane; it was successful, and so panic-stricken became the ruffians that they abandoned a portion of their whisky in their flight. In the annals of Kansas the abandonment of whisky always denotes extreme and desperate demoralization in the ruffian ranks. A cannon was secured.

Lane established a camp three miles from Fort Saunders. As soon as the Chicago party arrived at Topeka, which was on the 13th of August, he ordered them to this camp, where they arrived at 2 o'clock on the morning of the 14th. In the forenoon of this day the body of Major Hoyt was found, and preparations were made to

advance upon the fort. The Free-State men arrived there
at 2 o'clock in the afternoon, but the enemy had fled;
they left much plunder and some muskets and ammunition; the Free-State men burned the fort. On the 16th
Fort Titus, near Lecompton, was attacked by the Free-
State men, and the garrison captured. The gun captured
at Franklin had been supplied with ammunition by gathering up the type of the *Herald of Freedom* scattered about
the streets at the sacking of Lawrence, and casting it into
balls. It was used with great effect upon Fort Titus, and
its reverberations so terrorized Governor Shannon that
he fled from Lecompton, and was found embarking upon
a mud-scow to cross the Kaw and escape in the jungles
of the north bottoms.

On the following day Governor Shannon came to Lawrence to conclude a peace in the interest of his ruffian
friends. The whole summer's harrying of the Free-State
settlers had not appealed to him, but after a few defeats
administered by these same settlers to his cut-throats he
came to plead their cause, and try to retrieve by treaty
what they had lost in battle. The treaty was concluded,
and prisoners exchanged. But this was not satisfactory
to the Missourians who had appealed to the people along
the border to gather for an invasion of the Territory.
Shannon saw that it would be impossible for him to make
any excuse to these when they arrived that would be satisfactory. The Kansas question had entered the campaign
for the Presidency. It was plainly seen by Pierce and Buchanan that if the Territory were not speedily quieted
Pennsylvania would vote against the Democratic candidate.
Shannon was ordered to accomplish this, and the storm of

civil war which he saw ahead of him rendered him impotent; he resigned his office, and fled from the Territory to escape assassination at the hands of his hopeful constituency of " Law and Order" party people. The executive authority now fell into the hands of Secretary Woodson. He was the willing tool of the ruffians; they could not make any request too brutal for him to refuse. It was determined to make clean work of the Free-State settlers in Kansas before the new Governor could arrive and undertake the pacification of the Territory. Atchison, Stringfellow and other Missourians gathered men for an invasion which was to be governed in its object by the motto, " Let the watchword be 'extermination, total and complete.' " About a thousand men were gathered at Little Santa Fe, in Missouri, and from this point moved into the Territory in the direction of Osawatomie. They sent a detachment of some three hundred and fifty men against this town; it arrived on the morning of August 30th.

The battle here was lost by the Free-State men, who were commanded by John Brown, but the defense of the town was so heroic that from that day he was known as Osawatomie Brown. The best account of the battle is his own report:[5]

" Early in the morning of the 30th of August the enemy's scouts approached to within one mile and a half of the western boundary of the town of Osawatomie. At this place my son Frederick (who was not attached to my force) had lodged, with some four other young men from Lawrence, and a young man named Garrison, from Middle creek. The scouts, led by a Pro-Slavery preacher named White, shot my son dead in the road, while he—as I have since ascertained—supposed them to be friendly. At the same time they butchered Mr. Garrison, and badly mangled one of the young men from Lawrence, who came with my son, leaving him for dead. This was not far from sunrise. I had stopped during the night about two and one-half miles from them, and nearly one mile from Osawatomie. I had no organized force, but only some twelve or fifteen new recruits, who were ordered to leave their preparations for breakfast and follow me into the town, as soon as this news was brought me.

"As I had no means of learning correctly the force of the enemy, I placed twelve of the recruits in a log house, hoping we might be able to defend the town. I then gathered some fifteen more men together, whom we armed with guns; and we started in the direction of the enemy. After going a few rods we could see them approaching the town in line of battle, about half a mile off, upon a hill west of the village. I then gave up all idea of doing more than to annoy [them], from the timber near the town, into which we were all retreated, and which was filled with a thick growth of underbrush; but I had no time to recall the twelve men in the log house, and so we lost their assistance in the fight. At the point above named I met with Captain Cline, a very active young man, who had with him some twelve or fifteen mounted men, and persuaded him to go with us into the timber, on the southern shore of the Osage, or Marais des Cygnes, a little to the northwest from the village. Here the men, numbering not more than thirty in all, were directed to scatter and secrete themselves as well as they could, and await the approach of the enemy. This was done in full view of them (who must have seen the whole movement), and had to be done in the utmost haste. I believe Captain Cline and some of his men were not even dismounted in the fight, but cannot assert positively. When the left wing of the enemy had approached to within common rifle-shot, we commenced firing, and very soon threw the northern branch of the enemy's line into disorder. This continued some fifteen or twenty minutes, which gave us an uncommon opportunity to annoy them. Captain Cline and his men soon got out of ammunition, and retired across the river.

"After the enemy rallied we kept up our fire, until, by the leaving of one and another, we had but six or seven left. We then retired across the river. We had one man killed—a Mr. Powers, from Captain Cline's company—in the fight. One of my men, a Mr. Partridge, was shot in crossing the river. Two or three of the party who took part in the fight are yet missing, and may be lost or taken prisoners. Two were wounded; namely, Dr. Updegraff and a Mr. Collis. I cannot speak in too high terms of them, and of many others I have not now time to mention.

" One of my best men, together with myself, was struck by a partially spent ball from the enemy, in the commencement of the fight, but we were only bruised. The loss I refer to is one of my missing men. The loss of the enemy, as we learn by the different statements of our own as well as their people, was some thirty-one or two killed, and from forty to fifty wounded. After burning the town to ashes and killing a Mr. Williams they had taken, whom neither party claimed, they took a hasty leave, carrying their dead and wounded with them. They did not attempt to cross the river, nor to search for us, and have not since returned to look over their work." [6]

The Missourians returned to their encampment. Lane sent a force of about one hundred and fifty men against this camp. After exchanging a few shots with their assailants the forces under Atchison and others returned in great haste to Missouri. But they did not remain there long. Woodson issued a proclamation declaring the Ter-

ritory in a state of insurrection, and calling out all the
Territorial militia,—which was in fact an invitation to the
ruffians to invade Kansas and complete the "extermination" of settlers opposed to slavery. Governor Geary was
hurrying to the Territory, and found companies on their
way in obedience to these calls; one company embarked
on the Governor's boat, at Glasgow, Mo., and carried a
brass cannon. On his way from Leavenworth to Lecompton he detected a member of the bogus Legislature in the
act of plundering Free-State men, and this hopeful legis-
lator advanced upon the Governor's party with the intention of robbing it, and was only deterred by the appearance of a wagon in the distance.[7]

The invasion of Kansas progressed as favorably as the
Pro-Slavery leaders could expect. By the 15th of September there were twenty-seven hundred men surrounding Lawrence, under the command of Atchison, Stringfellow, Reid, and others. The number of volunteers the
Free-State men were able to assemble to oppose this army
of invasion did not exceed three hundred. Brown was
offered the command of these, but declined. He preferred
to fight in the ranks. But he was looked upon as the
most capable military man present, and the people relied
upon him for their safety should they be attacked. Brown
assembled them one afternoon and addressed them as follows:

"GENTLEMEN: It is said there are twenty-five hundred
Missourians down at Franklin, and that they will be here
in two hours. You can see for yourselves the smoke they
are making by setting fire to the houses in that town. Now
is probably the last opportunity you will have of seeing

a fight, so you had better do your best. If they should come up and attack us, don't yell and make a great noise, but remain perfectly silent and still. Wait till they get within twenty-five yards of you; get a good object; be sure you see the hind sight of your gun,—then fire. A great deal of powder and lead and very precious time is wasted by shooting too high. You had better aim at their legs than at their heads. In either case be sure of the hind sights of your guns. It is from the neglect of this that I myself have so many times escaped; for if all the bullets that have been aimed at me had hit, I should have been as full of holes as a riddle." [8]

Sounder and more patriotic advice was never given a little band gathered to battle for their homes. But Governor Geary succeeded in turning back these barbarous invaders before they could attack Lawrence. He called to his assistance the United States troops and marched to the camp of the Missourians, where he met their leaders. After much grumbling, swearing, threatening, and disorderly wrangling, they held a meeting to devise some excuse to present to their sodden followers for turning back. After resolving that they had come to drive out Lane and his hireling army, they reached the core of the controversy in the following preamble: " Whereas, we have here met and conferred with Governor Geary, who has arrived in the Territory since we were here called, *and who has given us satisfactory evidence of his intention and power to execute the laws of the Territory."* They returned to Missouri, but their routes were marked with burning homes, plundered farms, and murdered citizens.

So ended the campaign of the Pro-Slavery party of

Kansas and Missouri in 1856 for the enforcement of the bogus laws. Had not political conditions in the East demanded its suppression, the Administration would have assisted it to a successful termination. When the hordes rolled back across the border their opportunity to crush Kansas was forever gone; it was never again in their power to stifle liberty. While many an outrage was yet to be perpetrated upon the Free-State men, freedom was assured when the congregated barbarians turned from the walls of the noble town of Lawrence, whose people were so patriotic and liberty-loving that nothing could subdue or overcome them.

Had not John Brown and his faithful followers lurked in thicket and swamp, like the great guerrilla, Marion, of South Carolina, ready to defend a home or settlement here, and attack a band of murderers there, it is uncertain whether the result could have been attained in this time. The people of Kansas honor the memory of the old hero who without money and without price, at the peril of his life and the sacrifice of his son, alone of the leaders of the people, ranged the land and entreated the harried and discouraged settlers to continue the fight for freedom till help should come, and who exhorted them to charge

"Once more unto the breach, dear friends, once more."

His fame was great. Pottawatomie and Osawatomie were talked of in every ruffian camp, and the terror of the name of Old John Brown increased all along the border. He believed himself raised up of God to break the jaws of the wicked. He cared no more for political policy than for personal abuse or the laudations of men. He gave no account to man of his actions. He sought no counsel in the assemblies of men; he cared nothing for their praises or condemnations. He held himself accountable to God alone, and as he understood His will he tried to execute it. He cared nothing for law when it stood in the way of right and humanity. He was a revolutionist as were the fathers of 1776. He was the oracle of the doctrine enunciated in the Declaration of Independence. He believed it agreed perfectly with the Sermon on the Mount, and he believed that it were better that his generation perish than that a syllable of either should fail. Only such men are truly great.

NOTE 1.—Carlyle's *Past and Present*.

NOTE 2.—The Covenant, list of names and by-laws are given in the *Life and Letters of John Brown*, F. B. Sanborn, pp. 287, 288, 289, 290.

NOTE 3.—"There would be no advantage in my making anything of a mystery about this man. His real name was Aaron Dwight Stevens. A few months before this time, he was serving as a bugler in Col. Sumner's regiment of U. S. Dragoons. Being greatly provoked, he struck an officer. A court-martial condemned him to be shot. The sentence was commuted to three years' imprisonment. He escaped in the spring of 1856. Came to Topeka as Chas. Whipple, and was elected Captain of a Free-State company there. Was afterwards promoted Colonel of the Second Regiment, and commanded under Lane at Hickory Point, Sept. 13, 1856. In 1859 he went to Harper's Ferry with old John Brown—being third in command. On the night of October 16 they captured the U. S. armory at that place; and in the fight, the next day, Stevens was shot down on the street while bearing a flag of truce. His wounds were supposed to be mortal; but he recovered, and was executed March 2d, 1860."— *Reader's Journal*.

NOTE 4.—This differs materially from the accepted version of the death of Major Hoyt. I was given this account by John Armstrong, Esq., of Topeka. Mr. Armstrong was one of the very first settlers in Douglas county; he was a member of the Lawrence "Stubbs," (a Free-State military company,) and was one of the men who searched for and found the shallow grave of Major Hoyt. He knew Hoyt well, and was evidently informed of every movement undertaken or to be undertaken against the camps of Buford. He says that this is the true account of the matter. I have greatly condensed his account. Mr. Armstrong was one of the founders of the city of Topeka.

"The following is copied from an article on David Starr Hoyt, written by William B. Parsons, and published in the *Kansas Magazine* of July, 1872—Vol. II, p. 45:

"'After a few weeks, Hoyt returned to Lawrence, and entered heart and soul into the stirring events which followed. In June he went with a white flag into a Border-Ruffian fort in the south part of Douglas county, known as Fort Saunders, and while returning, still under the protection of the flag, was basely murdered by the men with whom he had been treating. Such was the boasted "chivalry."

"'Hoyt was among the earliest and bravest of the Kansas martyrs. He left his home with the impression fastened in his mind that he should be called upon to give up his life somewhere on the Kansas prairies, and the thought never quickened his pulse, or produced the quiver of a muscle.'"—*"Annals of Kansas," D. W. Wilder, p. 101, edition of 1875.*

Mr. Parsons is in error as to the time. He says it was in the month of June that he was killed. It was in August.

NOTE 5.—One of the first settlers of Osawatomie was O. C. Brown. He was not related to John Brown. He was a prominent Free-State man, and stood high in the councils of the Free-State party. He was given the name "Osawatomie," and for some time was known as "Osawatomie Brown." He disappeared for a time from the Kansas conflict. As John Brown was the most noted man in that region, those not knowing the different Browns called him "Osawatomie" Brown. When his fame spread through all the land he came to be everywhere known as "Osawatomie Brown," or "Old Osawatomie Brown," and often as "Old John Brown of Osawatomie." The Pro-Slavery Missourians almost always called him "Old Brown" or "Old Osawatomie Brown." In *Butler's Book* he is called "Pottawatomie Brown."

NOTE 6.—John Brown, in *Life and Letters of John Brown*, F. B. Sanborn, p. 318.

———

NOTE 7.—"The Governor and party crossed the Stranger river about noon, thirteen miles from Leavenworth, at a place called Alexandria. This town consists of two houses, used as a postoffice and stores. Several whisky-barrels, with their heads broken in, lay in the road. A young man in attendance gave a deplorable account of the robbery. He said the attack was made by about one hundred and fifty of Lane's men, all mounted, who came with two wagons, which they filled with goods, broke open the postoffice box and robbed it of letters and postage stamps, and destroyed such articles as they could not carry away. The proprietor, to save his life, had fled to the hills and hid himself in the bushes, and he was threatened with death if he should give information concerning the robbery. The Governor, who had been accustomed to examine 'moccasin-tracks,' made a careful investigation of the premises, and at once assured Lieutenant Drum that the statements of his informant were false. He pointed out distinctly the fact that the traces upon the ground indicated the late presence of certainly not over a dozen horsemen. He then ordered the young man to take a seat in the ambulance, to point out the direction taken by the robbers, and hastened in pursuit of them. Along the road were exhibited fearful evidences of ruffian violence. Almost every house had been destroyed, and the sites they had occupied were marked only by solitary chimneys standing in the midst of heaps of ashes. The first dwelling approached was about three miles from Alexandria, where the Governor halted and inquired of the settler if he had seen a large body of men pass during the morning. He promptly answered that only six horsemen had passed that way, about half an hour previous. The Governor then asked the man in company why he had attempted to mislead him with a lying statement. The fellow had nothing to reply, and, after a severe rebuke, was permitted to return to Alexandria. As a reward for having told the truth, the settler's house was attacked a day or two after, and burned to the ground; his wife and half a dozen children being turned out upon the open prairie, and his crop of corn destroyed.

"The Governor increased his speed, and having traveled two miles farther, upon reaching an elevated piece of ground saw six horsemen crossing the prairie at the distance of about half a mile. Upon observing the carriage, they turned toward it, putting their horses to a gallop, with the evident intention to attack and rob it. As they came within a few hundred yards, and preparations were being made to give them a warm reception, the covered wagon ascended the hill, thus exhibiting the character and strength of the Governor's party, when the intending assailants turned and fled in the opposite direction. They were pursued by the sergeant, the only mounted man in the company, and a more interesting chase was never witnessed. The horses were put to their utmost speed, their tails standing straight out, and making time rarely equaled on a race-course. Four of them succeeded in reaching a wooded ravine, but the other two, whose horses were not equal to that rode by the sergeant, were overtaken and commanded to halt. Upon being questioned, they represented themselves as Free-State men who had been driven from their homes by a party of border ruffians. The sergeant, however, recognized them as two of a party of six men whom he had that morning seen leave Leavenworth City. It was subsequently learned that the leader of the party was a citizen of Missouri; a prominent member of the Legislative Assembly of Kansas, and the alleged author of most of the odious election and test laws passed by that body during its session of 1855. This person has boasted that he 'pressed' from Free-State men several valuable horses, which he had carried for safe-keeping into Lexington, Missouri."—*"History of Kansas," John H. Gihon, pp. 118, 119.*

NOTE 8.—This is an exact report of what Brown said. It was taken down as he spoke, by Colonel Richard J. Hinton, who was present as the reporter for Eastern newspapers. Colonel Hinton was a stenographer or shorthand writer, and one of the ablest correspondents sent to Kansas. He identified himself with the Free-State party, and rendered valuable services; afterward he served in the Kansas regiments in various capacities through the war. He has written much and well of the early days here. One of his best works is *John Brown and His Men.* This address can be seen in *Life and Letters of John Brown,* F. B. Sanborn, p. 335.

CHAPTER XI.

FAREWELL TO KANSAS.

Eleven slaves are now set free,—
A kindly stroke for those who fell,
A just and righteous parallel,—
Their freedom won; and strange to tell,
Kansas has gained her liberty.

Not on far Afric's burning sand,
When age on age has come and gone,
And people searching in the throng
Which passing centuries prolong,
Ask for some hero proud and grand,

The theme for master sculptor's hand,
Whose ancient glory and renown
The waiting multitude shall crown,
Will there remote appear John Brown;—
But will be found in every land

His glory heralded by seers,—
In marble cut; by poets sung;
And his rude image shall be hung
Round the charmed neck, and every tongue
Shall praise him as a saint of years.
    —*Joel Moody's "The Song of Kansas."*

John Brown did not intend to remain permanently in
Kansas, so far as we now know; it is believed that he did
not come with that purpose. It seems that he only "turned
aside" for a time from his life-work to take up the sword

for Kansas. But it is by no means certain that he did not finally come to see the possibility of his remaining in the State he helped to redeem and rescue. There is little doubt that he at one time contemplated striking his final blow at slavery from Kansas—that he studied long and seriously the establishment of the stations in the Indian Territory and Texas that he eventually concluded to undertake in the Appalachians. At least three purposes moved him to come to Kansas. The first was, to assist his children in the battle to make Kansas free and in the defense of their lives and property. The second was, to seek every opportunity to attack the institution of slavery. The third was, to gain practical experience in guerrilla warfare. The latter was essential to the success of the great design so long and so devoutly intended by him.[1]

When the hordes from Missouri had rolled back from the walls of Lawrence, Governor Geary devoted himself in good faith to dispersing all armed bands in the Territory. There were indictments against John Brown for resistance to the bogus laws, or treason, and any strict construction of his duty would compel the Governor to bring him to trial; but he did not want the hero of Osawatomie captured, for he did not know what to do with him. To have dealt harshly with him would have aroused the Free-State men to resistance. He intimated to Brown's partisans that he should consider it a favor if they would in some way prevent his officers from meeting him. It is by no means certain that he did not request his friends to induce Brown to quit the Territory for a season, in order that there might remain no possibility of his arrest. By Governor Geary's efforts the campaign waged so persistently and relentlessly against the Free-State men of Kansas for the preceding six months was rendered ineffectual. There was some hope that the settlers would be protected in their homes. Brown consented to go East in September; but he did not relinquish any purpose he had formed in relation to slavery, or even Kansas; on the contrary, he labored diligently in these causes during his absence from the Territory. He left Kansas in September, probably about the 15th. He had his old wagon and ox team, and in this clumsy conveyance he rode much of the time, for he was sick. His progress was slow; and he was pursued for a time by the United States troops, but had no trouble in evading them. He followed the trail over which Lane's Army of the North had marched in.

Brown remained a fortnight at Tabor, Iowa, and when his health improved he continued his journey, arriving in Chicago about the 25th of October. Here the National Kansas Committee purchased him a suit of clothes. He visited the various committees formed in the Eastern States to assist in the settlement of Kansas; he hoped to procure the means to arm a considerable number of men. He had in mind the great work of his life, and never for a moment neglected it; and on this trip he secured the custody of two hundred Sharps' rifles then at Tabor, Iowa, and these he finally carried with him to Harper's Ferry.

The committees were able to do but little for him; and finding this condition of affairs, he determined to make appeals directly to the people. He spoke in many New England towns. In Massachusetts there was a movement to have the Legislature appropriate twenty-five thousand dollars in the aid of Kansas work. The committee having this matter in charge requested him to appear before them and deliver an address. This he did. He arraigned the Administration, and described the conditions existing in Kansas and the trials Free-State people were compelled to bear in that Territory. He said:

"I saw, while in Missouri, in the fall of 1855, large numbers of men going to Kansas *to vote,* and also returning after they had so done; as they said.

"Later in the year, I, with four of my sons, was called out, and traveled, mostly on foot and during the night, to help defend Lawrence, a distance of thirty-five miles; where we were detained, with some five hundred others, or thereabouts, from five to ten days—say an average of ten days—at a cost of not less than a dollar and a half per day, as wages; to say nothing of the actual loss and suffering occasioned to many of them, by leaving their families sick, their crops not secured, their houses unprepared for winter, and many without houses at all. This was the case with myself and sons, who could not get houses built after returning. Wages alone would amount to seven thousand five hundred dollars; loss and suffering cannot be estimated.

"I saw, at that time, the body of the murdered Barber, and was present to witness his wife and other friends brought in to see him with his clothes on, just as he was when killed.

"I, with six sons and a son-in-law, was called out, and traveled, most of the way on foot, to try and save Lawrence, May 20 and 21, and much of the way in the night. From that date, neither I nor my sons, nor my son-in-law, could do any work about our homes, but lost our whole time until we left, in October; except one of my sons, who had a few weeks to devote to the care of his own and his brother's family, who were then without a home.

" From about the 20th of May, hundreds of men, like ourselves, lost their whole time, and entirely failed of securing any kind of a crop whatever. I believe it safe to say that five hundred Free-State men lost each one hundred and twenty days, which, at one dollar and a half per day, would be—to say nothing of attendant losses— ninety thousand dollars.

"On or about the 30th of May, two of my sons, with several others, were imprisoned without other crime than opposition to bogus legislation, and most barbarously treated for a time, one being held about a month, and the other about four months. Both had their families on the ground. After this both of them had their houses burned, and all their goods consumed by the Missourians. In this burning all the eight suffered. One had his oxen stolen, in addition."

The Captain, laying aside his paper, here said that he had now at his hotel, and would exhibit to the committee, if they so desired, the chains which one of his sons had worn, when he was driven, beneath a burning sun, by Federal troops, to a distant prison, on a charge of treason. The cruelties he there endured, added to the anxieties and sufferings incident to his position, had rendered him, the old man said, as his eye flashed and his voice grew sterner, "a maniac—yes, a MANIAC."

He paused a few seconds, wiped a tear from his eye, and continued his narration:

"At Black Jack, the invading Missourians wounded three Free-State men, one of them my son-in-law; and a few days afterward one of my sons was so wounded that he will be a cripple for life.

" In June, I was present and saw the mangled and disfigured body of the murdered Hoyt, of Deerfield, Mass., brought into our camp. I knew him well.

" I saw the ruins of many Free-State men's houses, in different parts of the Territory, together with grain in the stack, burning, and wasted in other ways, to the amount, at least, of fifty thousand dollars.

"I saw several other Free-State men, besides those I have named, during the summer, who were badly wounded by the invaders of the Territory.

"I know that for much of the time during the summer, the travel over portions of the Territory was entirely cut off, and that none but bodies of armed men dared to move at all.

"I know that for a considerable time the mails on different routes were entirely stopped; and notwithstanding there were abundant troops in the Territory to escort the mails, I know that such escorts were not furnished, as they ought to have been.

"I saw while it was standing, and afterwards saw the ruins of, a most valuable house, the property of a highly civilized, intelligent, and exemplary Christian Indian, which was burned to the ground by the Ruffians, because its owner was suspected of favoring Free-State men. He was known as Ottawa Jones, or John T. Jones.

"In September last, I visited a beautiful little Free-State town called Stanton, on the north side of the Osage (or Marais des Cygnes, as it is sometimes called), from which every inhabitant had fled for fear of their lives, even after having built a strong log house, or wooden fort, at a heavy expense, for their protection. Many of them had left their effects, liable to be destroyed or carried off, not being able to remove them. This was to me a most gloomy scene, and like a visit to a sepulcher.

"Deserted houses and cornfields were to be found in almost every direction south of the Kansas river.

"I have not yet told all I saw in Kansas.

"I once saw three mangled bodies, two of which were dead, and one alive, but with twenty bullet and buckshot holes in him, after the two murdered men had lain on the ground, to be worked at by flies, for some eighteen hours. One of these young men was *my own son*."

The stern old man faltered. He struggled long to suppress all exhibition of his feelings, and soon, but with a
subdued, and in a faltering, tone continued:

" I saw Mr. Parker, whom I well knew, all bruised
about the head, and with his throat partly cut, after he
had been dragged, sick, from the house of Ottawa Jones,
and thrown over the bank of the Ottawa creek for dead.

"About the first of September, I, and five sick and
wounded sons, and a son-in-law, were obliged to lie on
the ground, without shelter, for a considerable time, and
at times almost in a state of starvation, and dependent
on the charity of the Christian Indian I have before
named, and his wife.

" I saw Dr. Graham, of Prairie City, who was a prisoner with the Ruffians on the 2d of June, and was present
when they wounded him, in an attempt to kill him, as he
was trying to save himself from being murdered by them
during the fight at Black Jack.

" I know that numerous other persons, whose names I
cannot now remember, suffered like hardships and ex-
posures to those I have mentioned.

" I know well that on or about the 14th of September,
1856, a large force of Missourians and other Ruffians,
said by Governor Geary to be twenty-seven hundred in
number, invaded the Territory, burned Franklin, and,
while the smoke of that place was going up behind them,
they, on the same day, made their appearance in full view
of, and within about a mile of, Lawrence; and I know of
no reason why they did not attack that place, except that
about one hundred Free-State men volunteered to go out
and did go out, on the open plain before the town, and give
them offer of a fight, which, after getting scattering shots
from our men, they declined, and retreated back towards
Franklin. I saw the whole thing. The Government troops,
at this time, were at Lecompton, a distance of twelve
miles only from Lawrence, with Governor Geary; and

yet, notwithstanding runners had been dispatched to advise him, in good time, of the approach and setting out of the enemy, (who had to march some forty miles to reach Lawrence,) he did not, on that memorable occasion, get a single soldier on the ground until after the enemy had retreated to Franklin, and been gone for more than five hours. This is the way he saved Lawrence. And it is just the kind of protection the Free-State men have received from the Administration from the first." [2]

Brown visited his family at North Elba, N. Y., but did not remain long at home; he returned to New England early in March, and continued his work on the platform. He met with some encouragement; eighty dollars was given him in three nights by two towns in Connecticut. One of these towns was Canton, where his father and mother were brought up. The old granite monument of his grandfather, John Brown, of Revolutionary fame, stood in the burial-ground there, though the old patriot had been buried on the banks of the Hudson. The people agreed to send the venerable monument to North Elba, to be there set up and inscribed with the name of his son Frederick, and other names as occasion arose. The monument was sent, and was an object of great interest to the many who visited the grave of the martyr in after-years. At Hartford and Canton Brown read from his manuscript an appeal for assistance; this appeal explains his objects, and shows that he was then contemplating greater things:

" I am trying to raise from twenty to twenty-five thousand dollars in the free States, to enable me to continue my efforts in the cause of freedom. Will the people of Connecticut, *my native State,* afford me some aid in this undertaking? Will the gentlemen and ladies of Hartford,

where I make my first appeal in this State, set the example
of an earnest effort? Will some gentleman or lady take
hold and try what can be done by small contributions from
counties, cities, towns, societies, or churches, or in some
other way? I think the little beggar-children in the
streets are sufficiently interested to warrant their contrib-
uting, if there was any need of it, to secure the object.
I was told that newspapers in a certain city were dressed
in mourning on hearing that I was killed and scalped in
Kansas, but I did not know of it until I reached the place.
Much good it did me. In the same place I met a more cool
reception than in any other place where I have stopped.
If my friends will hold up my hands while I live, I will
freely absolve them from any expense over me when I am
dead. I do not ask for pay, but shall be most grateful for
all the assistance I can get." [3]

It was while in Connecticut at this time that Brown
contracted for the construction of a thousand pikes, which
he afterwards carried with him to Harper's Ferry. He
visited many of the principal cities on this second visit
to New England, and addressed large audiences. He also
made the personal acquaintance of the men most prominent in the work of aiding Kansas; and he met the abolitionists then laboring in their way to free the slaves.
Eli Thayer was much impressed with his services to
the cause of freedom, and did not ascertain until he was
an independent candidate for Congress, in 1860, when
he was in opposition to his party, which was then engaging in the mighty conflict for the preservation of the
Union, that Brown was a detriment to the cause of liberty
in Kansas. He offered Brown a home in a "boom town"
enterprise in what is now West Virginia, at the mouth of

the Big Sandy river, called Ceredo, and which was a failure.

Brown received most encouragement from the Massachusetts State Committee. It proposed to obtain an appropriation of one hundred thousand dollars to be used for relief in Kansas; to organize a force, "well armed and under control of the famous John Brown, to repel Border-Ruffian outrage and defend Free-State men." In the explanation of its objects it was recited that "many of the Free-State leaders, being engaged in speculations, are willing to accept peace on any terms. Brown and his friends will hold to the original principle of making Kansas free, without regard to private interests." This is just what Brown had been doing in Kansas, and what opposition there was in the Free-State ranks in the Territory to Brown came from his strict adherence to these original principles. But with all his efforts, the results in New England was disappointing to him. His chagrin found expression in the following quaint document:

"OLD JOHN BROWN'S FAREWELL

TO THE PLYMOUTH ROCKS, BUNKER HILL MONUMENTS, CHARTER OAKS, AND UNCLE TOM'S CABINS.

"He has left for Kansas; has been trying since he came out of the Territory to secure an outfit, or, in other words, the means of arming and thoroughly equipping his regular minute-men, who are mixed up with the people of Kansas. And he leaves the State with a feeling of deepest sadness, that after exhausting his own small means, and with his family and his brave men suffering hunger, cold, nakedness, and some of them sickness, wounds, imprisonment, and others death; that, lying on the ground for months in the most sickly, unwholesome, and uncomfortable places, some of the time with sick and

wounded, destitute of any shelter, hunted like wolves, and
sustained in part by Indians; that after all this, in order
to sustain a cause which every citizen of this 'glorious
Republic' is under equal moral obligation to do, and for
the neglect of which he will be held accountable by God,—
a cause in which every man, woman, and child of the
entire human family has a deep and awful interest,—
that when no wages were asked nor expected, he cannot
secure, amid all the wealth, luxury, and extravagance of
this 'heaven-exalted' people, even the necessary supplies
of the common soldier. 'How are the mighty fallen!'

"I am destitute of horses, baggage-wagons, tents, harness, saddles, bridles, holsters, spurs, and belts; camp
equipage, such as cooking and eating utensils, blankets,
knapsacks, intrenching-tools, axes, shovels, spades, mat-
tocks, crowbars; have not a supply of ammunition;
have not money sufficient to pay freight and traveling
expenses; and left my family poorly supplied with common necessaries.

"Boston, April, 1857."

John Brown was working with method to accomplish
an end—perfecting· arrangements to accomplish the design he had cherished for more than twenty years. He
had not yet disclosed this plan to anyone—perhaps in its
more definite outlines so far as they were fixed, not even
to his wife. He made the acquaintance, in April, 1857,
of Hugh Forbes, who was an Englishman late from Italy,
where he had been a silk merchant and a follower of
Garibaldi. In one of the downward turns of the cause
of his leader he found it necessary to flee, and, leaving
his wife and daughter in Paris, he sought the hospitable
shores of America. He was a fencing-master, and claimed
an extensive knowledge of military tactics and guerrilla

warfare. He proposed to Brown to translate a French work on street-fighting and other varieties of desultory tactics, and print it for the use of his army. To this Brown was favorable, and he furnished the means to bring out the work, believing that it would prove of great service to his men. Forbes was also employed, or taken on some terms not now well understood, to instruct the army to be raised and equipped by Brown to carry out his intentions. He was to come to Tabor, Iowa, in May, 1857, but did not arrive until the 9th of August. Being dissatisfied, he left there early in November, and went East, where he divulged such of Brown's plans as had been made known to him. These revelations were made to prominent public men, and to persons who had assisted Brown and were in sympathy with his designs.[4]

From Tabor, Iowa, Brown came to Kansas, arriving at the farm of E. B. Whitman, a little south of Lawrence, on the 5th of November. He intended to remain but a short time, and his object was to enlist men skilled in the rough guerrilla warfare of the Kansas border in his army of invasion of Virginia.[5] His presence was made known to few, for it was feared that he might be arrested on the old indictments for treason or conspiracy. From Lawrence he went to the farm of Daniel Sheridan, south of Topeka. There he was joined by John E. Cook, Richard Realf, and Luke F. Parsons. He and J. H. Kagi visited Manhattan. With the persons named, and "Colonel Whipple," or Aaron D. Stevens, Charles W. Moffett, and Richard Richardson, a colored man of intelligence, Brown left Kansas for Iowa late in November. They arrived without incident, and soon afterward the whole company were moved to the Quaker community at Springdale, Iowa, and were given a heartfelt welcome by the good people of that place. The gratitude and approval of humanity are due the Quakers of every part of America for their services in effecting the abolition of slavery. They were the first body to oppose the institution in both Europe and America, and were ever in advance in this righteous cause as the work for its consummation dragged slowly along. No black man or woman or child fleeing from a crushing and degrading bondage with bloody-fanged dogs crying on the trail at the instance of the minions of the laws of the nation, ever knocked in vain at a Quaker door. The underground railroad ran from one Quaker settlement to another, and was always safest where the Friends were most numerous, and to them the distress-cry of the fugitive black man was a call from God that was never unheeded.

The company of John Brown gathered at Springdale consisted of eleven men,—John Brown, Owen Brown, Aaron D. Stevens, John Henri Kagi, John Edwin Cook, Richard Realf, Charles P. Tidd, William Leeman, Luke F. Parsons, Charles W. Moffett, and Richard Richardson. During the winter George B. Gill, Steward Taylor, Edwin Coppoc and Barclay Coppoc joined the little army. John Brown installed Aaron D. Stevens in the position of military instructor, left vacant by the desertion of Forbes. As soon as provision for his men for the winter was completed, Brown returned East; this was in January, 1858. He stopped in Ohio to see his son John, and from there he went to the home of Frederick Douglass, in Rochester, N. Y. He made his home with Douglass for a time, and while there, drew up his constitution for a provisional government. He began also to disclose to his friends his plans for the future—very cautiously at first, and by vague hints and suggestions rather than by direct avowal. He inquired of Theodore Parker by letter: "Do you think any of my Garrisonian friends, either at Boston, Worcester, or any other place, can be induced to supply a little 'straw,' if I will absolutely make 'bricks' ?"[6] He desired something less than a thousand dollars. "He wishes to avoid publicity, and will not see his family. Meantime he is staying with Fred Douglass under the *nom de guerre* of N. Hawkins. He 'expects to overthrow slavery' in a large part of the country," wrote Edward Morton to F. B. Sanborn.[7] He wrote Sanborn: "My reasons for keeping quiet are such that when I left Kansas I kept it from every friend there; and I suppose it is still understood that I am hiding somewhere in the Territory." These were his reasons for not going to Boston, or even passing through Albany. He was at the home of Gerrit Smith, near Peterboro, N. Y., February 20th, 1858. Here he was met by Mr. Sanborn, who says that on the evening of Washington's birthday "the whole outline of Brown's campaign in Virginia was laid before our little council, to the astonishment and almost the dismay of those present." The discussion continued till past midnight, "but nothing could shake the purpose of the old Puritan. Every difficulty had been foreseen and provided against in some manner; the grand difficulty of all—the manifest hopelessness of undertaking anything so vast with such slender means—was met with the text of Scripture: 'If God be for us, who can be against us?' He had made nearly all his arrangements: he had so many men enlisted, so many hundred weapons,—all he now wanted was the small sum of money. With that he would open his campaign in the spring, and he had no doubt that the enterprise 'would *pay*,' as he said."

On the following day the question was again taken up. Brown carried his point. "You see how it is," said Gerrit Smith to Mr. Sanborn; "our dear old friend has made up his mind to this course, and cannot be turned from it. We cannot give him up to die alone; we must support him." [8] He went by the way of Brooklyn to Boston at the instance of Mr. Sanborn, arriving there on the 4th of March. His visit to Boston was made secretly. He saw Theodore Parker, who encouraged him but was not sanguine of the success of his effort. The amount of money required was given him, and he considered his journey successful at every point. He was in communication with Forbes, and seems to have anticipated no serious trouble from his course. When the success of his plans seemed so nearly complete—when, climbing up from the devious defiles of the valley of disappointments and vexations, he saw from the height of his mountain-top the broad plains of peace and freedom unfold in a panorama at his feet, he wrote to his wife and children in the rude home in the frozen forests of the Adirondacks: "The anxiety I feel to see my wife and children once more, I am unable to describe. I want exceedingly to see my big baby and Ruth's baby, and to see how that little company of sheep look about this time. The cries of my poor sorrow-stricken, despairing children, whose 'tears on their cheeks' are ever in my eyes, and whose sighs are ever in my ears, may however prevent my enjoying the happiness

I so much desire. But, courage, courage, courage!—the great work of my life (the unseen Hand that 'guided me, and who has indeed holden my right hand, may hold it still,' though I have not known Him at all as I ought) I may yet see accomplished (God helping), and be permitted to return, and 'rest at evening.' " [9]

John Brown and his son, John Brown, jr., were in Philadelphia, where a conference was held with a number of colored men. They went from thence to Connecticut, and from there, by the way of New York, to North Elba. They remained but a few days, and returned to Peterboro, arriving at Gerrit Smith's April 2d. Mr. Smith fully approved the arrangements made for the invasion of Virginia, and "was buoyant and hopeful about it, and showed great animation and interest." From Peterboro they went to Rochester, where they separated. John Brown went to St. Catherine's, Canada, early in April, writing from that place to his son John, from whom he had parted at Rochester, April 8th. There were many fugitive slaves in St. Catherine's, and he was probably looking among them for additions to his little army. A certain Harriet Tubman, a colored woman of much influence, was there at the time, and she seems to have aided him in this work. But he did not remain long in Canada. He went to Iowa, and from Springdale wrote his wife on the 27th of April. He had come to transfer his army to Chatham, Canada West, which he accomplished quickly, for he wrote from that town to his wife, May 12th. The Provisional Constitution had been adopted here before the letter to his wife was written. It began with the following preamble: "*Whereas,* Slavery throughout its entire existence in the

United States, is none other than a most barbarous, unprovoked, and unjustifiable war of one portion of its citizens upon another portion—the only conditions of which are perpetual imprisonment and hopeless servitude or absolute extermination—in utter disregard and violation of those eternal and self-evident truths set forth in our Declaration of Independence." [10]

But at this moment, when it seemed that all things were turning to favor the rapid consummation of John Brown's life-purpose, unexpected developments forced a postponement of the expedition for many months. Forbes continued to talk of Brown's plans. He gave information to Senators in Washington and influential persons in New England. The result was that Mr. Smith, Theodore Parker, Mr. Sanborn and those knowing his full plans wrote him that the expedition must be deferred for a year. Brown met Mr. Stearns in New York about the 20th of May. He went to Boston, where he was assured that he would be furnished two or three thousand dollars for the execution of the plan in the following winter. In the meantime it was believed best for him to return to Kansas, for, as Forbes did not know that Virginia was the objective point of Brown's expedition, his return to the Territory and the resumption of the old warfare there would serve to contradict Forbes's revelations. He left Boston June 3d, "with five hundred dollars in gold, and liberty to retain all the arms," visited North Elba, passed through Ohio and Iowa into Nebraska, and reached Lawrence on the 25th of June, 1858. He was warmly welcomed by his friends and the people of Kansas generally; among these were the correspondents of the Eastern newspapers. Redpath records at length a conversation "which lasted nearly the whole afternoon." He was accompanied by Kagi, and they returned to Kansas, as Kagi gave out, because of the betrayal of their plans by Forbes. On Monday, the 26th, Brown and Kagi left Lawrence for southern Kansas to visit Mr. Adair and other friends near Osawatomie, and also to consult with Captain James Montgomery.

The Marais des Cygnes massacre had occurred on May 19th. Trouble had existed in Linn and Bourbon counties for a long time. When the Free-State people settled in the Kansas Valley and northern Kansas in such numbers that the danger from invasions from Missouri ceased and civil order appeared, the worst characters among the ruffians betook themselves to these counties, and made their headquarters at Fort Scott. Among them were Clark and the Lieutenant Brockett who was captured with Captain Pate. In 1858 the Free-State men had increased in Linn county to the point that they could take the initiative. Pro-Slavery men occupying the claims from which Free-State men had been driven were made to leave. The feelings of each party toward the other were very bitter. The leader of the Pro-Slavery people was Charles A. Hamilton. He made up a list of some sixty Free-State men whom he intended to kill. He had lived on a claim near the Missouri line and near the little town of Trading Post, but was at this time living in Missouri. He was the commander of a company of ruffians known as the "Bloody Reds." On the 19th of May he rode over the line, gathered up eleven of his neighbors, all unarmed, and many of them inoffensive and peaceable, formed them in line in a gloomy gulch and shot them. Four were instantly killed, and all the survivors but one desperately wounded. The ruffians mounted their horses and fled, and Hamilton was never again heard of " by anyone familiar with this bloody crime." A blacksmith named Snyder had saved himself from the same fate by resisting with his shotgun. Brown went to the point where these murders were committed.[11] It was believed for some time that he had purchased the claim upon which Snyder's shop was located, and that he had built a strong fort upon it, called Fort Snyder; but this he never did. He enlisted a few men, among them many of the foremost in the Territory. He assumed the name of Shubel Morgan, and his volunteers were known as " Shubel Morgan's Company." The nine rules for the government of the company are characteristic of the stern and Puritanical character of Brown, and they are yet preserved in the library of the Historical Society. Augustus Wattles and James Montgomery were privates in this company commanded by " Shubel Morgan."

The company saw considerable service during the summer. Governor Denver posted some soldiers in the vicinity of the camp, which was near Trading Post. On the 23d of July Brown wrote that some of the soldiers of this company had offered him their services, and that he had declined them. Afterwards there was an attempt to capture Brown, and this duty was intrusted to the United States troops. There was a sharp engagement between Brown's company and these troops at Fox's Ford, on Big Sugar creek, in which a number were wounded on each side. The troops were commanded by a Captain Farnsworth. Brown and his men are said to have disguised themselves as stone-masons, and worked for some time on a stone house being built by Augustus Wattles. Farnsworth and his command stopped at the house of Mr. Wattles one day for dinner or water or under some other pretext, but really because they suspected that these stone-cutters were Brown and his men. Brown was then concealed in the loft of Mr. Wattles's cabin. While Mr. Wattles and Captain Farnsworth discussed the desperate courage of Old John Brown he was lying with his eye at a rent in the wall not ten feet away, listening to the young officer, who boasted that he would make him prisoner yet. He remained for more than an hour, and it afforded Mr. Wattles much amusement to keep the officer always on the subject, as he knew that Brown was listening to all he said.

During the summer he was for a time sick with an ague; this so weakened him that he was unable to remain in camp. He went to the home of his brother-in-law, the Rev. Mr. Adair, where he was very ill from an attack of typhoid fever. It was the 10th of September when he could again write to his friends. He returned to camp as soon as he was again well enough to bear the hardships of the camp life, but he wrote that he was anxious to reëngage in preparation for the invasion of Virginia.

On Sunday, December 19, 1858, a negro man came from Missouri to Brown's camp and begged that his wife and family be rescued from slavery before they were sold to be carried South. The following Monday night Brown, with a number of men from his company, made a foray into Missouri, and secured these slaves, eleven in number, and carried them into Kansas. They were carried to the Pottawatomie and kept in a cabin on the open prairie for more than a month, while every ravine and thicket swarmed with people searching for them. No one thought of their being concealed in the deserted old cabin in plain view of a number of houses, and they escaped without detection. This raid was the occasion which caused the writing of the famous communication known as "Old Brown's Parallels," which is as follows:

"OLD BROWN'S PARALLELS.

"TRADING POST, KANSAS, Jany, — 1859.

"GENTS: You will greatly oblige a humble friend by allowing me the use of your columns while I briefly state Two paralells in my poor way. Not One year ago Eleven quiet citizens of this neighborhood (Viz) Wm Robertson, Wm Colpetzer, Amos Hall, Austin Hall, John Campbell Asa Snyder, Thos Stilwell, Wm Hairgrove, Asa Hairgrove, Patrick Ross, and B. L. Reed, were gathered up from their work, & their homes by an armed force (under One *Hamilton*) & without trial; or opportunity to speak in their own defense were formed into a line & all but one shot Five killed, & Five wounded. One fell unharmed pretending to be dead. All were left for dead. Now I inquire what action has ever since (the occasion in May last) been taken by either the President of the United States; the Governor of Missouri: the Governor of Kansas or any of their tools: or by any proslavery *or administration man?*

"Now for the other parallel. On Sunday the 19th of December a Negro man called Jim came over to the Osage settlement from Missouri & stated that he together with his Wife, Two Children, & another Negro man were to be sold within a day or Two & beged for help to get away. On Monday night of the following day Two small companies were made up to go to Missouri & forcibly liberate the Five slaves *together with other slaves*. One of those companies I assumed to direct. We proceeded to the place surrounded the buildings liberated the slaves; & also took certain other property supposed to belong to the Estate. We however learned before leaving that a portion of the articles we had taken belonged to a man living on the plantation as a tenant & who was supposed to have no interest in the Estate. We promptly restored to him *all we had taken* so far I believe. We then went to another where we freed Five more slaves, took some property; & Two *white* men. We moved all slowly away into the territory for some distance & then sent the White men back telling them to follow us as soon as they chose to do so. The other company freed One female slave took some property; & as I am informed killed One White man (the master) who fought against the liberation.

" Now for a comparison. Eleven persons are forcibly restored to their *natural; & unalienable* rights with but one man killed; & all ' Hell is stirred from beneath.' It is currently reported that the Governor of Missouri has made a requisition upon the Governor of Kansas for the delivery of all such as were concerned in the last named *'dreadful outrage':* the Marshall of Kansas is said to be collecting a posse of Missouri (not Kansas men) at West Point in Missouri a little town about Ten Miles distant to 'enforce the laws,' & and all proslavery conservative Free State dough faced men & administration tools are filled with holy horror.

Respectfully Yours,
JOHN BROWN." [12]

The Governor of Missouri offered a reward for the capture and delivery of John Brown, and this was supplemented by a reward offered by James Buchanan, President of the United States, of two hundred and fifty dollars. Brown immediately had printed a small handbill in which he publicly proclaimed that he thereby offered a reward for Buchanan, declaring that if any lover of his country would deliver that august personage to him, well tied, at Trading Post, he would willingly pay such patriot the sum of two dollars and fifty cents. It is said that reflection upon the matter afterwards convinced him that this sum was more than the President was actually worth for any purpose.

Brown now prepared to leave Kansas. He was anxious to be on his way to Virginia. He had taken an old wagon from the master in Missouri when he rescued the slaves. This was concealed in a rocky gorge some distance from the old cabin on the prairie where the slaves were kept. It was of a peculiar pattern, and almost covered with chains—chains here, and chains there, chains everywhere —and they made a deafening rattle and clangor when the old wagon was in motion. About January 20, 1859, Brown put his negroes into this wagon, hitched to it the two yoke of oxen taken from the slave-owner, and set out for Canada. He was accompanied for a short distance by some friends from the Pottawatomie; but they soon turned back to their homes. The slaves had little idea of the distance to Canada. Perhaps they expected to arrive there in a day or two.

"Jim, who was driving an ox team, 'supposed to belong to the estate,' asked one of the liberators, ' How far is it to Canada?'

" ' Twenty-five hundred miles.'

" '*Twenty-five hundred!* Laws-a-massa! Twenty-five hundred miles! No git dar 'fore spring!' cried Jim, as, raising his heavy whip and bringing it down on the ox's back, he shouted impatiently, 'Whoa-haw, Buck; git up dar—g'lang, Bill!' " [13]

The audacity and daring of the man is shown in the commencement of this journey. He was almost alone. A price was on his head. His conveyance was such as to attract attention anywhere, and the slowest known to traffic or travel. His route ran near the capital of the Territory, where he was wanted on many a charge. He had little or no food, and was clad in thin cotton garments worn by him during the summer. But his stout heart knew no fear. He pushed forward, the chains of the old wagon rattling as it rolled over the prairie or plunged into ravines and draws. But he cared not for chains so long as they bound no slave. And he knew where to find his friends. At the house of Major James B. Abbott he tarried for a short time. He avoided Lawrence, and came to Topeka by the way of Auburn, on the Wakarusa. Here he remained a day or two, at the house of Daniel Sheridan, and some supplies of food and clothing were given him. He crossed the Kansas river in the night, and was entertained by Cyrus Packard, Esq., a Free-State man from Maine. He left the house of his friend before daylight, and followed on his way to Canada the old trail made by Lane's Army of the North. [14] Beyond Holton he was threatened by a posse, commanded by Dr. J. N. O. P. Wood, of Lecompton, and numbering some forty men. These were reinforced by some Atchison parties. He sent a messenger to Topeka for help, and some thirty-five men responded, but before they arrived the posse was routed. The last battle fought by the old Puritan on Kansas soil resulted in the ignominious defeat of his enemies. After having been reinforced by the party from Atchison, they supposed it impossible for Brown to escape them. There were forty-two of them, and they advanced to capture Brown's camp. At this moment Brown and seven men came out of a wood and opened fire. Never were men more surprised. They turned and fled in great disorder; some were unhorsed. These were so terror-stricken that they seized the tails of the horses ridden by their frightened comrades, and disappeared over the prairie "just hitting the high places." Four of the party were captured by Brown. They were retained some days and released on the Nebraska side of the State line. They requested that their horses be returned to them, but Brown assured them that they could well afford to walk back to Kansas. This last battle of the slave-owners with Brown in Kansas was called derisively, "the Battle of the Spurs," by Richard J. Hinton, then a Kansas correspondent for Eastern newspapers, and an ardent Free-State man and champion of freedom. The battle has always been called by the name given it by Colonel Hinton.

Brown passed through the State of Iowa during the month of February. At Tabor he was not well received. At Springdale, on the 25th, he was furnished food and clothing for his fugitives and charged nothing for their entertainment. He addressed "full houses for two nights in succession," and a small sum of money was realized by the collections. His notes for these addresses yet exist, and are characteristic of the man.[15] At Iowa City he was assailed by the postmaster, with the following result:

" In the midst of a crowd on the street-corner a quiet old countryman was seen listening to a champion of slavery, who was denouncing Brown as a reckless, bloody outlaw,—a man who never dared to fight fair, but skulked and robbed, and murdered in the dark, adding, 'If I could get sight of him I would shoot him on the spot; I would never give him a chance to steal any more slaves.' 'My friend,' said the countryman in his modest way, 'you talk very brave; and as you will never have a better opportunity to shoot Old Brown than right here and now, you can have a chance.' Then, drawing two revolvers from his pockets he offered one to the braggart, requesting him to take it and shoot as quick as he pleased. The mob orator slunk away, and Brown returned his pistols to his pocket." [16]

Brown carried his fugitives through Chicago to Detroit, where he crossed with them into Canada. From Canada he went to Cleveland, Ohio, where he sold the horses taken from the enemy in the " Battle of the Spurs." He explained that the title might be defective, but this did not affect the price secured. When his business in Cleveland was transacted, he went on to his home in North Elba. He remained there but a short time, and went on to New England. He went by the way of Peterboro, N. Y., where he stopped to consult Gerrit Smith. He spent his birthday, the last that came to him in this world, with Mr. Sanborn, at Concord, Massachusetts. Then he went to Boston to begin his preparations to go upon his expedition to attack slavery in Virginia.

NOTE 1.—Redpath insists almost vehemently that it was never John Brown's purpose to make Kansas his place of residence. I regard Redpath as not the best authority upon this subject, as well as upon some others connected with the life of Brown. There are letters written by members of his family which show at least that the coming of the family to Kansas was contemplated. If he had finally concluded to attempt in Arkansas and Texas what he purposed in Virginia, he would have brought his family to Kansas.

NOTE 2.—*Annals of Kansas*, D. W. Wilder, pp. 153, 154, 155.

NOTE 3.—The paper from which Brown read is in the library of the Kansas Historical Society. It is long, and is a valuable historical document. This quotation is from *Life and Letters of John Brown*, F. B. Sanborn, p. 379.

NOTE 4.—*John Brown and His Men*, Richard J. Hinton, and *Life and Letters of John Brown*, F. B. Sanborn, have good accounts of Hugh Forbes and his relations with John Brown.

NOTE 5.—I know a number of men now living in Kansas who were invited to become members of Brown's army of invasion. Among these I remember Mr. Edward P. Harris, who came to Kansas one of Lane's Army of the North, and one of the best known and most respected of the old pioneers. He is one of the best printers in America, and his reputation as a proof-reader is second to none. Richard Realf requested him to go to Harper's Ferry with Brown, but Mr. Harris, while willing to fight border ruffians in Kansas, could not see his way clear to oppose the authority of the United States in Virginia. Colonel Thomas E. Scudder is another man who was invited to go, and who refused on the same ground.

NOTE 6.—*Life and Letters of John Brown*, F. B. Sanborn, p. 435.

NOTE 7.—*Life and Letters of John Brown*, F. B. Sanborn, p. 437.

NOTE 8.—For these quotations, see *Life and Letters of John Brown*, F. B. Sanborn, pp. 436, 437, 438, 439.

NOTE 9.—Letter of John Brown to his family, in *Life and Letters of John Brown*, F. B. Sanborn, p. 441.

NOTE 10.—The best copy published of this remarkable instrument is to be found in *John Brown and His Men*, Richard J. Hinton, beginning on page 619.

NOTE 11.—For accounts of the Marais des Cygnes massacre see *Kansas in 1858*, W. P. Tomlinson; and the account written for the Kansas State Historical Society by Ed. R. Smith, Esq., of Mound City, and published in the *Kansas Historical Collections*, Vol. VI, p. 365, and following.

NOTE 12.—This is given just as Brown wrote it. The original is in the library of the Kansas Historical Society. It was first published in the *New York Tribune* and the *Lawrence Republican*. The original shows some interlineations made with pen and some made with pencil. Mr. Sanborn believes those made with pen were made by Kagi. Mr. E. P. Harris was a compositor in the *Republican* office when the copy was received. The changes and additions made with pencil, now to be seen on the original, in the library of the State Historical Society, and the changes in orthography, were made by Mr. Harris, as he informs me. He also changed the punctuation. These changes all appear on the original copy in the handwriting of Mr. Harris. The paper as edited by Mr. Harris has been used as the copy of this valuable communication, and may be found in most all the biographies of John Brown. By comparing one of those with this the additions will readily appear.

The original paper bears some evidences that it was contemplated that some one else, probably Kagi, should make additions to it. There are spaces left to be filled if thought necessary; one of these follows the list of victims of the Marais des Cygnes massacre, and another is at the close. The only word in the original not in the copy as printed herein is the word "party." This is the last word, and is below the space and next to the signature. There is no connection between it and what precedes it in Brown's handwriting, and it is in his handwriting. Mr. Harris made it a part of the last sentence in the copy as published generally.

NOTE 13.—*Life of Captain John Brown*, James Redpath, p. 220.

NOTE 14.—Miss G. Packard, of Topeka, writes me:

"My father, Cyrus Packard, came from Maine to Kansas, in the spring of 1857. He lived about three miles north of Topeka, and John Brown frequently made his house his stopping-place, when traveling with slaves. I remember once, in the fall of 1858, that he came in the middle of the night with a large company, among whom was a babe who had been born on the road. My brother and I were little children, and were wakened in the night by the unwonted noise.

We got up and dressed and started to go downstairs, but found the door locked; and our curiosity was so great that we looked down through space around the stove pipe, and saw a great crowd of black people moving about. My brother-in-law, coming upstairs just then, concluded that we might as well be downstairs; so we were permitted to go about among the fugitives. I looked at John Brown with a great deal of interest. Col. Whipple and Kagi were with him. My mother and sister were bustling about, cooking as good a meal as they could under the circumstances. Before morning they were loaded into the covered wagons, and were well under way before daylight. Another time, word was brought to Topeka that John Brown was besieged by Missourians, and a company of men made a forced march to his relief. They suffered so much that by the time they got back they were entirely exhausted. One of them, one Captain Henry, came into my father's house and sank down. He was stricken with a violent fever and only lived a week, during which time he was unconscious. A friend of his, a Mr. Emerson from Topeka, helped take care of him, and closed his eyes for his last long sleep.

"This Mr. Emerson was quite a genius in his way. He was not a religious man, but was a very strong temperance man. He stammered in conversation. One time there was a company of fugitive slaves here, and there was a discussion as to how they were to be guided safely to the Queen's dominions. There was a plan that Mr. Emerson and Rev. L. Bodwell should impersonate Missourians, and take them through Missouri as their slaves. Mr. Emerson said to Mr. Bodwell, 'Y-y you c-can d-do the d-drinking, and I w-wi-will d-do the s-sw-swear-swearing.' "

NOTE 15.—*Life and Letters of John Brown*, F. B. Sanborn, p. 489.

NOTE 16.—*Life and Letters of John Brown*, F. B. Sanborn, p. 491.

CHAPTER XII.

THE KENNEDY FARM.

Are your hands lifted towards the sun,
  What time our onsets wax and wane?
Do you see troops of angels run
  In shining armor o'er the plain?
I know not; but I know, full sooth,
  No wrath of hell, nor rage of man,
Nor recreant servant of the Truth,
  Can balk us of our Canaan.
                              —*Richard Realf.*

John Brown succeeded in obtaining from his friends in New England and New York a sum of money considered by him sufficient to warrant his moving forward in the enterprise he believed himself called of God to undertake for humanity. He bore the burdens of the poor and oppressed as they groaned in bitter bondage, cried under the merciless lash, and shrieked in the bloody jaws of the fierce hounds which pulled them down in their flight towards a land of refuge and freedom.

The summer of 1859 was spent in moving the arms from Ohio and other points to the vicinity of Harper's Ferry, providing a temporary base of operations, enlisting men for his little army, and in becoming familiar with the topography of the country in which he intended to carry on his warfare against the "sum of all villainies."

Chambersburg, Pennsylvania, was made the first point

of concentration. This town is some fifty miles north of Harper's Ferry; and at that time there was no railroad connecting the two towns. When the rifles arrived there from Ohio and the pikes from Connecticut, it was necessary to transport them to the rendezvous on the Potomac in wagons. Brown himself drove the teams on many of these trips to remove the arms.

On June 23d Brown wrote his family from Akron, Ohio, and between that date and the 30th of the same month he made his way to Chambersburg; for at that time he wrote to Kagi, " We leave here to-day for Harper's Ferry, via Hagerstown." There were with him at this time his sons Owen and Oliver, and Jerry Anderson. John E. Cook was already living in Harper's Ferry, where Brown and his companions appeared July 3d. He began the search for a suitable location for his rendezvous, and on the 4th was directed by a Marylander to the farm belonging to the heirs of Dr. Booth Kennedy, some five miles from Harper's Ferry, and on the Maryland side of the Potomac. There were two houses on this farm, both standing back from the highway, which was then little used; one of these houses was almost concealed by thickets which grew between it and the road. The place was admirably adapted to Brown's purposes. He represented that he was a farmer, from New York; that the frosts had ruined his crops, and that he desired to come to a country more favorable in climate to his business. He wished to rent a farm until he could become sufficiently acquainted with the country to not be at a disadvantage in buying. He rented the farm until the following March, paying therefor the sum of thirty-five dollars, and agreeing

to care for some live-stock still on the farm, belonging to
the heirs.   He gave as his name, Isaac Smith, and the
transaction was made in the name of I. Smith & Sons.

When the constitution was adopted in Chatham, Canada, a provisional government was formed and its officers
elected: Captain John Brown was made Commander-in-
chief; John Henri Kagi was elected Secretary of War;
Richard Realf, Secretary of State; and Owen Brown,
Treasurer.   This government was not to become fully op-
erative until after the invasion of Virginia and a considerable number of slaves had been liberated, when it was
to be proclaimed in the fastnesses of the Appalachians—
in the inaccessible, abrupt and wooded hills of the Blue
Ridge ranges.   It was never intended to be the government of any body of people in Canada, but was to be
the fundamental law of Brown's men and the accessions
to their body in Virginia and other Southern States.   His
plans contemplated an advance from Harper's Ferry,
south, through the, rugged hills, ultimately into the very
heart of the slave territory.   A guerrilla warfare was to
be waged against slave-owners; slaves were to be liberated,
armed, and turned against their masters, who were to
be kidnapped and only restored to freedom upon their
manumission and release of a stipulated number of slaves.
Forts were to be established at points difficult of access
and favorable for defense; these were to be in charge of
armed men, and as near one another as circumstances demanded,—at first some five miles intervening.   The descent upon the plantations was to be made from these
fortified camps; their location was to be made known to
such slaves as could be safely intrusted with the informa-

tion, and were to serve as asylums or posts of refuge for the slaves who from any cause fled from any master. Slavery was declared by Brown to be a state of war between master and slave, consequently any armed force in the interest of the slave was entitled by the rules of war to support from the enemy if it could be seized. On this theory and this alone did he forcibly take horses, implements, arms and food from the slave-owners and their allies in Kansas and Missouri. In this battle against slavery in the Appalachians he expected to prey upon the masters for food and all other supplies necessary for the maintenance of this warfare and for the welfare of those he liberated.

John Brown believed that the little garrisons of these mountain forts could resist largely superior forces, and if defeated that they could make their way through the pathless woods to another station. He expected that bloodhounds would be placed on his trail in these forays upon the plantations, but he believed they could be killed, and that the pursuit would not be pressed by the planters. He believed he might persuade the planters, or some of them, to assist him and coöperate with him when he had made slaveholding unprofitable because of the uncertainty of value and insecurity of property in slaves. It was his hope to eventually extend his provisional government over all the hill-country of the South,—from Harper's Ferry to Alabama, maintain his position, and carry this guerrilla warfare successfully forward until the abolition of slavery should be accomplished.

The original plans of Brown did not contemplate such attacks as he afterwards made upon Harper's Ferry.

—22

While the movement was to be inaugurated at that point, the attack upon the town and capture of the Federal property there were perhaps not included in the original design. The forts were to be established in the peaks and crags and the warfare commenced by silent and swift movements and sudden retreats similar to his forays into Missouri. The mystery surrounding his movements, the uncertainty of the extent of the conspiracy, the sudden and unexpected development and appearance of it, and the number engaged in it, would have been mighty factors in its favor. While it is certain that he never could have succeeded as he hoped, he might have accomplished much. The value of the Appalachians for such purposes was recognized by General Washington, who declared that if he was defeated on the Atlantic seaboard he would retire to these mountains and continue the war. Brown's determination to attack Harper's Ferry was an error, but this action led ultimately to the accomplishment of all he had hoped for, although in a very different way from what he expected. It was the inauguration of a new and different manner of fighting slavery. It so widened the breach that compromise was impossible—really the first great practical step in the battle for emancipation. It is probable that an examination of the highlands in the immediate vicinity revealed no sites for forts to his liking. It was September before he spoke to his men of any modification of his plans, and first to his son Owen. But Frederick Douglass visited him at Chambersburg in August, at his request. Brown made known to him his change of purpose and his intention to attack the town of Harper's Ferry as the opening or initial blow of his

campaign against slavery in its own country. Douglass
tried to dissuade him, but in vain. Brown urged Douglass
to join him in the campaign, but Douglass declined to
take any part in it. All of Brown's men opposed the new
order, and so much was urged against it that John Brown
resigned as Commander-in-chief, though he was immediately reëlected. From that time, opposition to the attack
upon the town and the seizure of the Federal property
ceased, and the new plan was acquiesced in.

The Government received warning of the intended invasion of Virginia for the purpose of creating insurrection among the slaves about the 25th of August, but it
seems that little attention was given this communication
conveying the information, as it was anonymous.[1] And
the country had some intimation of what might shortly
take place, but neither the Government nor the public
comprehended these warnings nor heeded them in the
least.[2] And when the blow descended, the country was
as much surprised as if nothing had been publicly said
of an insurrection.

The little band at the Kennedy farm grew slowly. Additions arrived singly, or by twos and threes. Oliver
Brown's wife and Anne, the daughter of John Brown,
were brought from North Elba to prevent suspicion, which
might (and did) arise at sight of so many strange men on
the farm. The women were to keep watch, and warn of
danger. The men remained in the upper story of the large
house during the day, where they drilled and studied the
science of war. Sometimes they read, but time went
heavily with them by day; at night they descended from
their loft to walk about the fields and over the hills.

Sometimes the girls gathered autumn wild-flowers and made nosegays, which they sent aloft to cheer the weary hours of the grim and waiting warriors. When at the farm John Brown went to church, and held converse with his neighbors when he saw them. He spent much time on the road to and from Chambersburg. He was often at Harper's Ferry, and soon gained a perfect knowledge of the surrounding country.[3] He even visited the armory and gun-factory.

The men composing John Brown's army of invasion were from various places. A brief sketch of them must here suffice.

1. JOHN BROWN, Commander-in-chief.

2. WATSON BROWN, Captain. Son of John Brown.

3. OLIVER BROWN, Captain. Son of John Brown.

4. OWEN BROWN, Captain and Treasurer. Son of John Brown.

5. WILLIAM THOMPSON. Son of Roswell Thompson; born in New Hampshire, in August, 1833. Married in the fall of 1858 to Mary Brown, who was not related to the family of John Brown. His sister Isabel was married to Watson Brown; and Henry Thompson, his elder brother, was married to Ruth, the daughter of John Brown.[4]

6. DAUPHIN THOMPSON. Brother of William Thompson. Lieutenant. Was born April 17, 1838. He was "very quiet, with fair, thoughtful face, curly blonde hair, and baby-blue eyes." Slain at Harper's Ferry.

7. JOHN HENRY KAGI. Born March 15, 1835, in Bristol, Trumbull county, Ohio. His father had come from the Shenandoah Valley, in Virginia, to Ohio. He was

cold in manner, rather coarse of fiber and rough in appearance, an agnostic, and mentally the ablest man in John Brown's army. Was very brave and determined. Was a lawyer. When he was young his father went to California, but returned and settled on Camp creek in Otoe county, Nebraska. Came to Kansas in 1856, arriving at Topeka July 4th, where he witnessed the dispersal of the Legislature by Colonel Sumner. Immediately identified himself with the Free-State forces, and became one of John Brown's most devoted followers. Bore the title of Secretary of War in the provisional government; next in command to John Brown; was adjutant. Slain at Harper's Ferry.

8. AARON DWIGHT STEVENS. Born in Lisbon, New London county, Connecticut, March 15, 1831. His great-grandfather, Moses Stevens, was an officer in the war of the Revolution, and his grandfather was a soldier in the War of 1812. Served through the Mexican War, and was honorably discharged. In 1851 he enlisted in the regular army, joining the regiment of dragoons commanded by Colonel Sumner, and served in the capacity of bugler; in this service he was in Wyoming, Colorado, Kansas, Nebraska, and New Mexico. Struck an officer for brutally punishing a comrade; was court-martialed and ordered to be shot, but his sentence was commuted to three years' imprisonment at hard labor. Escaped, and concealed himself in the Delaware Reserve, from whence he came to Topeka early in 1856. He gave his name as "Charles Whipple," and served in the Free-State forces as Captain, where he was known as Captain Whipple. Met John Brown August 7, 1856, at the Ne-

braska line, when Lane's Army of the North marched into
Kansas. Became one of Brown's bravest and most devoted
followers. He was an ideal soldier, six feet and three
inches high, finely formed, of impressive appearance, very
intelligent, and brave as a lion. Unmarried. Captured,
and executed in the following March.

9. JOHN E. COOK. Born in Haddam, Connecticut, in
1830. Of an old Puritan family which was quite wealthy.
Five feet and seven inches in height, handsome, quick in
movement, an incessant talker, blue-eyed, and had curly
blonde hair. A devoted follower of Brown, though considered indiscreet. Was the one man who believed that
it was best to attack the town of Harper's Ferry. Was
sent to that town in advance of others, and lived in the
city. Passed much of his time in gathering information
about slaves, and perhaps in communication with them,
although this is denied by the family of Brown. It is
reasonable to believe that he had found that the slaves
would not rise at the first appearance of Brown, though
he believed they would flock to the standard when the blow
had been struck. Was married, and had wife and one
child in Harper's Ferry up to within a month of the
attack. One of his sisters married a Mr. Willard, who
was, in 1859, Governor of Indiana. Cook escaped from
Harper's Ferry, but was captured at Chambersburg, returned to Virginia, tried and convicted, made a confession,
and was hanged.

10. CHARLES PLUMMER TIDD. Captain. Born in Pa-
lermo, Waldo county, Maine, in 1832. Five feet nine
inches high, strong and broad-shouldered. Dark eyes and
beard, and black hair. Was sharp in retort, and over-

bearing. Came to Kansas in 1856. Was turned aside by the blockade of the Missouri river, and came into the Territory through Iowa and Nebraska. Met John Brown and his sons, Owen and Oliver, at Tabor, Iowa. Was ever after a faithful follower of Brown, and was fully trusted by him. He and Cook were particularly warm friends. Opposed the attack on Harper's Ferry. Escaped, and enlisted in a Massachusetts regiment, in the Civil War, and died in service.

11. WILLIAM H. LEEMAN. Lieutenant. Was born in Maine March 20, 1839. In 1856 he determined to go to Kansas, and left Massachusetts in June of that year, in the party led by Dr. Cutter. Was turned back by the Missouri blockade, and found his way to Kansas through Iowa. Joined John Brown's Regulars, September 9, 1856, and was thereafter one of his trusted followers. Was in the Springdale (Iowa) school of instruction. Slain at Harper's Ferry.

12. BARCLAY COPPOC. Born in Salem, Ohio, January 4, 1839, of Quaker parents, who moved to Springdale, Iowa. Young Coppoc was in Kansas a short time in 1856. Drilled in the Springdale school. Although young, he seems to have been trusted by John Brown. Escaped from Harper's Ferry, and was killed in a wreck on the Hannibal & St. Joseph Railroad caused by rebels, who sawed the bridge timbers partly off.

13. EDWIN COPPOC. Lieutenant. Born near Salem, Columbiana county, Ohio, June 30, 1835. Elder brother of Barclay Coppoc. Hung in Virginia December 16, 1859. Was brave and generous, "honorable, loyal, and true."

14. ALBERT HAZLETT. Lieutenant. Born in Indiana county, Pennsylvania, September 21, 1837. Came to Kansas in 1857, perhaps as early as May. Located in Linn county, and was an ardent Free-State man. Was a follower of Montgomery. When John Brown appeared there he attached himself to the old hero's little band, and was one of the men who went into Missouri to liberate the eleven slaves. Escaped from Harper's Ferry, but was captured near Chambersburg, and returned to Virginia as William Harrison; tried there, and executed on the 16th of March, 1860.

15. JEREMIAH G. ANDERSON. Lieutenant. Born in Putnam county, Indiana, April 17, 1833. His ancestors were officers in the War of the Revolution, and were Virginians and slaveholders; they removed to Kentucky, and from there to Wisconsin, and finally to Indiana. Anderson came to Kansas in the fall of 1857, and purchased a claim on the Little Osage. He was a strong Free-State man, and bore his part in the troubles in southeastern Kansas. Killed at Harper's Ferry by a bayonet-thrust of one of the marines. "One of the prisoners described Anderson as turning completely over against the wall [to which he was pinned by the bayonet] in his dying agony. He lived a short time, stretched on the brick walk without, where he was subjected to savage brutalities, being kicked in body and face, while one brute of an armed farmer spat a huge quid of tobacco from his vile jaws into the mouth of the dying man, which he first forced open."

16. FRANCIS JACKSON MERRIAM. Born November 17, 1837, in Framingham, Massachusetts. His family had been for a previous generation opposed to slavery. Mer-

riam came to Kansas, but seems to have borne little part
in the struggle here, as he did not arrive before 1858.
Was ardent in his desire to fight slavery, and solicited
service under John Brown. Was educated; had some
money. Escaped from Harper's Ferry after the attack;
afterwards settled in Illinois, and enlisted in the Union
army. Died November 28, 1865.

17. STEWARD TAYLOR. Born in Uxbridge, in the prov-
ince of Ontario, Canada, October 29, 1836. Left his home
to go to Kansas, in his youth, but was seriously ill for
some time in Missouri. After he recovered he visited Arkansas, and finally went to Iowa. Here he worked in a
wagon factory, and became acquainted with George B.
Gill, Esq., who introduced him to John Brown. From
Iowa he went to Chatham, Canada, where he attended
the convention which adopted the provisional constitution.
After this he was one of John Brown's most ardent followers. Killed at Harper's Ferry.

18. SHIELDS GREEN. Fugitive slave from Charleston,
S. C. Joined Brown at Chambersburg, having come there
with Frederick Douglass, August 19th; was known as the
"Emperor," but how he obtained this name is not now
known. Was very brave. Captured with John Brown,
and executed December 16, 1859.

19. DANGERFIELD NEWBY. Free negro, married to a
slave woman living some thirty miles from Harper's
Ferry. Became acquainted with Brown in Canada. Was
killed at Harper's Ferry. His wife was immediately
sold to a dealer in Louisiana, and was living there some
years since.

20. JOHN A. COPELAND. Free negro; lived at Ober-

lin, Ohio. Seems to have been induced by friends there to join Brown, and was given money to pay his expenses to Chambersburg. Was captured, and executed on the 16th of December, 1859.

21. LEWIS SHERRARD LEARY. Free negro; married, and lived in Oberlin, Ohio. Said to have been the first Oberlin recruit to Brown's army. Was furnished money to go from Oberlin to Chambersburg, and accompanied John A. Copeland to that town. Was killed at Harper's Ferry.

22. JOHN ANDERSON. A free negro from Boston. Killed at Harper's Ferry. Nothing definite is known of this man. There is a question as to who he was, where he came from,—even that there was such a man in Brown's company.

23. OSBORN P. ANDERSON. Negro; born free, in Pennsylvania. Was a printer, and was working in Chatham, Canada, at his trade, when he met John Brown. Became one of his most devoted followers. Was a man of some ability, and of undoubted courage. Fought bravely at Harper's Ferry, and escaped. Afterwards he wrote an interesting account of the foray into Virginia, entitled "A Voice from Harper's Ferry." It is one of the most reliable and valuable accounts prepared of that invasion. Anderson enlisted in the Union army, and fought through the Civil War; he died in Washington City in 1871.

Others had been expected; they did not arrive in time to take part in the attack. Some of the men afterwards said the assault was made some days before the time first fixed for it, and this prevented the assembling of the full force. John Brown, jr., wrote on the 8th of September: "From what I even had understood, *I had sup-posed you would not think it best to commence opening the coal-banks before spring, unless circumstances should make it imperative.*" [5] It is very probable that the attack was hastened by some information which made Brown believe that to delay was to be fatal to his enterprise. Francis Jackson Merriam was the last accession to Brown's army to arrive at the Kennedy farm.

NOTE 1.—The letter was directed to John B. Floyd, Secretary of War. It is given, in full, in *Life and Letters of John Brown,* F. B. Sanborn, p. 543.

NOTE 2.—See Gerrit Smith's letter of August 27, 1859, published in full in *Life and Letters of John Brown,* F. B. Sanborn, p. 544.

NOTE 3.—Osborn P. Anderson's book, "A Voice from Harper's Ferry," is the best authority for the matters connected with the Kennedy farm.

NOTE 4.—*John Brown and His Men,* Richard J. Hinton, is the best authority extant upon the men who went with John Brown to Harper's Ferry. What is here said of them is principally compiled from Colonel Hinton's valuable work.

NOTE 5.—The correspondence between Brown and his men was worded in a blind way, which would not have betrayed them had a letter fallen into unfriendly hands. The people who unavoidably saw the pikes were led to believe they were parts of mining implements.

CHAPTER XIII.

THE SEIZURE OF HARPER'S FERRY.

Our hearts are as nothing—our gashes and scars
    Are worn without boastings and shammings:
What have men who have climbed to the steeps of the stars
    To do with Earth's vauntings and claimings?
But the Altars of Righteousness reared on the mounds
    Where our canonized heroes lie sleeping—
Not a stone must be touched while the sun swings his rounds,
    And our sabers are still in our keeping!
                                    —*Richard Realf.*

The 16th of October, 1859, was Sunday. The day was cloudy and lowering, and the night brought darkness, cold, and finally rain. John Brown had returned from Philadelphia during the previous Friday night. On Sunday morning "he arose earlier than usual, and called his men to worship." The day was a busy one. The men were assembled in council at ten o'clock, and for some time their enterprise was discussed. The constitution was read by Stevens, and those who had not done so before were sworn by Brown to support it and the new government they were about to undertake battle to establish. Commissions were given those officers who had not before received them. During the afternoon Brown formulated and published eleven orders for the present government of the men in their coming attack. It was a serious, solemn day, and each man realized that grave work lay ready to

(348)

his hand, the result of which would be fraught with momentous consequences to himself and others. John Brown had looked for this day and prayed for its coming for a quarter of a century. What it had for him he did not know; he was conscious of his own rectitude; and he held high and noble purposes,—for the result he was willing to trust God.

At eight o'clock the men were ordered to arm themselves, and were told that they were to proceed to the Ferry. Only twenty of the twenty-three went, for by the first of the eleven orders Owen Brown, F. J. Merriam and Barclay Coppoc were left at the farm to guard the arms until they could be removed to the school-house within two miles of the Ferry and on the Maryland side of the Potomac. The wagon was driven to the door, and some pikes, a sledge-hammer and a crowbar were placed in it. Then Brown "put on his old Kansas cap," and climbed into the wagon; after which he said to the men, who were ranked in marching order, "Come, boys." [1] He led the way to the main road, driving down the rugged path, the old wagon rattling over the road-worn stones, making a noise which sounded loud and harsh to the men, now wrought to high nerve-tension. The men marched in couples, each couple a given distance in the rear of that in advance, John E. Cook and Charles P. Tidd leading the column.[2] It was the order that anyone met in the highway should be held until the column had passed on or the men had concealed themselves until the wayfarer could be conducted away from the line of march. If they were overtaken by a traveler the orders were the same. The lonely road, shut out from the dull light of the over-

cast sky by the somber branches of beech and oak draped
in autumn mists, proved to be solitary and unfrequented
by nocturnal wanderers. The men were unmolested and
undiscovered, and they marched in melancholy silence
down to the bridge over the Potomac at Harper's Ferry.

Harper's Ferry is built in the fork of the Potomac and
Shenandoah rivers. The manufacturing portion of the
town is along the river-banks. Here are two streets, one
leading up each river. Back of these river streets the
land rises abruptly to a considerable height, and forms a
sort of uneven plateau, upon a part of which the residence
portion of the town is situated. This plateau increases
in height as it recedes from the junction of the rivers.
At some points its sides are perpendicular, or even over-
hanging, and a short distance up the rivers it rises to many
times the height of the tallest buildings along the water's
edge. The whole country bears the aspect of bold rugged-
ness, and the swift waters of the troubled rivers tumbling
over stony and broken beds swirl together fiercely and
lend a sense of savageness to the general visage of nature
there. The bridge runs from the point between the rivers,
with a down-stream diagonal course to the Maryland side.
There was a bridge across the Shenandoah, from the
town to the bluffs on the opposite side. The armory was
near the Virginia terminal of this bridge, with the railroad between it and the Potomac river. The arsenal was
a short distance up the Potomac, immediately on its bank,
and between the railroad and the river. The rifle-works
were on an island in the Shenandoah river, something
like a half-mile from its junction with the Potomac, and
that distance from the other Federal buildings. The

engine-house was a part of the arsenal and armory, although a little distance up the Potomac. The arsenal yard extended to the Shenandoah. There seems to have been a musket-factory something more than a quarter of a mile up the Potomac.

It was the duty of John E. Cook and Charles P. Tidd to tear down or cut the telegraph wires on the Maryland side of the Potomac during the night, and to do the same on the Virginia side when the town was captured. When for this purpose they left the ranks of the advancing army, Kagi and Stevens remained in advance. These secured the watchman at the bridge, and when the little band entered this thoroughfare, covered and inclosed like a house, they strapped their cartridge-boxes outside their coats and unmasked their Sharps' rifles, which until now they had concealed. Watson Brown and Steward Taylor were directed to guard the bridge and hold it until morning, and until they were relieved. Brown then drove his wagon to the gate of the armory; he was accompanied by his fourteen remaining men, and they arrived at the armory gate about half-past ten o'clock. They forced the armory gate with a crowbar, ran into the building, and secured one of the watchmen there. Brown sent Kagi and Copeland to capture the rifle-works. They were successful, and captured the watchmen at that place; they sent these to Brown, at the armory. The captured watchmen and bridge-guard were guarded by Jeremiah G. Anderson and the younger Thompson. Brown himself mounted guard at the armory gate, assisted by two men. Hazlett took possession of that part of the armory known as the arsenal. By one o'clock of Monday morning, the 17th, Brown had complete possession of Harper's Ferry and all the arms of the Federal Government then at that place; this was accomplished without firing a gun or shedding blood. He then sent Stevens, Cook, and four others up the turnpike towards Charlestown, to bring in Colonel Lewis W. Washington and his slaves. As they started upon this errand the night mail train on the Baltimore & Ohio Railroad came down the Potomac on its way from Wheeling to Baltimore. This train was stopped at the bridge by Watson Brown and Steward Taylor. This was the cause of the first bloodshed. The train porter, a free negro named Hayward, who lived at Harper's Ferry, went out to ascertain the cause of the arrest of the train and to search for the bridge-guard. When he appeared on the bridge he was halted by Brown's men, and instead of complying with this order he turned and fled. He was fired upon by Brown and Taylor, one shot striking him in the back; from the effect of this wound he died in a few hours. The train was detained until morning dawned. This was the first mistaken move of Brown at Harper's Ferry; no wires should have been cut until this train was well out of the town toward Baltimore, and it should have been allowed to pass without any knowledge of Brown's presence at Harper's Ferry.

In the gray light of the dull morning, which broke chill and damp, the expedition sent up the Potomac arrived with Colonel Washington and other slave-owners, and with the Colonel's large four-horse wagon. The Cavalier was met and welcomed by the stern old Puritan who had sent for him. "You will find a fire in here, sir; it is rather cool this morning," was his greeting. The slaves brought in were armed with pikes, but seem to have done little to aid Brown.[3] Some of them may have remained with him for a short time, but they evidently escaped as soon as possible. This was the first real disappointment of Brown. The slave-owners were added to the prisoners already held; and the wagon in which they arrived was immediately dispatched to the Kennedy farm to remove the arms remaining there to the school-house, two miles from the town, to be from there distributed to the slaves, who it was hoped would come in numbers to the aid of Brown as soon as they heard of the presence of the invaders.

As the morning advanced the people began to move about the streets in pursuit of their daily vocations. As they appeared they were captured and taken to the armory; by ten o'clock these prisoners numbered some sixty. Many of them were workmen who came down to their daily toil in the armory and rifle-works. One was a bartender in a near-by hotel. Brown exchanged this man for breakfast for his men and prisoners.

The train carried the news of an insurrection at Harper's Ferry, and the startling intelligence that the town was in the hands of the rebels. From a military point of view Brown blundered constantly after he gained possession of the armory and town. The first mistake was the capture of the train; the second was to allow it to proceed. Brown said he did this to relieve the anxiety of passengers on the train and their relatives, as well as those of the men in charge of the train. To have made any sort of success Brown should have destroyed the Federal buildings and arms, as well as the railroad and other bridges, and then have fled to the mountains. If he had

—23

done this, his blow would have been surrounded with such
mystery and followed by such destruction that, for a time,
rumor, magnifying a thousand-fold his forces, pursuit
would have been paralyzed. He could have escaped, and
from his view the expedition would have been something
of a success. His plans contemplated a quick abandonment of the town, and he was urged by Kagi, Stevens and
others to comply with this understanding and agreement.
Why he delayed to do so he did not himself know. He
gave as his reason that he "wanted to allay the fears of
those who believed we came here to burn and kill." "For
this reason," he said, " I allowed the train to cross the
bridge, and gave them full liberty to pass on. I did it
only to spare the feelings of those passengers and their
families, and to allay the apprehensions that you had got
here in your vicinity a band of men who had no regard
for life and property, nor any feelings of humanity."
The real cause of his delay was the failure of the slaves to
flock to his standard. He strained his eyes in vain for
the sight of crowds of them flocking over the hills and
along the valleys to take up arms for themselves. He delayed in waiting for them until it was too late to escape.
Perhaps he expected no general uprising; in fact, he says
he did not expect or desire that; but he certainly expected
a very considerable accession of negroes to his ranks at
Harper's Ferry. But his expectation was not reasonable.
The slaves were unacquainted with him; they had not
heard of him. The negro is suspicious, and the slaves had
been ground down for centuries; there was no widespread
determination to fight for freedom, perhaps no thought of
such determination. The war proved that the negro was

not ripe for rising; the white man forced the issue which gave to the black man his freedom.[4]

At noon, on Monday, it was barely possible for Brown to have escaped; after that his fate was fixed. Troops began to arrive. By one o'clock it was impossible for him to assemble his men, and it was necessary that each man fight from the position he then occupied; he could secure no other. Those in the arsenal just across the street from the engine-house could not join their leader; those on the Maryland side of the Potomac could not come to his assistance. By three o'clock Kagi and his companions were forced to abandon the rifle-factory, and were all killed or captured. Militia and citizens were firing from every point of vantage. Colonel Robert E. Lee arrived from Washington at the close of the day, but only the engine-house remained in possession of the invaders at that time; this was defended by Brown and six men, two of whom were wounded. Hazlett and Osborn P. Anderson yet remained in the arsenal, but could do nothing, and they finally escaped. Upon the arrival of Colonel Lee a flag of truce was sent to Brown, and his surrender demanded. He replied "that he knew what that meant—a rope for his men and himself; adding, 'I prefer to die just here.'" This flag was carried in by Captain J. E. B. Stuart, who had met Brown and detained him a short time in Kansas. Stuart recognized him, and from this meeting his identity became known. Stuart returned at daylight the following morning, but Brown had not changed his mind, and still answered, "No; I prefer to die here." Lee began his attack at once. The door failed to yield to the force of hammers, and a long ladder was grasped by its rungs by a file of men on each side of it; they battered down the door and pushed back the barricade against it. During this assault upon the door, Brown, seeing the hopelessness of further resistance, cried out that he surrendered. His assailants did not hear him, and perhaps their course would not have been changed if they had. A Lieutenant Green was the first to enter the engine-house, and was greeted with a shower of balls. Colonel Washington pointed out Brown; he "sprang about twelve feet at him, giving an under-thrust of his sword, striking Brown about midway the body, and raising him completely from the ground. Brown fell forward with his head between his knees, while Green struck him several times over the head, and, as I then supposed, split his skull at every stroke." [5] Brown was pinned to the ground with bayonets, one of which passed through his left kidney, and he was supposed to be dead.

"The fight was over; the work was done. John Brown was a prisoner, surrounded by politicians, soldiers, reporters, and vengeful spectators. His son, Owen, with his followers, Cook, Tidd, Barclay Coppoc, and F. J. Merriam, as also Albert Hazlett and O. P. Anderson, on their own account, were fugitives. Of these, Cook and Hazlett were captured, tried, and executed. Stevens, Edwin Coppoc, Copeland and Shields Green were hung; while Oliver and Watson Brown, William and Dauphin Thompson, John H. Kagi, William Leeman, Steward Taylor, Lewis S. Leary, Jeremiah G. Anderson, and Dangerfield Newby were killed in combat or as prisoners." [6]

John Brown had failed because he departed from his well-matured plans. He erred when he determined to

abandon the plan of twenty years and make the attack.
When the attack was made, some success might have en-
sued had he kept to his design to abandon the town soon
after daylight. By a few minutes past noon all possibility
of even escape was gone. All that could then be done was
to fight to the end, and desperately and grimly did he
do this. Colonel Washington bore witness to his bravery.
Governor Wise said, "And Colonel Washington said that
he—Brown—was the coolest man he ever saw in defying
death and danger. With one son dead by his side, and
another shot through, he felt the pulse of his dying son
with one hand and held the rifle with the other, and
commanded his men with the utmost composure, encourag-
ing them to be firm, and to sell their lives as dearly as
possible." When John Brown was carried out and placed
in the yard with the dead and dying, it seemed that
he had failed. For a day or two he may have feared so
himself; but this did not long continue.

> " God moves in a mysterious way,
>   His wonders to perform ;
> He plants his footsteps in the sea,
>   And rides upon the storm."

He was enabled to see God's hand. "All our actions,
even all the follies that led to this disaster, were decreed
to happen, ages before the world was made," he said.
When the scaffold was erected before his eyes he saw
it erected in God's mercy and in the execution of His
plans. He saw that the journey of his life had been directed to it by One that was mightier than he. That
unto him it was now to be given to die a martyr for
humanity, for his brother, for the poor, the despised, the

bondman, the oppressed. Such an exceeding weight of glory is apportioned to few men in this world. He saw the scaffold baptized in the blood of brave men fighting by his side, and as it arose it was consecrated by the groans and tears of children and mothers and fathers wailing in a bitter thralldom. He had faithfully labored in the vineyard of his Master, and now his reward was come, and a greater reward than has fallen to many other men.

NOTE 1.—The pamphlet of Osborn P. Anderson is the best authority that I find on the closing days of Brown and his men at the Kennedy farm, and also of the events which took place at Harper's Ferry. He saw what he wrote, and while it gives us the impression that the slaves came to Brown's aid, this may be pardoned in one who was writing of the first struggle of the new revolution for the liberation of his race. Anderson seems to have been a brave man, as indeed were all the men who followed Brown to Harper's Ferry. He was ready and willing to die for his own people, if his death were required.

NOTE 2.—Their work was to destroy the telegraph lines, and when these were reached and they left the column for that purpose, Stevens and Kagi were left in the front.

NOTE 3.—Speaking of the suitability of the spear or pike for a weapon for the negro, General Benjamin F. Butler said:

"Reverting to the subject of arming the negroes, I said to him that I thought it might be possible to start with a sufficient number of white troops, and avoiding a march which might deplete their ranks by death and sickness, to take them in ships and land them somewhere on the Southern coast. These troops could then come up through the Confederacy, gathering up negroes, who could be armed at first with arms that they could handle, so as to defend themselves and aid the rest of the army in case of rebel charges upon it. In this way we could establish ourselves down there with an army that would be a terror to the whole South.

"He [the President] asked me what I would arm them with. I told him John Brown had intended, if he got loose in the mountains of Virginia, to arm his negroes with spears and revolvers; and there was a great deal in that. Negroes would know how to use those arms, and Southern troops would not know how to meet their use of them, and they could be easily transported in large numbers and would require no great expense or trouble in supplying ammunition.

"'That is a new idea, General,' said he.

"'No, Mr. President,' I answered, 'it is a very old one. The fathers of these negroes themselves, fought their battles in Africa with no other weapon save a club.'"—"*Butler's Book*," *Benjamin F. Butler, p. 579*.

NOTE 4.—It is not meant to say here that the negro acted in any different manner than would any other enslaved race. Nor is it meant to say that he had not the courage to fight. After the war began he fought for his freedom as he had the opportunity. But the war for his liberation was of the white man's creation, and due in small degree to any effort of the black man, though Douglass and others did all they could, and aided much the cause.

NOTE 5.—Statement of Captain Daingerfield, one of Brown's prisoners, published in most of the biographies of Brown. This is quoted from *Life and Letters of John Brown*, F. B. Sanborn, p. 559.

NOTE 6.—*John Brown and His Men*, Richard J. Hinton, p. 307.

The details of the fight of Virginia against Brown and his men are too long for insertion here; space forbids it. Colonel Hinton's work, above referred to, is one of the best in this respect.

CHAPTER XIV.

TRIAL OF CAPTAIN JOHN BROWN.

Portia.   Why, this bond is forfeit;
And lawfully by this the Jew may claim
A pound of flesh, to be by him cut off
Nearest the merchant's heart.—Be merciful:
Take thrice thy money; bid me tear the bond.
 Shylock. When it is paid according to the tenour.—
It doth appear you are a worthy judge;
You know the law; your exposition
Hath been most sound: I charge you by the law,
Whereof you are a well-deserving pillar,
Proceed to judgment. By my soul I swear,
There is no power in the tongue of man
To alter me. I stay here on my bond.
 Antonio. Most heartily do I beseech the court
To give the judgment.
 Portia.   Why then, thus it is:
You must prepare your bosom for his knife.
 Shylock. O noble judge! O excellent young man!
 Portia. For the intent and purpose of the law
Hath full relation to the penalty
Which here appeareth due upon the bond.
 Shylock. 'Tis very true. O wise and upright judge!
How much more elder art thou than thy looks!
 Portia. Therefore lay bare your bosom.
 Shylock.   Ay, his breast;
So says the bond—doth it not, noble judge?—
Nearest his heart; those are the very words.

. . . .

 Portia. You, merchant, have you anything to say?
 Antonio. But little; I am arm'd and well prepar'd.—
      —*Shakespeare's "Merchant of Venice."*

John Brown was immediately closely questioned. No mistake can be charged to him after his capture. His mind cleared at once; his duty to humanity and himself stood out distinct and clearly defined. Doubts and hesitation fled. His statements and avowals were frank, very full, and very ingenious. No man ever said more precisely what he intended to say than did John Brown to his inquisitors in Virginia. Interrogators were numerous and of all ranks, and they came at all times, both by night and by day. Governor Wise, shortsighted, and with no understanding at all of what this foray meant, stood in the presence of one of the heroes of the ages with mind now cleared by the revelation of God's purpose, and received plain and simple statements which it took four years of war to make him understand. Vallandigham, the pusillanimous, slimy, cringing demagogue and malignant blatherskite, the Ohio doughface, hurried to Harper's Ferry, broke in abruptly upon the wounded man, interrupted the Southern inquisitors, bullied the old hero for a short time, and retired in discomfiture but with the hope that his zeal for the slave-owners had been noted, and that he should be rewarded by them when they should come to distribute the offices. Having no fixed principles, nor the remotest conception of right, honor and truth, he could have no comprehension of an action growing out of a deep conviction of justice and a desire to sacrifice even one's life for the benefit of humanity. He evidently expected guarded and reluctant replies from Brown, or perhaps a refusal to talk. Then he could have said to the Virginians, " Here is a great mystery. The people of the North, and especially of Ohio, are implicated without exception other than the Democratic party. I join hands with you in meting out political punishment." But nothing was concealed. Brown was anxious to talk— anxious to have his intentions fully known. Strange man!—incomprehensible! The more he explained his intentions the more did he befog the mediocres and the doughface.

In the long interview he was literally weltering in his blood. His wounds had not been dressed, and he believed himself near death by reason of them. But he was courteous, affable, kind, explicit, sublime.

A bystander. Do you consider this a religious movement?

Brown. It is, in my opinion, the greatest service man can render to God.

Bystander. Do you consider yourself an instrument in the hands of Providence?

Brown. I do.

Bystander. Upon what principle do you justify your acts.

Brown. Upon the Golden Rule. I pity the poor in bondage that have none to help them: that is why I am here; not to gratify any personal animosity, revenge, or vindictive spirit. It is my sympathy with the oppressed and the wronged, that are as good as you, and as precious in the sight of God. . . . I want you to understand that I respect the rights of the poorest and weakest of the colored people, oppressed by the slave system, just as much as I do the most wealthy and powerful. That is the idea that has moved me, and that alone. We expected no reward except the satisfaction of endeavoring to do for those in distress—the greatly oppressed—as we would be done by. The cry of distress, of the oppressed, is my reason, and the only thing that prompted me to come here.[1]

"Never before, in the United States, did a recorded conversation produce so sudden and universal a change of opinion. Before its publication, some, who subsequently eulogized John Brown with fervor and surpassing eloquence, as well as the great body of the press and people who knew not the man, lamented that he should have gone insane,—never doubting that he was a maniac; while, after it, from every corner of the land came words of wonder, of praise rising to worship, and of gratitude mingled with sincerest prayers for the noble old hero. Enemies and friends were equally amazed at the carriage and sayings of the wounded warrior. 'During his conversation,' wrote a Southern pro-slavery reporter to a Southern pro-slavery paper, 'no signs of weakness were exhibited. In the midst of enemies whose home he had invaded; wounded and a prisoner; surrounded by a small army of officials and a more desperate army of angry men; with the gallows staring him full in the face, Brown lay on the floor, and, in reply to every question, gave answers that betokened the spirit that animated him. The language of Governor Wise well expresses his boldness when he said: "He is the gamest man I ever saw." I believe the worthy Executive had hardly expected to see a man so act in such a trying moment.' "

" 'Such a word as *insane*,' said an eloquent speaker, unconsciously uttering the opinion of the people of the North, 'is a mere trope with those who persist in using it; and I have no doubt that many of them, in silence, have already retracted their words. Read his admirable answers to Mason and others. How they are dwarfed and defeated by the contrast! On the one side, half-brutish, half-timid questioning; on the other, Truth, clear as lightning, crashing into their obscure temples. They are made to stand as Pilate or Gessler and the Inquisition. Probably all the speeches of all the men whom Massachusetts has sent to

Congress for the last few years do not match, for manly directness and force, and for simple truth, the few casual remarks of John Brown on the floor of the Harper's Ferry engine-house,—that man whom you are about to send to the other world; though not to represent *you* there. He is too fair a specimen of a man to represent the like of us. Who, then, were his constituents? Read his words understandingly, and you will find out. In his case there is no idle eloquence. Truth is the inspirer and earnestness the polisher of his sentences. He could afford the loss of his Sharps' rifle while he retained the faculty of speech—a rifle of far straighter sight and longer range." [2]

Some people profess to believe that John Brown was insane. There is no evidence anywhere that he was insane or mentally deranged. Replying to this imputation, he himself said: "I may be very insane; and I am so, if insane at all. But if that be so, insanity is like a very pleasant dream to me. I am not in the least degree conscious of my ravings, of my fears, or of any terrible visions whatever; but fancy myself entirely composed, and that my sleep, in particular, is as sweet as that of a healthy, joyous little infant." [3] One of the most eloquent men ever in Kansas public life says: "All men who rise to the height of purest patriotism and absolute unselfishness, who are ready to die for their principles, have been charged in their day and age as impractical, and mentally unbalanced. This is said of Luther, Melanchthon, and Columbus, and inventors like Fulton, Morse, Howe, and even of our own Edison. *It is the explanation mediocrity offers for greatness.*" [4]

John Brown and his men were captured on the property of the United States, by the United States marines, but they were left to be dealt with by the State of Virginia. On the 19th of October, Brown, Stevens, Coppoc and Shields Green were conveyed to Charlestown, the county seat of Jefferson county, Virginia, (now in West Virginia.) The formal committal occurred on the 20th, upon charges sworn to by Governor Wise and two other witnesses, accusing them of "feloniously conspiring with each other; and other persons unknown, to make an abolition insurrection and open war against the Commonwealth of Virginia." A writ was issued to the sheriff, commanding him to summon and convene a preliminary court of examination on the 25th. At half-past ten o'clock on that day the court assembled. It consisted of eight persons,—justices of the peace,—and was presided over by a Colonel Davenport. The prisoners were brought in, "presenting a pitiable sight, Brown and Stevens being unable to stand without assistance." Brown's eyes were almost closed from the inflammation caused by his wounds; his hearing was so impaired that he could hear but indistinctly, and was unable to gather the words or even the import of his judges or his counsel. The only man with a comprehension of what was taking place in that Virginia court was John Brown. He was not deceived with promises of a fair trial. He said—"Virginians: I did not ask for quarter at the time I was taken. I did not ask to have my life spared. The Governor of the State of Virginia tendered me his assurance that I should have a fair trial; but under no circumstances whatever will I be able to attend to my trial. If you seek my blood, you can have it at any moment without this mockery of a trial. . . If we are to be forced with a mere form,—a trial for execution,—you might spare yourselves

that trouble. I am ready for my fate. I do not ask a trial.
I beg for no mockery of a trial—no insult—nothing but
that which conscience gives or cowardice would drive you to
practice. I ask again to be excused from the mockery of a
trial. I do not know what the special design of this examination is. I do not know what is to be the benefit of it
to the Commonwealth. I have now little further to ask,
other than that I may be not foolishly insulted, only as
cowardly barbarians insult those who fall into their
power." [5] He did not ask that his fate be different from
what he knew it must. His only concern was that his
objects and intentions should be clearly and truthfully
shown.

The court presented an indictment against Brown, containing three counts, as follows:

Conspiracy with slaves for the purpose of insurrection;
Treason against the Commonwealth of Virginia; and
Murder in the first degree.

The trial was set for the following day, October 26th.
The attorney for the Commonwealth charged that he was
feigning sickness, to obtain delay and gain time. On the
report of the jail surgeon that he could endure the ordeal,
the trial was ordered to proceed. The court assigned him
counsel, two resident members of the bar. The North sent
counsel for Brown, but no expectation of fairness was
entertained by him, and his attorneys had no hope of
accomplishing anything in his favor.[6] He took little interest in the matter, but lay on his pallet with his eyes closed
most of the time. When his attorneys thought to benefit
his case by filing a plea of insanity in his behalf, he
"raised himself up in bed" and repelled it with scorn and

indignation. John Brown was one of the sanest men that
ever lived. He said: "I will add, if the court will allow
me, that I look upon it as a miserable artifice and pretext
of those who ought to take a different course in regard to
me, if they took any at all, and I view it with contempt
more than otherwise. As I remarked to Mr. Green, insane
prisoners, so far as my experience goes, have but little
ability to judge of their own sanity; and if insane, of
course I should think I knew more than all the rest of the
world. But I do not think so. I am perfectly unconscious
of insanity, and I reject, so far as I am capable, any attempts to interfere in my behalf on that score." [7]

When the Commonwealth had closed, Brown asked a
short delay, and this was refused. Thereupon his Virginia
counsel deserted him. Attorneys from the North arrived,
and assumed control of the defense. But no one expected
that anything would come of efforts to get him justice.
The cause was given to the jury late in the afternoon of
Monday, October 31st, and after an hour's deliberation
a verdict was returned of guilty as charged in the indictment.

John Brown said not a word.

On the second day of November he was brought into
court to hear his sentence. "He still walked with difficulty,
every step being attended with evident pain. His features
were firm and composed, but within the dimly lighted court
room, showed wan and pallid. He seated himself near
his counsel, and resting his head upon his hand, remained
motionless, apparently the most unheeding man in the
room. He sat upright with lips compressed, looking direct
into the chilled stern face of the judge as he overruled the

exceptions of counsel. When directed by the clerk to say 'why sentence should not be passed upon him,' John Brown rose slowly to his feet, placing his hands on the table in front of him, and leaning slightly forward, in a voice singularly quiet and self-controlled, with tones of marked gentleness and a manner slow and slightly hesitating, made this memorable speech." [8]

"I have, may it please the court, a few words to say: In the first place, I deny everything but what I have all along admitted,—the design on my part to free the slaves. I intended certainly to have made a clean thing of that matter, as I did last winter, when I went into Missouri and took slaves without the snapping of a gun on either side, moved them through the country, and finally left them in Canada. I designed to have done the same thing again, on a larger scale. That was all I intended. I never did intend murder, or treason, or the destruction of property, or to excite or incite slaves to rebellion, or to make insurrection.

"I have another objection: and that is, it is unjust that I should suffer such a penalty. Had I interfered in the manner which I admit, and which I admit has been fairly proved (for I admire the truthfulness and candor of the greater portion of the witnesses who have testified in this case), had I so interfered in behalf of the rich, the powerful, the intelligent, the so-called great, or in behalf of any of their friends,—either father, mother, brother, sister, wife, or children, or any of that class,—and suffered and sacrificed what I have in this interference, it would have been all right; and every man in this court would have deemed it an act worthy of reward rather than punishment.

"This court acknowledges, as I suppose, the validity of the law of God. I see a book kissed here which I suppose is

the Bible, or at least the New Testament. That teaches me
that all things whatsoever I would that men should do
to me, I should do even so to them. It teaches me further,
to 'remember them that are in bonds, as bound with them.'
I endeavored to act up to that instruction. I say, I am yet
too young to understand that God is any respecter of persons. I believe that to have interfered as I have done—as I
have always freely admitted I have done—in behalf of His
despised poor, was not wrong, but right. Now, if it is
deemed necessary that I should forfeit my life for the furtherance of the ends of justice, and mingle my blood further with the blood of my children and with the blood of
millions in this slave country whose rights are disregarded
by wicked, cruel, and unjust enactments,—I submit; so
let it be done.

"Let me say one word further.

"I feel entirely satisfied with the treatment I have received on my trial. Considering all the circumstances, it
has been more generous than I expected. But I feel no
consciousness of guilt. I have stated from the first what
was my intention, and what was not. I never had any design against the life of any person, nor any disposition to
commit treason, or excite slaves to rebel, or make any
general insurrection. I never encouraged any man to do
so, but always discouraged any idea of the kind.

"Let me say, also, a word in regard to the statements
made by some of those connected with me. I hear it has
been stated by some of them that I have induced them to
join me. But the contrary is true. I do not say this to
injure them, but as regarding their weakness. There is not
one of them but joined me of his own accord, and the
greater part of them at their own expense. A number of
them I never saw, and never had a word of conversation
with, till the day they came to me; and that was for the
purpose I have stated.

"Now I have done!" [9]

—24

NOTE 1.—This is only a short quotation from the conversation. It was reported and published by the newspapers; perhaps the New York *Herald* had the best report of it. Much of it can be found in *The Life of Captain John Brown*, by James Redpath; and in *Life and Letters of John Brown*, by F. B. Sanborn.

NOTE 2.—*Life of Captain John Brown*, James Redpath, p. 275.

NOTE 3.—John Brown, in a letter to Hon. D. R. Tilden, November 28, 1859, from the Charlestown jail, quoted here from *Life and Letters of John Brown*, F. B. Sanborn, p. 609.

NOTE 4.—*Lecture on John Brown*, J. K. Hudson, Topeka.

NOTE 5.—Associated Press report; quoted here from *John Brown and His Men*, Richard J. Hinton, p. 339.

NOTE 6.—George Henry Hoyt, of Boston; Mr. Chilton, of Washington; Judge Griswold, of Cleveland, Ohio. George Sennott, of Boston, defended the other prisoners.

NOTE 7.—Quoted from *Life and Letters of John Brown*, F. B. Sanborn, p. 574.

NOTE 8.—*John Brown and His Men*, Richard J. Hinton, p. 362.

NOTE 9.—Quoted from *John Brown and His Men*, Richard J. Hinton, p. 362.

CHAPTER XV.

COURT TO SCAFFOLD.

I cannot remember a night so dark as to have hindered the coming day, nor a storm so furious or dreadful as to prevent the return of warm sunshine and a cloudless sky. But, beloved ones, do remember that this is not your rest,—that in this world you have no abiding-place or continuing city.

—*John Brown, to his Wife and Children.*

So far as can now be determined, it is believed that John Brown was well pleased to have his trial ended. He expected no different result. There was no disappointment in the verdict for John Brown. He knew from the first that surrender or capture meant "a rope for his men and himself," and for that reason he preferred to die with gun in hand. It was impossible for Virginia to have done differently with John Brown. The old hero knew this. While he seems to have made no distinction between the forays into Missouri and Virginia, they were, in nature, entirely different. It was his purpose to have remained in Virginia or other Southern States. He attacked, captured, and tried to hold the town of Harper's Ferry, or portions of it. He was guilty of conspiracy. He invaded Virginia. He slew Virginians. He sent flags of truce and demeaned himself as a soldier, and he complained when he was not accorded the rights of an enemy in civilized warfare. No State can suffer the invasion of its soil by a hostile armed force. Such a violation must be punished; such invasion suppressed. Otherwise the dignity of the State passes away and authority disappears. It has always been held that such offenses against States should be sternly and re-lentlessly dealt with. In this instance it was imperative that Virginia do promptly one of two things—execute John Brown and his companions, or free her slaves. There could be no evasion, no hesitation; there was no escape. And while the trial of Brown was unfair, it was as fair as he expected, and as fair as he had reason to except. Perhaps, after all, there was very little violence done the precedents of judicature in the disposition of political prisoners, or of persons who have assailed polit-ical institutions; such trials have never been in exact accord with law. It was not reasonable for John Brown to expect to escape punishment by Virginia. When he said surrender meant "a rope for himself and men," he certainly expected to pay with his life the full penalty which he knew Virginia would exact. Brown complained that his execution was to be judicial murder. This con-clusion must have been reached after the deep contempla-tion of the injustice done him by the non-observance and non-accord of all the legal rights he felt himself entitled to in his trial. But this conclusion can scarcely be con-curred in. Virginia's action was legally right and mor-ally wrong. The motto of sovereignty has always been:

> "You must not think
> That we are made of stuff so flat and dull
> That we can let our beard be shook with danger,
> And think it pastime."

In the state of public opinion prevailing in Virginia

and the entire South, Virginia could not adopt abolition
for her slaves. For a quarter of a century the popularity
of the institution had been increasing in that portion of
the United States where it existed, and the aggressions of
the slave-power upon the free territory of the country
remaining unpeopled was one of the causes of Brown's
presence at Harper's Ferry. And while the execution of
John Brown was thus not left to the discretion of Virginia, the saving of the institution of slavery for the
time being by this act only postponed the day when the
fetters would fall from all the slaves. And this day was
made more and more inevitable by the very act upon which
the lease of life of the institution temporarily hung. Virginia was compelled to hang John Brown to preserve
slavery, but his death did more to forward universal emancipation than his life could ever have accomplished had he
had all the successes he hoped for. And while Slavery
legally executed John Brown, it could not escape the consequences of that act. It acted by virtue of accredited
authority and recognized enactments, which, though ever
so wrong in spirit, must be the rule of action for state
and municipality until repealed. John Brown struck at
the root of the wrong. He acted upon the eternal principles of justice; he brought these principles into conflict—active and aggressive conflict—with an accredited
wrong and an evil and injustice which existed by authority. Such has been the burden borne by every reformer
in all the ages. The task has been this—only this—
nothing more. And it has almost invariably required the
blood of the reformer to cause his reformation to take
root. "Without the shedding of blood there is no re-

mission," has been the law of human progress. If there was any one great truth, universal in its application, known to Brown, it was the principle contained in this text. So, when the scaffold rose before his eyes, he saw in the temporary victory of Slavery over the powers he had succeeded in setting against it its ultimate defeat and annihilation. He spent the remaining days allowed him in laying broad and deep the lines of this conflict, which he saw was inevitable, and which it was given him to see would end in a triumph for justice and the principles he had devoted his life to forwarding, and for which he gladly and joyously went to the scaffold.

"Christ saw fit to take from me the sword of steel after I had carried it for a time, but He has put another in my hand, ('the sword of the Spirit;') and I pray God to make me a faithful soldier wherever He may send me—not less on the scaffold than when surrounded by my warmest sympathizers," he wrote to his old teacher. With the new weapon given him he continued to fight to the end. The forces of his new warfare ranged themselves under his command, and from the time of his arraignment until his execution he suffered no defeat, but enjoyed victory every hour. He had anticipated all the cost, whatever occurred. In the letter above referred to he says: "And before I began my work at Harper's Ferry, I felt assured that in the *worst event* it would certainly *pay*." Thus was he enabled to go back to his dungeon in the spirit of a conqueror; he had looked at the gallows before he began his work, and the scaffold had no terrors for him. The ancient precept of the Brown family, "An old man should have more care to end life well than to live long," was exemplified in him. His work, he was in faith, would bear much fruit in the realm of slavery; "I have many opportunities for faithful plain-dealing with the more powerful, influential, and intelligent classes in this region, which I trust are not entirely misimproved," he wrote. The spirit in which he entered the new field is well exemplified in the reply to a Quaker lady who wrote him expressing her sympathy for his condition: "And may the Lord reward you a thousand fold for the kind feeling you express toward me; but more especially for your fidelity to the 'poor that cry, and those that have no help.' For this I am a prisoner in bonds. It is solely my own fault, in a military point of view, that we met with our disaster. I mean that I mingled with our prisoners and so far sympathized with them and their families that I neglected my duty in other respects. But God's will, not mine, be done. You know that Christ once armed Peter. So also in my case I think He put a sword into my hand, and there continued it so long as He saw best, and then kindly took it from me. I mean when I first went to Kansas. I wish you could know with what cheerfulness I am now wielding the 'sword of the Spirit' on the right hand and on the left. I bless God that it proves 'mighty to the pulling down of strongholds.' " And to his brother he wrote: " I am quite cheerful in view of my approaching end,—being fully persuaded that I am worth inconceivably more to hang than for any other purpose."

He was loaded with fetters—chained to the floor of his prison. Armed guards walked before his dungeon-door day and night, and they had orders to shoot him at once upon any attempt at rescue. He was wounded and sick; his time to live was limited to a month. He had no expectation that it would be extended a minute; the effort for a new trial he regarded as a mere froth of "attorney-logic." He was without education; of rhetoric he knew nothing. But the world waited for his every sentence, and the words most sought for and hung upon came from the prison at Charlestown, and not from the temple of justice there, nor from the Governor's mansion in Richmond. His words stirred the North. He was known before he went to Harper's Ferry; after his imprisonment there, and his condemnation, his name was upon every tongue. Before, they knew him as a brave soldier fighting ruffianism in Kansas; now, they saw him stand as a martyr for the poor. "I feel just as content to die for God's *Eternal Truth, and for suffering humanity's, on the scaffold as in any other way;* and I do not say this from any disposition to 'brave it out.' No; I would readily *own* my wrong, were I *in the least convinced of it.*" In this spirit he spent his last days: "Under all these terrible calamities, I feel quite cheerful in the assurance that God reigns and will overrule all for His glory and the best possible good. I feel no consciousness of guilt in the matter, nor even mortification on account of my imprisonment and irons." He encourages his family in this same letter: "Never forget the poor, nor think anything you bestow on them to be lost to you. . . . Remember them that are in bonds as bound with them. . . . 'These light afflictions, which are but for a moment, shall work out for us a far more exceeding and eternal weight of glory.'" And he adds in the postscript: "Yesterday, November 2,

I was sentenced to be hanged on December 2, next. Do not grieve on my account. I am still quite cheerful."

His wife desired very much to visit him. This he at first opposed, on account of the feeling against him in Charlestown and the fear that she would be insulted and insolently treated. But on the 16th of November he wrote: " If you feel sure that you can endure the trials and the shock which will be unavoidable (if you come), I should be most glad to see you once more. . . . If you do come, defer your journey till about the 27th or 28th of this month."

John Brown rejoiced that " he was counted worthy to suffer in God's cause." He wrote to T. B. Musgrove: "Men cannot imprison, or chain, or hang the soul. I go joyfully in behalf of millions that 'have no rights' that this great and glorious, this Christian Republic 'is bound to respect.' Strange change in morals, political as well as Christian, since 1776! I look forward to other changes to take place in God's good time, fully believing that 'the fashion of this world passeth away.' " This was his constant theme. He wrote his cousin, the Rev. Luther Humphrey: " I suppose I am the first since the landing of Peter Brown from the ' Mayflower' that has either been sentenced to imprisonment or to the gallows. But, my dear old friend, let not that fact alone grieve you. You cannot have forgotten how and where our grandfather fell in 1776, and that he, too, might have perished on the scaffold had circumstances been but a very little different. The fact that a man dies under the hand of an executioner (or otherwise) has but little to do with his true character, as I suppose. John Rogers perished at the stake, a great and good man, as I suppose; but his doing so does not prove that any other man who has died in the same way was good or otherwise. . . . No part of my life has been more happily spent than that I have spent here; and I humbly trust that no part has been spent to better purpose. I would not say this boastingly, but thanks be unto God, who giveth us the victory through grace.

" I should be sixty years old were I to live to May 9, 1860. I have enjoyed much of life as it is, and have been remarkably prosperous, having early learned to regard the welfare and prosperity of others as my own. I have never, since I can remember, required a great amount of sleep; so that I conclude that I have already enjoyed full an average number of working-hours with those who reach their threescore years and ten. I have not yet been driven to the use of glasses, but can see to read and write quite comfortably. But more than that, I have generally enjoyed remarkably good health. I might go on to recount unnumbered and unmerited blessings, among which would be some very severe afflictions, and those the most needed blessings of all. And now, when I think how easily I might be left to spoil all I have done or suffered in the cause of freedom, I hardly dare to wish another voyage, even if I had the opportunity."

There were matters of concern to him now (about the 20th of November) taking place in and about Charlestown. Incendiary fires destroyed buildings almost every night. And Governor Wise was in daily receipt of threatening letters. John Brown had no friends in the vicinity of Charlestown, but he felt sure that it would be charged that his friends caused the fires. They were doubtless kindled by persons who desired to keep the people in a frenzy against the invaders, that a rescue or a pardon would be impossible. Some foolish and mistaken friend in the North may have written letters of ominous import to Governor Wise, but no one regretted it so much as did John Brown.

He retained his interest in the affairs of the little farm in the gloomy woods of the North, and complains that they do not write him whether any of their crops had matured or not. His thoughts were never of himself: "I have no sorrow either as to the result, only for my poor wife and children," he wrote a minister, November 23d. And to this minister he also wrote, " You may wonder, Are there no ministers of the gospel here? I answer, No. There are no ministers of Christ here. These ministers who profess to be Christian, and hold slaves or advocate slavery, I cannot abide them. My knees will not bend in prayer with them while their hands are stained with the blood of souls." He said to the others that the prayers of such ministers were an abomination to his God.

It was made known to John Brown before he died that friends would aid in the education of his children. When consulted about this matter he always made practical replies, and was never once tempted to suggest for them anything more than the useful. The industrious housewife is the foundation upon which rests the Republic, not upon the women of fashion, wealth, ease and leisure. These care for nothing but vanity. They are the butterflies of our country, and are entirely useless. But the wife who bears and brings up children, who cooks their food, designs their clothing, weeps with them, prays with them, rejoices with them, carries them and their troubles in her own life day by day,—she is the foundation-stone of American liberty. On this subject he wrote: " I feel disposed to leave the education of my dear children to their mother, and to those dear friends who bear the burden of it; only expressing my earnest hope that they may all become strong, intelligent, expert, industrious, Christian housekeepers. I would wish that, together with other studies, they may thoroughly study Dr. Franklin's ' Poor Richard.' I want them to become matter-of-fact women."

John Brown's wife visited him; she was permitted to eat dinner with him in his cell. His body was delivered to her after his execution.

There is little more to be said. John Brown died as he had lived—brave, and free from fear of any kind. On the morning of his execution he took a tender but cheerful farewell of his companions in bonds and in arms. He gave them each a small coin, except Hazlett. He visited Stevens last: "Good-by, Captain," he said; "I know you are going to a better land." "I know I am," replied Brown.

John Brown was put into a furniture wagon, in which was his own black-walnut coffin; the jailer, Mr. Avis, who had been very kind to Brown, and the driver, a man named Hawks, being the other occupants. The wagon was surrounded by cavalry, which escorted it to the field where the gallows was standing, something like half a mile away. Here there were a large number of soldiers going through military maneuvers, and assembled to prevent

the rescue of Brown. He was calm, perfectly self-pos-
sessed. He was asked if he thought he could endure the
ordeal, and replied, "I can endure almost anything but
parting from friends; that is very hard." In speaking
of fear, on the road to the scaffold, he said: "It has
been a characteristic of me, from infancy, not to suffer
from physical fear. I have suffered a thousand times
more from bashfulness than from fear." "You are a
game man, Captain Brown," said an attendant. He replied, "Yes, I was so trained up; it was one of the lessons
of my mother; but it is hard to part from friends, though
newly made." "You are more cheerful than I am, Captain Brown," said his friend. The stern old hero replied,
"Yes, I ought to be."

The wagon halted at the scaffold, and the troops opened
file. Brown descended from the wagon, saluted the Mayor
and Mr. Hunter, and ascended the scaffold stairs. I shall
let an eye-witness describe the execution.

"His demeanor was intrepid, without being braggart.
. . . John Brown's manner gave no evidence of tim-
idity. He stood upon the scaffold but a short time, giving
brief adieus to those about him, when he was properly
pinioned, the white cap drawn over his face, the noose
adjusted and attached to the hook above, and he was
moved, blindfolded, a few steps forward. It was curious
to note how the instincts of nature operated to make him
careful in putting out his feet, as if afraid he would walk
off the scaffold. The man who stood unblenched on the
brink of eternity, was afraid of falling a few feet to the
ground!

"Everything was now in readiness. The sheriff asked

the prisoner if he should give him a private signal before
the fatal moment.   He replied, in a voice that sounded to
me unnaturally natural,—so composed was its tone, and
so distinct its articulation,—that 'it did not matter to him,
if only they would not keep him too long waiting.'   He
was kept waiting, however; the troops that had formed
his escort had to be put into their proper position, and
while this was going on he stood for some ten or fifteen
minutes blindfolded, the rope about his neck, and his feet
on the treacherous platform, expecting instantly the fatal
act; but he stood for this comparatively long time upright
as a soldier in position, and motionless.   I was close to
him, and watched him narrowly, to see if I could detect
any signs of shrinking or trembling in his person, but
there was none.   Once I thought I saw his knees tremble,
but it was only the wind blowing his loose trousers.   His
firmness was subjected to still further trial by hearing
Colonel Smith announce to the sheriff, ' We are all ready,
Mr. Campbell.'   The sheriff did not hear or did not comprehend, and in a louder tone the same announcement was
made.   But the culprit still stood steady until the sheriff,
descending the flight of steps, with a well-directed blow
of a sharp hatchet severed the rope that held up the trap-
door, which instantly sank sheer beneath him.   He fell
about three feet; and the man of strong and bloody hand,
of fierce passions, of iron will, of wonderful vicissitudes,
the terrible partisan of Kansas, the capturer of the United
States Arsenal at Harper's Ferry, the would-be Catiline
of the South, the demi-god of the abolitionists, the man
execrated and lauded, damned and prayed for, the man
who, in his motives, his means, his plans, and his suc-

cesses, must ever be a wonder, a puzzle and a mystery, John Brown, was hanging between heaven and earth."

This was written by J. T. L. Preston, of the Military College of Lexington, Virginia, a few hours after the execution. He adds: "In all that array there was not, I suppose, one throb of sympathy for the offender. Yet the mystery was awful—to see the human form thus treated by men—to see life suddenly stopped in its current, and to ask one's self the question without answer, 'And what then?' "

John Brown's body was taken to North Elba. As it was lowered into the grave the preacher repeated the words of Paul:

"I have fought the good fight; I have finished my course; I have kept the faith: henceforth there is laid up for me a crown of righteousness, which the Lord, the righteous Judge, shall give me; and not to me only, but unto all that love His appearing."

The South always maintained that the attack on Harper's Ferry was the beginning of the Civil War. On March 30th, 1860, Victor Hugo wrote:

"Slavery in all its forms will disappear. What the South slew last December was not John Brown, but Slavery. Henceforth, no matter what President Buchanan may say in his shameful message, the American Union must be considered dissolved. Between the North and the South stands the gallows of Brown. Union is no longer possible: such a crime cannot be shared."

John A. Andrew was the war Governor of Massachusetts. When John Brown was executed he said of him:

"Whatever may be thought of John Brown's acts, John Brown himself was right."

The world acquiesces in the verdict thus rendered, and accepts it as true.

_____

MURAT HALSTEAD'S DESCRIPTION OF THE EXECUTION OF JOHN BROWN.

[This sketch was written by the eminent journalist, Murat Halstead, for the *New York Independent*. It was published in the *Topeka Mail and Breeze*, December 9, 1898.]

The execution of John Brown was on the second of December, 1859; the scene, in a field a furlong south of Charlestown, seven miles from Harper's Ferry. The sensation caused by the John Brown raid was something wonderful. The excitement of the whole country was out of all proportion to the material incidents. The shock was because the feeling of the people that the slavery question had reached an acute stage and demanded uncompromising attention, was general, and there was apprehension that there were conditions upon the country of "unmerciful disaster"—a public sensibility that an immense catastrophe was impending.

As a correspondent of the *Cincinnati Commercial,* to write the story of the hanging of old John Brown, I carried letters from Dr. Dandridge, cousin of Colonel Washington, to that gentleman, and from the Hon. George H. Pendleton, to the superintendent of the Harper's Ferry rifle-works of the United States. On the journey I fell in with the Baltimore police scouts, who by command of the Governor of Virginia had explored "the abolition counties of Ohio" in search of military organizations, made up in violation of the peace and dignity of the United States, for "another raid on Virginia."

When we reached Harper's Ferry the station was in the hands of the military, and I was driven about at the point of the bayonet for some time before finding a place to stand and wait a few minutes. There was a hole ragged with splinters at the corner of the station-house, constructed of plank, but put together with tongue-and-groove, said to mark the course of "the ball from a yager with which old Brown killed a man." Inside Brown's fort was a plain red stain on the whitewashed brick wall, the blood of Brown when, overpowered, he was wounded with a cutlass and thrust down with a strong hand. There was a curved red streak and a few long hairs where the gashed head of the old man had been rubbed against the whitened bricks. The superintendent of the rifle-works was a cautious official. He took a member of the Legislature of Pennsylvania and myself in his carriage, and putting on a belt with two revolvers we were driven along a good turnpike through a pleasant country to the county seat, where Brown was tried and was the next day to be executed. By the roadside there were marks of fire, the burning of stacks, and the explanation, " The niggers have burned the stacks of one of the jurors who found Brown guilty." There was no reference to the fact that the superintendent took his pistols with him for a daylight drive over seven miles of turnpike through a highly cultivated country. That was taken as a matter of course. There was greater alarm among the people of Virginia than could be accounted for by comparison with the experience of communities into which the slave element did not enter.

—25

It was doubtless that deep sense of insecurity that widened into awful alarms at the suggestion of slave insurrections —the fact that society was permeated with stories of West-Indian wars of races, especially the traditions, more terrible than history, of the San Domingo horrors. The town, then and always to be distinguished as the place of the trial of John Brown, and his death, was crowded with the troops of Virginia, and there was a marked absence of the people of the surrounding country. The uniforms of the militia of Virginia were as various as the companies were numerous. There was no uniformity of dress or weapons. There were a troop of cavalry, a battery of field guns, and about two thousand infantry, the whole under the command of General Taliaferro, whose headquarters were at the Washington House. There was the palpable excitement of conscious history-making, and trifling incidents magnified by common consent.

The fact about myself best known was that I had a letter from Dr. Dandridge to Colonel Lewis Washington, and one from George H. Pendleton to the Harper's Ferry superintendent. My connection with an "abolition newspaper" was quite subordinated, but there were many inquiries as to my "views" of the John Brown raid, and I did not insist upon attempting to vindicate the old farmer, so suddenly and strangely a world's hero. Indeed, the close contact with the events of the raid made it difficult to resist the impression that Brown was an unbalanced man, one whose exaltation was akin to insanity. The philosophy, the philanthropy, the martyrdom, the religion of humanity, the spiritual sanctification, and immense romantic and tragic interpretations placed upon the raid of "The Man of Osawatomie" by Victor Hugo and Ralph Waldo Emerson, the latter declaring that "the gallows was made glorious like the cross," had in the immediate presence of the miserable skirmishing and the shedding of the blood of men who were, by all the customary tests, kindly disposed to be orderly, neighborly, humane, become obscure, belonging to the sentimental, the imaginative, and the impossible.

Late in the evening Mrs. Brown arrived in a dingy hack, escorted by the horsemen who became known in the war that was on two years later as "the Black Horse Cavalry." As the carriage approached the jail the artillery, which had been arranged on either side of the door, was trundled across the street and turned about, the muzzles open-mouthed upon the prison. There was much parade and shuffling of military figures in the execution of this maneuver, and then Mrs. Brown was taken to her husband's cell, when he was reported to have repeated to her often the admonition, "My dear, you must keep your sperrets up"—"sperrets" pronounced as here spelled; but a very strict and close guard was kept upon the pair.

As the evening wore on, General Taliaferro was seated surrounded by his staff, in the public room of the hotel. A young man, tall and lithe, and wearing a military dress, rushed up to him and said hurriedly in my hearing: "General, I am told, sir, and believe, that Henry Ward Beecher is coming here to-morrow to pray on the scaffold with old Brown, and I pledge you my word if he does he shall be hanged along with Brown." The General stared coldly and said with deliberation and severe dignity: "If Mr. Beecher comes, as you say, I pledge my word of

honor, sir, that while I live not a hair of his head shall be
harmed, sir; not one hair of his head shall be harmed."

On the morning of the execution the troops were early
stirring. The murmur of camps filled the air. There
were no visitors trailing along the roads, to be witnesses of
the solemn function. It was forbidden. The people far
and near were ordered to be alert at home. Therefore,
when the hollow square of the military companies was
formed about the scaffold there was not even a fringe of
civil spectators. There were reporters, surgeons, three or
four politicians of distinction, and one woman on the roof
of a house nearly a quarter of a mile distant. The Hon.
James M. Ashley was in the town with Col. Henderson of
Kansas, and introduced him as "the worst of the border
ruffians," an announcement usually received with appro-
bation of the humor in it and of the fact also. Ashley had
just dropped in from the West, and was held to be of those
interested in the care of Mrs. Brown and her Quaker escort from Philadelphia. A story has been largely circulated that as Brown left the jail he kissed a colored child,
and there are paintings and poetry to that effect. When
he stepped out of the prison there was not a group other
than military in sight. I was not on the spot at the moment, but saw the street before the jail filled with guns
and soldiers and horses, staff officers and officials, and no
one else during the morning. I had walked, before Brown
came out, to the vicinity of the scaffold where the militia
companies were marching into the positions assigned them.
The most striking horseman on the field, Turner Ashley,
galloped around bearing orders and giving directions,
mounted on a spotted stallion with a wonderful mane and

tail, flowing like white silk from neck and rump, almost
sweeping the ground. The Colonel and his horse—and the
horsemanship of the Colonel was worthy his steed—were a
gallant show. Ashley was killed in battle, defending for
his State the Valley of the Shenandoah. There seemed to
be no attainable end of the evolution of the troops in preparation for the ceremony. I distinctly remember in the
movement the gaunt, severe figure of an officer whose command was a company of bright boys. It was the contrast
between the stern man and the gay youths that formed a
picture for me, and I heard the word as they passed—
" Lexington Cadets." The man was Prof. Jackson, later
the Confederate hero, " Stonewall."

The day was extremely beautiful and mild. The highly
cultivated farms, the village, the broad landscape, browned
by the frosts of November, framed in the ranges of the
Blue Ridge—blue indeed, a daintily defined wall, of a
blue shade more delicate than the sky. Though it was
"the day of Austerlitz" as the days of the season are
marked, the clover in the stubble was green, and the
ground so warm and dry the reporters reclined upon it
with comfort and exchanged observations in the spirit of
levity with which the representatives of the press relieve,
when witnesses of true tragedies, the strains upon their
vitality.

The procession from the jail to the scaffold was brilliant. The General commanding had a staff more re-
splendent than that of Field Marshal Moltke and King
William, when they rode together over their battlefields
in France. Old John Brown was seated on his coffin in
the bed of a wagon, of the fashion farmers call a wood

wagon, an open body and no cover. He wore a battered black slouch hat, the rim turned squarely up in front, giving it the aspect of a cocked hat. This was that his vision might not be impeded, and he looked with evident enjoyment upon the country, saying it was the first time he had the pleasure of seeing it. His words were repeated at the time. The man I saw as he was in the wagon and as he was helped upon the scaffold—he had about a dozen steps to ascend—his arms pinioned by ropes at the elbows, tied firmly, so that his hands were free while the upper arms were bound at his waist. He wore a baggy brown coat and trousers, and red carpet slippers over blue yarn socks, and stood firmly but in an easy attitude on the trap-door, that was sustained by a rope. Then a stout white cord of cotton, provided by some cotton planters who thought there was propriety in it—something symbolical in it—was placed over the iron-gray, sturdy head, the noose dropped easily around his neck and tightened so that it would not slip, but so as not to give physical discomfort. The face of the old man was toward the east, the morning light on it, and the figure perfectly in dress and pose, and all appointments, that of a typical Western farmer—a serious person upheld by an idea of duty—the expression of his features that of a queer mingling of the grim, and, to use a rural word, the peart. The white cap was pulled down, and still the troops were moving, falling into a hollow square—a formation that had not been rehearsed. This became tedious. Brown asked that there should be no delay. The suspense was distressing, and from the ascent of the scaffold to the fall of the trap and the sharp jerk upon the white cord, the time was nearly eighteen

minutes. This was not, though often stated, with the purpose of torture, but the delay of the military to get into
assigned places. Brown's hands gave the only sign of
emotion that possessed him. He was rubbing his thumbs
hard but slowly on the inside of his forefingers, between
the first and second joints, as one braces himself with a
nervous grasp upon the arms of a dentist's chair when a
tooth is to be drawn. It is no wonder Brown asked the
sheriff about the waiting. There was deep stillness as
the form of the victim plunged six feet and the rope
twanged as its burden lengthened a little and shivered.
Then the body began to whirl as the cord slackened and
twisted, and the rapid movement caused the short skirts of
the coat to flutter as in a wind. About a quarter of an
hour was spent by the surgeons climbing the stairs and
holding the suspended body to their ears, listening to see
if the heart continued to act. One of the reporters was
moved to say, as if he had prepared a deliverance and
was getting it off contrary to a better judgment, "Gentlemen, the honor of old Virginia has been vindicated."
There was no response to the sentiment.

The road to Harper's Ferry was soon filled with car-
riages at high speed. There was dust flying. In the yard
of a farm-house were a half-dozen lads playing soldier,
one beating a small drum. This was the highway along
which more than any other surged to and fro the armies of
the Nation and the Confederacy. Colonel Washington,
while on General Lee's staff, was killed in western Virginia by an Indiana sharpshooter, and I remember well
his stately presence, not unworthy to represent the name
he bore, and his courtesy and kindness to one who repre-

sented a newspaper and held there was no cause more
sacred in the world than that of the freedom of the Territories and the extinction of slavery; and the death of
Ashley, Pate and Wise seemed a grievous sacrifice of manhood.

Something more than ten years later, August, 1870, in
eastern France, I was with the German invaders of the
fair land of Lorraine, and one day as I looked upon a
division of the Grand Army of the Red Prince, a monstrous mass of men with the spikes of their helmets and
their bayonets glittering over them under a vast tawny
cloud of dust, I heard with amazement a deep-throated
burst of song in English, and it was:

"John Brown's body is moldering in the ground,
But his soul is marching on.
Glory, Hallelujah!"

The German invaders often sang magnificently while
marching. German soldiers in our army in the war
of the States returning to the Fatherland to fight the
French taught their comrades the splendid marching-song
which the legions of the North sang along the historic
highways of Virginia, that Father Abraham's boys were
coming and the soul of John Brown was marching on.
There is a bust of gold of Brown, presented his widow by
Victor Hugo, in the State Museum at Topeka, Kansas,
shown by the venerable superintendent, with an apology,
for it is a bad portraiture of the Hero of Osawatomie
and martyr of Harper's Ferry. It is the only likeness
of him giving the chief characteristic of his countenance
on the morning of his last day that I have seen, except in
the sketches taken for Harper's Weekly on the spot, by

Porte Crayon. The French makers of the golden bust
must have caught the keen lines of this artist's pencil,
showing the weirdness that had crept into Brown's strong
face when his eyes beheld unearthly scenes, his mind wan-
dering in the regions on the boundary of two worlds—he
must have seen cloud-capped domes not rounded by human
hands—invisible by mortal eyes unless introspectively.
One wonders whether the old farmer, as he waited on the
scaffold, could have beheld as in a dream—as one sees
at night in stormy darkness, when there is a flame of
lightning, a misty mountain-top—a vision incredible, but
not unsubstantial, of his own apotheosis and immortality.

SENATOR INGALLS ON JOHN BROWN.

The following quotation is from the article prepared
by Senator John James Ingalls for the *North American
Review*. After reviewing the sublime sayings of John
Brown, Senator Ingalls says:

" What immortal and dauntless courage breathes in this
procession of stately sentences; what fortitude; what pa-
tience; what faith; what radiant and eternal hope! No
pagan philosopher, no Hebrew prophet, no Christian
martyr, ever spoke in loftier and more heroic strains than
this "coward and murderer,"* who declared, from near
the brink of an ignominious grave, that there was no
acquisition so splendid as moral purity; no inheritance
so desirable as personal liberty; nothing on this earth
nor in the world to come so valuable as the soul, whatever
the hue of its habitation; no impulse so noble as an un-

*This article was written in reply to one published by David N. Utter, in which
Mr. Utter had called John Brown a " coward and murderer."

conquerable purpose to love truth, and an invincible determination to obey God.

"Carlyle says that when any great change in human society is to be wrought, God raises up men to whom that change is made to appear as the one thing needful and absolutely indispensable. Scholars, orators, poets, philanthropists, play their parts, but the crisis comes at last through some one who is stigmatized as a fanatic by his contemporaries, and whom the supporters of the systems he assails crucify between thieves or gibbet as a felon. The man who is not afraid to die for an idea is the most potential and convincing advocate.

"Already the great intellectual leaders of the movement for the abolition of slavery are dead. The student of the future will exhume their orations, arguments, and state papers, as a part of the subterranean history of the epoch. The antiquarian will dig up their remains from the alluvial drift of the period, and construe their relations to the great events in which they were actors. But the three men of this era who will loom forever against the remotest horizon of time, as the pyramids above the voiceless desert, or mountain-peaks over the subordinate plains, are Abraham Lincoln, Ulysses S. Grant, and Old John Brown of Osawatomie."

"My task is done—my song hath ceased—my theme
Has died into an echo; it is fit
The spell should break of this protracted dream.
The torch shall be extinguish'd which hath lit
My midnight lamp—and what is writ is writ.—

Farewell! a word that must be, and hath been—
A sound which makes us linger;—yet—farewell!
Ye! who have traced the pilgrim to the scene
Which is his last, if in your memories dwell
A thought which once was his, if on ye swell
A single recollection, not in vain
He wore his sandal-shoon and scallop-shell;
Farewell! with *him* alone may rest the pain
If such there were—with *you*, the moral of his strain!"

INDEX.

of hunted like wolves; a Bible-man and honest; he and his sons marched to relief of Lawrence May 22, 1856; names of the members of company of, 164; camped with his company on the claim of Captain Shore; favors continuing on to Lawrence; receives intelligence which causes him to return to the Pottawatomie settlements, 165; defamed by Leverett W. Spring, 170; surveying expedition of to Buford's camp described; death of determined upon, 178; return of to Pottawatomie described, 180; causes of his killing the Doyles and others stated by Judge James Hanway, 181, 182; was compelled to kill the Doyles and others or be killed, 183; message carried to; declaration of upon receiving message, 189; company of leaves for Pottawatomie, 190; actions of at Pottawatomie contradict statements of James Townsley, 192; what he told Governor George A. Crawford; how he spent May 24, 1856; gave the Doyles and others a trial, 193; statement of to E. A. Coleman, 196; statement of to Colonel Samuel Walker; sleeps under a tree; shoots at Walker, 198; object of in the Pottawatomie killings, 199; manner of killing the Doyles and others at Pottawatomie; did not kill any with his own hand, 200; manner of procedure of on the Pottawatomie, 200, 201, 202, 203; statements of Townsley proven erroneous, 202, 203; sensational and absurd charge against by James Christian, 203, 204; did he kill any man at Pottawatomie; did he and his men mutilate the dead there; unfairness of some Kansas writers towards, 205; moral of the Pottawatomie killings, 206; contributed more toward making Kansas free than did Eli Thayer, 207; understood better than any other that slavery had to be shot to death, 209; aided in his outfit for the Pottawatomie by the men in camp on Middle Ottawa creek, 210; absurd statements of Colonel James Blood concerning, 210, 211; had no need of assistance from Townsley or any other to find ruffian settlers on the Pottawatomie, 212; intended to kill George Wilson, 213; killed none with his own hand at Pottawatomié, 215; never contemplated "sweeping the creek," 218; declared that the Pottawatomie killing was by his order; returns to the camp on Middle Ottawa creek, 219; meeting of the settlers on the Pottawatomie not intended to condemn, 221; message from Pottawatomie sent to, 223; in Tappan's account, 224; statement of Charles Robinson that John Brown told him he did the Pottawatomie killing, 227; tribute of Charles Robinson to, 228; tribute of General Jo. O. Shelby to, 229; tribute of James F. Legate to, 230; a *hero*, not a *murderer*, 231; justification of by Judge James Hanway, 233; Spring comes to justify, 235; further justification by Hanway, 237; and by Charles Robinson, 238; company of did the killing at Pottawatomie; did not himself kill any, 238, 239; injustice of James Redpath to; action of at Pottawatomie tended to save Kansas; scorned double-dealing, 239, 240; fame of; Spring says Pottawatomie killing was beneficial to Kansas; justified by all the Free-State settlers on the Pottawatomie, 240, 241; justified by Senator Ingalls; D. W. Wilder upon, 242; action of saved lives of the Free-State settlers on the Potta-

—26

—27

Sevier. John. schooled on the frontier in the ways of men, 86.
Seward, William H., challenge of to the South, 53.
Shannon, Governor Wilson, appointed Governor of Kansas Territory; character of; his course; his flight from the Territory, 59; meets Governor Geary, 76; calls for troops to arrest Branson rescuers, 137; Missourians in consultation with, 139; plied with brandy by the commanders of the Free-State forces in the Wakarusa War, 146; given shares in the Lecompton town site, 159; orders Colonel Sumner to disperse armed bands, 262; frightened by the firing upon Fort Titus, 294.
Shelby, Isaac, schooled on the frontier in the ways of men, 86.
Shelby, General Jo. O., tribute of to John Brown; justifies the Pottawatomie killings, 229.
Sherbondy, Ellen, marries Jason Brown, 97.
Sheridan, Daniel, house of a stopping-place for John Brown, 316; visited by John Brown, 328.
Sherman, Henry, commonly known as "Dutch Henry," character of; account of, 160; the Doyles the tool of; Buford's men in communication with, 162; in Missouri when Lawrence was sacked, 167; found at camp of Buford's men, 178; one of the party to help burn the houses of the Free-State settlers on the Pottawatomie, 180; Rev. J. G. Pratt's account of; desire to kill the Rev. David Baldwin, 180, 181; threatens Free-State men, 237.
Sherman, John, one of the Congressional Committee to investigate Kansas affairs, 134.
Sherman, William, character of, 161; outrageous conduct of towards Morse, 165; warned by Frederick Brown to not molest the daughter of a Free-State settler, 177; cause of death of as stated by James Hanway, 181, 182; raised a red flag over his house when he heard of the sacking of Lawrence, 182, 183; Townsley's version of the death of, 201; statement of killing of, 214; was not mutilated, 218; warns Free-State settlers to leave the Pottawatomie settlements, 225; notifies Free-State men to leave the Pottawatomie settlements by a certain day, 229; a bad man, 230; in constant communication with Buford's men, 235; attempt to kill Morse, 236.
Shore, Captain Samuel T., had the Free-State forces camp upon his claim, 165; collects his men to fight Pate, 258; engages in battle of Black Jack, 259, 271; praised by John Brown for his bravery at Black Jack, 273.
Shore, Montgomery, information obtained from concerning the Doyles; sketch of, 177.
Slavery, at Jamestown, Va., 27; founders of our Republic opposed to, 28; measures to promote growth of, 29; infatuation of the South for, 30; statistics concerning, 32; unpopularity of in Appalachian America, 33; why it flourished in the South, 34; when abolished by the North, 40; intolerance concerning in the South, 40, 41; decadence of Virginia under, 43; declared the only issue in Kansas Territory by the Bogus Legislature, 120.
Slave trade, when abolished by the United States, 28.